I0828510

HISTORIC PHOTOS OF
PENNSYLVANIA

TEXT AND CAPTIONS BY LAURA E. BEARDSLEY

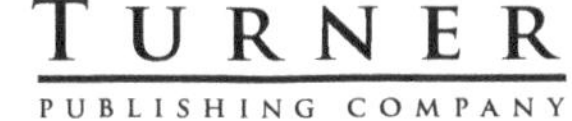

Williamsport, known in the nineteenth century as the "lumber capital of the world," reputedly had more millionaires per capita than any town in the country. Seen here at its peak at the end of the 1800s, Williamsport became the birthplace of Little League baseball in 1939.

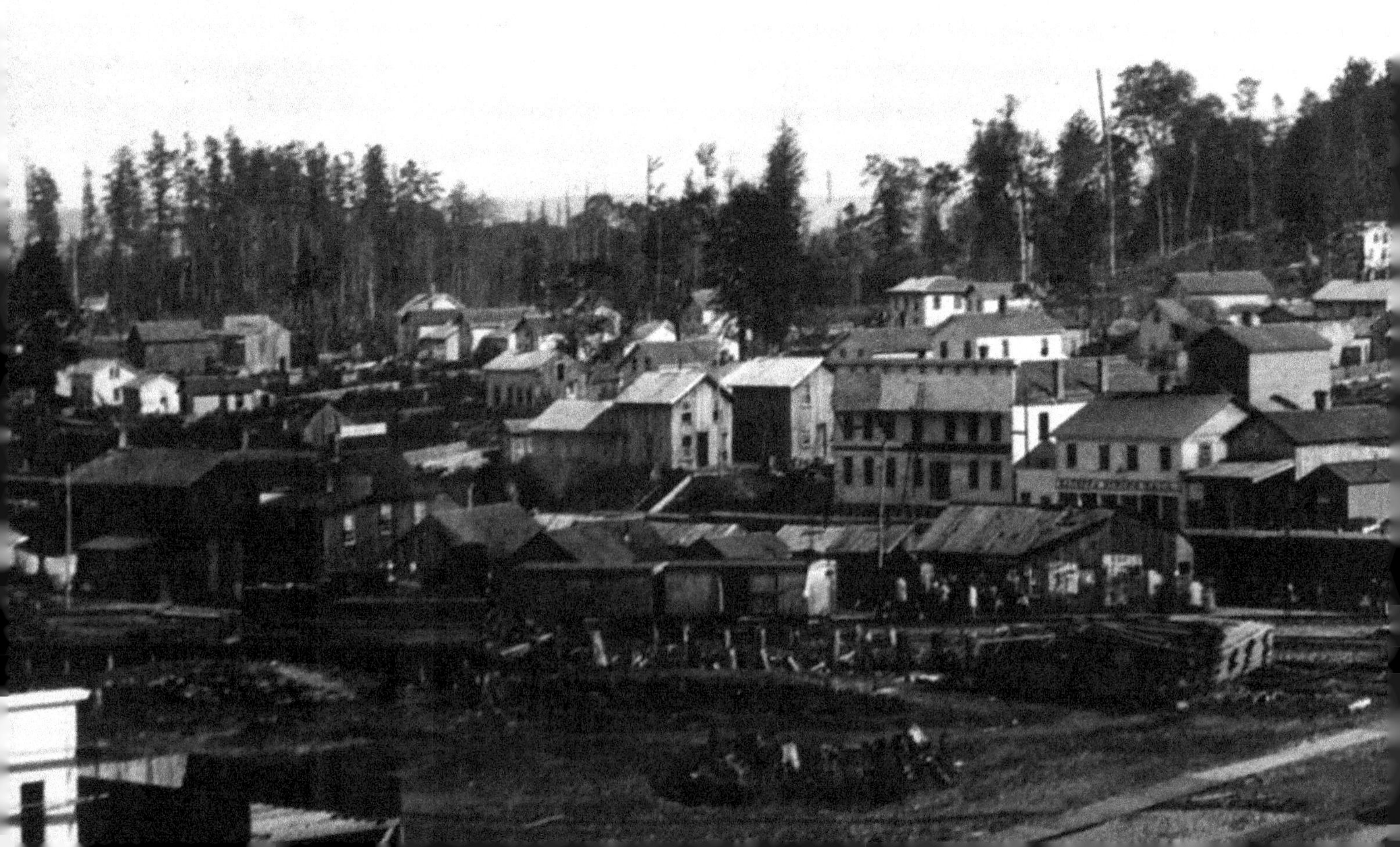

HISTORIC PHOTOS OF
PENNSYLVANIA

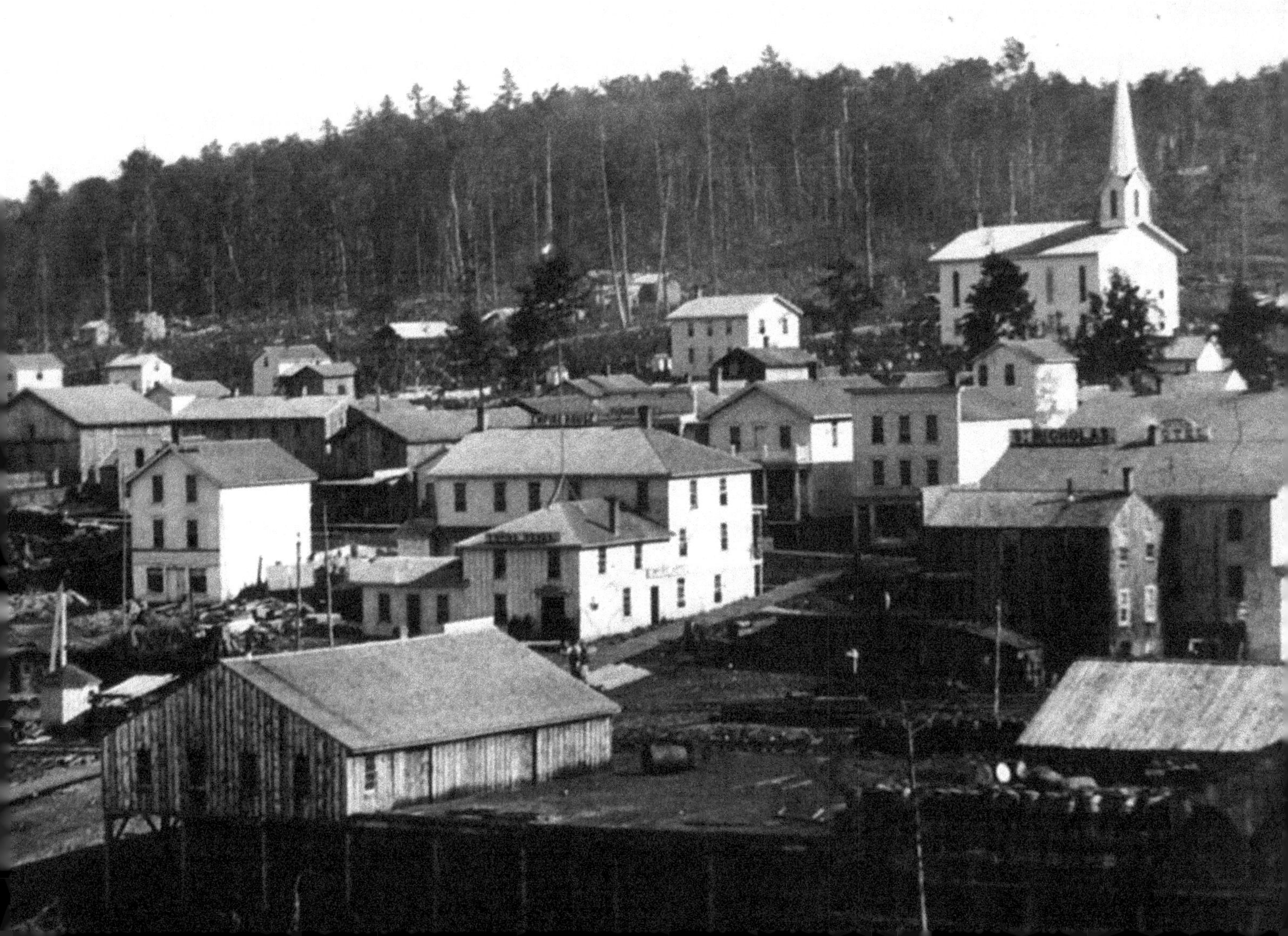

Turner Publishing Company
4507 Charlotte Avenue • Suite 100
Nashville, Tennessee 37209
(615) 255-2665

www.turnerpublishing.com

Historic Photos of Pennsylvania

Library of Congress Control Number: 2008908520

ISBN: 978-1-59652-515-3

ISBN-13: 978-1-68442-063-6 (hc)

Printed in the United States of America

09 10 11 12 13 14 15 16—0 9 8 7 6 5 4 3 2 1

Contents

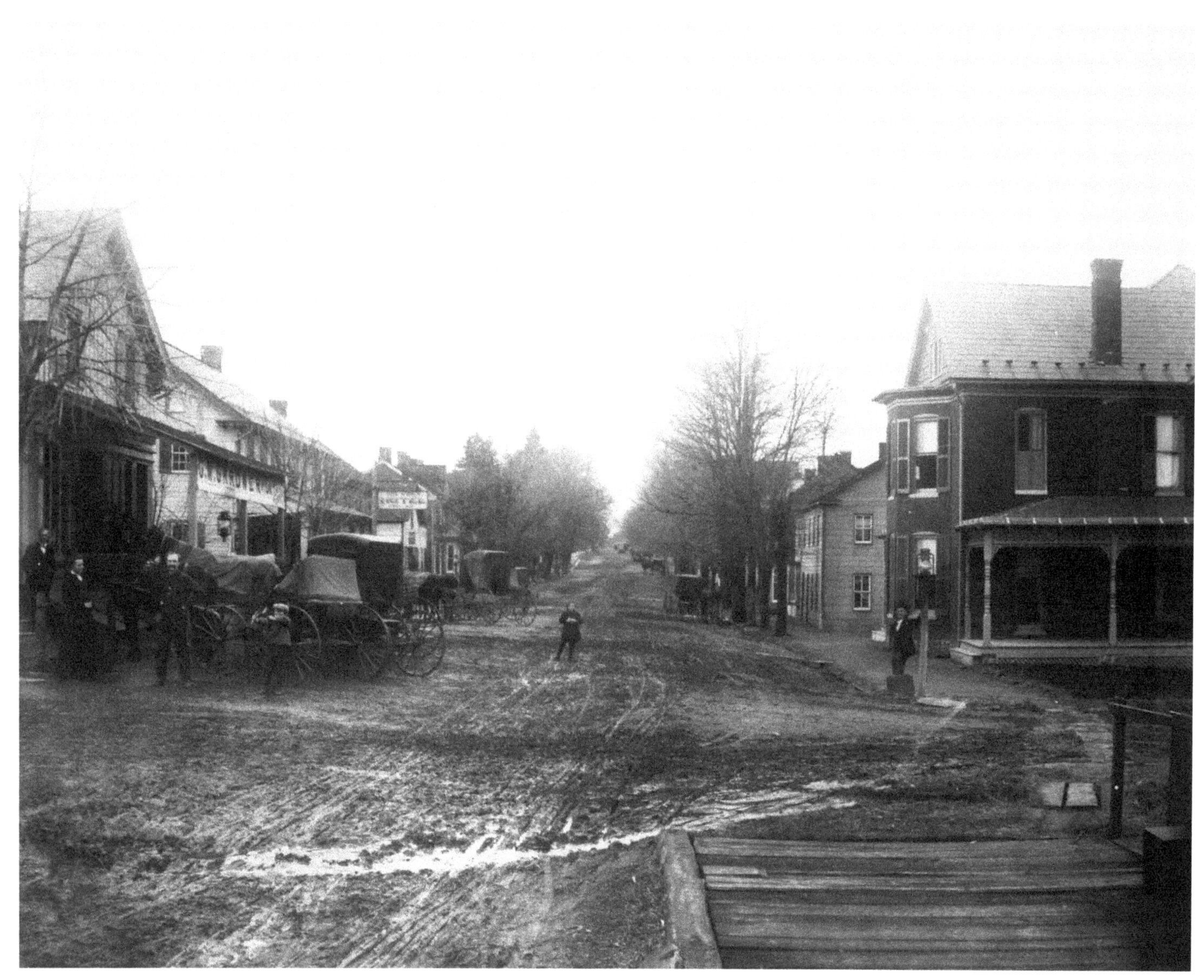

Local residents pose at the intersection of the Gettysburg and Harrisburg roads in York Springs, Adams County.

ACKNOWLEDGMENTS

This volume, *Historic Photos of Pennsylvania,* is the result of the cooperation and efforts of many individuals, organizations, and corporations. It is with great thanks that we acknowledge the valuable contribution of the following for their generous support:

Hershey Community Archives, Hershey, Pa.
Library and Archives Division, Sen. John Heinz History Center
Library of Congress
Temple University Libraries, Urban Archives, Philadelphia, Pa.
The Historical Society of Pennsylvania

PREFACE

Pennsylvania has thousands of historic photographs that reside in archives, both locally and nationally. This book began with the observation that, while those photographs are of great interest to many, they are not easily accessible. During a time when Pennsylvania is looking ahead and evaluating its future course, many people are asking, How do we treat the past? These decisions affect every aspect of the state—architecture, public spaces, commerce, infrastructure—and these, in turn, affect the way that people live their lives. This book seeks to provide easy access to a valuable, objective look into the history of Pennsylvania.

The power of photographs is that they are less subjective than words in their treatment of history. Although the photographer can make decisions regarding subject matter and how to capture and present it, photographs do not provide the breadth of interpretation that text does. For this reason, they offer an original, untainted perspective that allows the viewer to interpret and observe.

This project represents countless hours of review and research. The researchers and writer have reviewed thousands of photographs in numerous archives. We greatly appreciate the generous assistance of the organizations listed in the acknowledgments of this work, without whom this project could not have been completed.

The goal in publishing this work is to provide broader access to this set of extraordinary photographs that seek to inspire, provide perspective, and evoke insight that might assist people who are responsible for determining Pennsylvania's future. In addition, the book seeks to preserve the past with adequate respect and reverence.

With the exception of touching up imperfections that have accrued with the passage of time and cropping where necessary to accommodate format, no other changes have been made. The focus and clarity of many images is limited to the technology and the ability of the photographer at the time they were taken.

The work is divided into eras. Beginning with some of the earliest known photographs of Pennsylvania, the first section records photographs through the end of the nineteenth century. The second section spans the beginning of the twentieth century through World War I. Section Three moves from the 1920s through the 1940s. The last section covers the 1950s to recent times.

In each of these sections we have made an effort to capture various aspects of life through our selection of photographs. People, commerce, transportation, infrastructure, religious institutions, and educational institutions have been included to provide a broad perspective.

We encourage readers to reflect as they go walking in Pennsylvania, strolling through its parks, its countryside, and the neighborhoods of its cities. It is the publisher's hope that in utilizing this work, longtime residents will learn something new and that new residents will gain a perspective on where Pennsylvania has been, so that each can contribute to its future.

—*Todd Bottorff, Publisher*

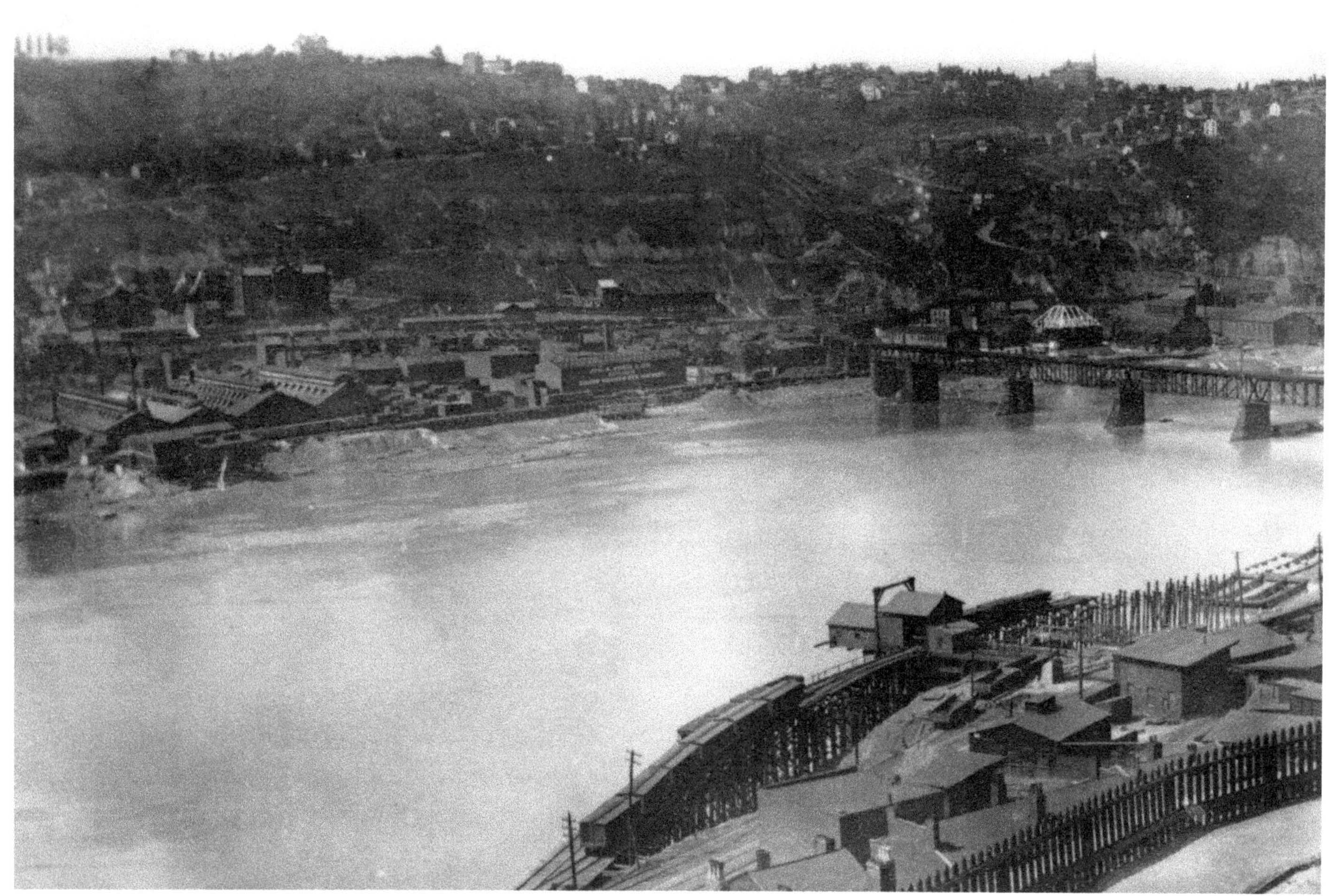

A view south from downtown Pittsburgh toward Mount Washington across the Monongahela River, 1888.

Birthplace of Greatness

(1839–1899)

When the first known surviving photograph taken in the United States was created in Philadelphia in 1839, it joined a long line of American firsts realized in Pennsylvania: first public protest against slavery (1688), first colonial constitution to guarantee freedom of conscience (1701), first turnpike (1795), first successful oil well (1859), and the first roller coaster (1879), to name just a few. Founded in 1682 by William Penn, a Quaker, as a haven for people of all faiths, Pennsylvania offered the demographic, economic, and natural resources to inspire great advances in industry, arts and sciences, and politics.

Following the earliest arrivals of colonists from Sweden, the Netherlands, and England, large numbers of Germans and Welsh settled in the vast areas of eastern and central Pennsylvania. Agriculture was preeminent, most notably the production of corn, wheat, rye, and flax, benefiting from excellent natural waterways and ideal soil and weather conditions.

Pennsylvania's political and cultural significance in the last quarter of the eighteenth century and into the nineteenth cannot be overstated. Birthplace of both the Declaration of Independence and the United States Constitution, the state would also lead the way in civil rights, education, finance, literature, and the arts. However, innovative exploitation of the natural resources available throughout Pennsylvania would ultimately cement its reputation as a great industrial giant.

By the 1830s, small manufacture gained in importance, with textiles, leather processing, shipbuilding, lumber harvesting, and publishing taking the lead as the state's major industries. As the Industrial Revolution expanded, the demand for iron grew until Pennsylvania was supplying half of all American iron to the nation's railroads and factories. Anthracite coal and natural gas, both discovered and heavily exploited in nineteenth-century Pennsylvania, fueled the iron and steel mills that contributed to the building of America's greatest cities and industries.

During the Civil War, battles were waged on Pennsylvania soil, and Pennsylvania industries gave their best efforts to the cause. Pennsylvania's abolitionist sentiments, influenced by its Quaker beginnings, inspired thousands from the state to serve. In the decades following the war, Pennsylvania's national political importance waned even as its industrial strengths brought great economic success. But with success came conflict, as laborers began to demand basic worker rights such as better pay and less dangerous working conditions, resulting in the earliest organized efforts of the labor movement.

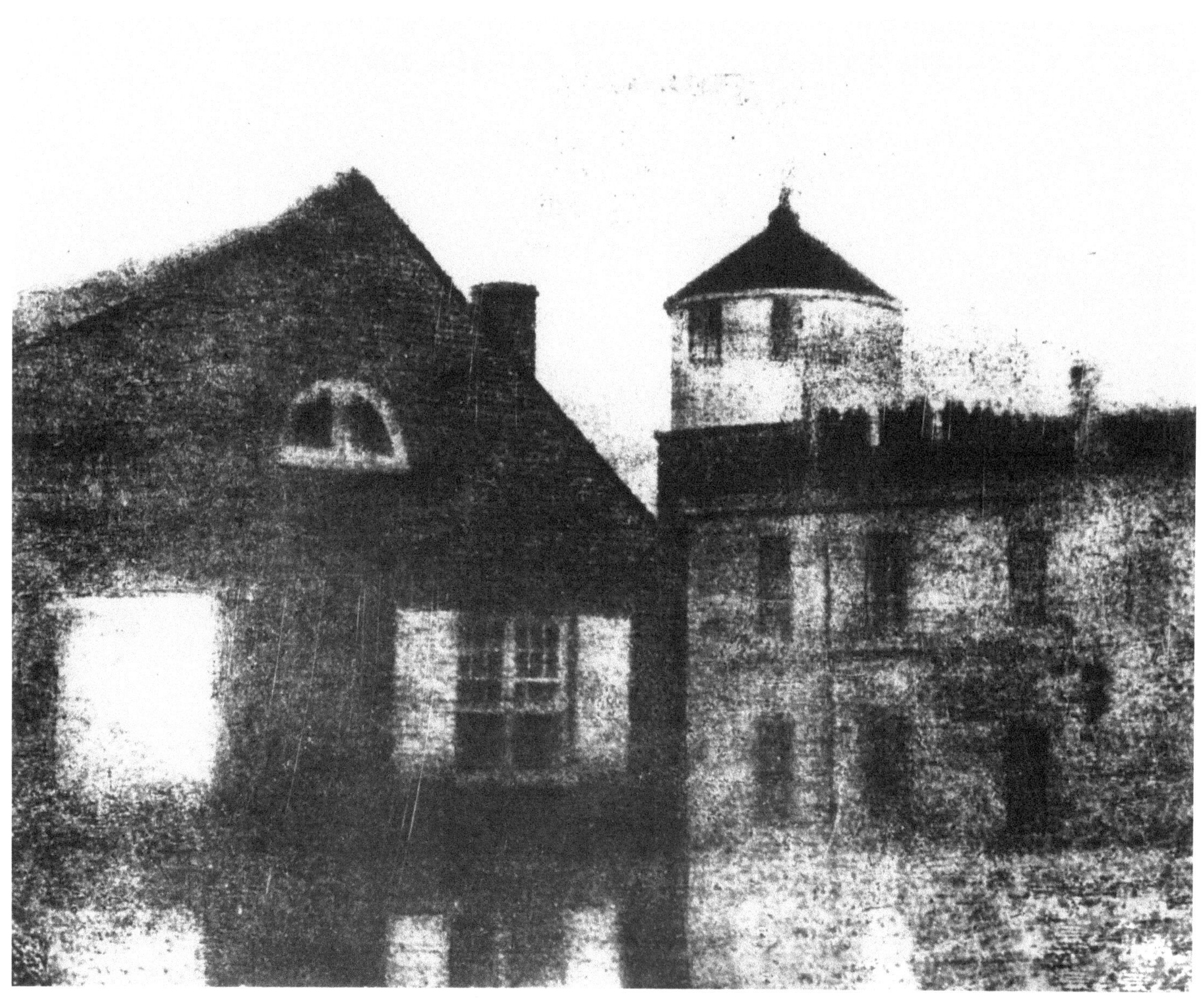

This unique view of Philadelphia's Central High School taken from a window of the United States Mint on September 25, 1839, is the oldest known photograph created in the United States. Amateur photographer and inventor Joseph Saxton created this daguerreotype after reading a brief description of the new photographic process in a local newspaper.

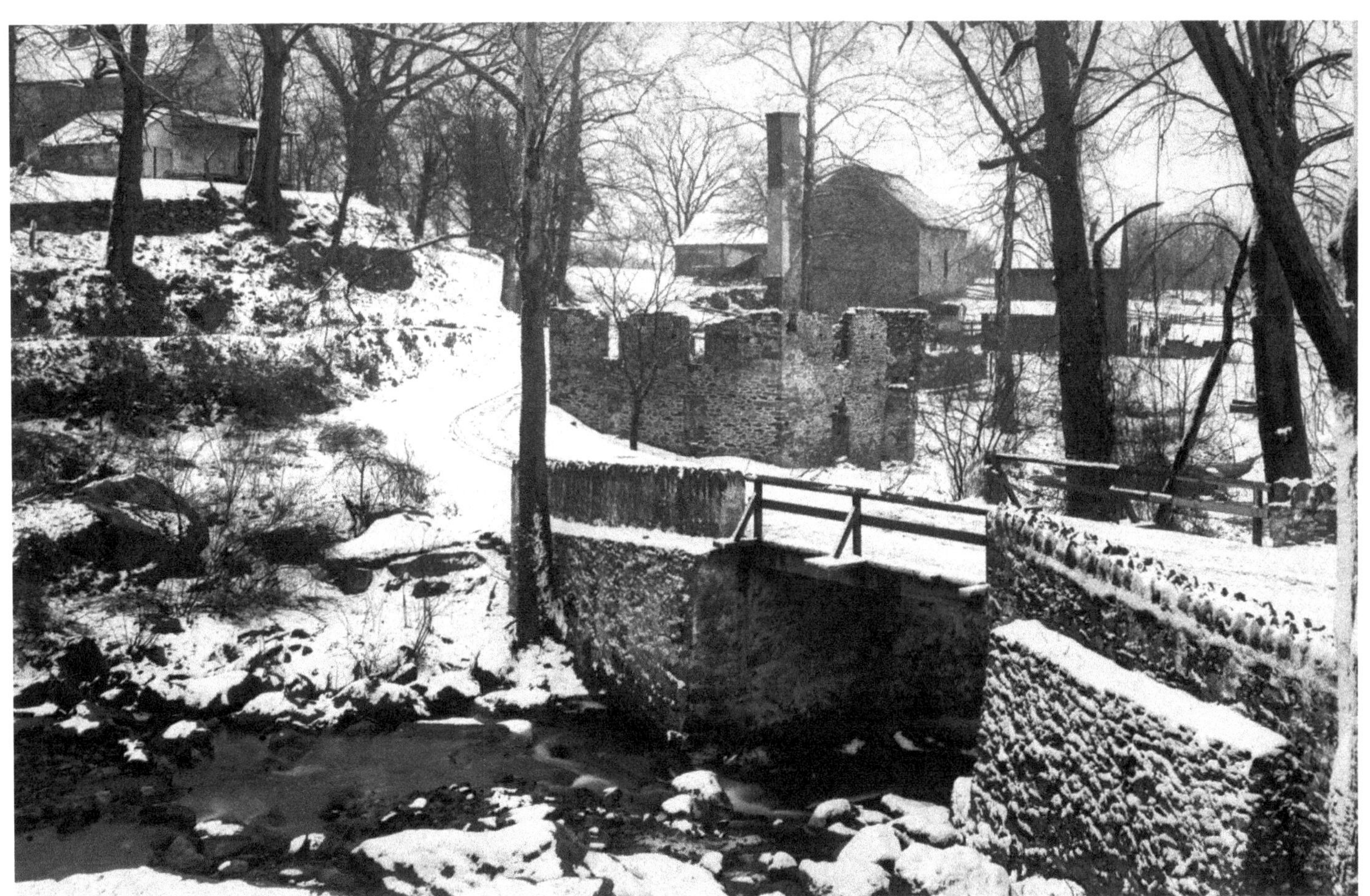

Sparsely settled by farmers and millers in the late 1600s, the town of Norwood in Delaware County grew into a bedroom community by the late 1870s. Connected to Philadelphia by an expanding freight and commuter railroad system, the town retained many features from its past, including the old mill seen here circa 1860.

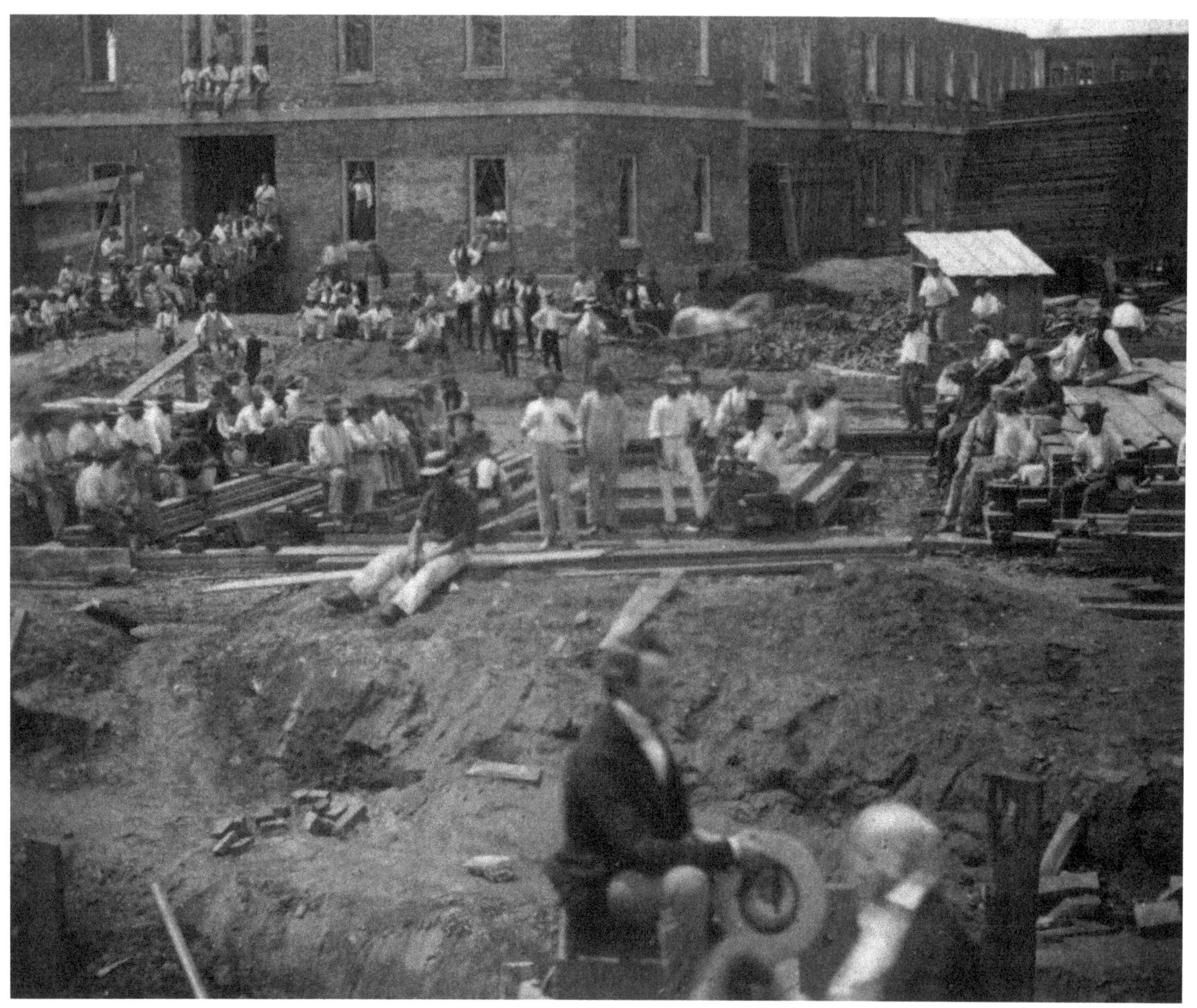

Workers pause for a photograph while building the Pennsylvania Hospital for the Insane in West Philadelphia, circa 1859. Also known as Kirkbride's Hospital after director Thomas Kirkbride, it was known for its innovative, humane treatment of the mentally ill.

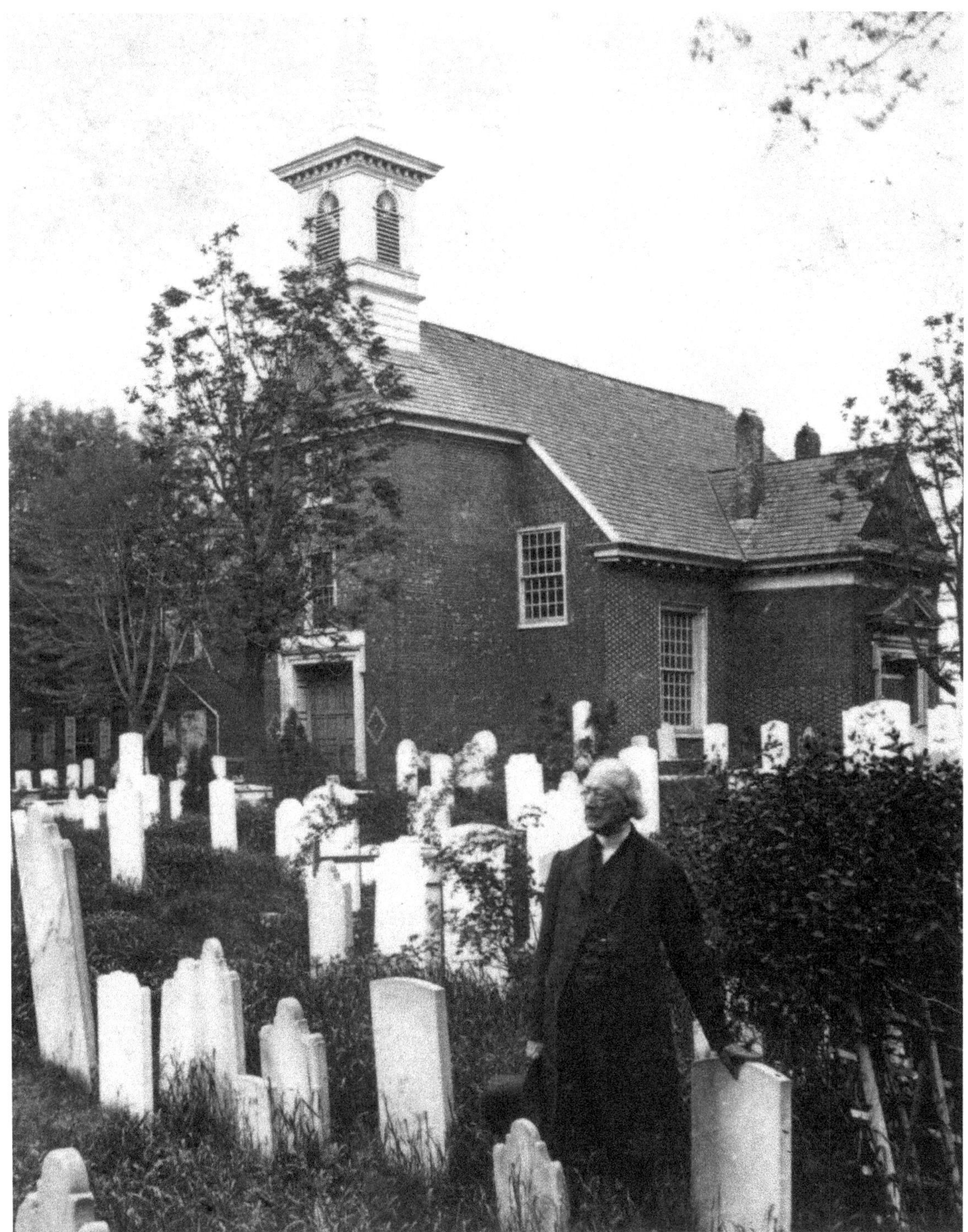

The Reverend Jehu Curtis Clay stands among the graves in the churchyard of Old Swedes (Gloria Dei) Church in Philadelphia, circa 1860. Built in 1700 by descendants of early Swedish missionaries and still an active Episcopal congregation, the church is the oldest in Pennsylvania.

After oil wells were first successfully drilled in northwest Pennsylvania in the late 1850s, hundreds of individual oil derricks like this one were built by prospectors hoping to strike it rich. Pennsylvania would ultimately supply half of the world's oil before the Texas oil boom in 1901.

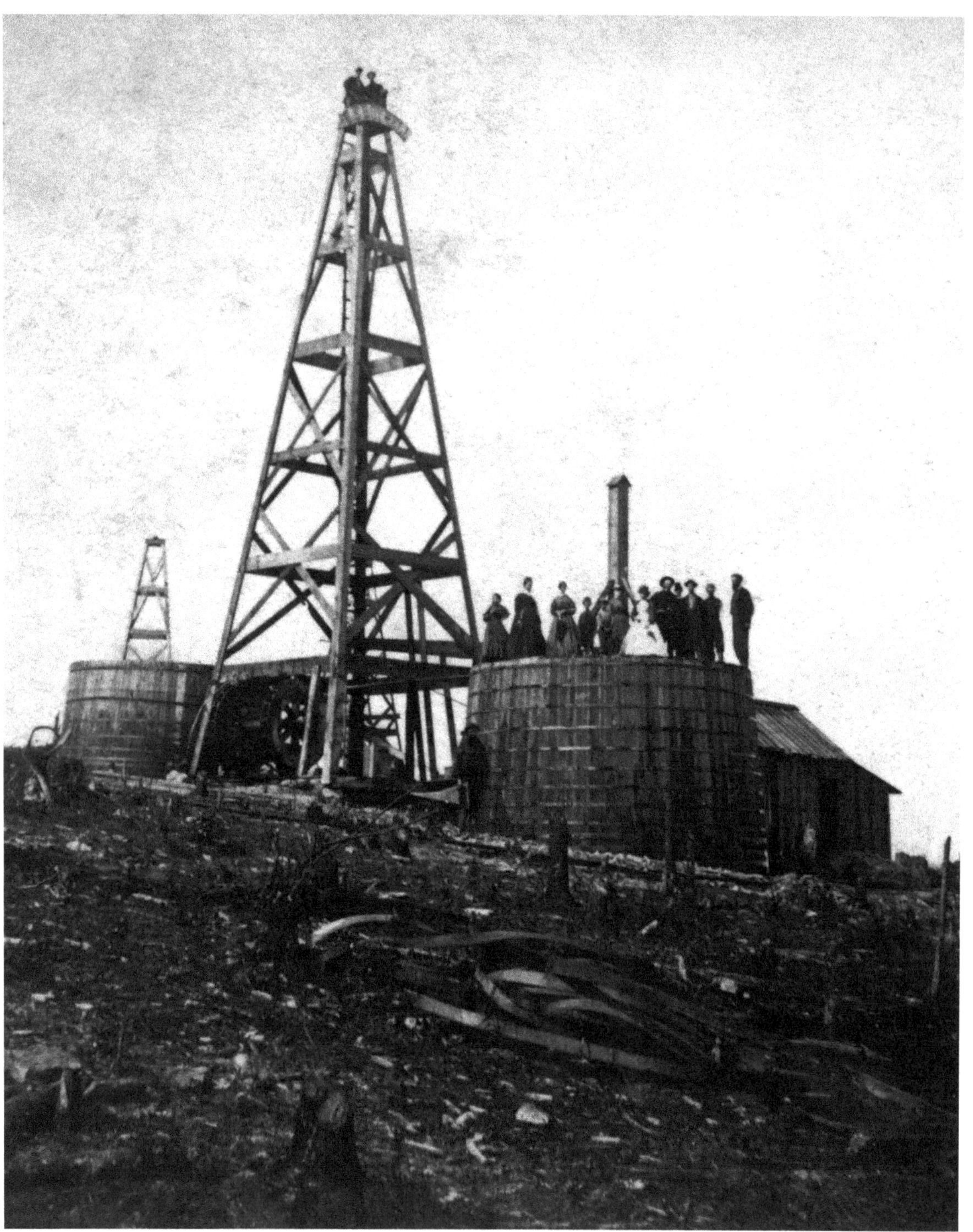

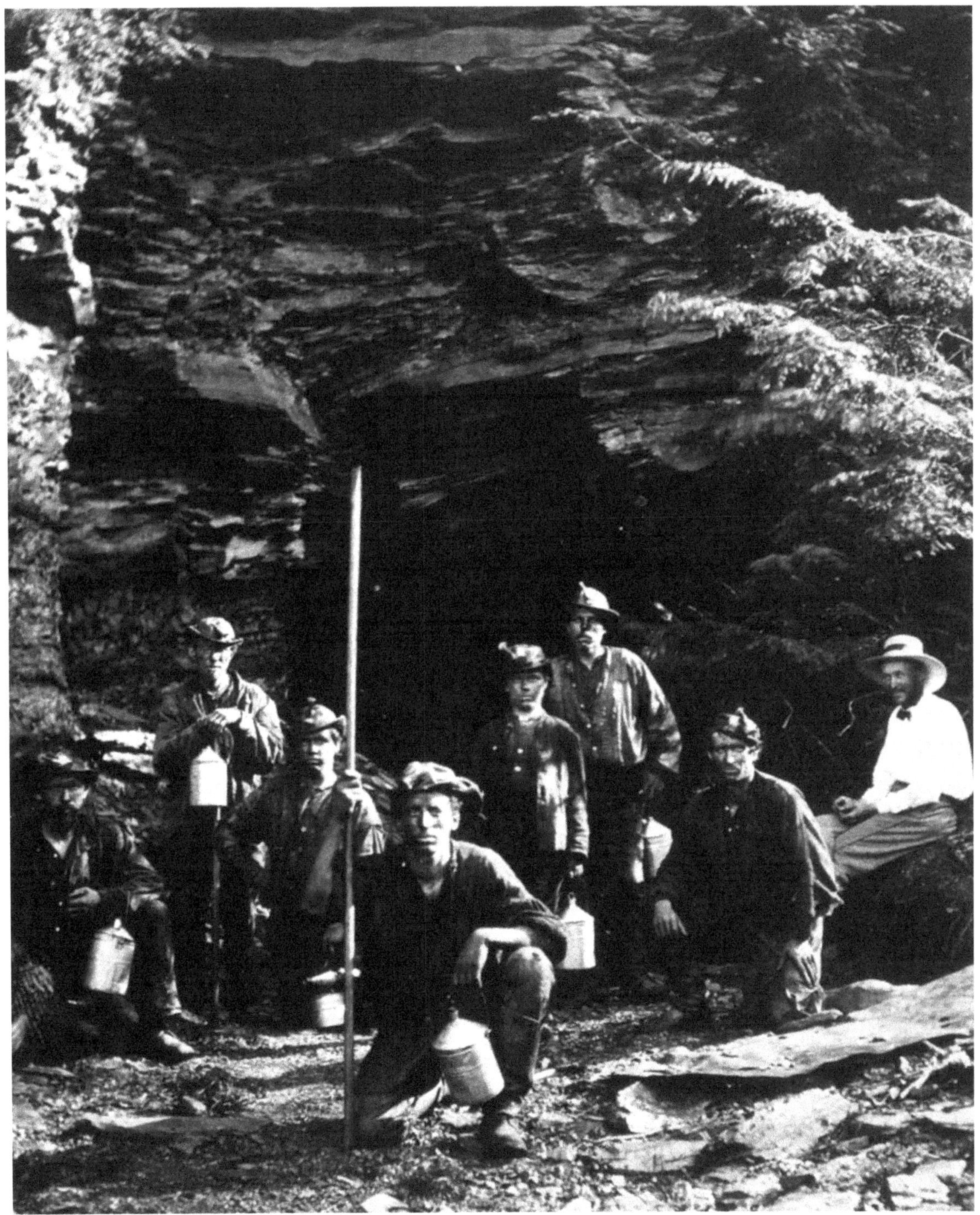

Anthracite coal was not successfully marketed until the mid-1800s, even though one of the world's great deposits of this highly efficient "hard" coal is found in the eastern and northeastern counties of the state. Photographed at the entrance to a natural cave, these men and boys in the Wyoming Valley illustrate how difficult early mining could be.

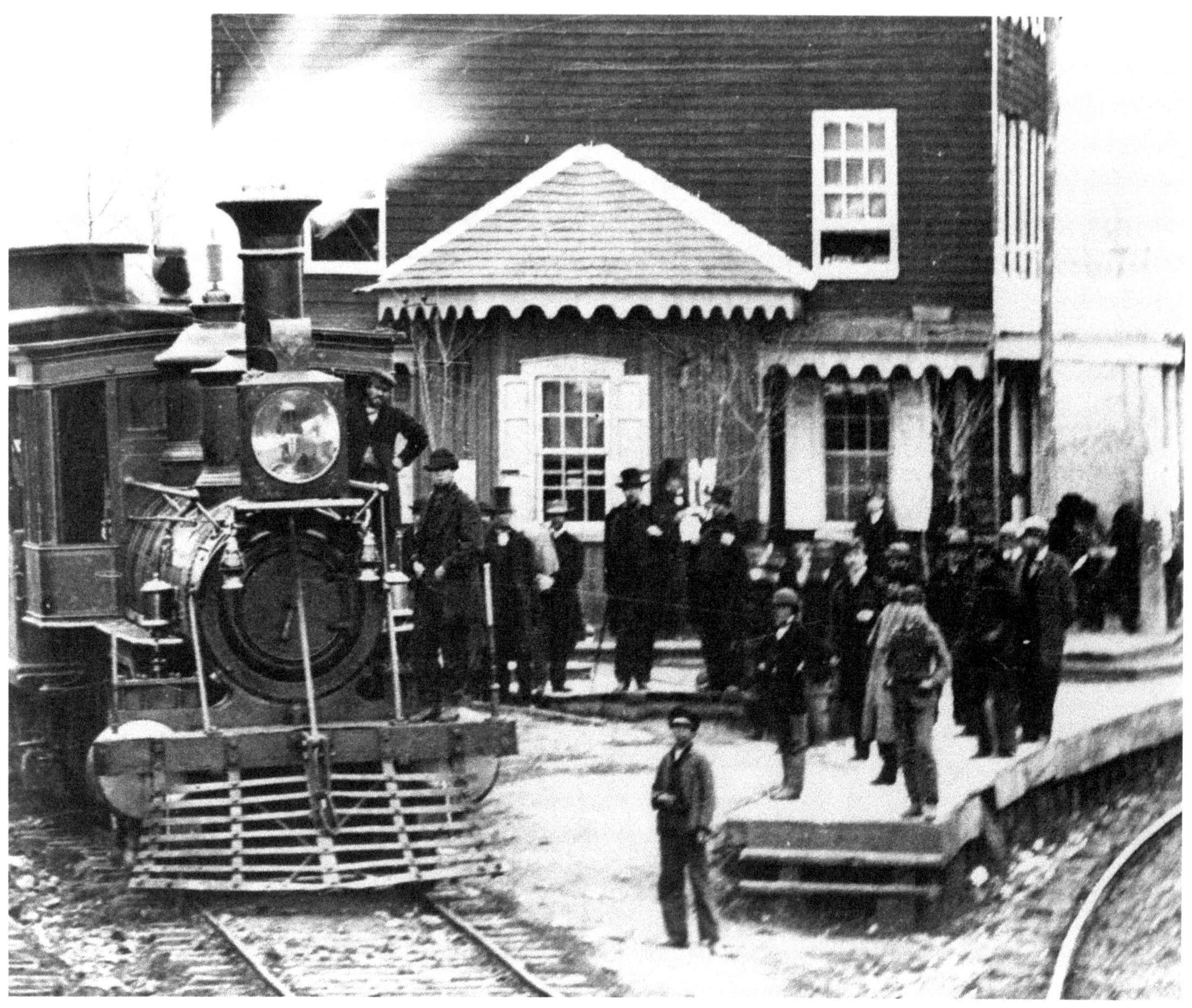

In November of 1863, Abraham Lincoln and a large number of dignitaries passed through Hanover Junction in York County on their way to and from Gettysburg, where Lincoln gave his famous address. It is believed that this photograph credited to Mathew Brady or his assistant documents one of those visits.

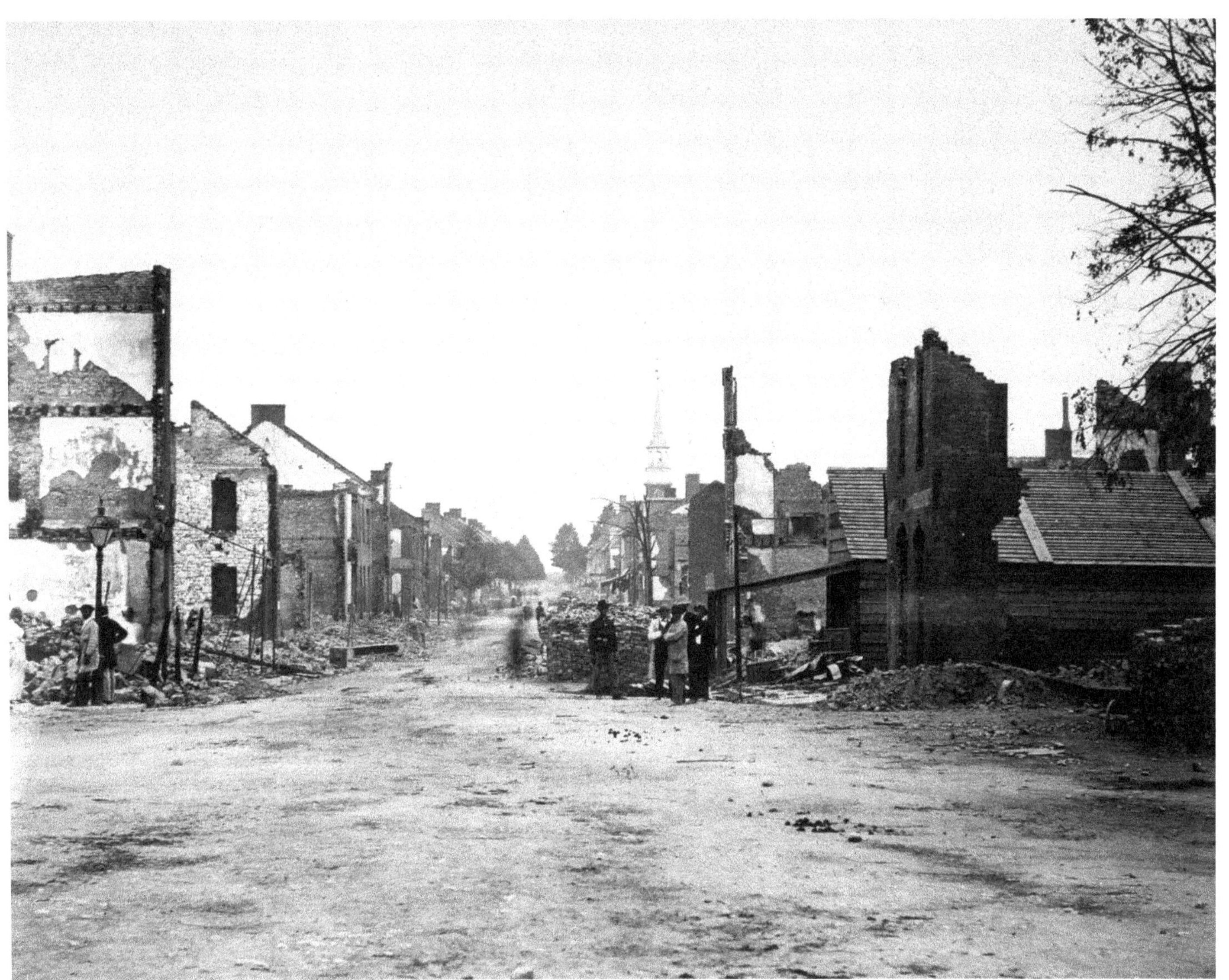

While the conflict at Gettysburg retains the most prominent place in modern memory, Chambersburg, just 16 miles north of the Mason-Dixon Line, was attacked and occupied by Southern forces three times during the Civil War. It recovered and remains today an active small town.

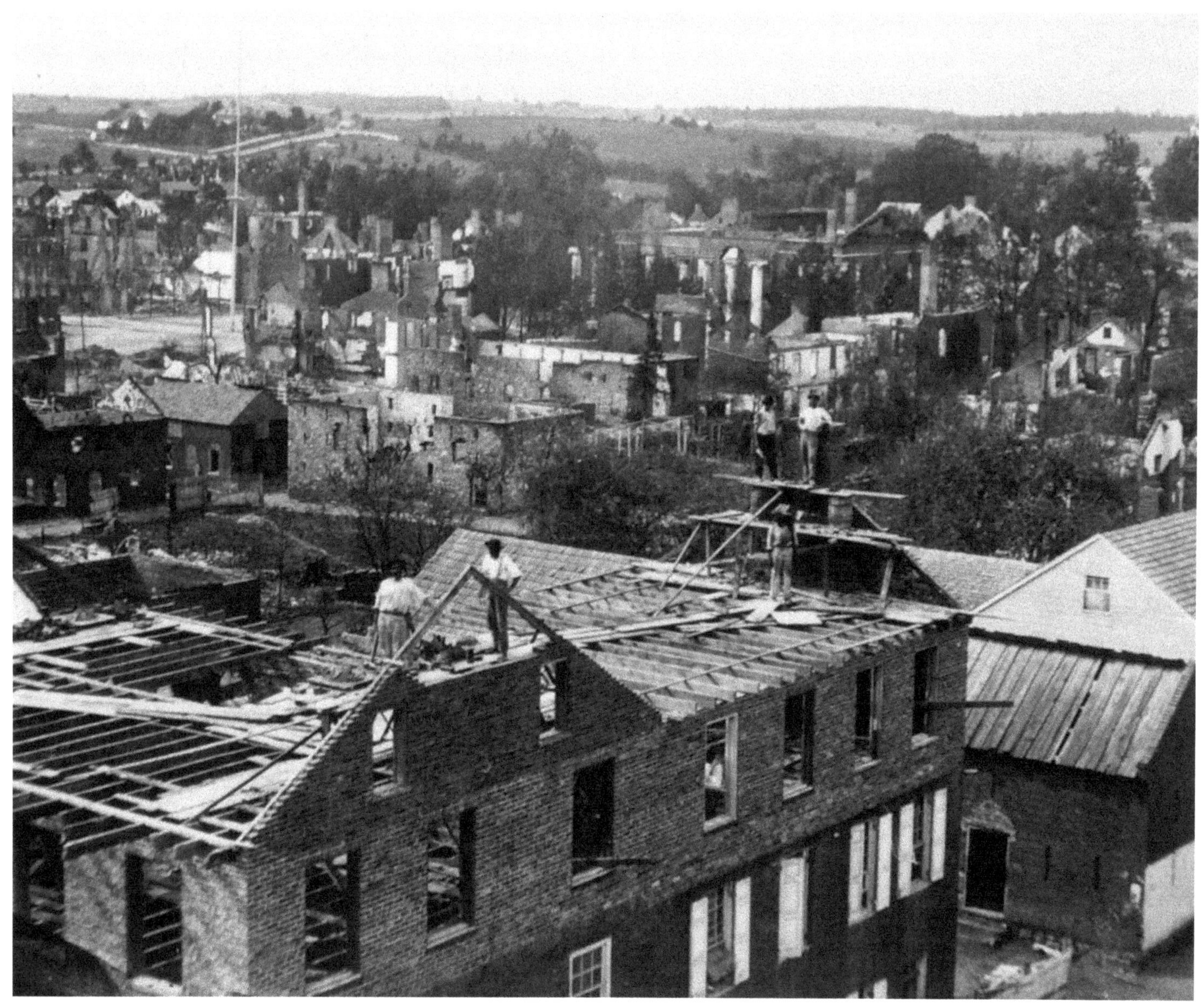

Carpenters work among the ruins of Chambersburg, destroyed by Confederate forces in July of 1864.

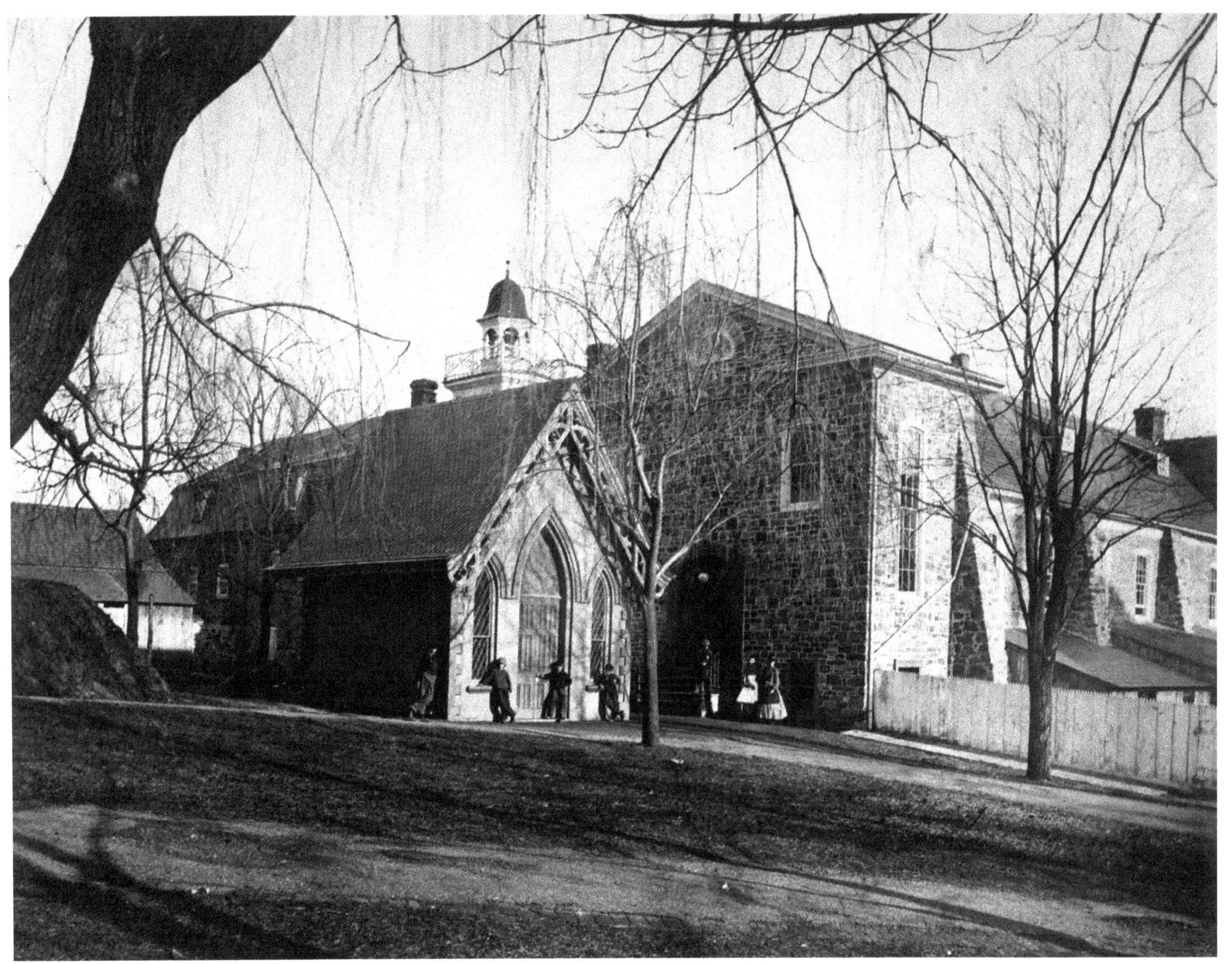

The Moravian Chapel, on the right, and its Gothic-style "dead house" were photographed in Bethlehem in 1866. In a practice characteristic to the Moravian sect, the deceased were placed in a dead house and guarded by the pallbearers while services were held in the chapel.

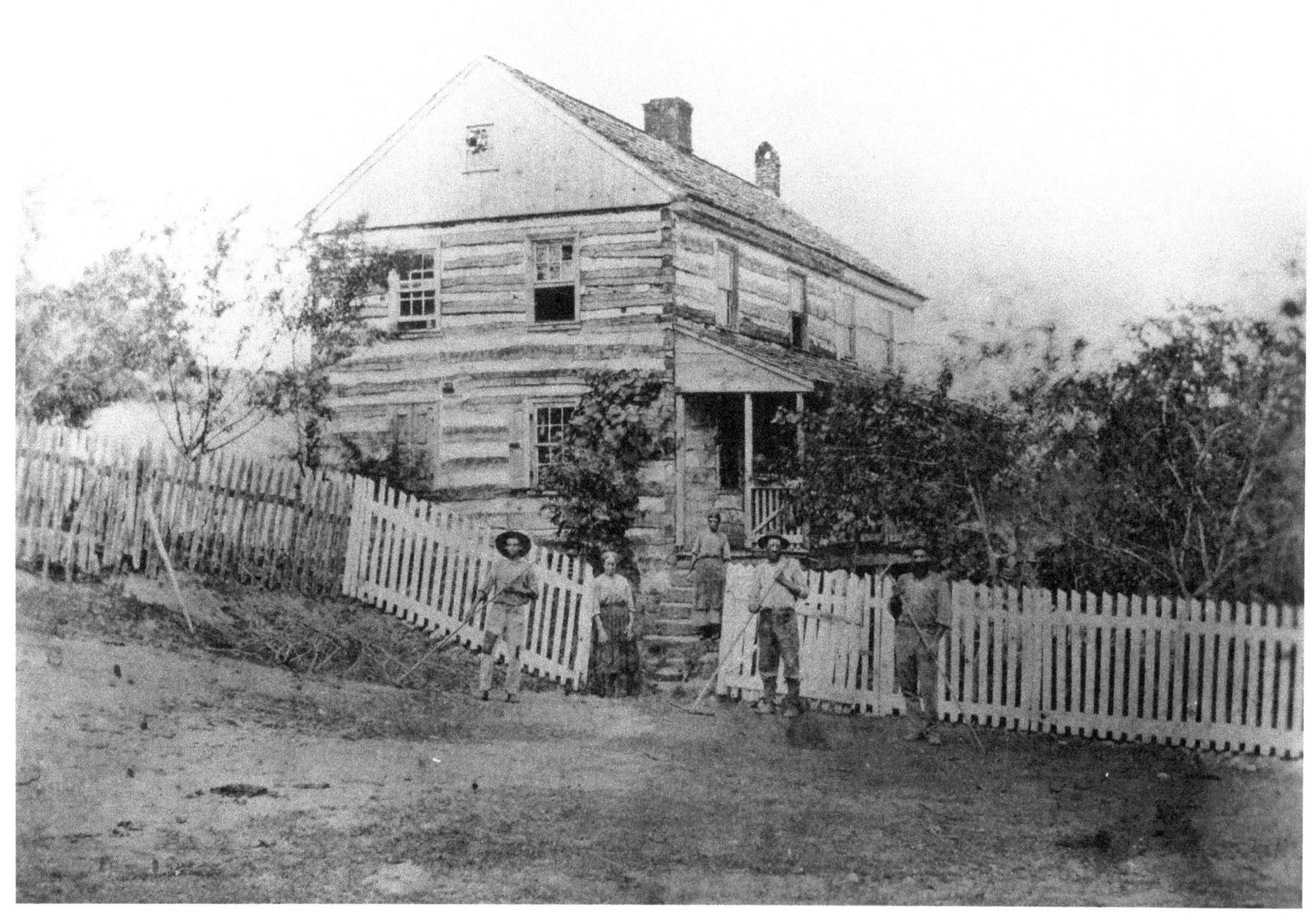

A family poses in front of their log house on Welsh Mountain in Lancaster County, circa 1870.

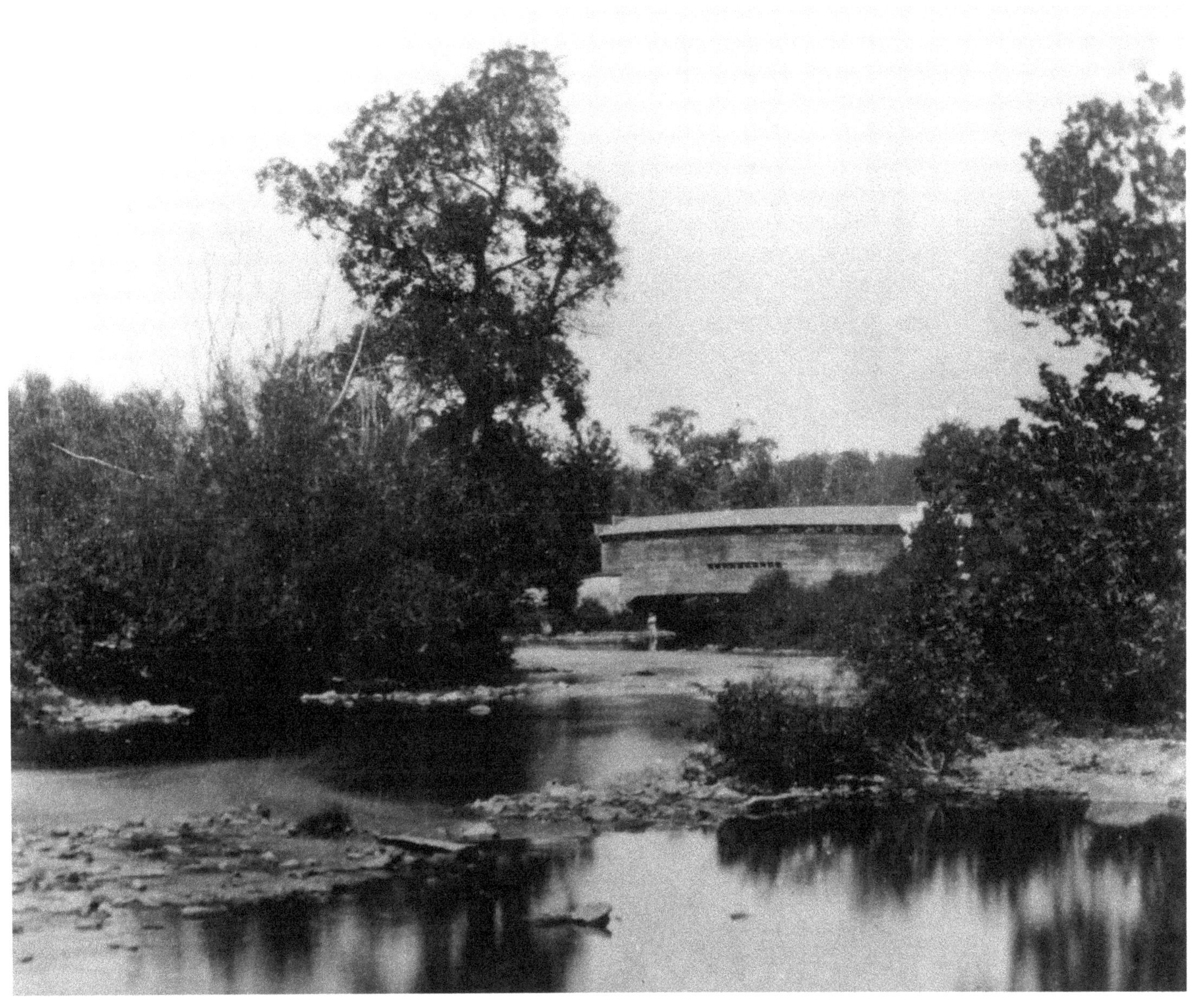

The Kennedy Covered Bridge, spanning the French Creek in Chester County, was built in 1856 and is seen here circa 1870. The bridge was destroyed by fire in 1985, and a replica was constructed on the site three years later.

A crew of four men attends a large, mounded charcoal burner in the Hopewell Furnace region, circa 1870. Charcoal was necessary in the cold-blast iron industry and was often produced by itinerants able to follow the wood-cutting crews in search of timber.

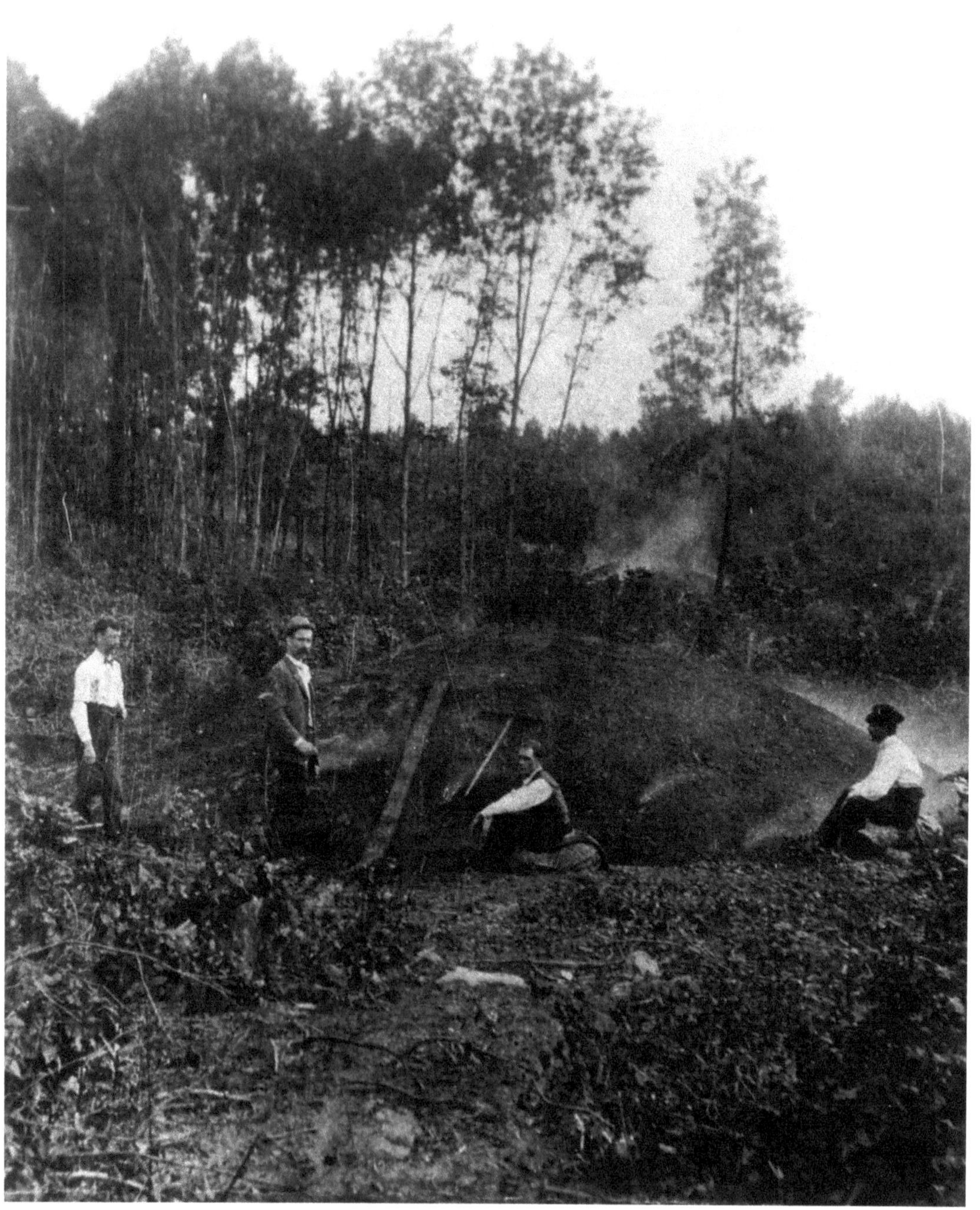

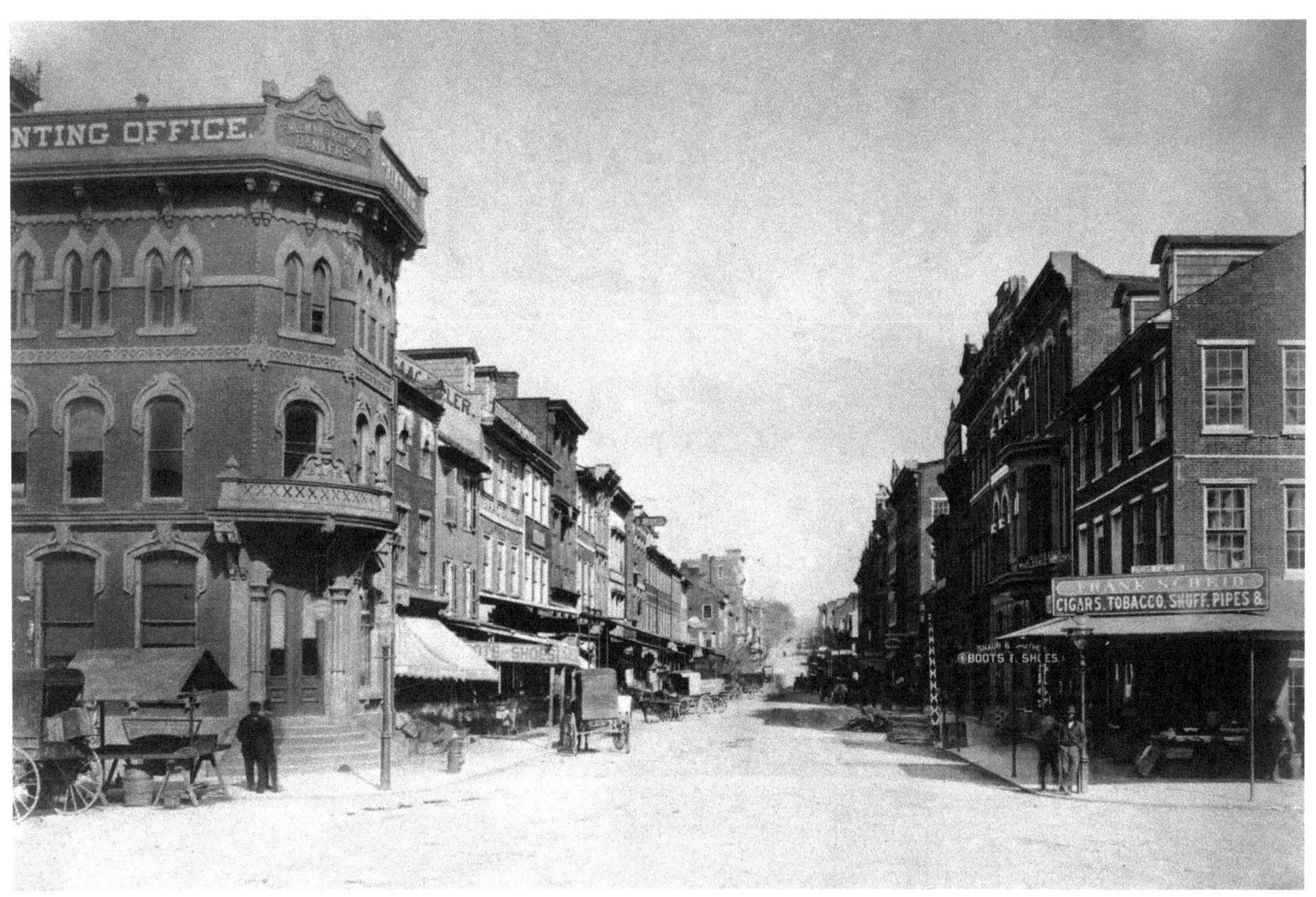

A view of East King Street near Center Square (now Penn Square) in Lancaster, circa 1875, highlights the "cigar factory" business of Frank Scheid.

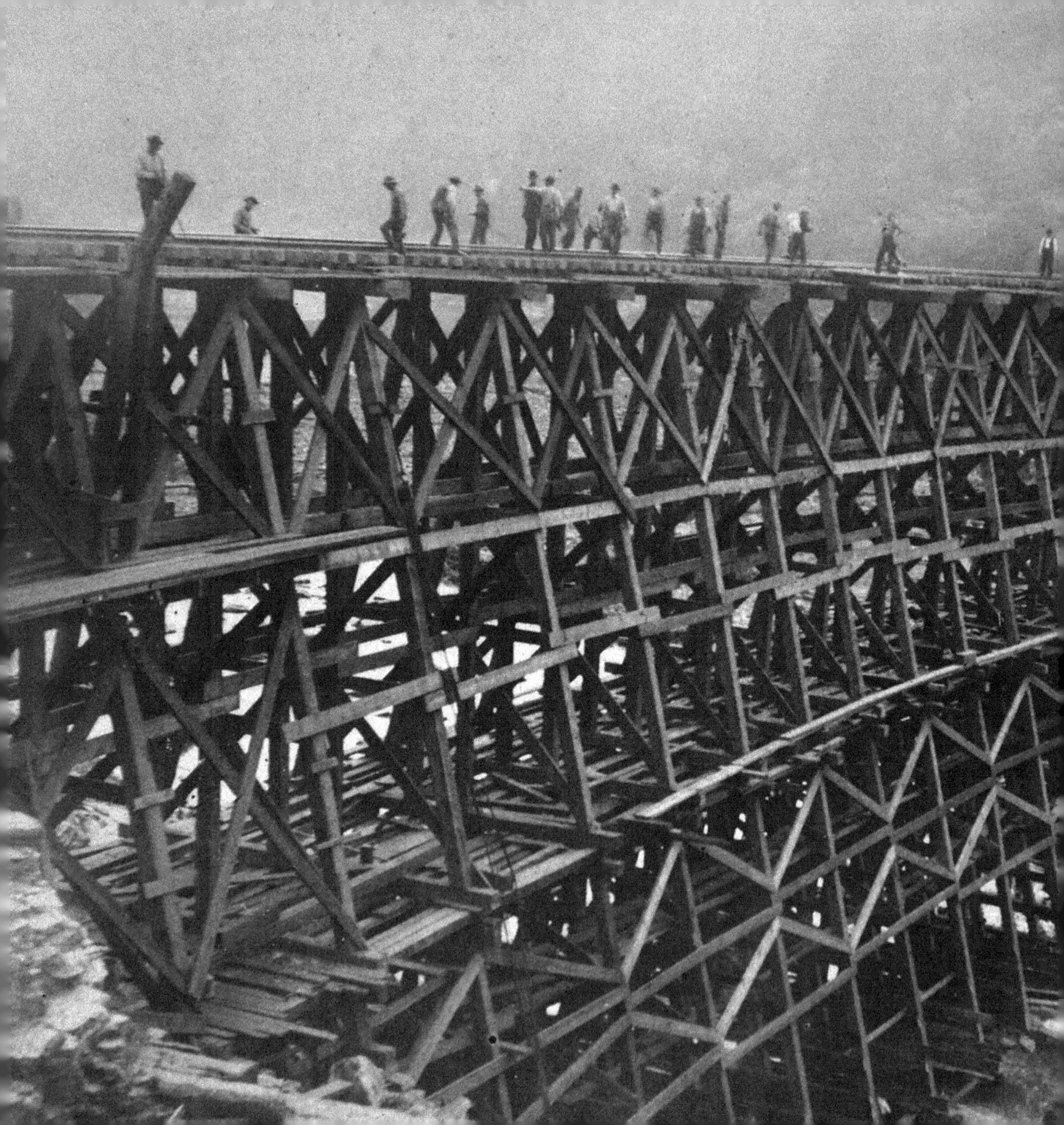

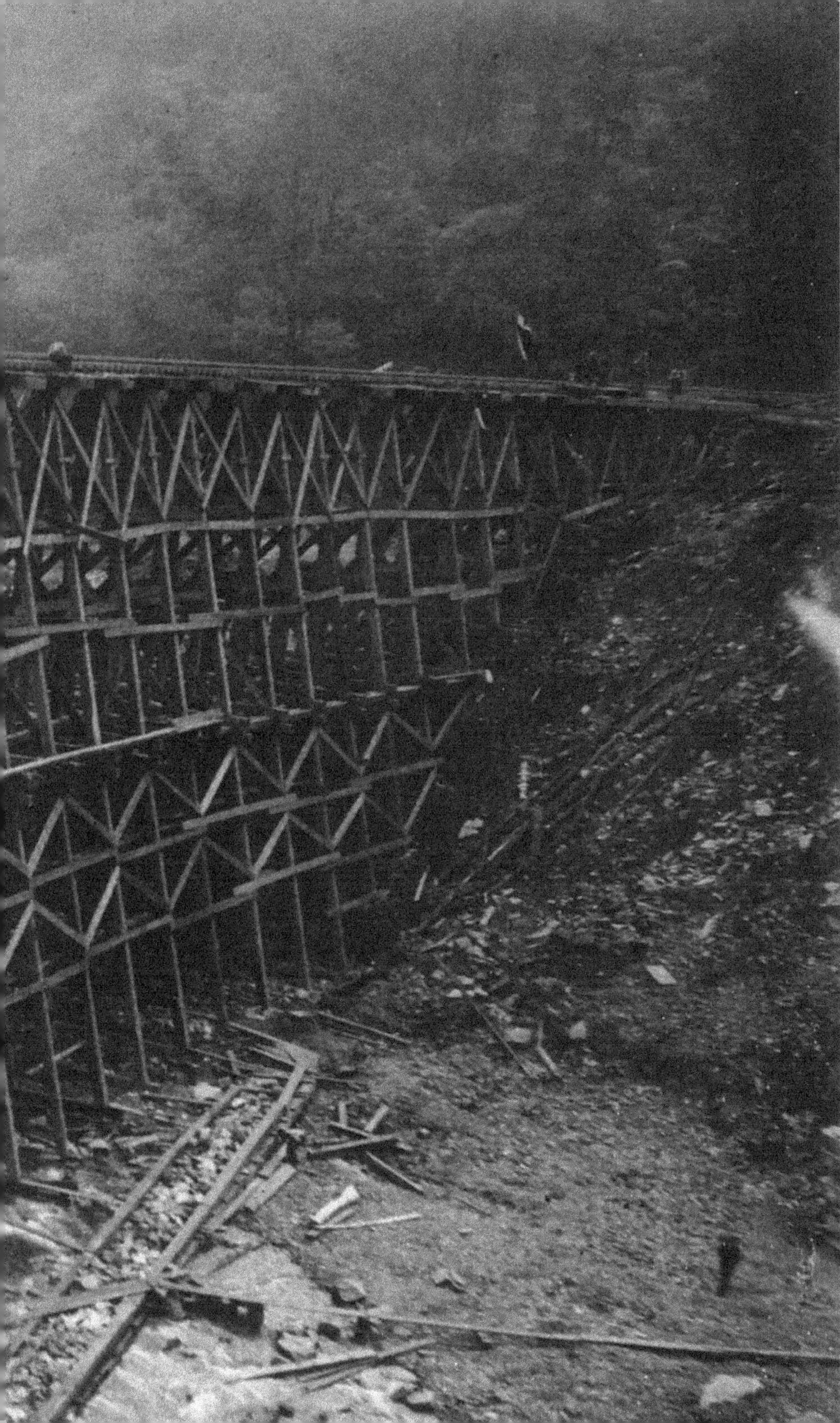

Men work to complete construction on a timber trestle intended for railroad use. Faced with dramatic mountain ranges and deep valleys throughout the state, railroad engineers frequently designed and constructed remarkable features like this one.

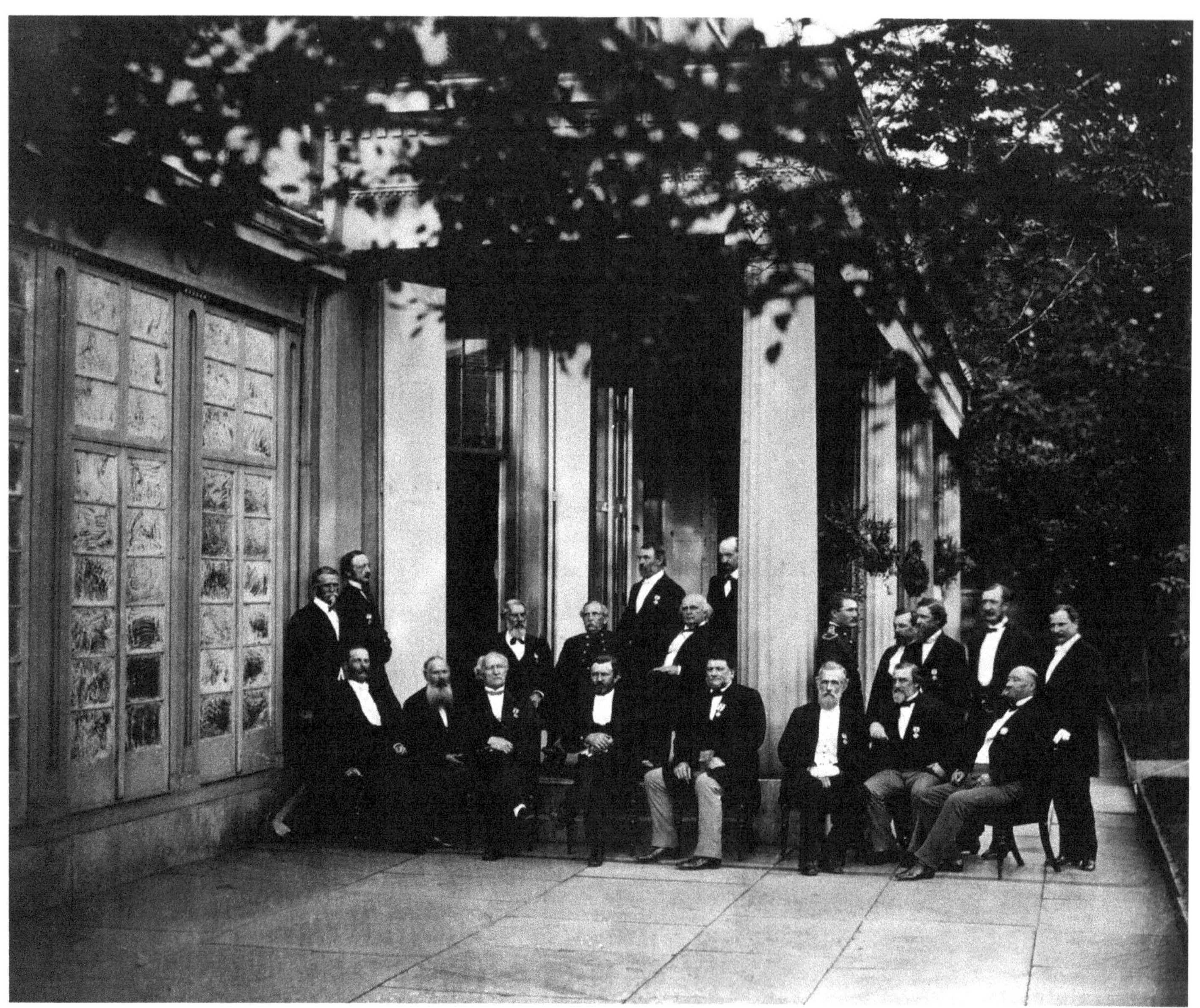

The Aztec Club, a social and entertainment club, was founded in 1847 in Mexico City by American officers occupying the city during the Mexican War. In this photo, members of the club are photographed at an anniversary dinner held at the home of General Robert Patterson, at Thirteenth and Locust streets in Philadelphia, in 1873. President Ulysses S. Grant is seated in the front row, fourth from the left.

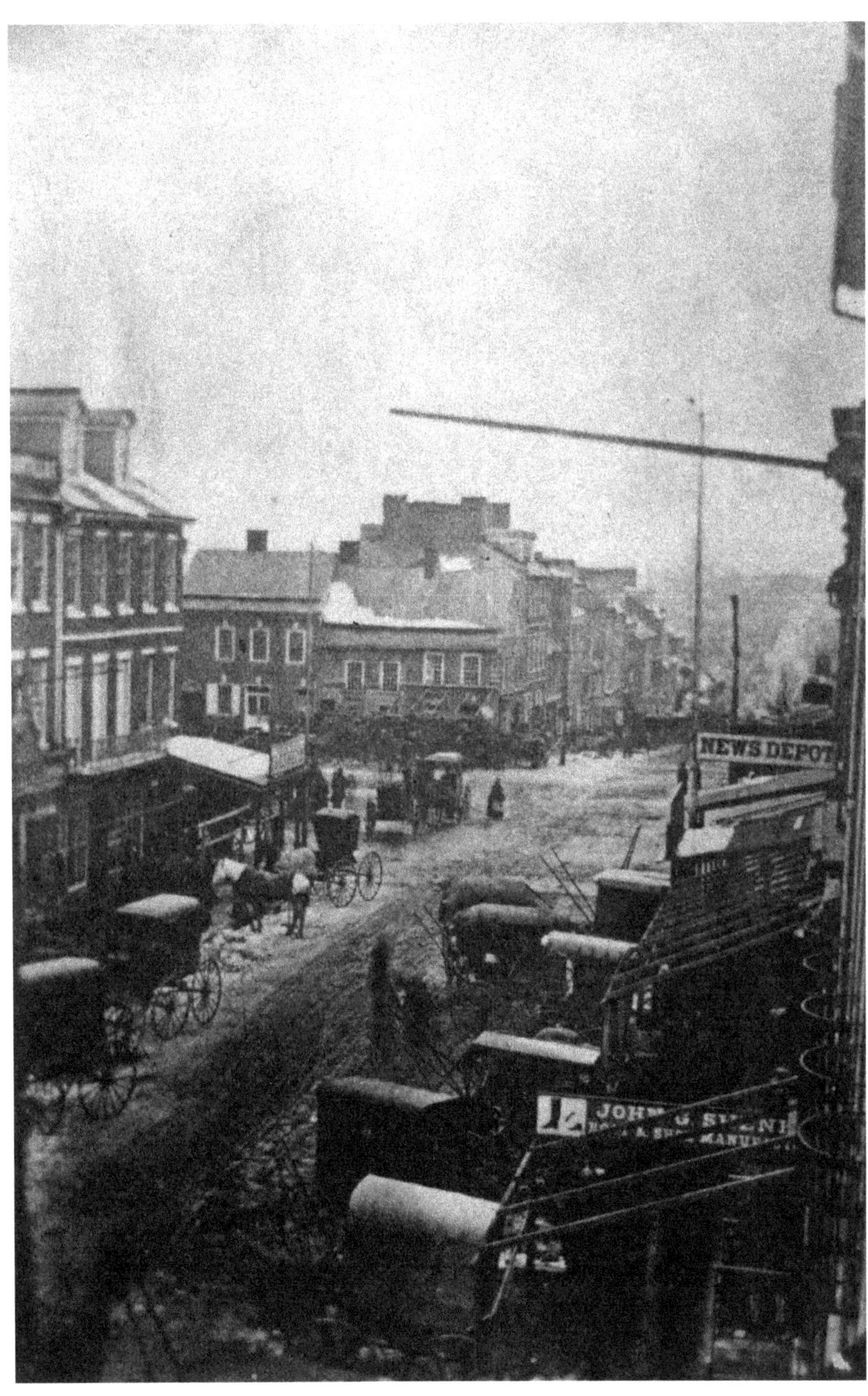

Snow blankets West King Street in Lancaster, originally known as Hickory Town, circa 1875.

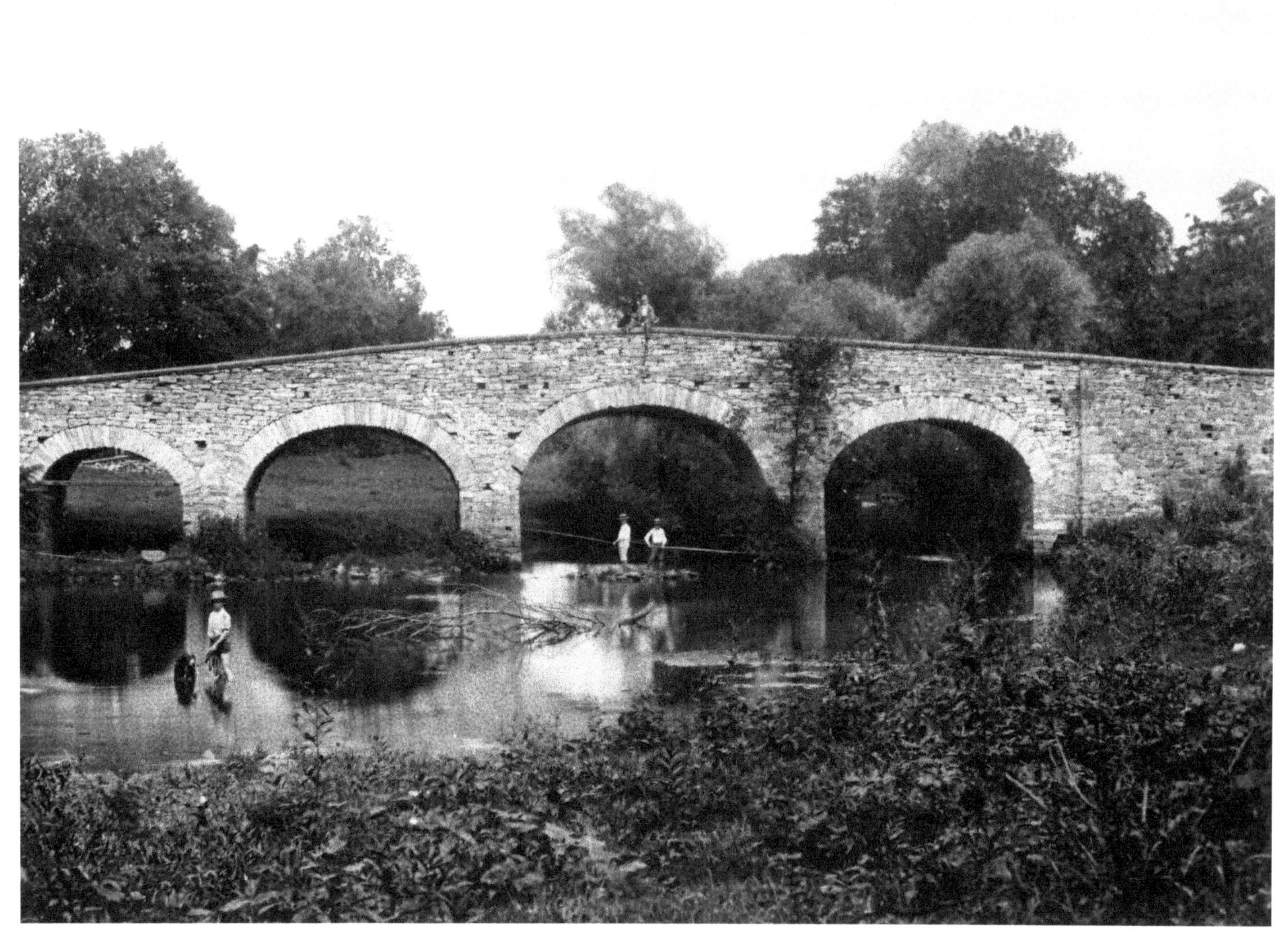

An old stone bridge on Cocalico Creek near Ephrata provides an ideal fishing spot in the 1870s.

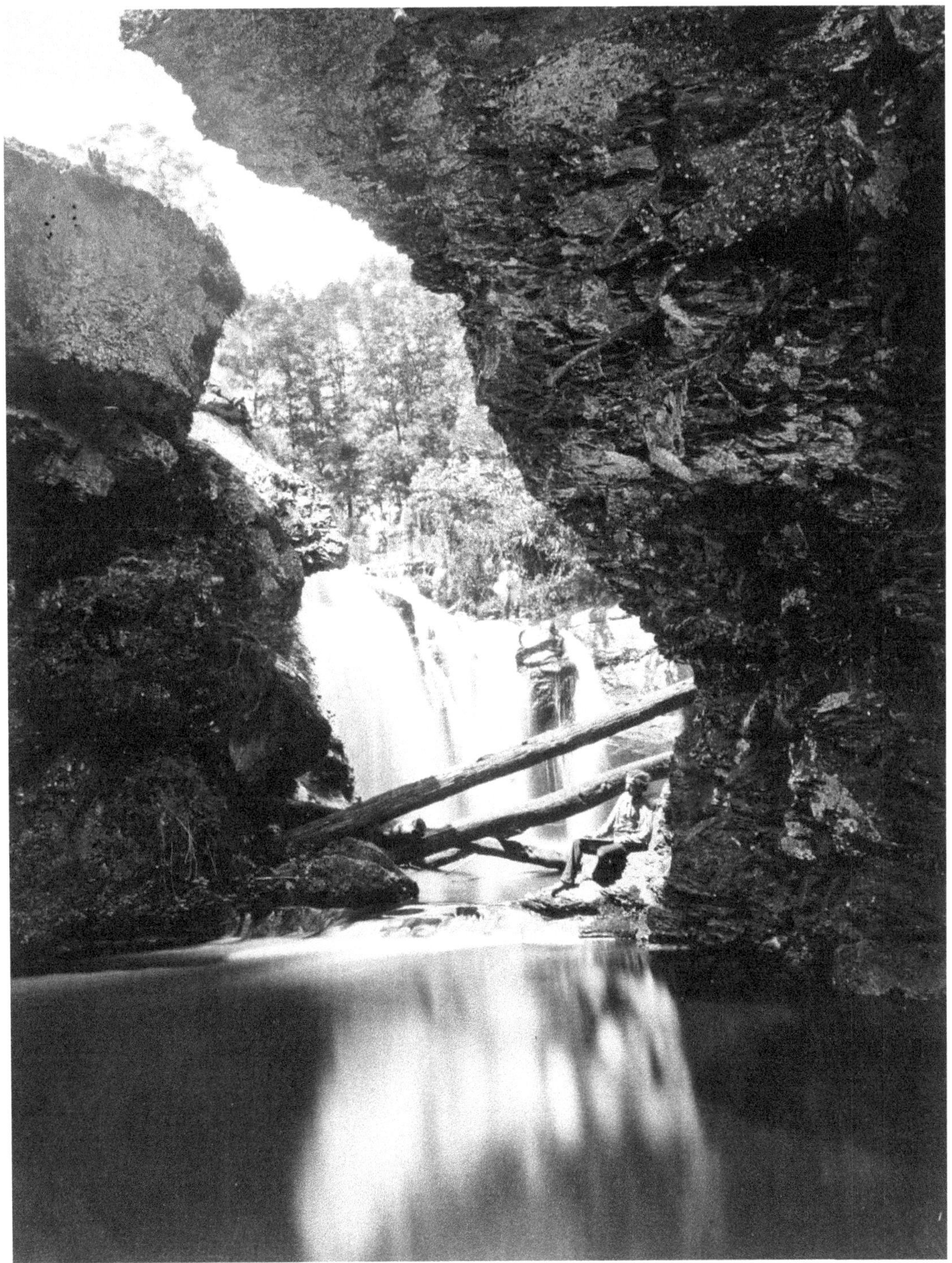

A hiker enjoys a secluded waterfall in Delaware Water Gap, along the boundary between Pennsylvania and New Jersey. By the latter half of the nineteenth century, the Delaware Water Gap region was a well-established summer resort area.

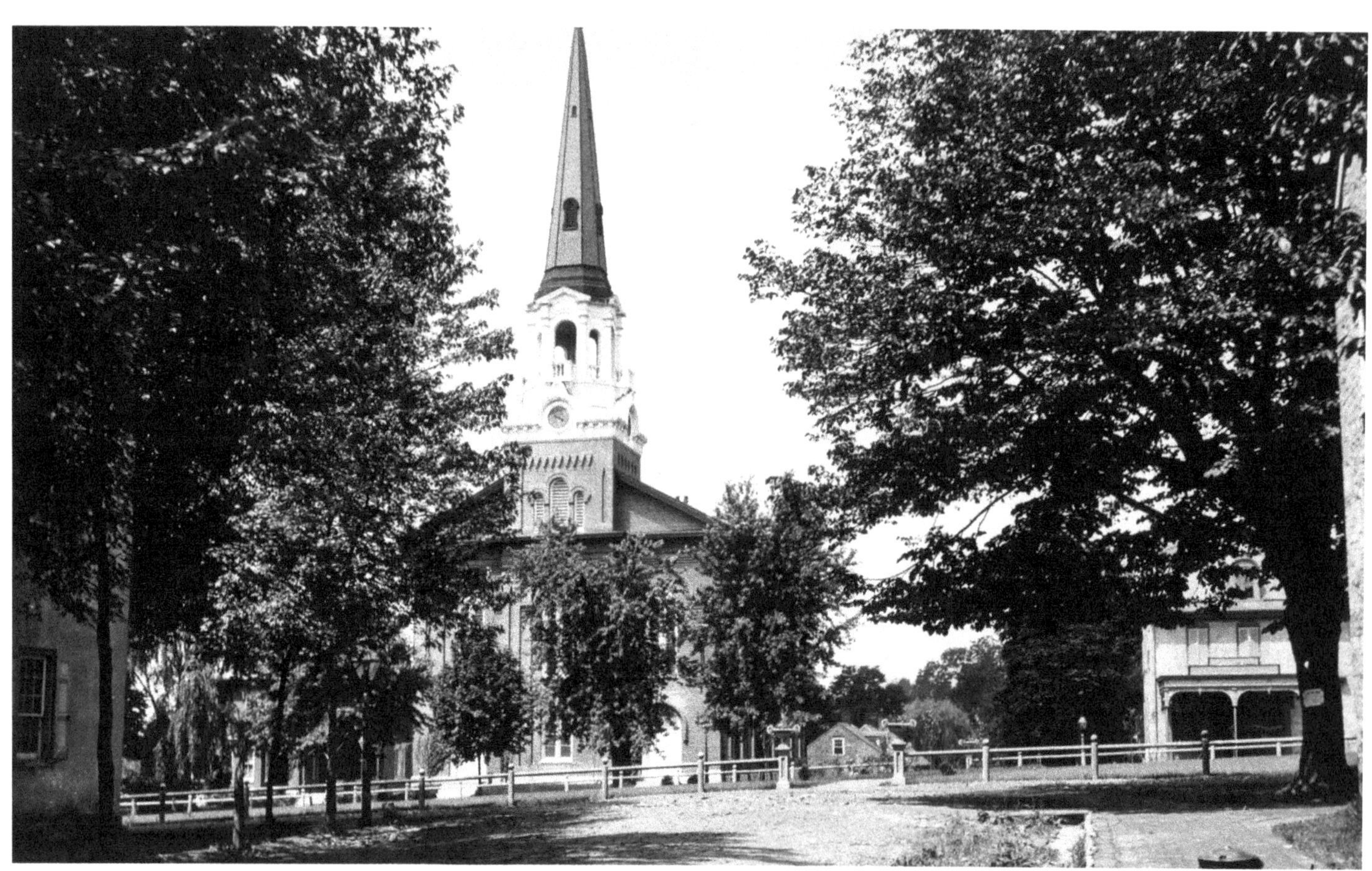

The Moravian Church in Nazareth, built in 1861, is seen here some years later. The earliest Moravians, a reformist sect that predated Martin Luther by 100 years, arrived in America in 1740 and temporarily settled in Nazareth. Within a year, they relocated to Bethlehem, which today serves as the Moravian Church's headquarters.

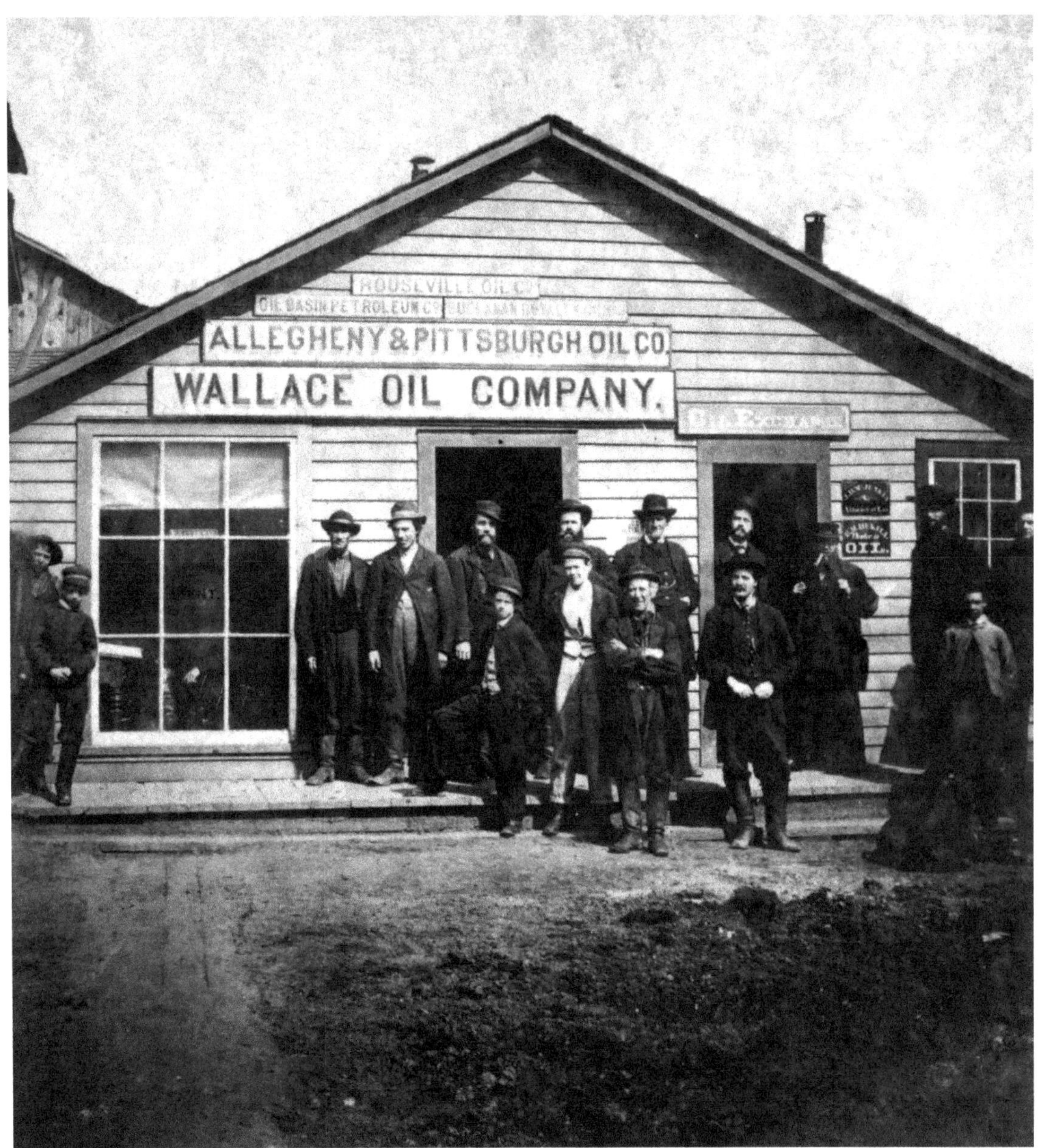

Within five years of the discovery of drillable oil in the counties of western Pennsylvania in 1859, hundreds of individual wells and small companies sprang up. Founded within a few months of each other in 1864, four oil companies share a headquarters in Rouseville, Venango County, a decade after the Civil War.

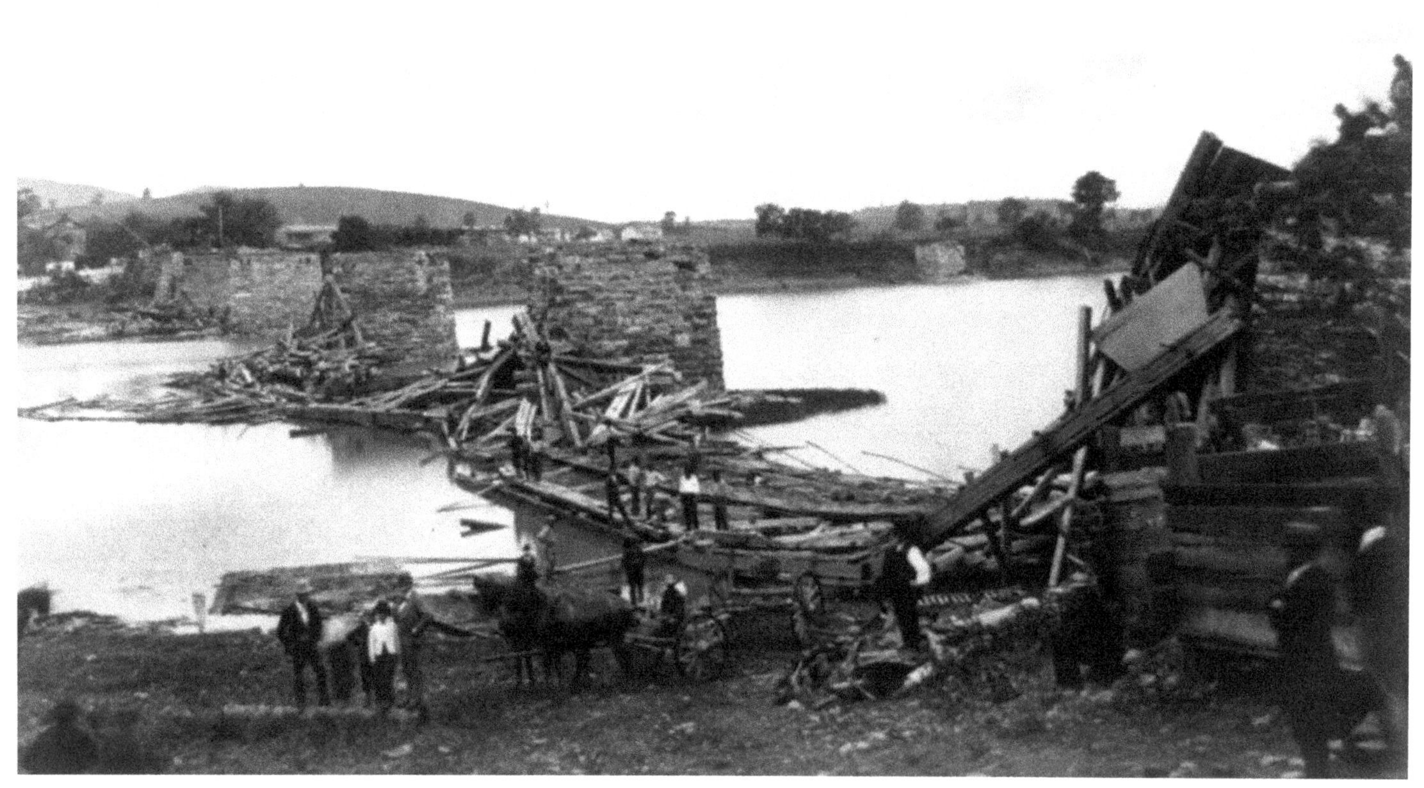

Men work to clear the remains of the Lewistown Bridge over the Juniata River after a tornado, July 4, 1874. Seven people were reported killed by the tornado, including three who were on this bridge or under it.

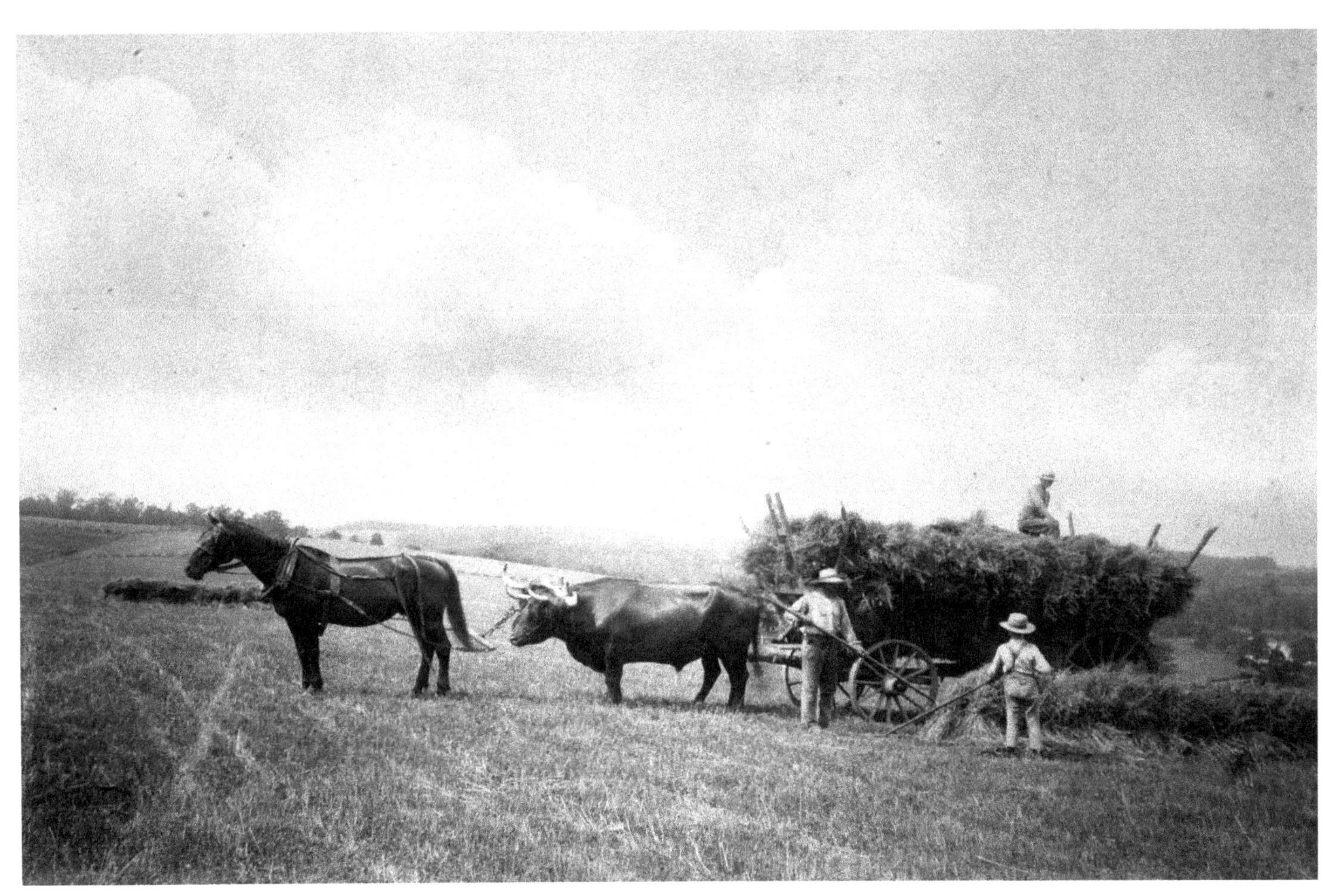

Farmers harvest straw in Chester County, 1880.

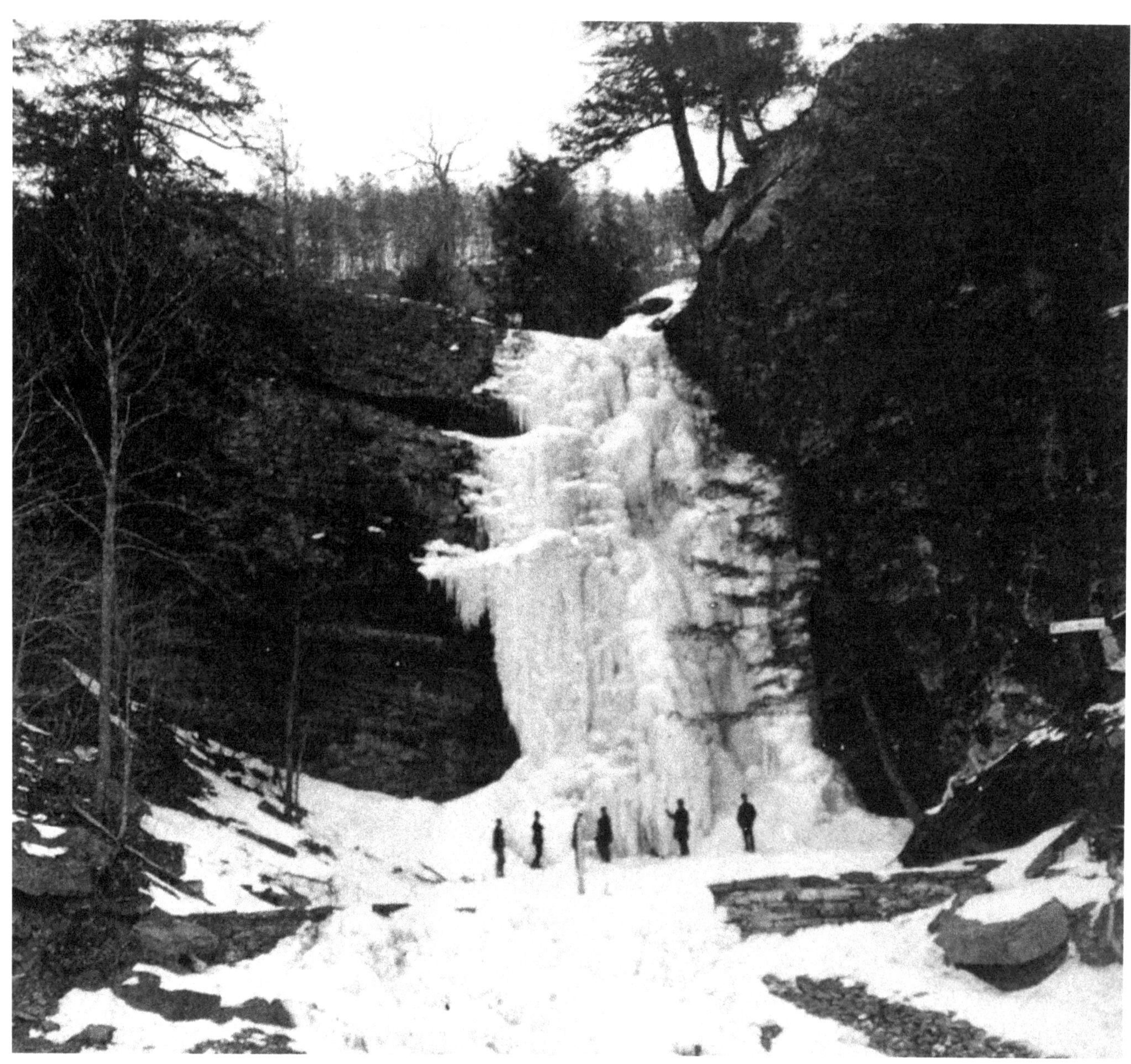

Visitors are dwarfed by a frozen falling spring near Campbell's Ledge, Luzerne County, in March 1875. The area remains a local fishing attraction.

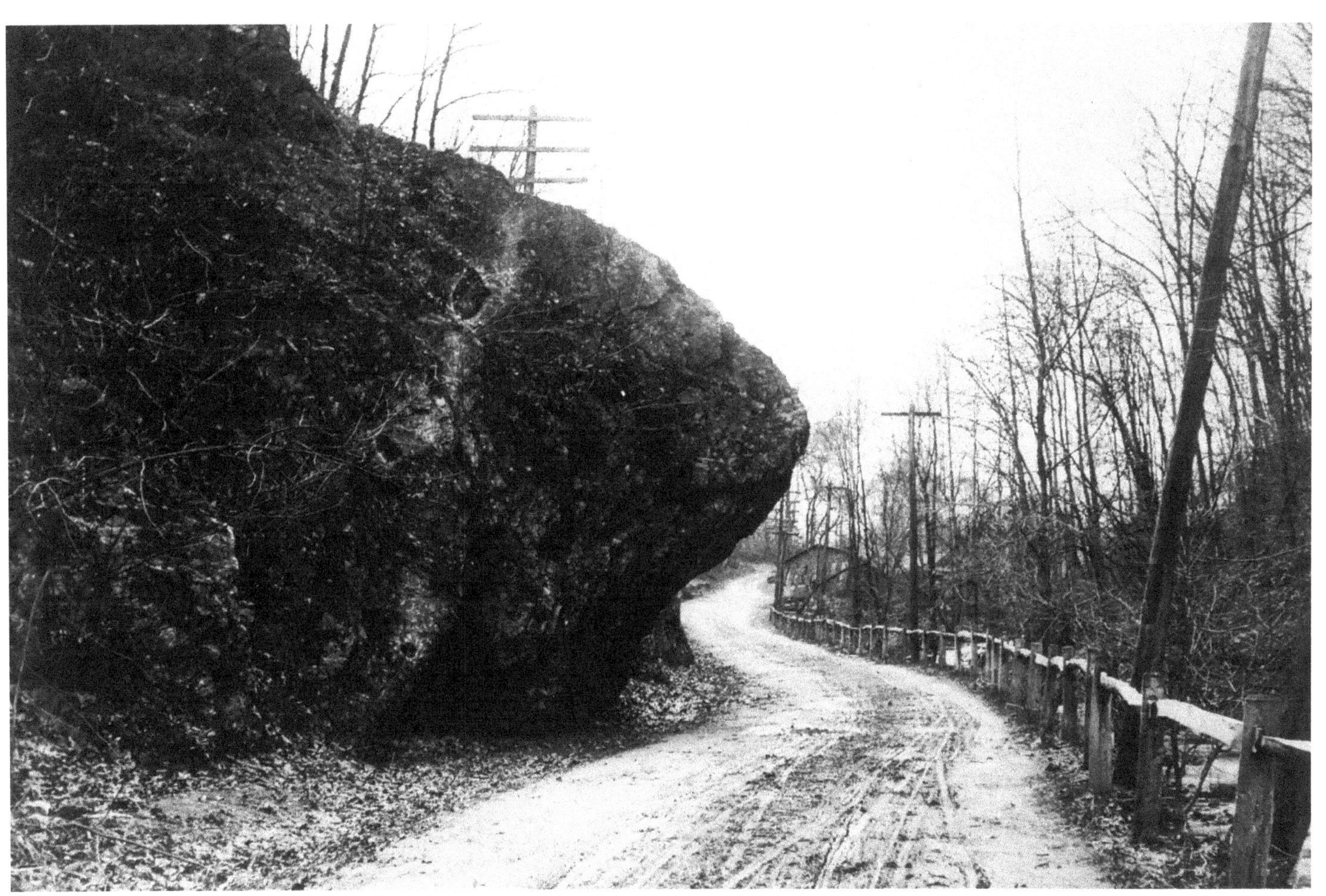

A road winds past the Overhanging Rock at Gulph Mills, circa 1890. It is believed that General George Washington and his army considered this location for a permanent winter encampment in December 1777. Instead, they rested here for one week and then went on to Valley Forge, where they remained until June 1778.

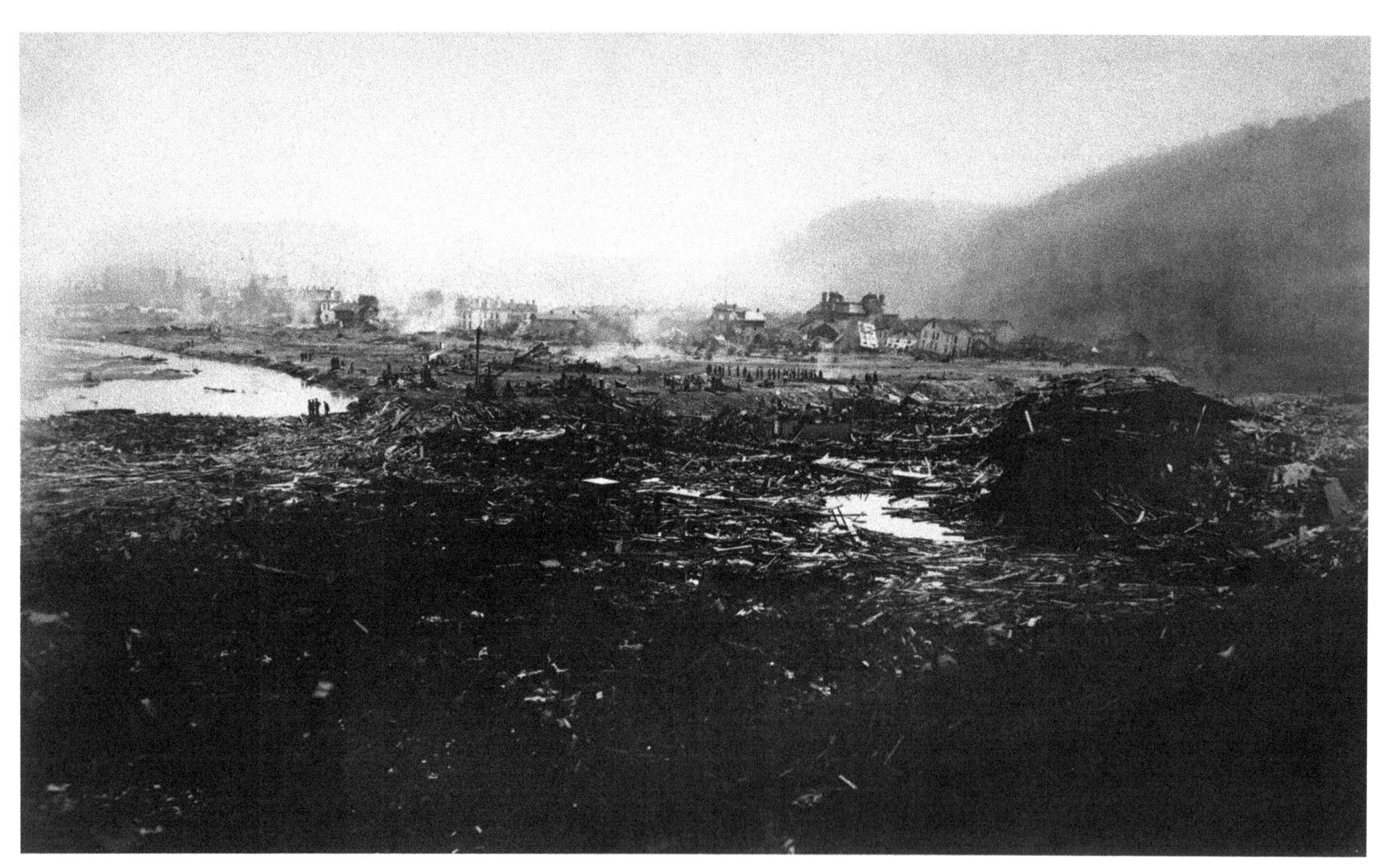

Devastation followed the collapse of the weakened South Fork Dam upstream from Johnstown, May 31, 1889. More than 2,200 people were killed as a result of the flood.

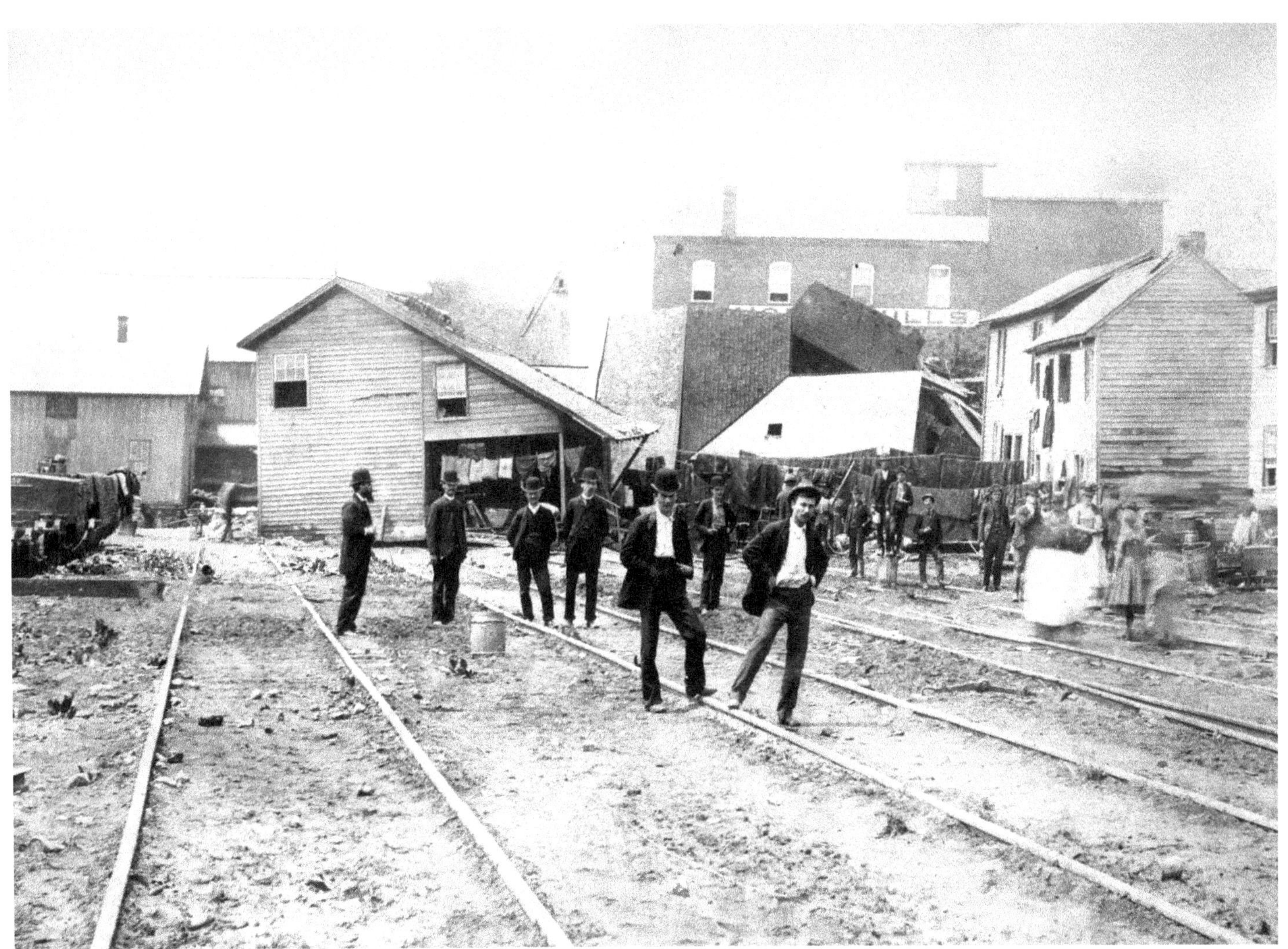

The devastation in Johnstown resulted in a tremendous influx of volunteers. The newly formed American Red Cross, led by Clara Barton, stayed in the town for five months and raised an unprecedented $3 million in the organization's first major disaster relief effort.

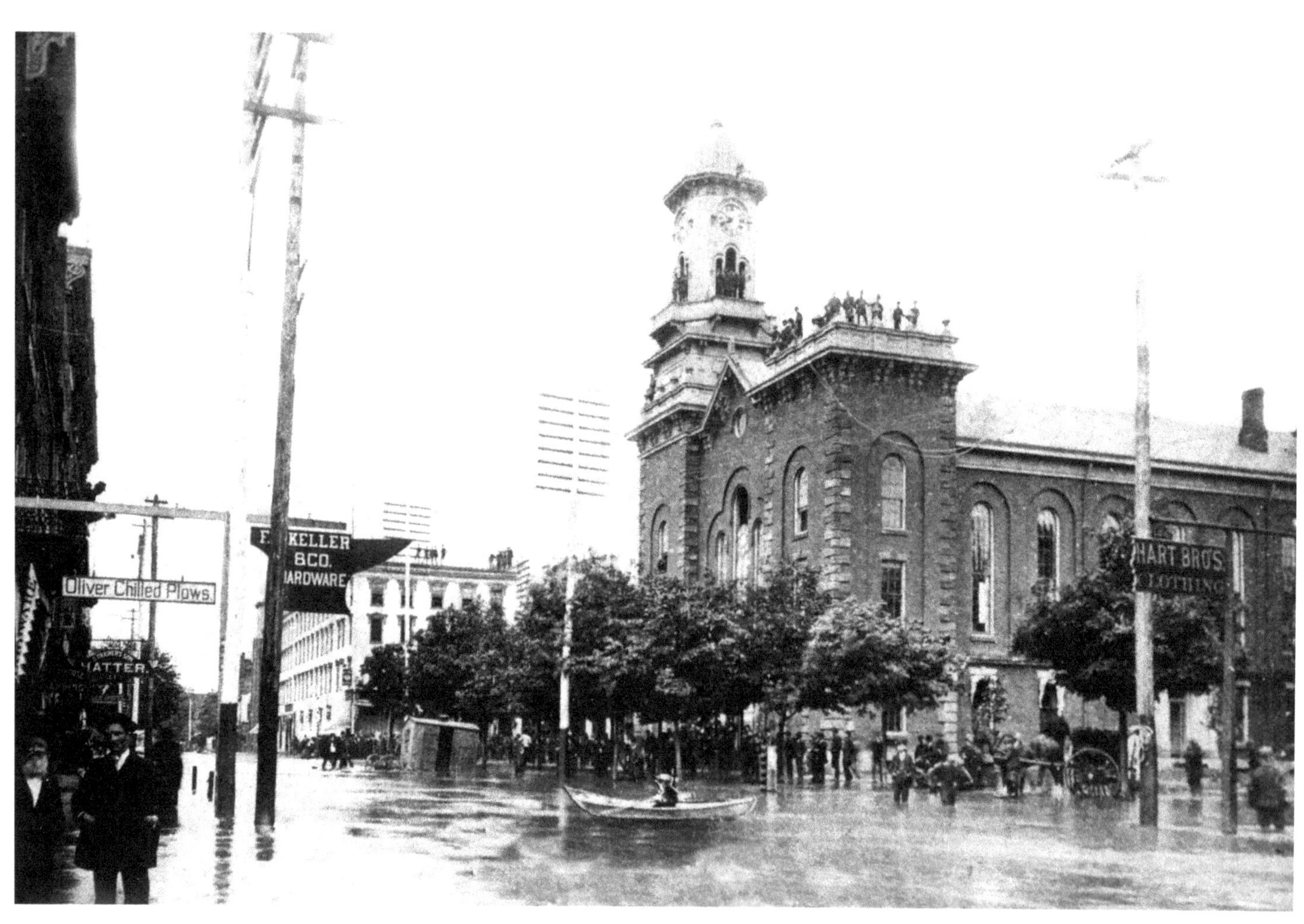

Occurring on the same date as the famous Johnstown flood but with far less catastrophic results, Williamsport, too, was inundated. Here, on June 1, 1889, residents walk through knee-high water and gather atop the County Courthouse.

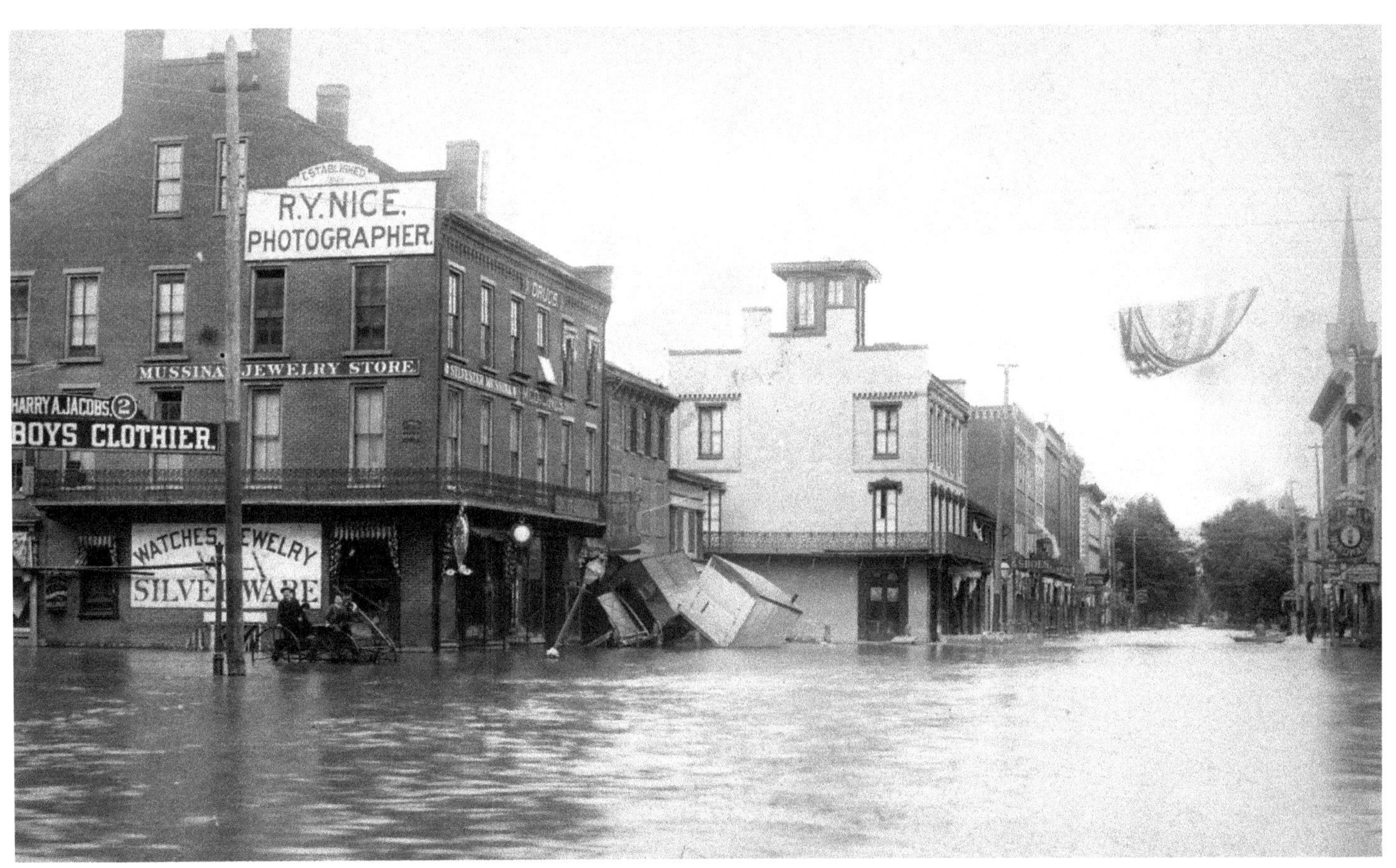

Four people keep themselves dry on a buggy at left in this image of Williamsport's Third Street, viewed east from Market Square, June 1, 1889.

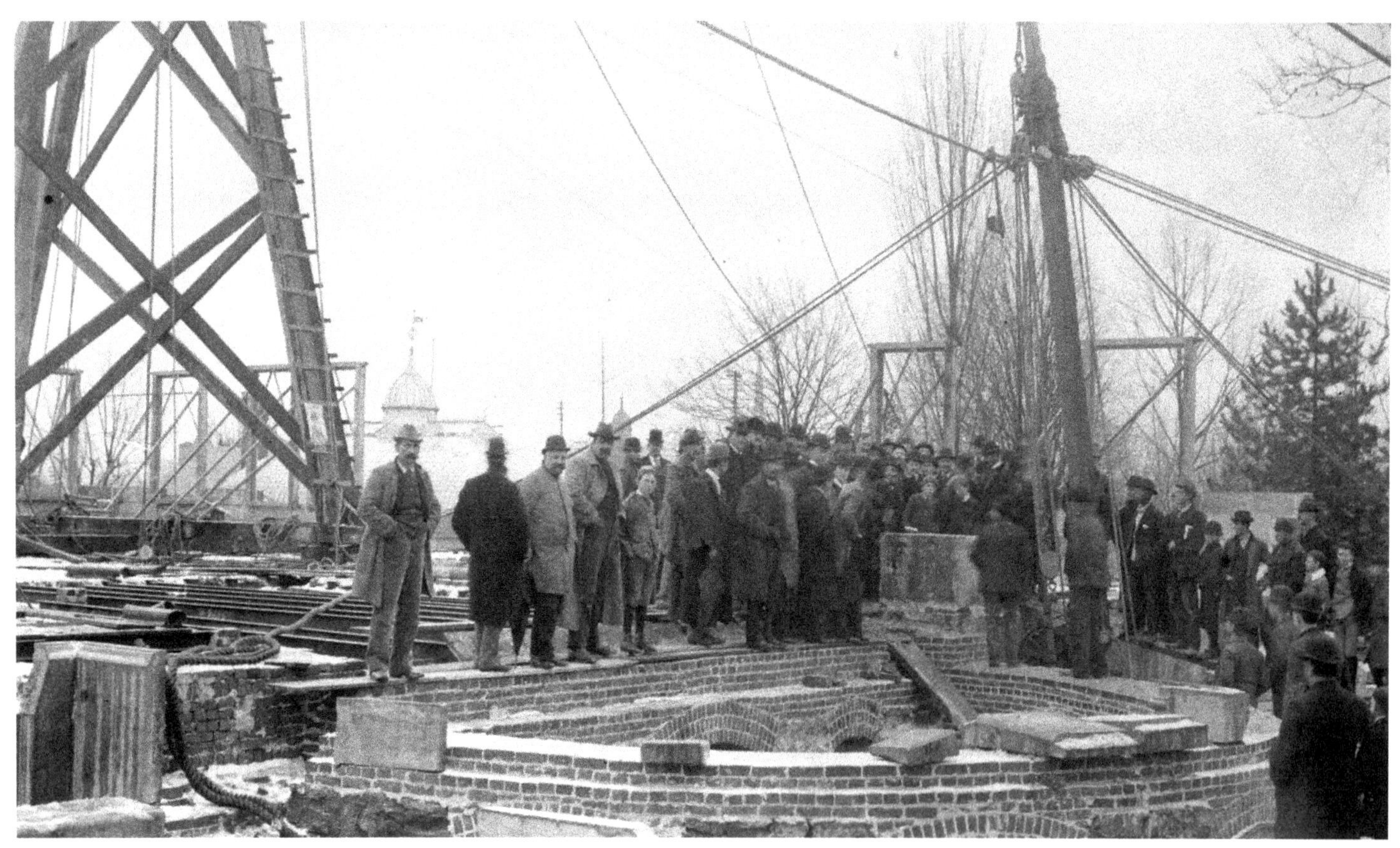

The cornerstone is laid to the new State Library and Executive Building in Harrisburg, December 15, 1893. The city was chosen the state capital in 1810, and the legislature moved there from Lancaster two years later.

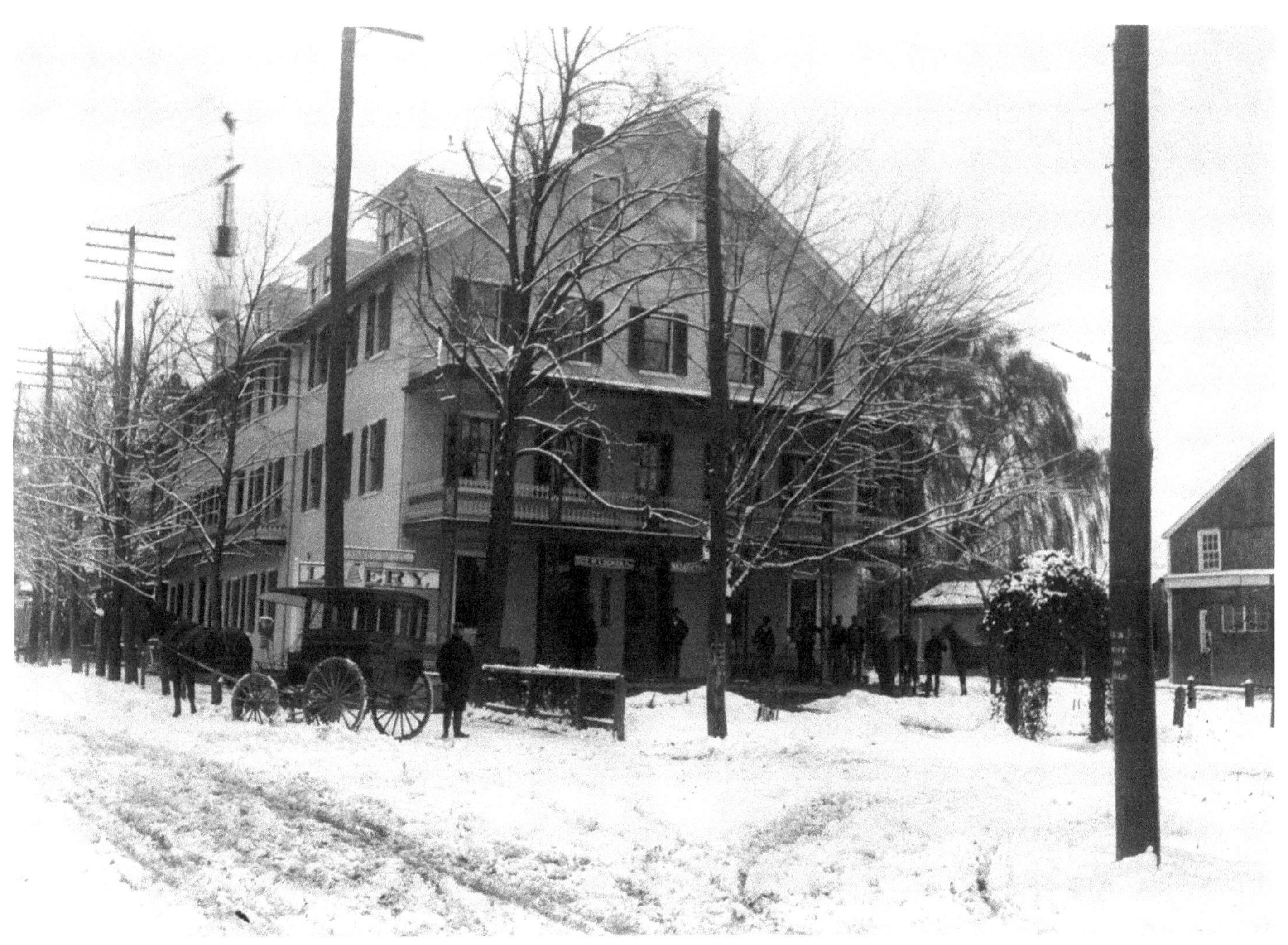

Visitors enjoy a snowy afternoon in front of the Nazareth Inn, at the intersection of South Main Street, Belvidere Street, and Mauch Chunk Street. The earliest inn at this location was constructed in 1771.

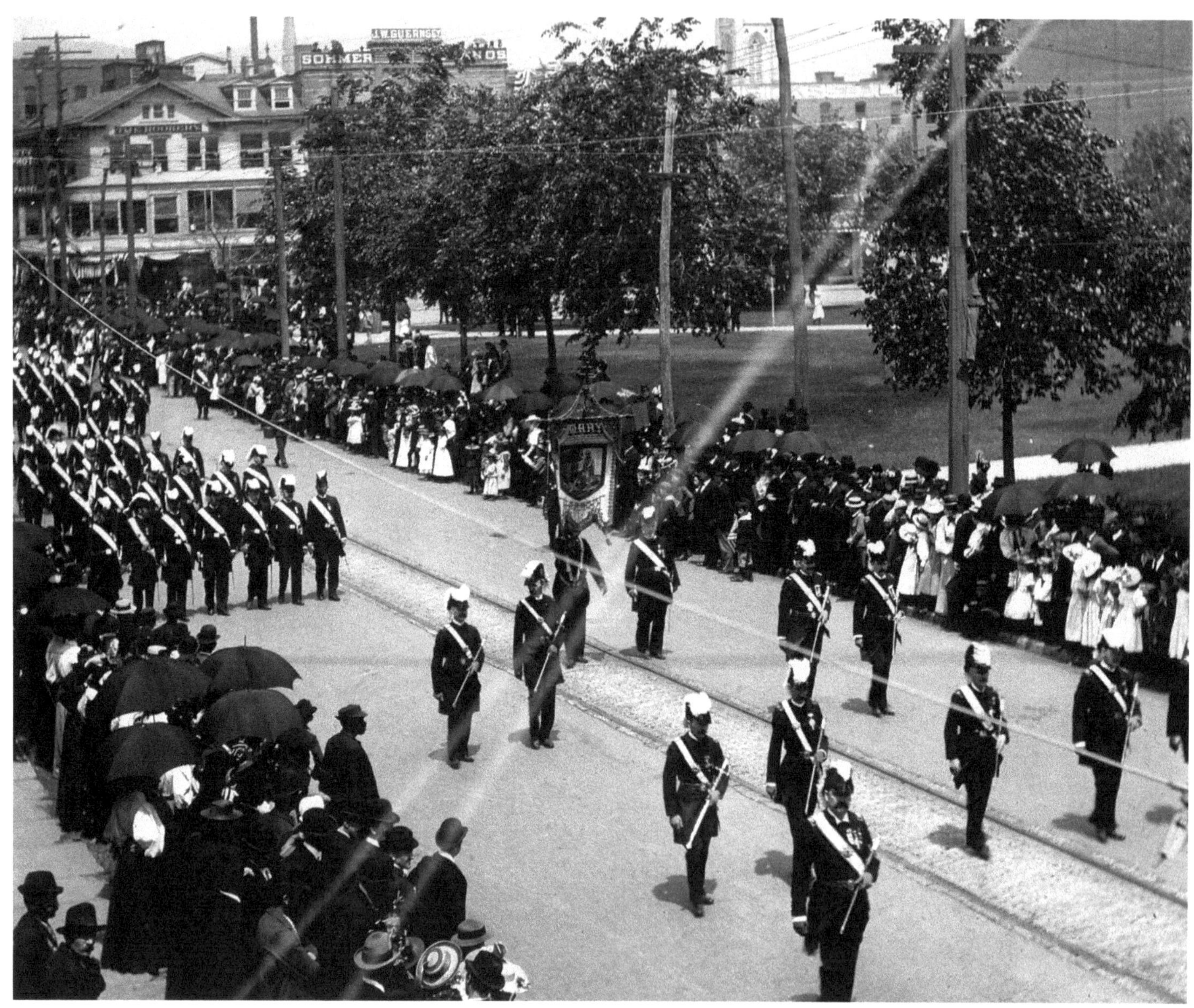

A religious parade passes onlookers on the streets of Scranton, circa 1890. In the background, a rooftop sign advertises the firm of J. W. Guernsey, a local music dealer.

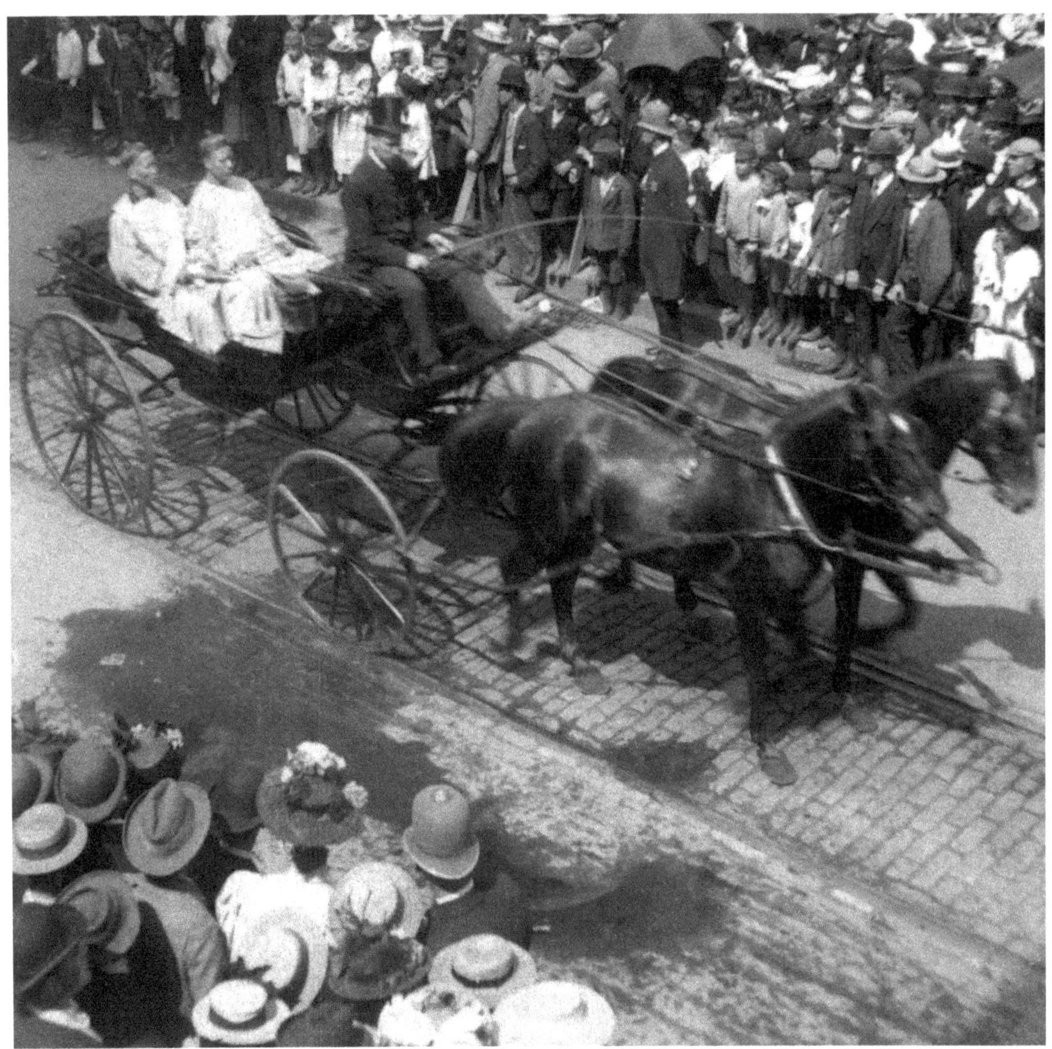

Chinese general and statesman Li Hung Chang rides in an open carriage with an attendant during a visit to Philadelphia in 1896. His visit to several American cities was an opportunity to advocate for changes in the anti–Chinese immigration laws passed in the 1880s.

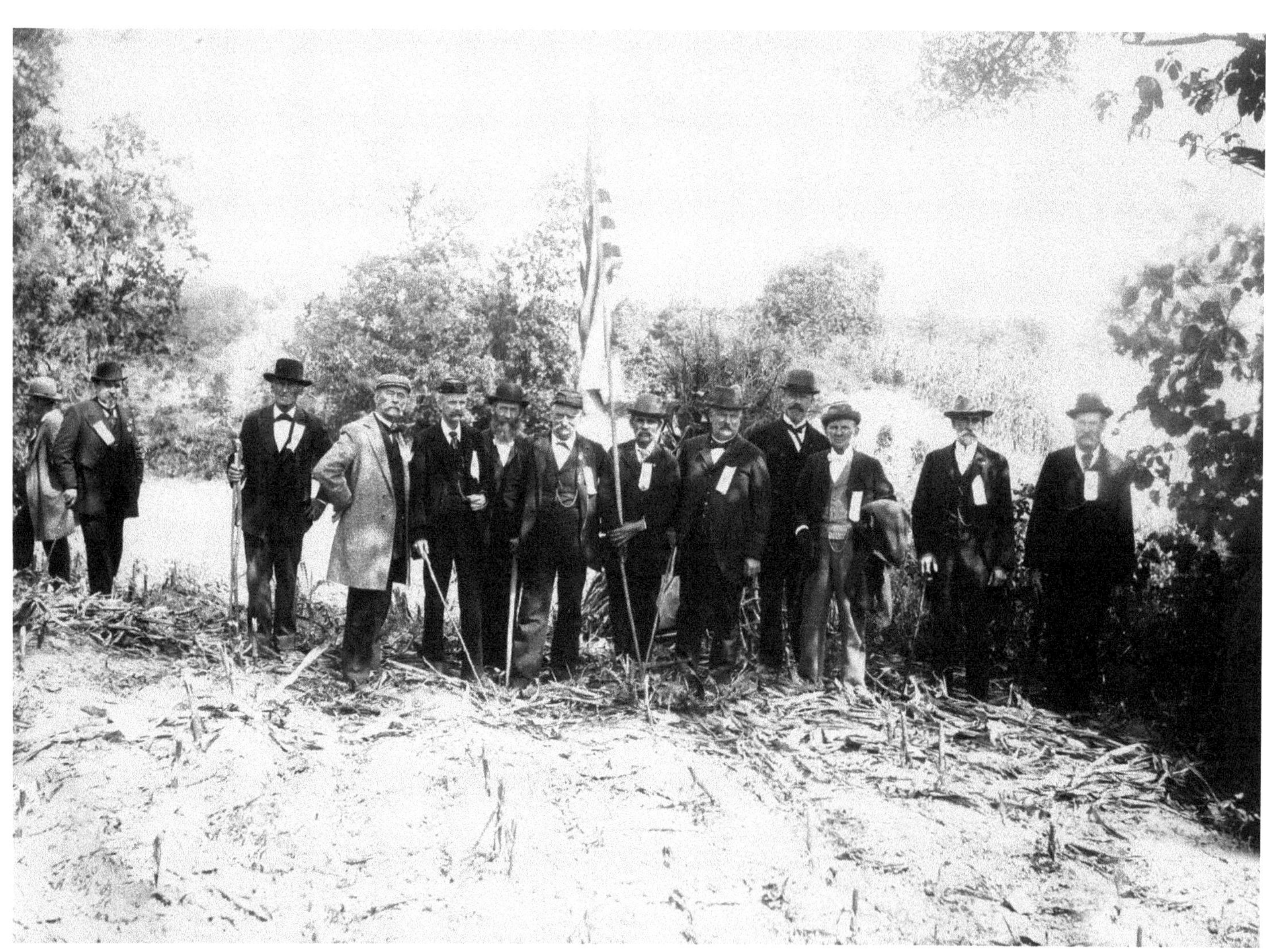

Surviving members of Company C of the 118th Regiment Pennsylvania Volunteers commemorate the 35th anniversary of the battle at Blackford's Ford, Maryland, that took place September 20, 1862. The 118th was nicknamed the "Corn Exchange Regiment" because the Philadelphia Corn Exchange, a brokerage house located at Second and Chestnut streets in Philadelphia, financed the regiment's formation.

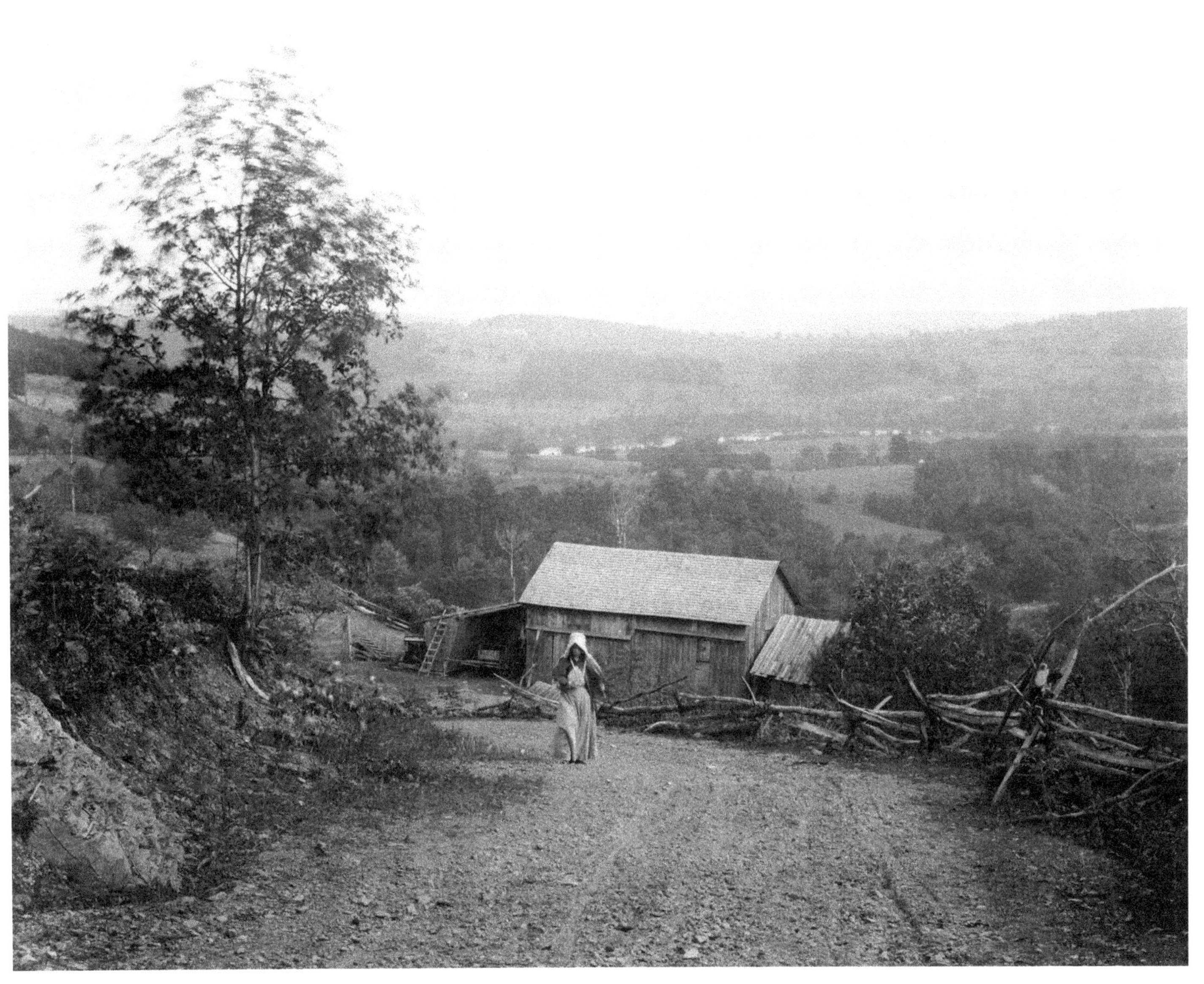

A woman walks up a valley road at Dingmans Ferry, Pike County, circa 1897.

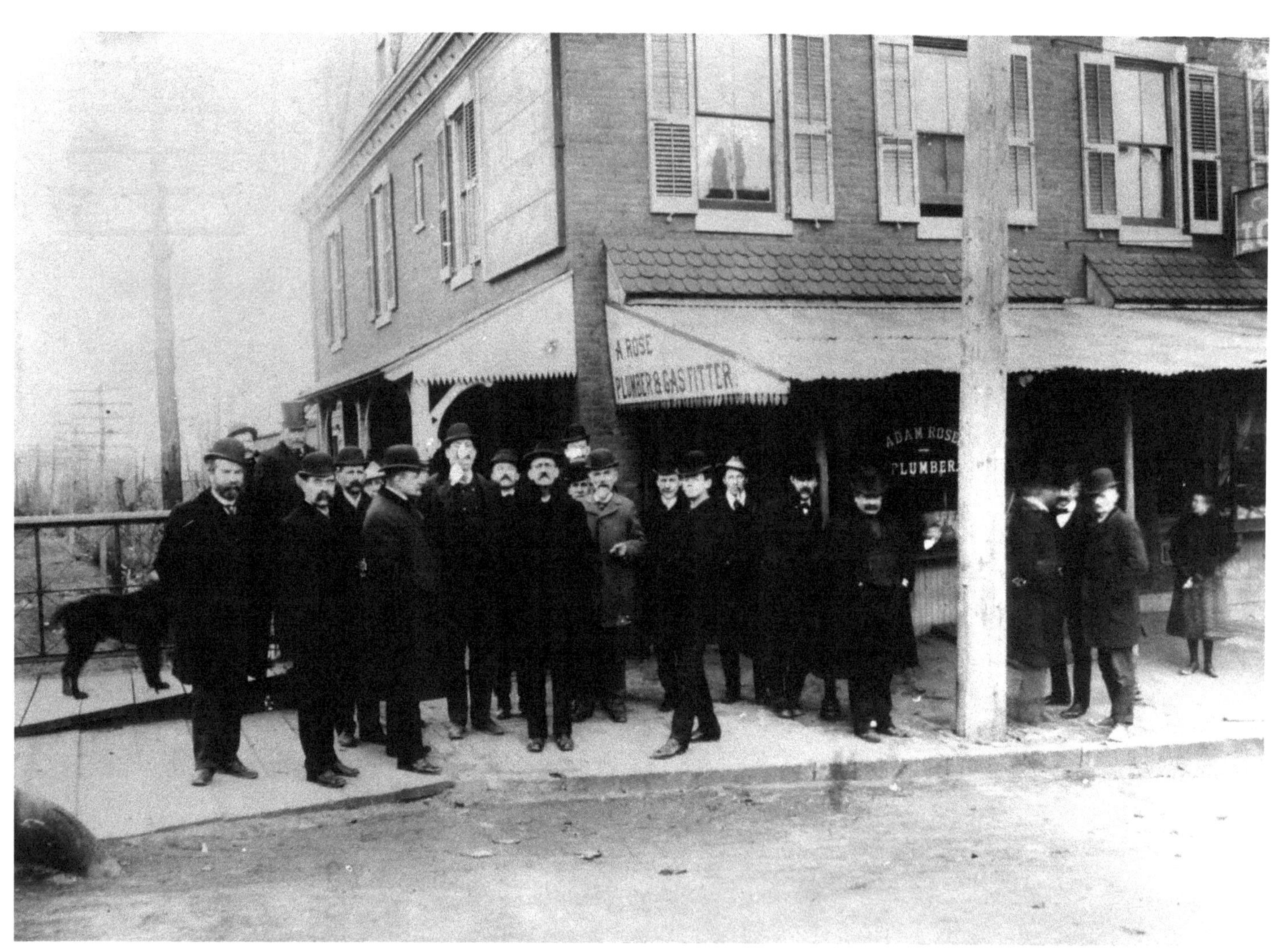

Local voters gather on Election Day 1897 in Sharon Hill, Delaware County.

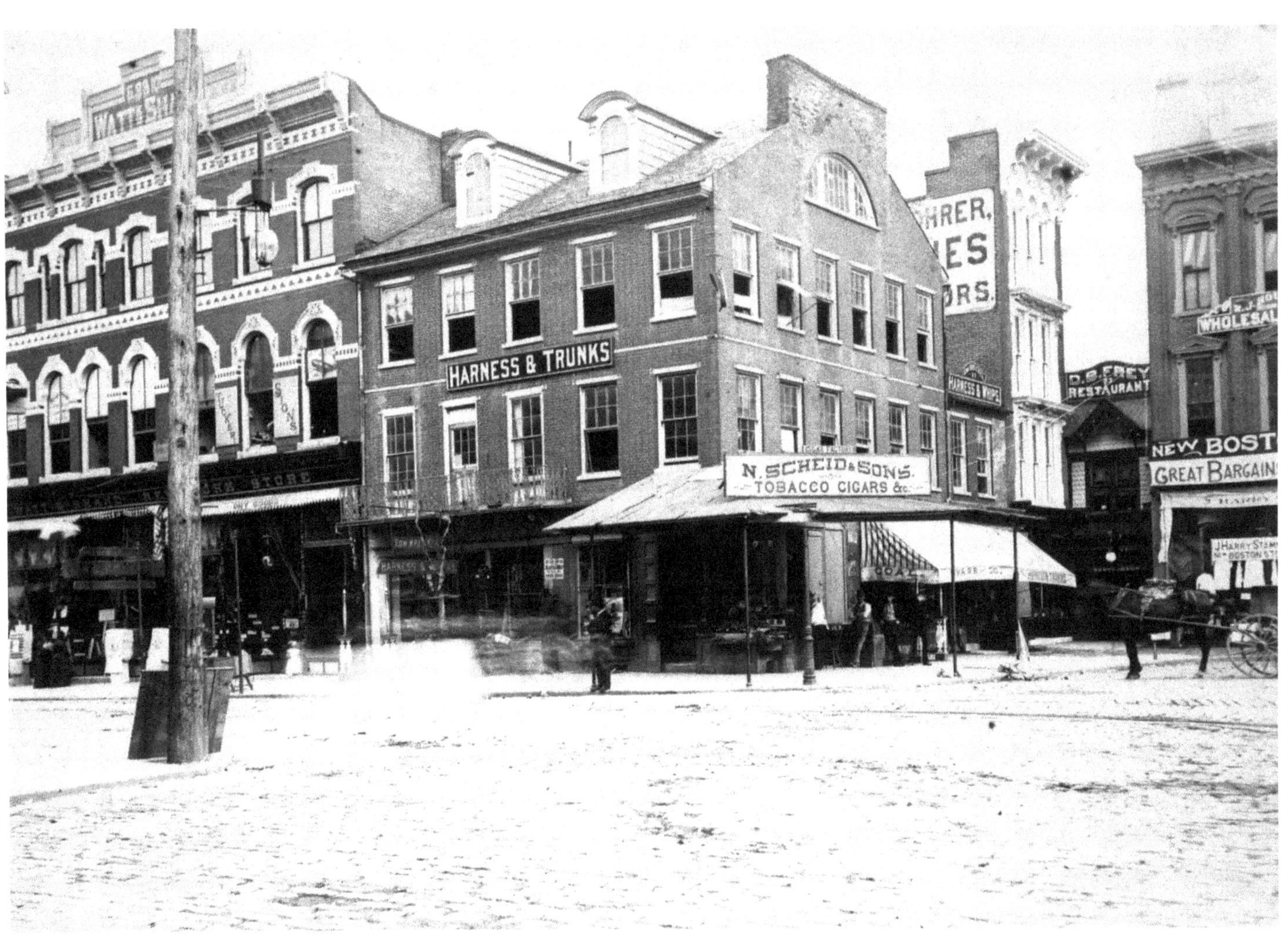

The southeastern corner at Center Square (now Penn Square) and Queen Street in Lancaster, sometime after 1898. The historic Watt & Shand department store stands at left.

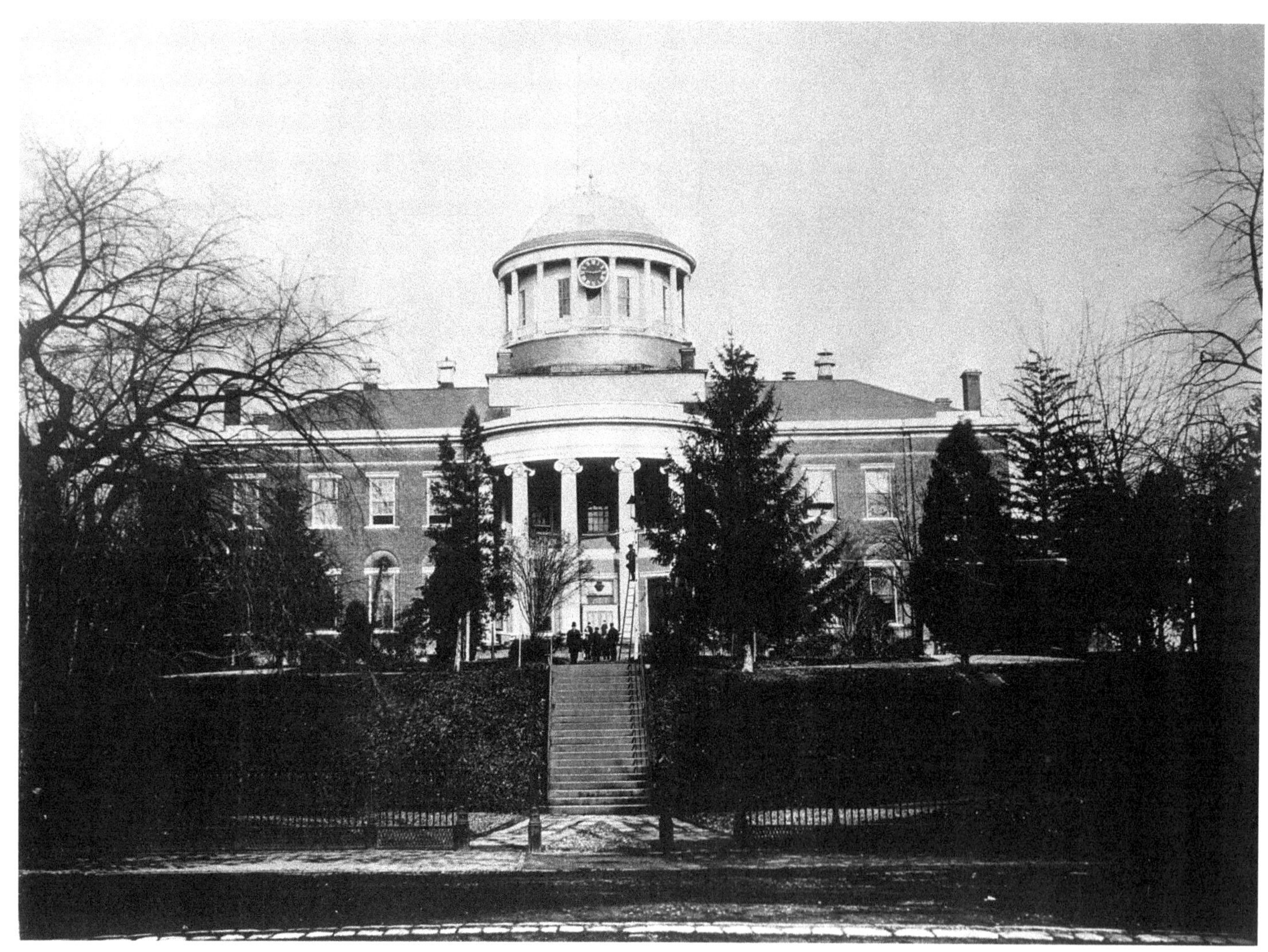

When the state seat of government was moved from Lancaster to Harrisburg in 1812, two fireproof capitol buildings were built to house the various state offices. Unfortunately (and perhaps ironically), in February of 1897 the main building seen here was lost to fire. The current Capitol was completed in 1906.

An Industrial Power

(1900–1919)

As the new century emerged, Pennsylvania held fast to its position as America's greatest manufacturing center, despite internal conflicts and increased competition from midwestern and western states. Pennsylvania led the country in textile and railroad manufacturing, while oil, steel, iron, and coal continued to drive large parts of the state's economy. These very industries provided essential support to the United States and its allies in World War I, drawing thousands of workers from across the country and from around the world to work in Pennsylvania's factories.

Where once English and German colonists led the way, new waves of immigrants from across Southern and Eastern Europe arrived, seeking work and opportunities not available in their homelands. Labor strife continued to mar relations between workers and management, aggravated in part by the influx of new immigrant workers considered to be cheaper labor by management and a threat to their own job security by the unions. Workers faced harsh conditions and little opportunity for advancement, while remote owners and management gained wealth and status. During a time of great violence, suspicion, and anger, President Theodore Roosevelt intervened in the anthracite strike of 1902 and established a precedent for nonviolent arbitration that has continued through the last century.

As the cities and manufacturing towns developed, so too did services to the growing populations. Free public schools, first envisioned and enacted in Pennsylvania in 1834, continued to expand, while libraries and colleges sought to attract new patrons by building branches and enlarging campuses. Streetcars and improved roads permitted easier travel to and from the attractions found in newly opened amusement parks and holiday resorts. Sports facilities attracted growing crowds, and amid much hoopla in 1906 a new State Capitol debuted in Harrisburg. The nature of life in Pennsylvania was quickly changing as the new century moved forward.

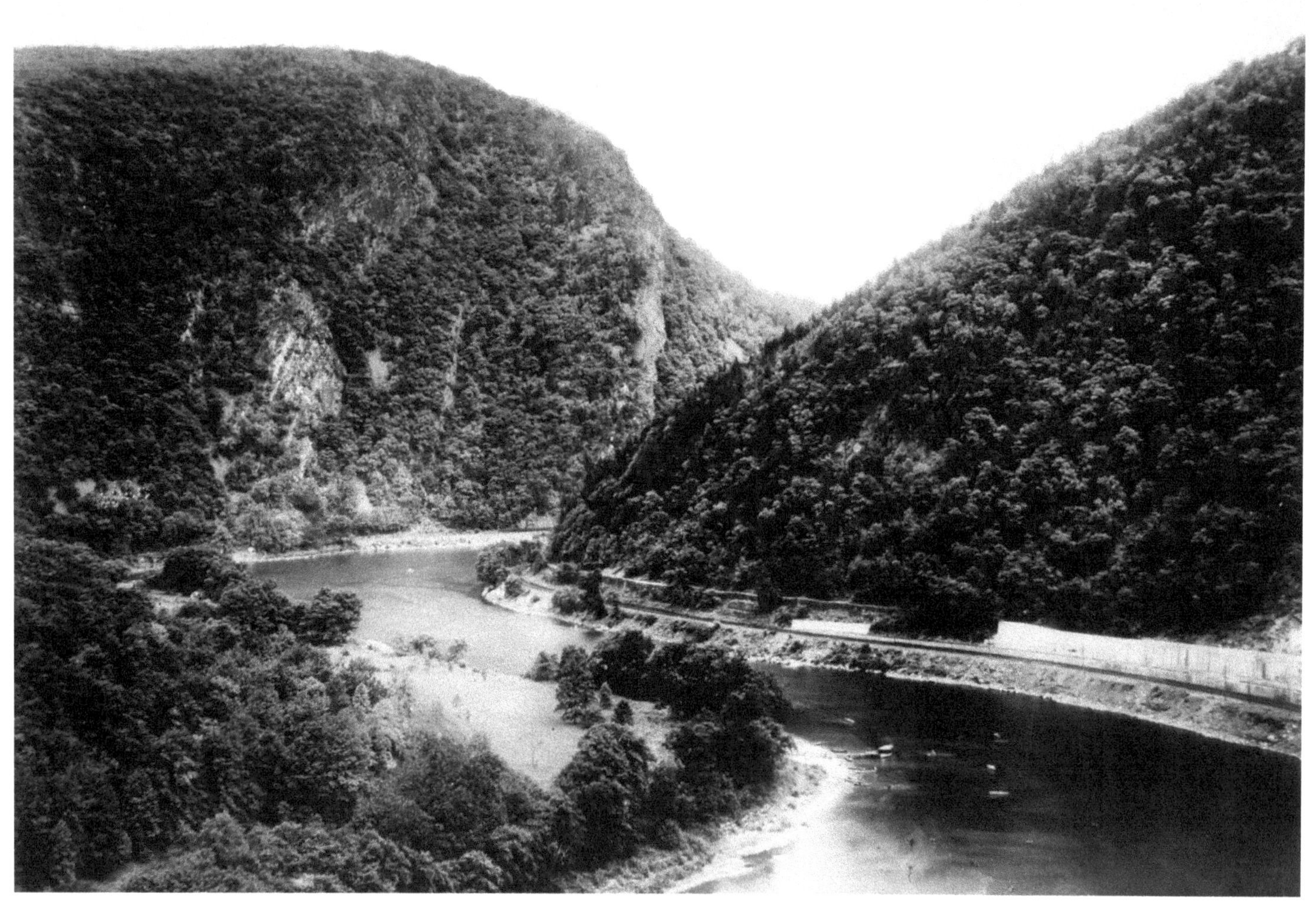

The Delaware Water Gap, where the Delaware River cuts through an Appalachian mountain ridge, circa 1900. The popular destination is currently a National Recreation Area, created in the 1960s to preserve 7,000 acres of land.

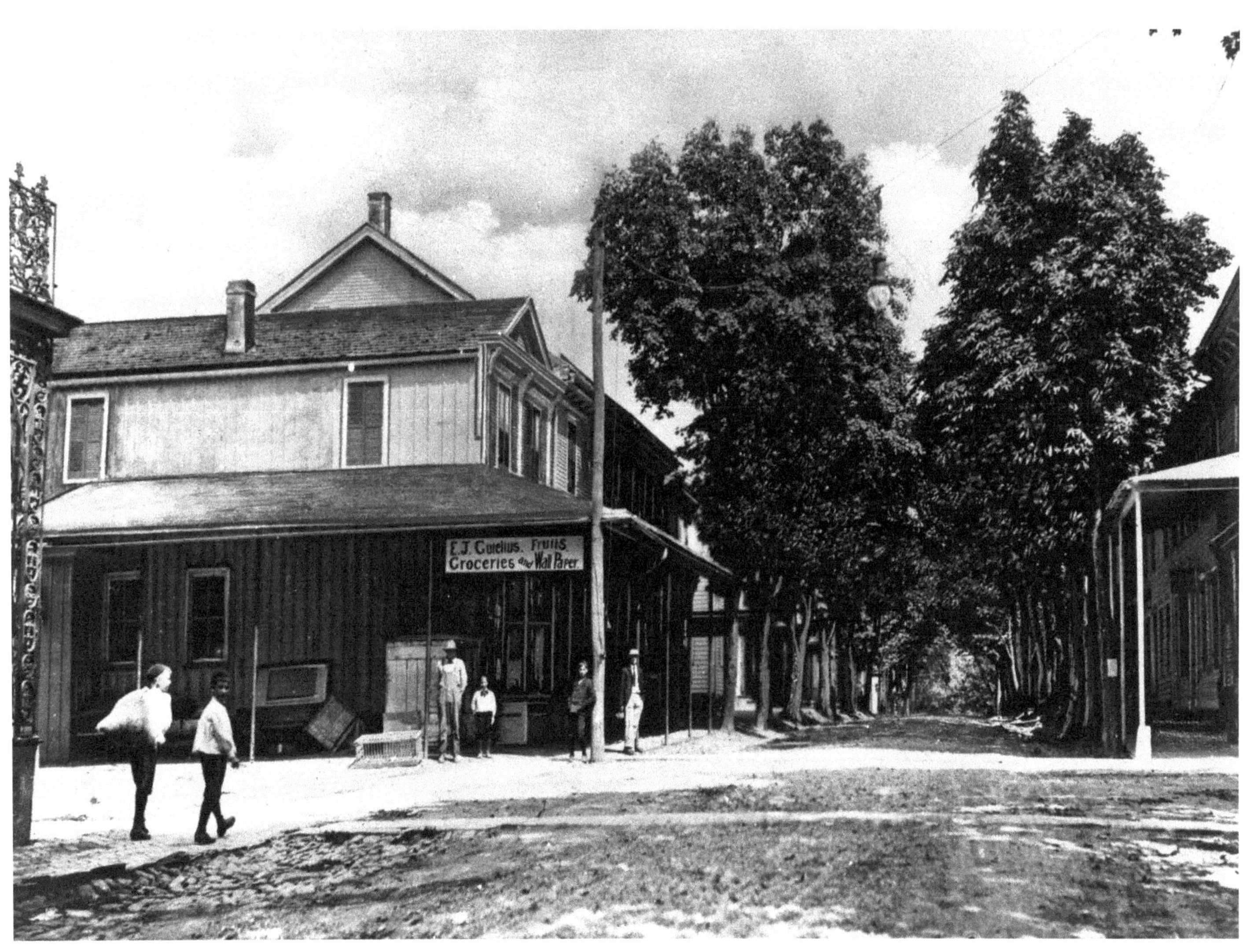

Several men and children pose in front of a grocery store (and wall paper dealer) at the corner of Fifth and Chestnut streets in Mifflinburg, Union County, circa 1900.

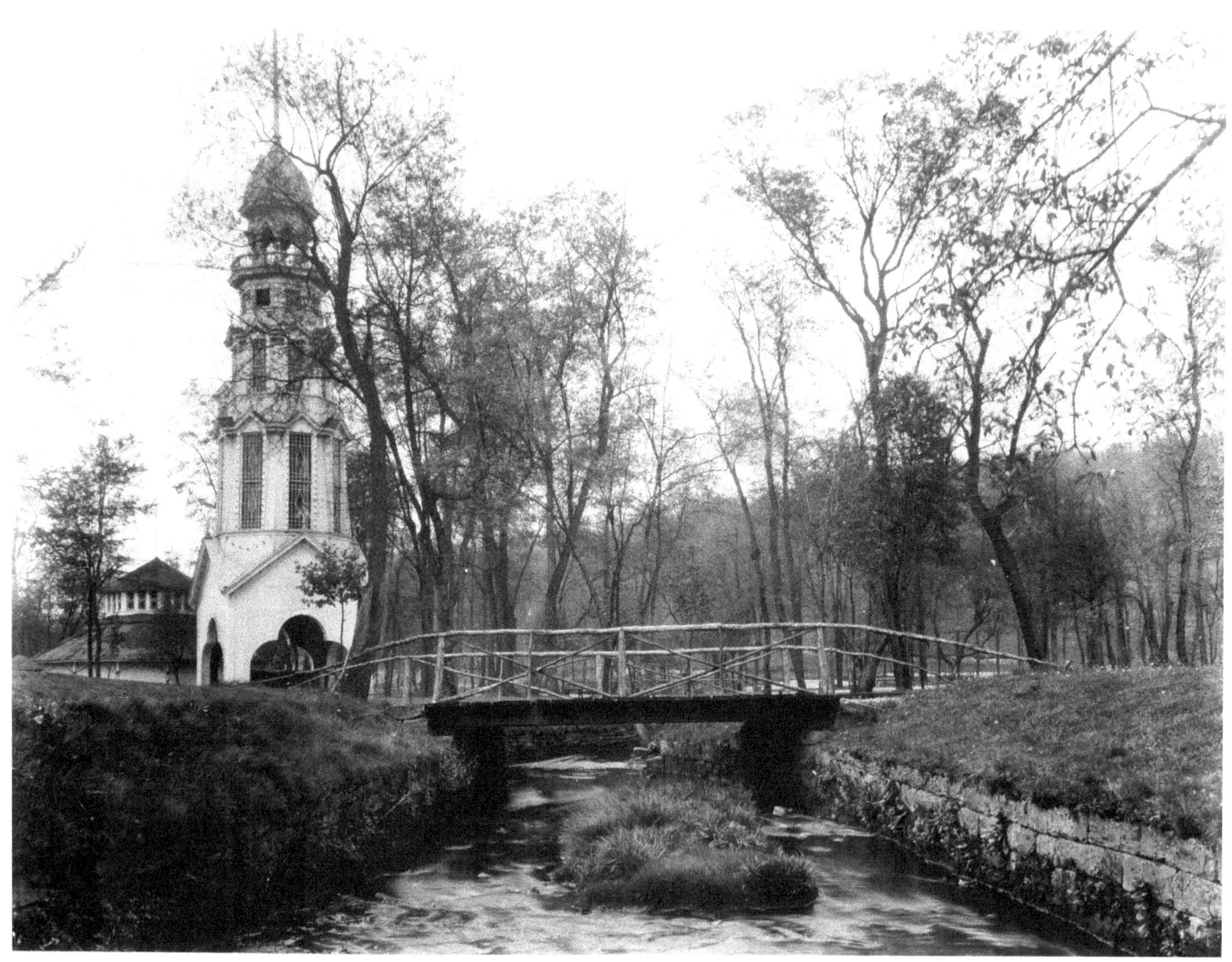

The Electric Tower looks out over Monarch Park, an amusement park in Oil City, circa 1905. Opened in 1896, the park featured a playground, regular band performances, and rides. By 1902 the 120-foot tower was fully electrified and lit with hundreds of light bulbs.

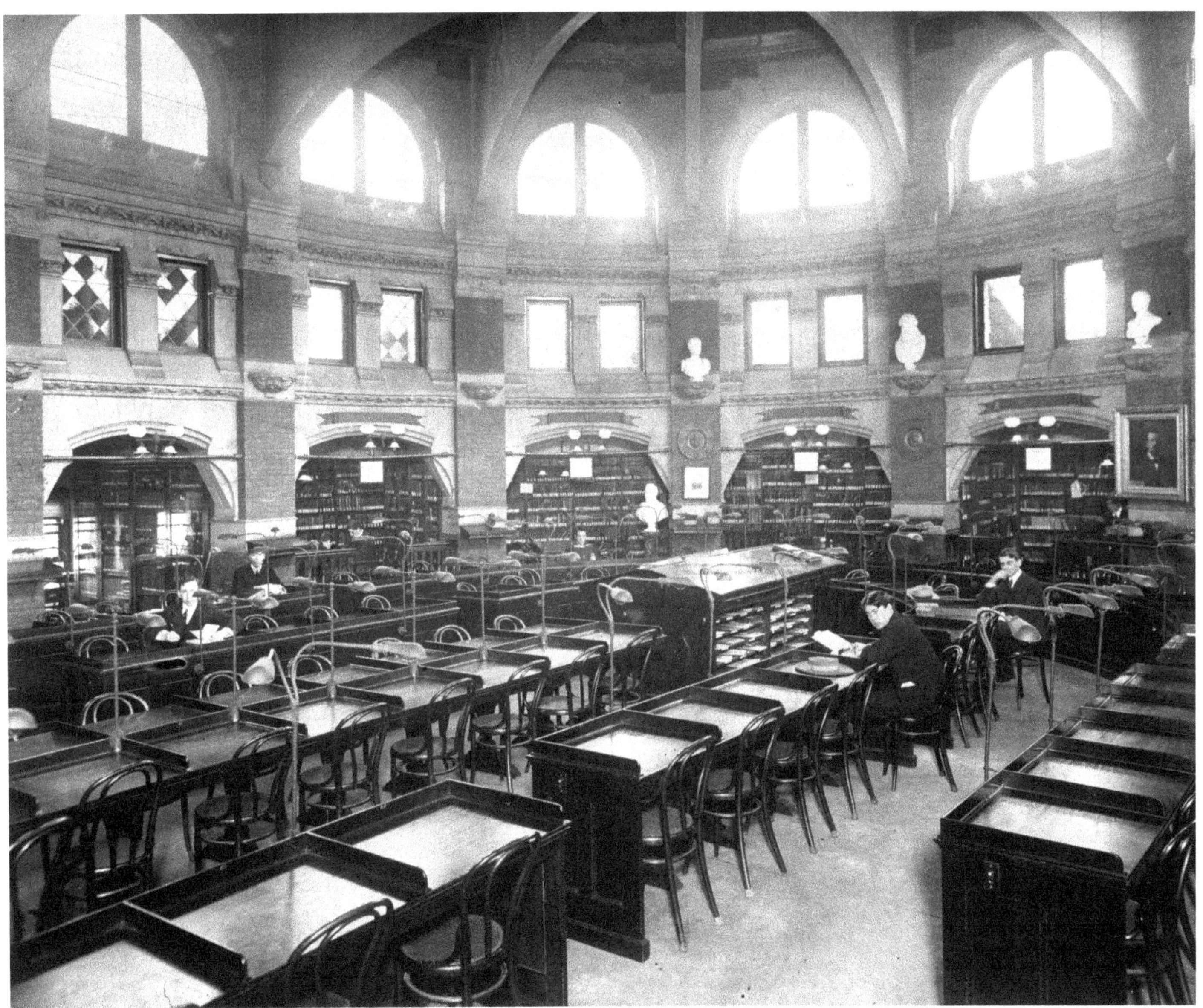

Students study in the reading room of the Victorian-era library of the University of Pennsylvania in Philadelphia, circa 1900. Designed by Frank Furness, the building represented a researched, practical approach to library design and use. By the 1960s the building was threatened with demolition, but has since undergone a complete restoration and is used as a fine arts library for the university.

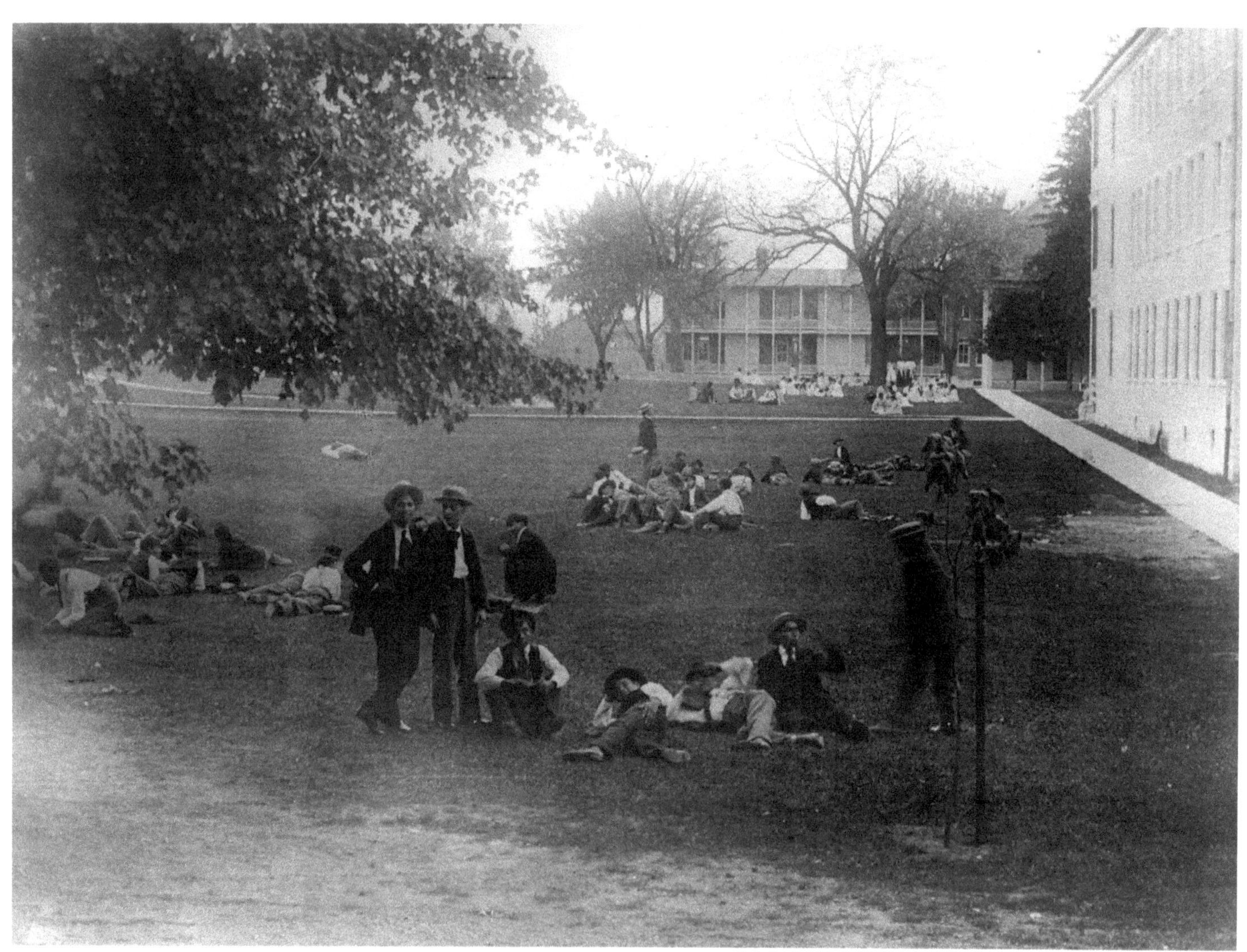

The Carlisle Indian Industrial School, seen here circa 1902, was founded in 1879 as a humane alternative to the prevalent harsh treatment of American Indian peoples and culture. By the time the school closed in 1918, more than 10,000 students had passed through its doors, but the school is viewed today as a failure because of its role in the damage inflicted on American Indian culture and identity by programs oriented toward assimilation.

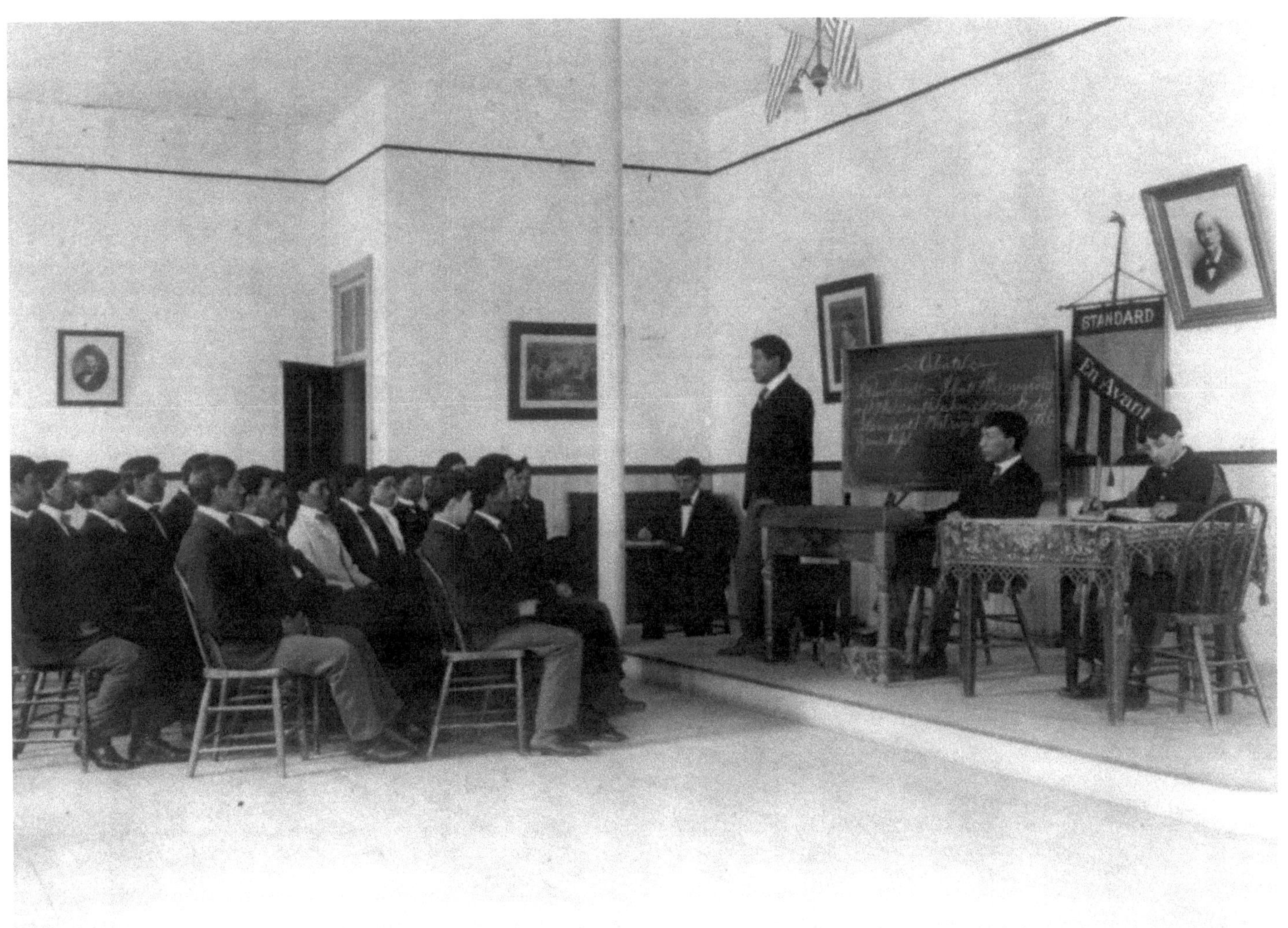

With assimilation as their goal, managers of the Carlisle Indian Industrial School required Native American children to abandon their tribal clothing, cut their hair, and participate in debate classes like this one. In the end, however, the school only achieved an 8 percent graduation rate.

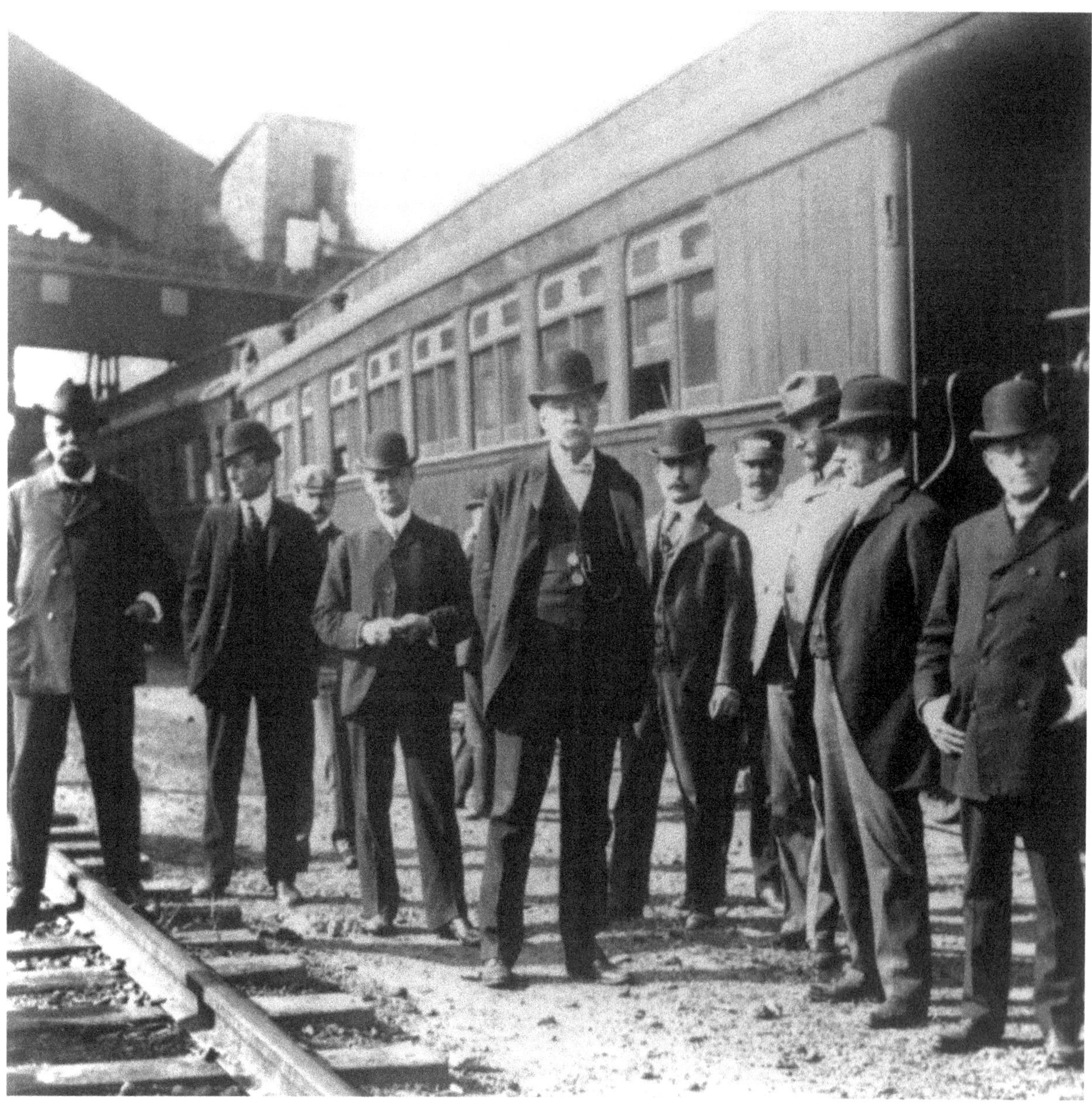

Following an 18-month coal miners' strike that brought violence and tensions throughout the anthracite coal regions of Pennsylvania, President Theodore Roosevelt appointed a Strike Arbitration Commission, seen here in 1902. The strike was quickly resolved, but labor conflicts continued for several decades.

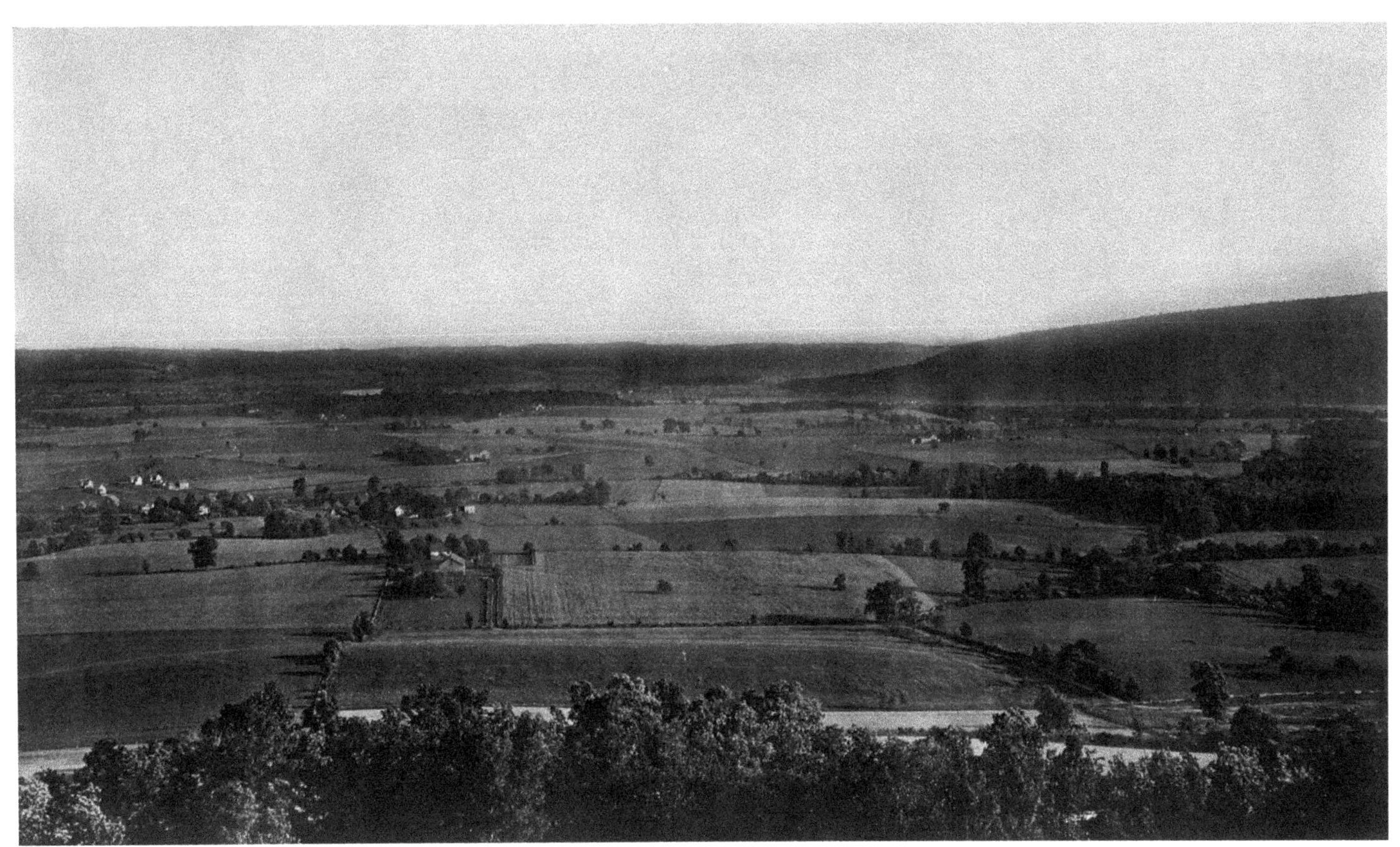

Bald Eagle Mountain and the Muncy Valley in central Pennsylvania, June 27, 1905.
The mountain remains one of the best birding sites in the state.

Following Spread: The Wabash Railroad Bridge spans the Monongahela River in Pittsburgh, 1905. The line's large terminal shed is visible at the center of the photo. Built in 1903 after much resistance from the city, the bridge would serve the Wabash Railroad until the company went bankrupt just five years later. Neglected in the years to follow, the bridge was demolished in 1948.

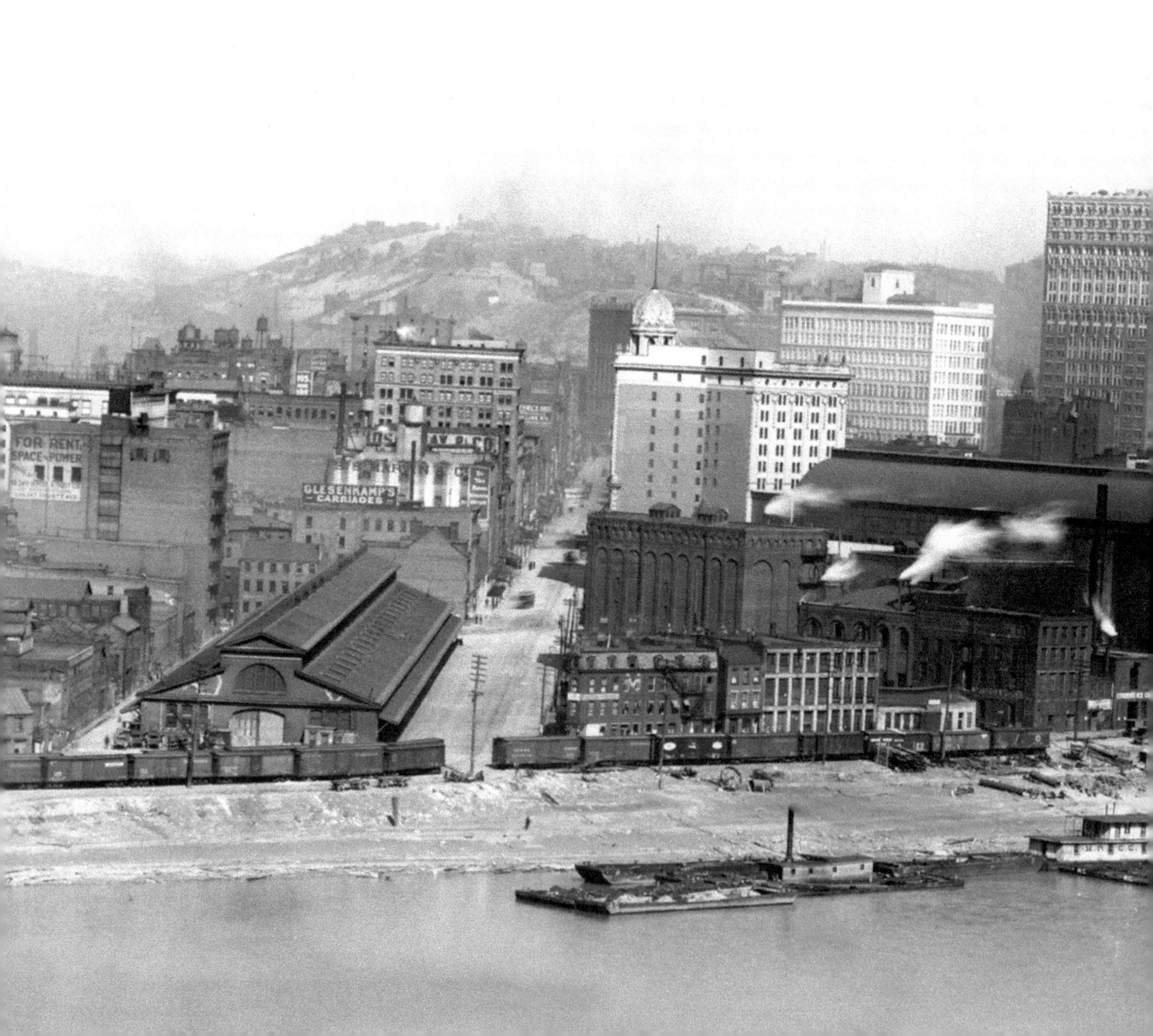
FOR RENT
SPACE—POWER
GLESENKAMP'S
CARRIAGES

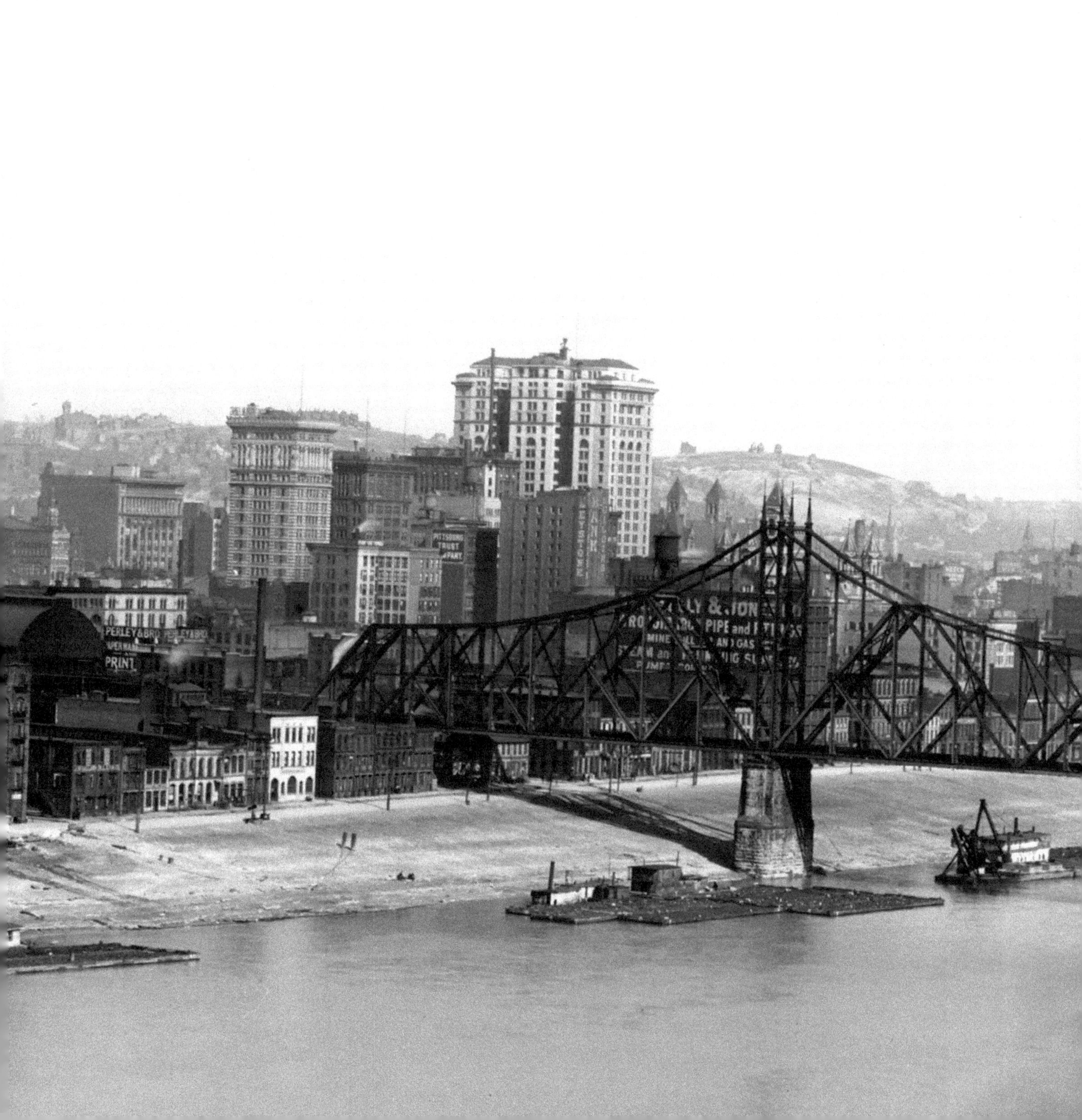
PERLEY & BRO
PRINT

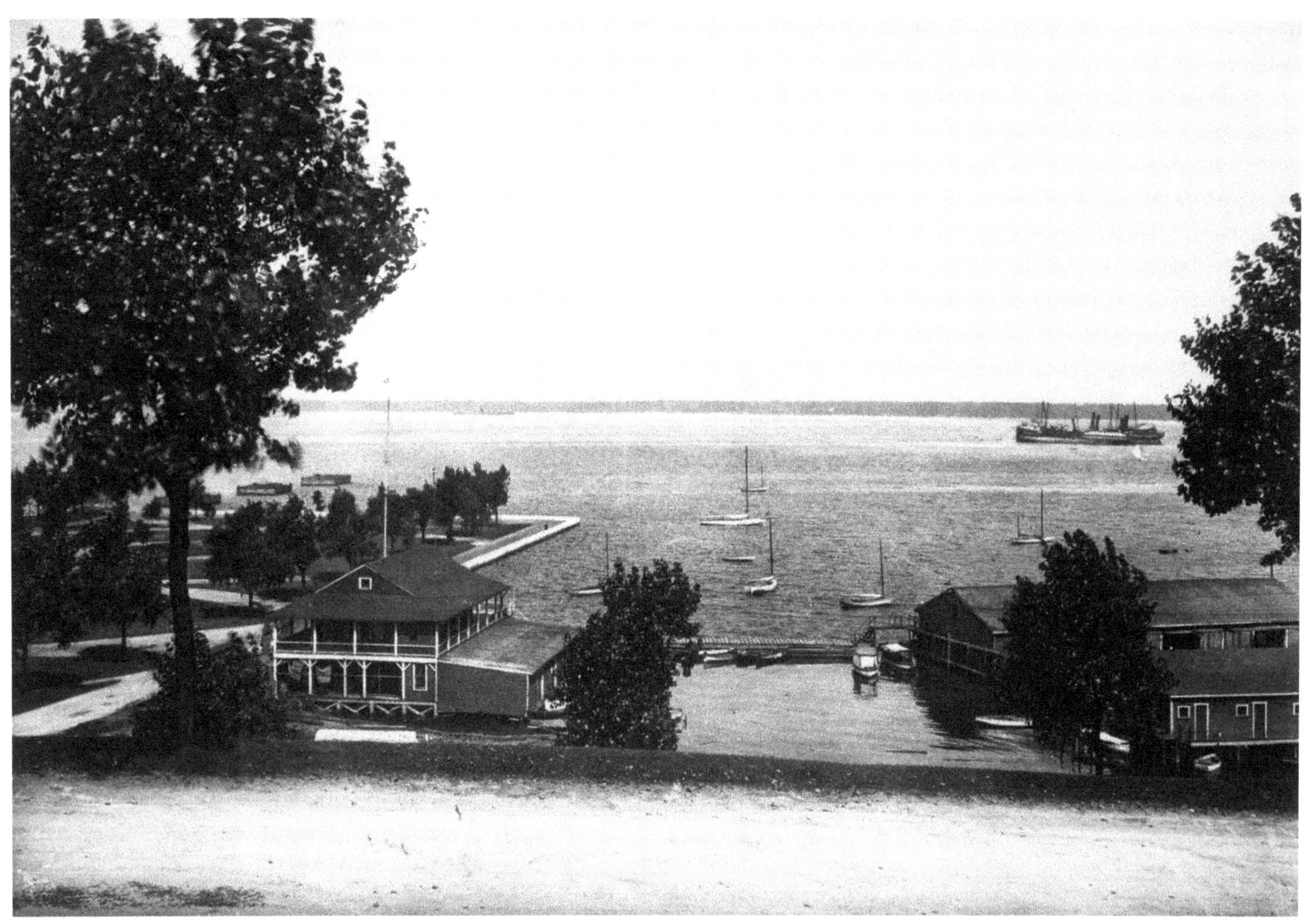

A view of Lake Erie overlooking the man-made ponds known as the Waterworks. Built in the first decade of the twentieth century to provide clean water to Erie residents, the ponds are now part of the Presque Island State Park.

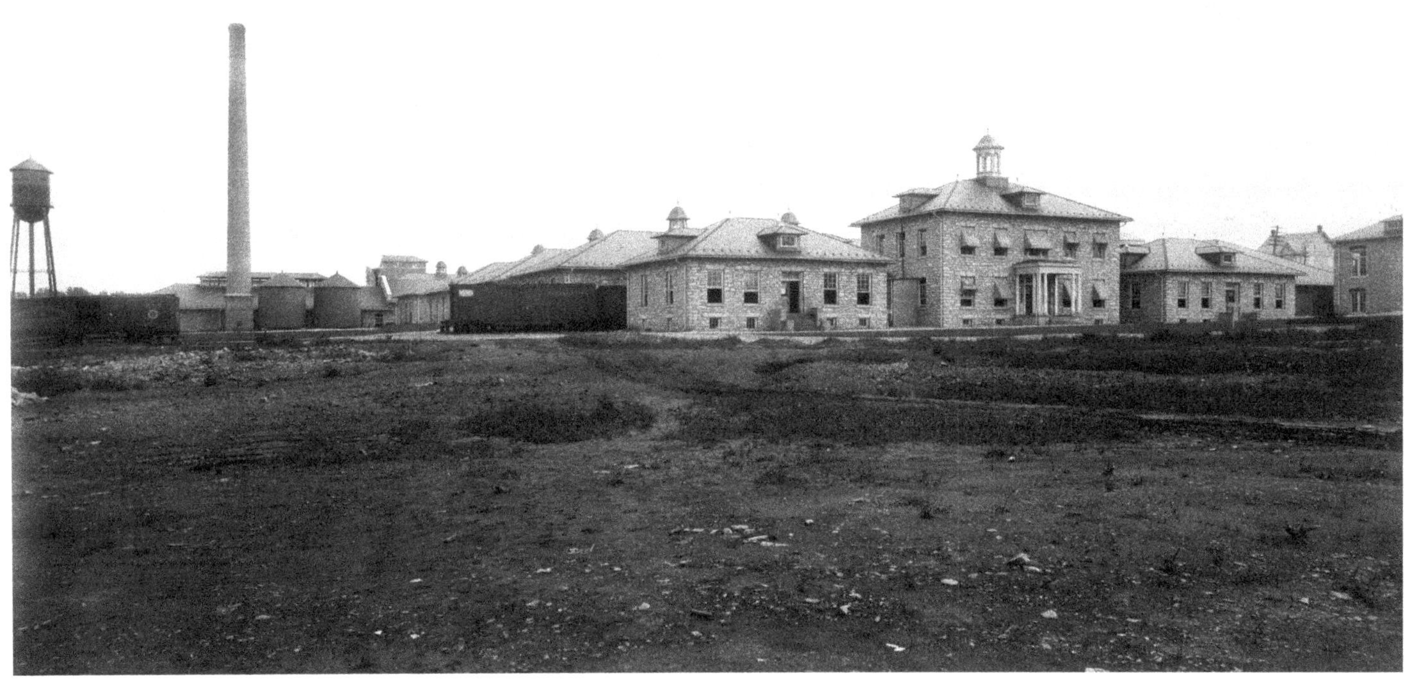

Having founded the Hershey Chocolate Company in Lancaster in 1894, and with Hershey's milk chocolate on the market by 1900, Milton Hershey decided to move his operation to Derry Township, where this Hershey office complex and the chocolate factory behind it opened in 1905.

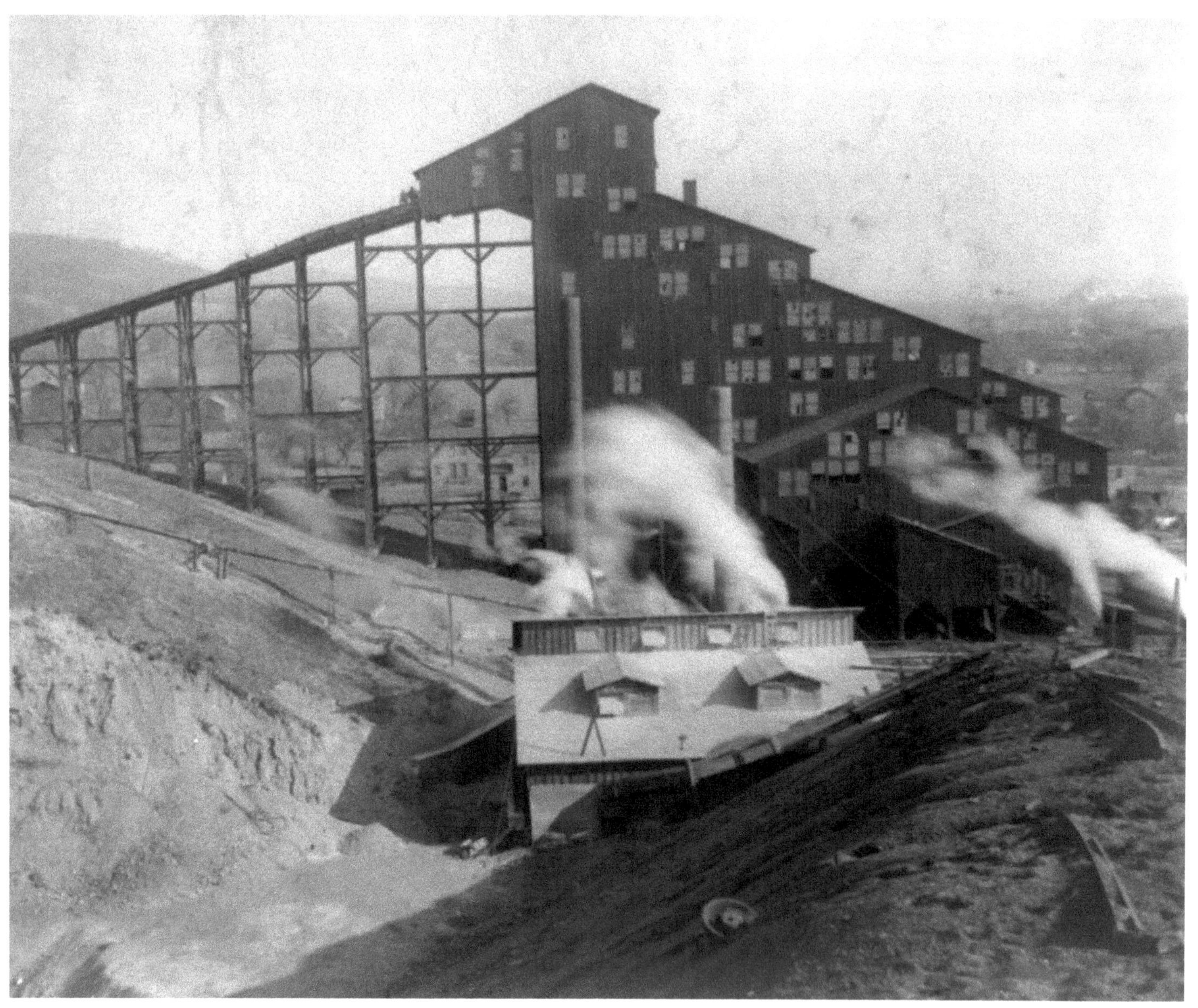

A massive coal breaker in Westmoreland County, 1905. Breakers are used to process raw chunks of mined coal and "break" them down into various sizes suitable for different furnaces. Slag and similar impurities are also removed.

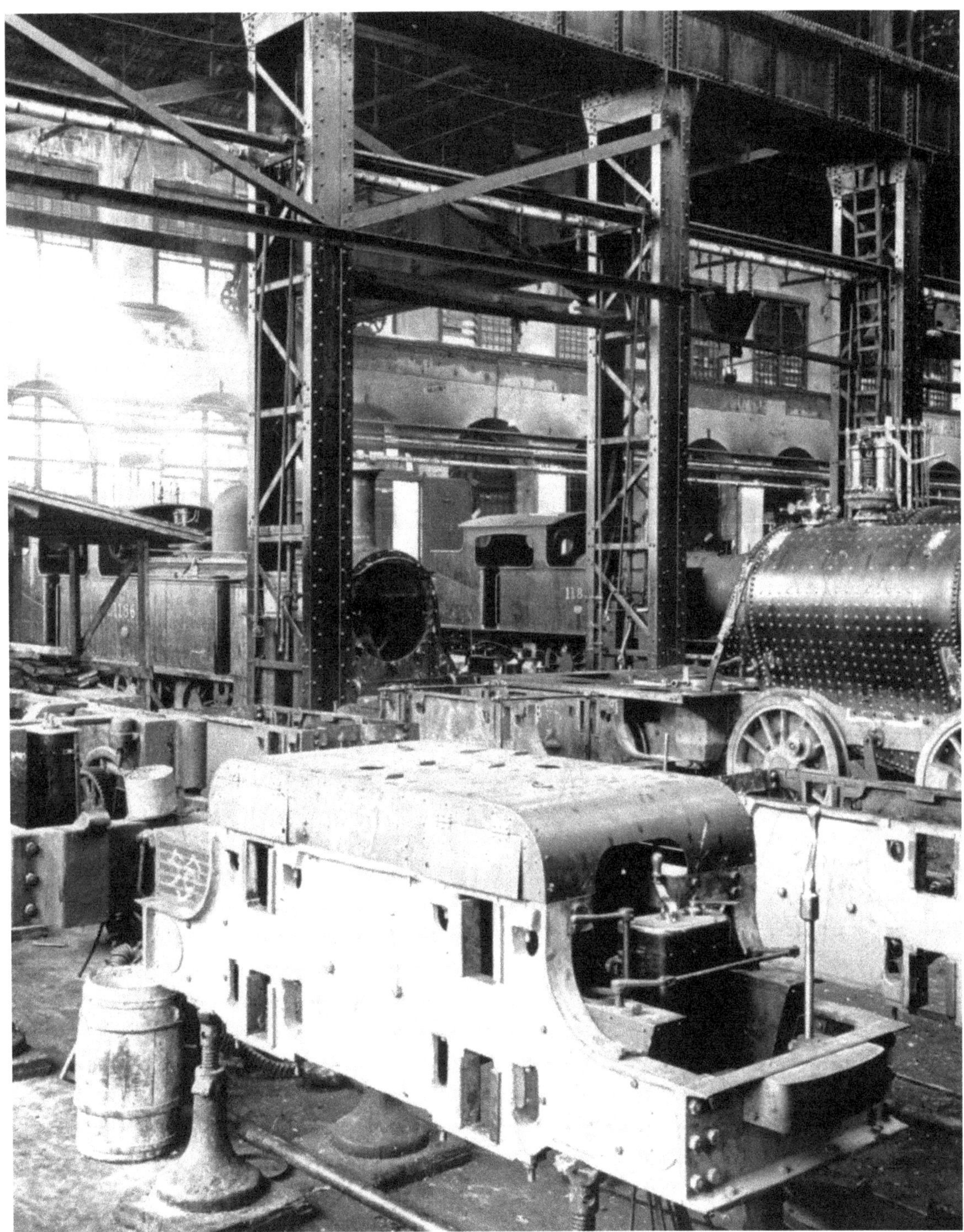

An electric locomotive for use in the mining districts is under construction at Baldwin Locomotive Works, Philadelphia, circa 1905. Founded in 1831 as a steam engine manufacturer, the Baldwin firm ultimately produced more than 70,000 locomotives before shutting down in 1956.

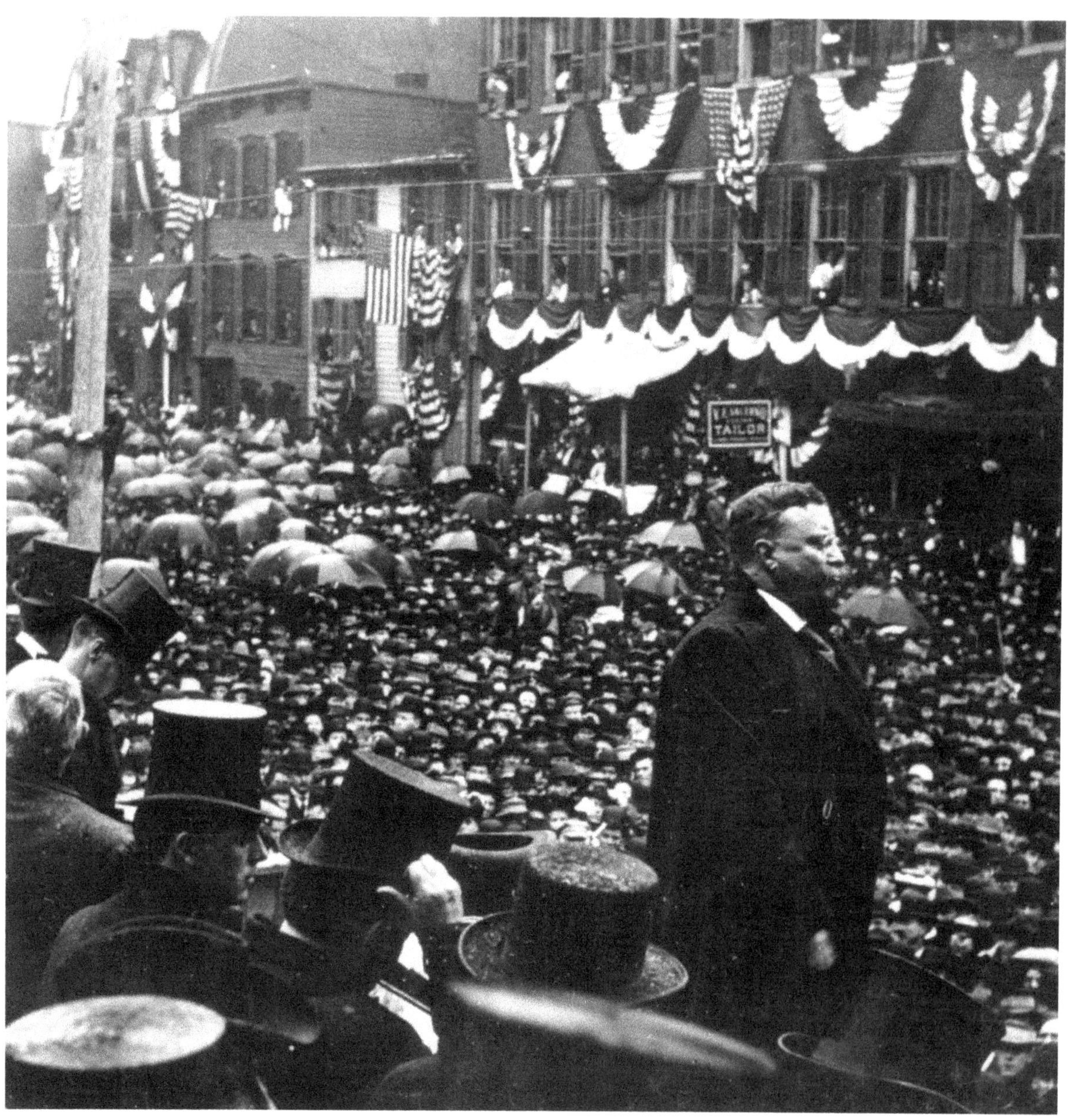

President Theodore Roosevelt, one of many important speakers during the opening ceremonies for the State Capitol in Harrisburg, October 4, 1906.

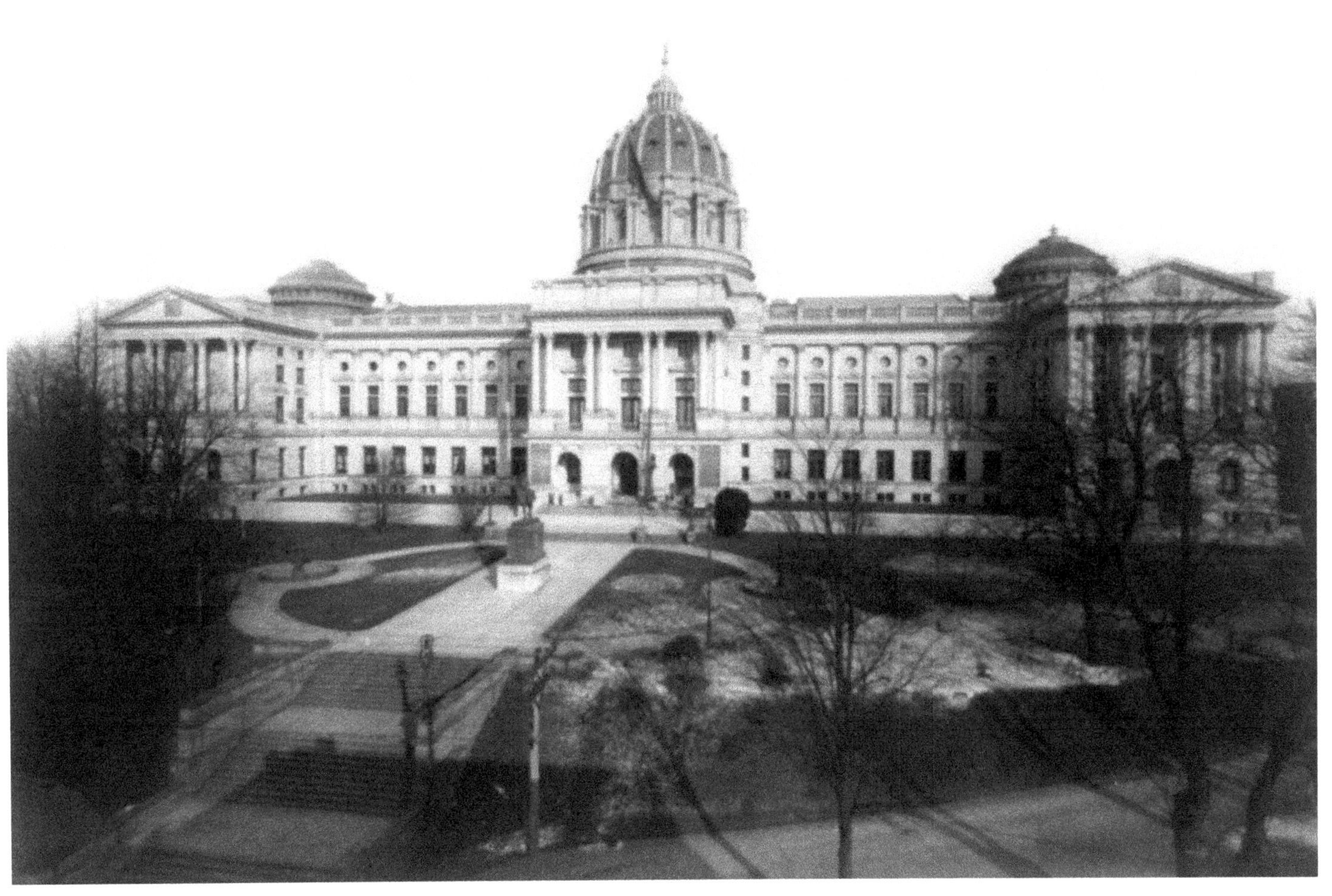

The newly completed State Capitol in Harrisburg. The building was designed by Joseph M. Huston, who took for inspiration such architectural models as St. Peter's Basilica in Rome.

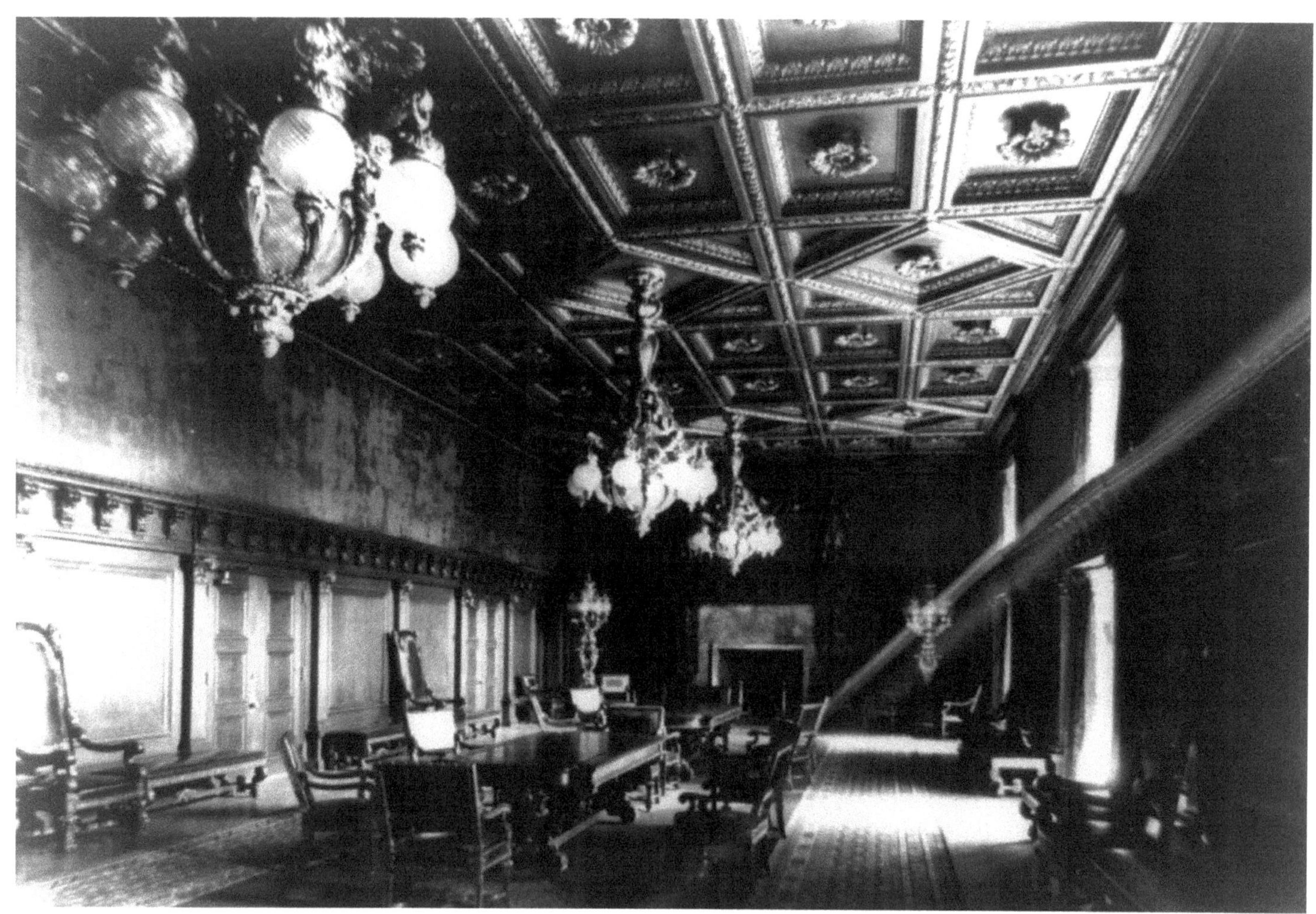

The lavishly decorated Governor's Reception Room in the State Capitol at Harrisburg as it appeared shortly after completion. A remarkable $8.6 million was spent to decorate and furnish the Capitol in time for the official opening in 1906. However, an investigation into the high costs resulted in the indictment for fraud and two-year incarceration of the state's auditor general and treasurer.

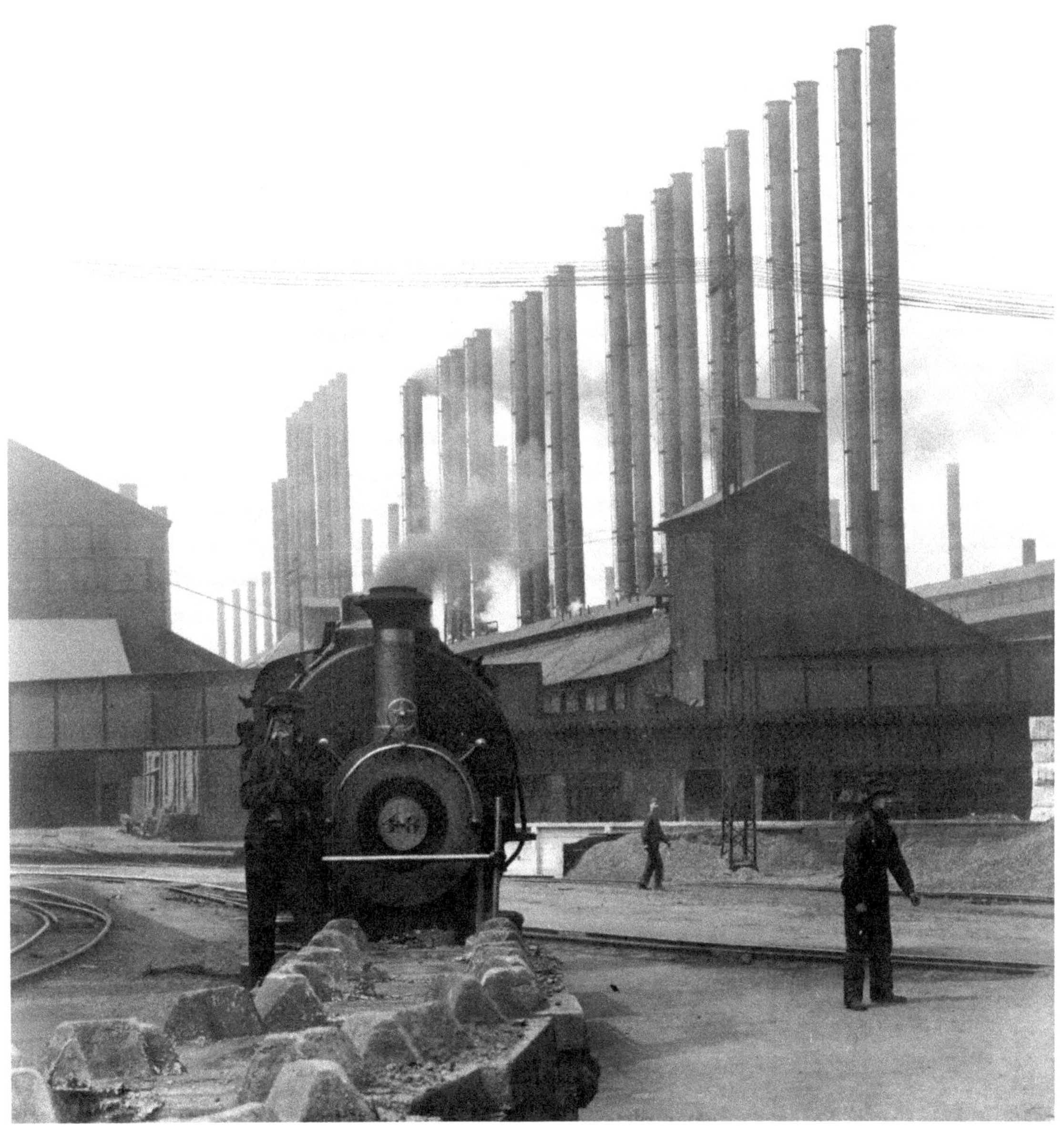

A freight locomotive waits in the yard of a steel plant in Homestead, circa 1907. Homestead, in Allegheny County, was the site of the violent and deadly steel strike of 1892 that was one of the first organized labor actions in the country. In a single day, 11 men were killed in conflicts between workers and the Pinkerton Detective Agency, hired by Carnegie Steel to end the strike.

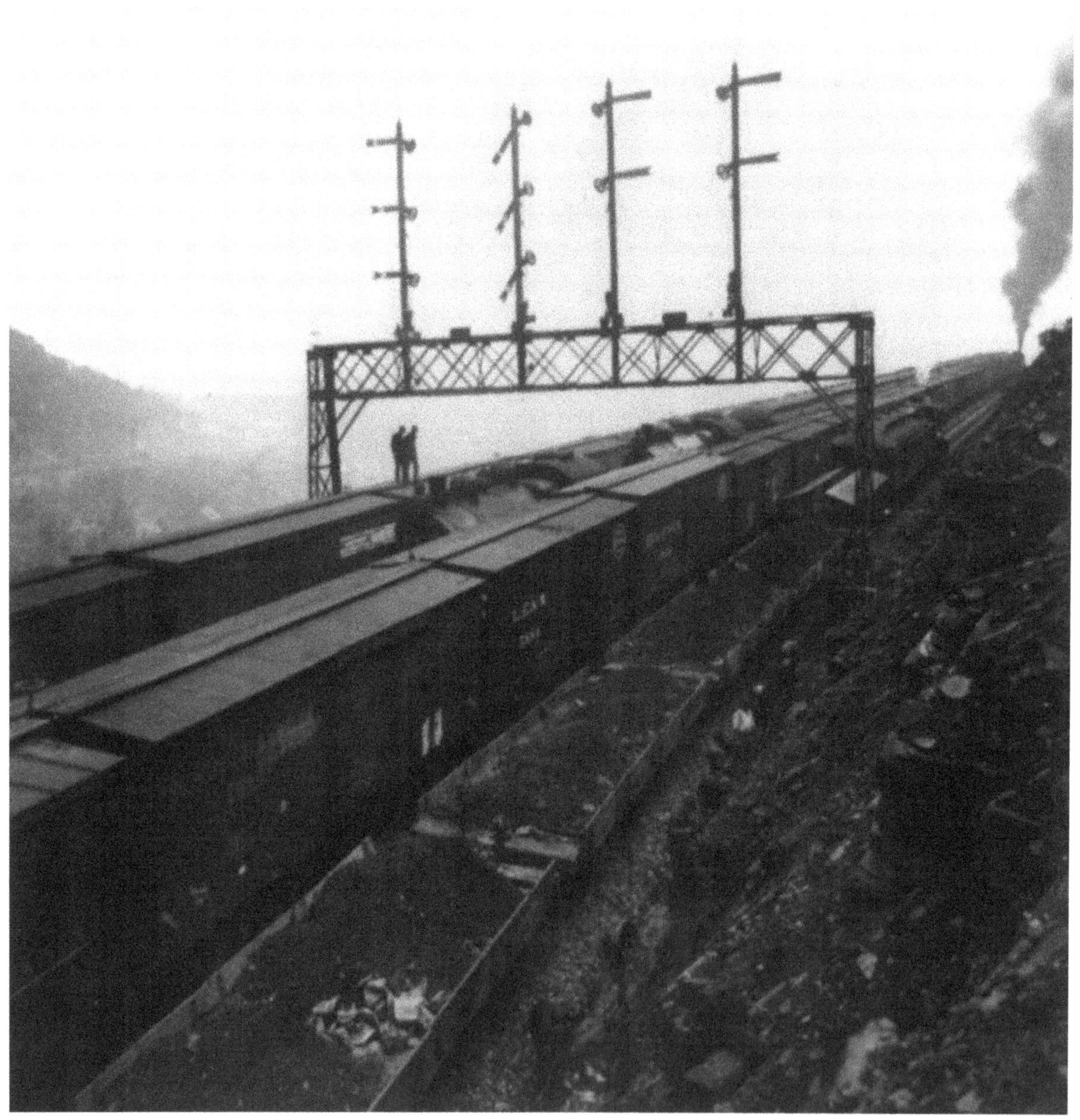

In a reflection of the massive quantity of coal moving along the Pennsylvania Railroad in the first decade of the twentieth century, four full freight trains sit abreast of one another on rails west of Altoona.

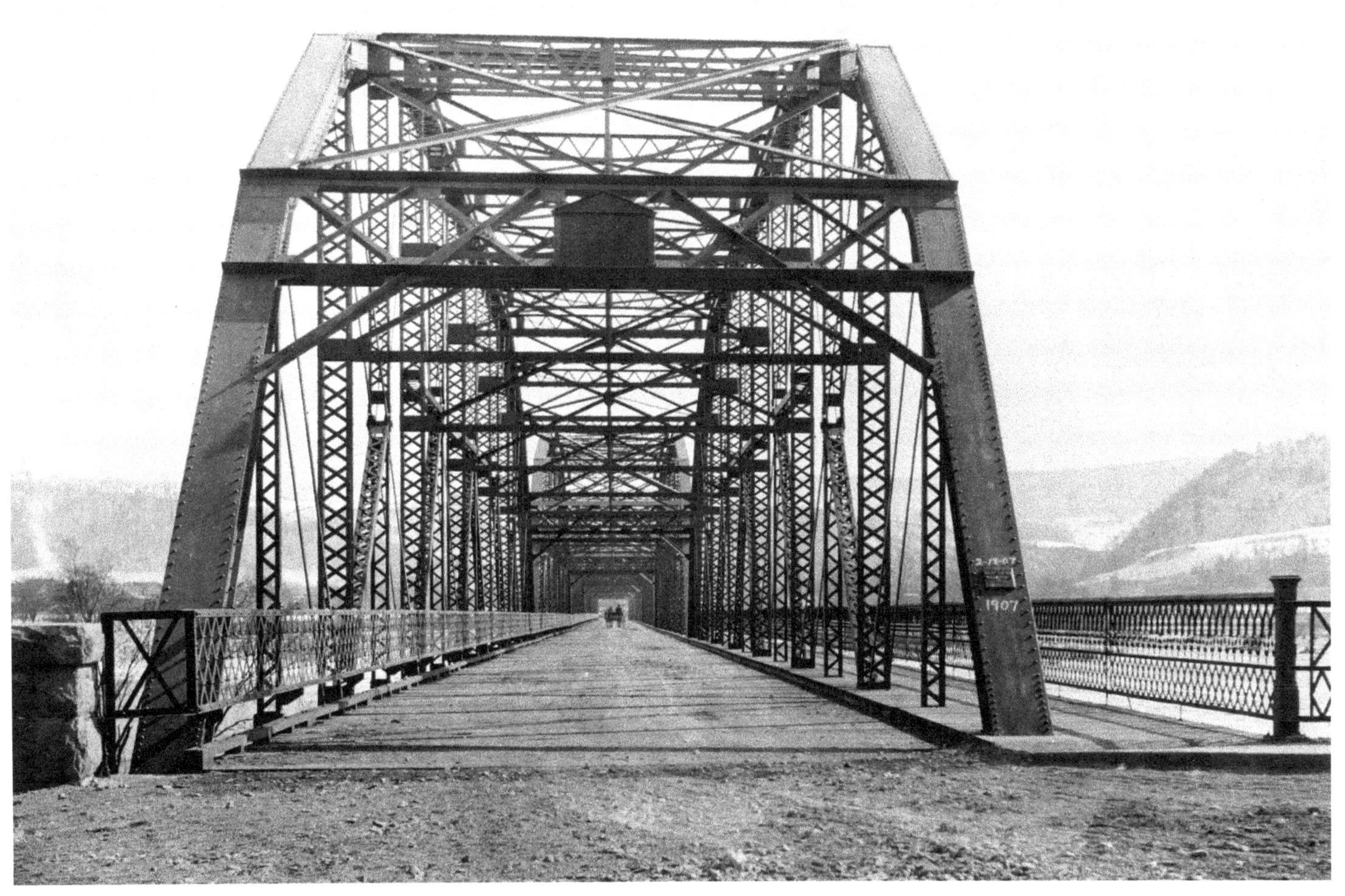

A bridge spans the Susquehanna River in Berwick, Columbia County, 1907. Berwick is home to the regionally known Wise Foods, manufacturers of potato chips.

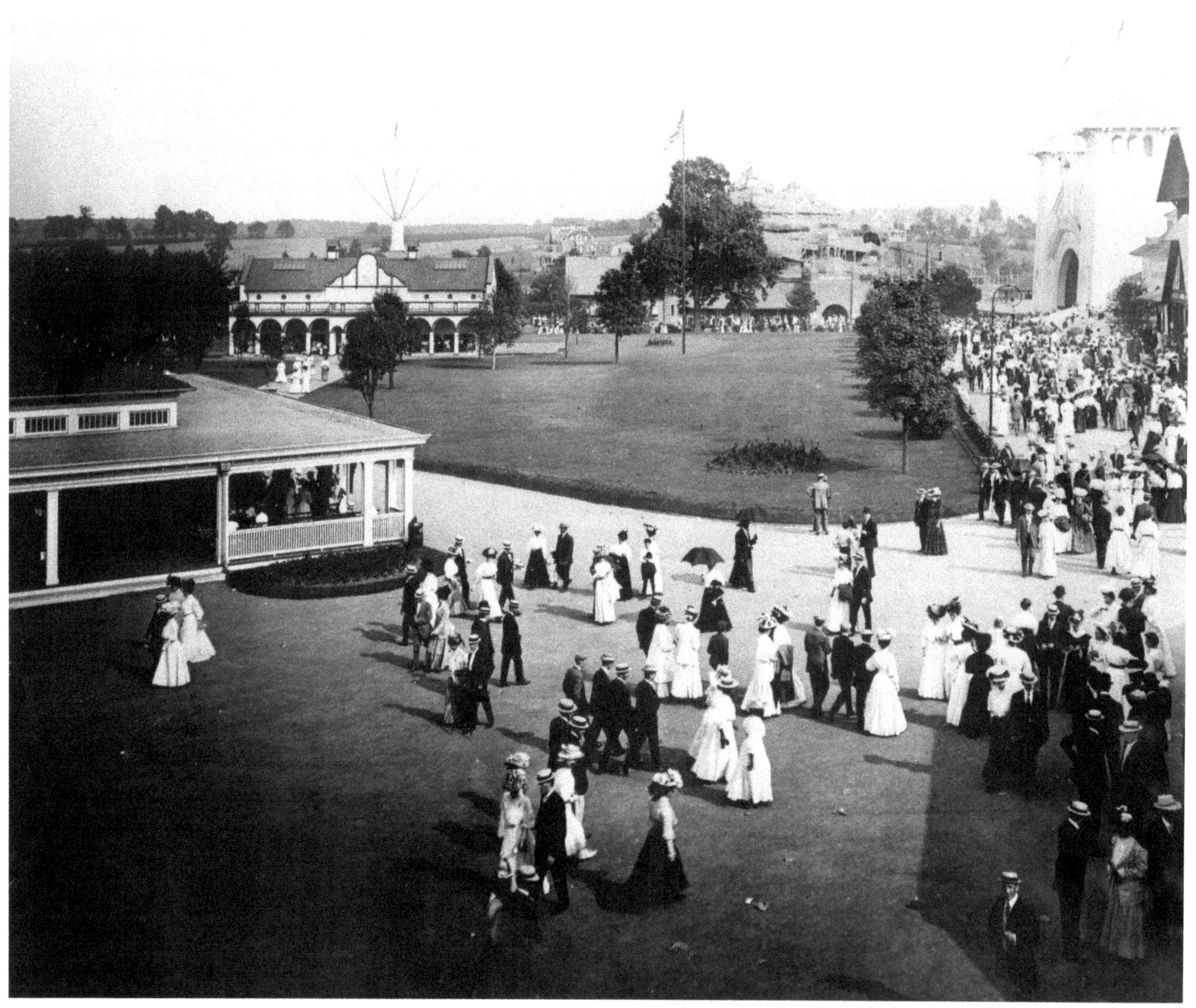

Willow Grove Park, a popular amusement park located north of Philadelphia, opened in 1896 and closed in 1975. Known as a "trolley park" because it was founded by the Philadelphia Rapid Transit Company in an effort to encourage the use of their trolley lines from the city, the park benefited from the growing number of middle-class families seeking varied forms of entertainment and leisure. Seen here circa 1907, the site is currently the location of the Willow Grove Park shopping mall.

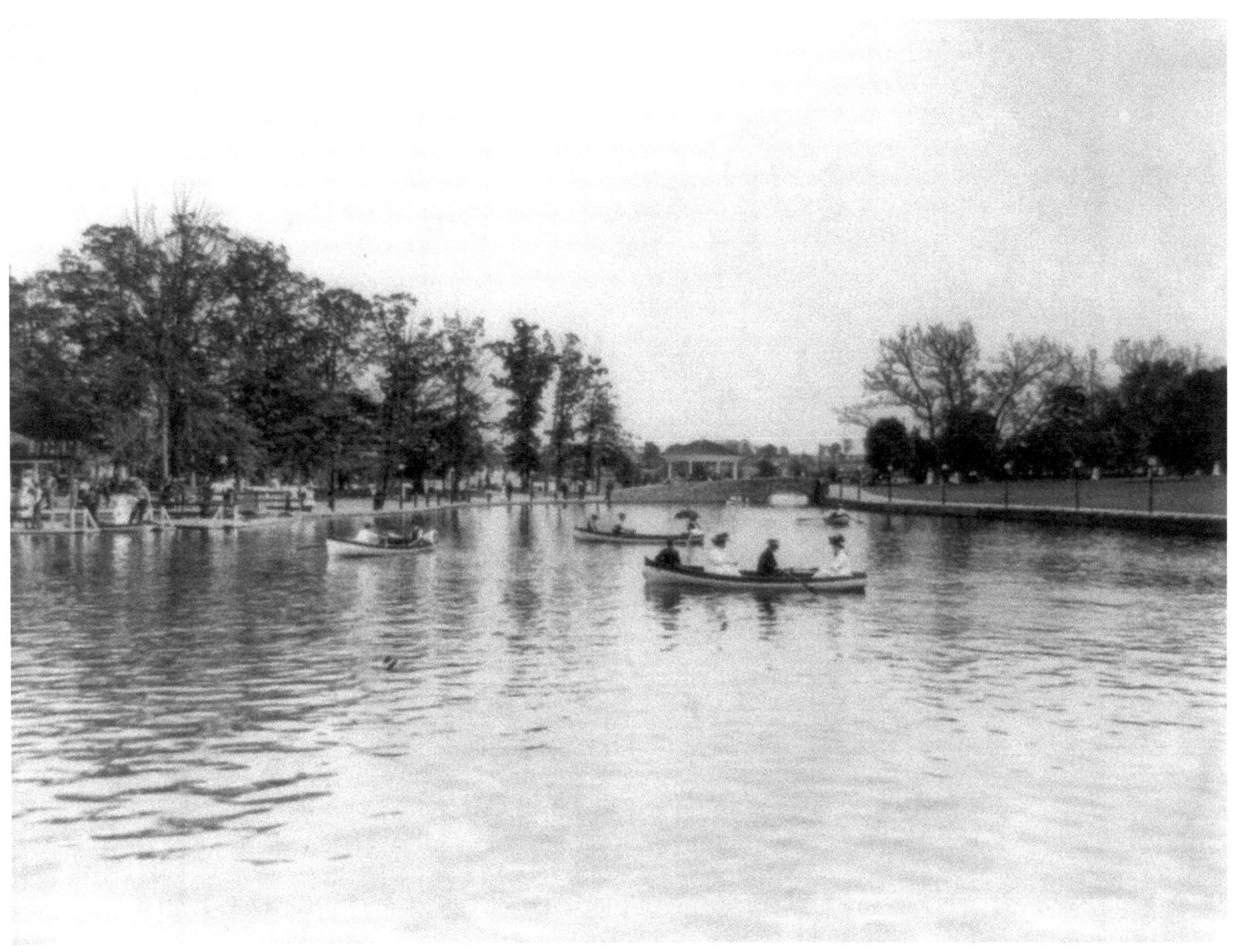

In addition to a world-famous music pavilion that featured performances by John Philip Sousa, Willow Grove Park offered amusement rides, landscaped and manicured walks, and a man-made lake with rowboats for rent.

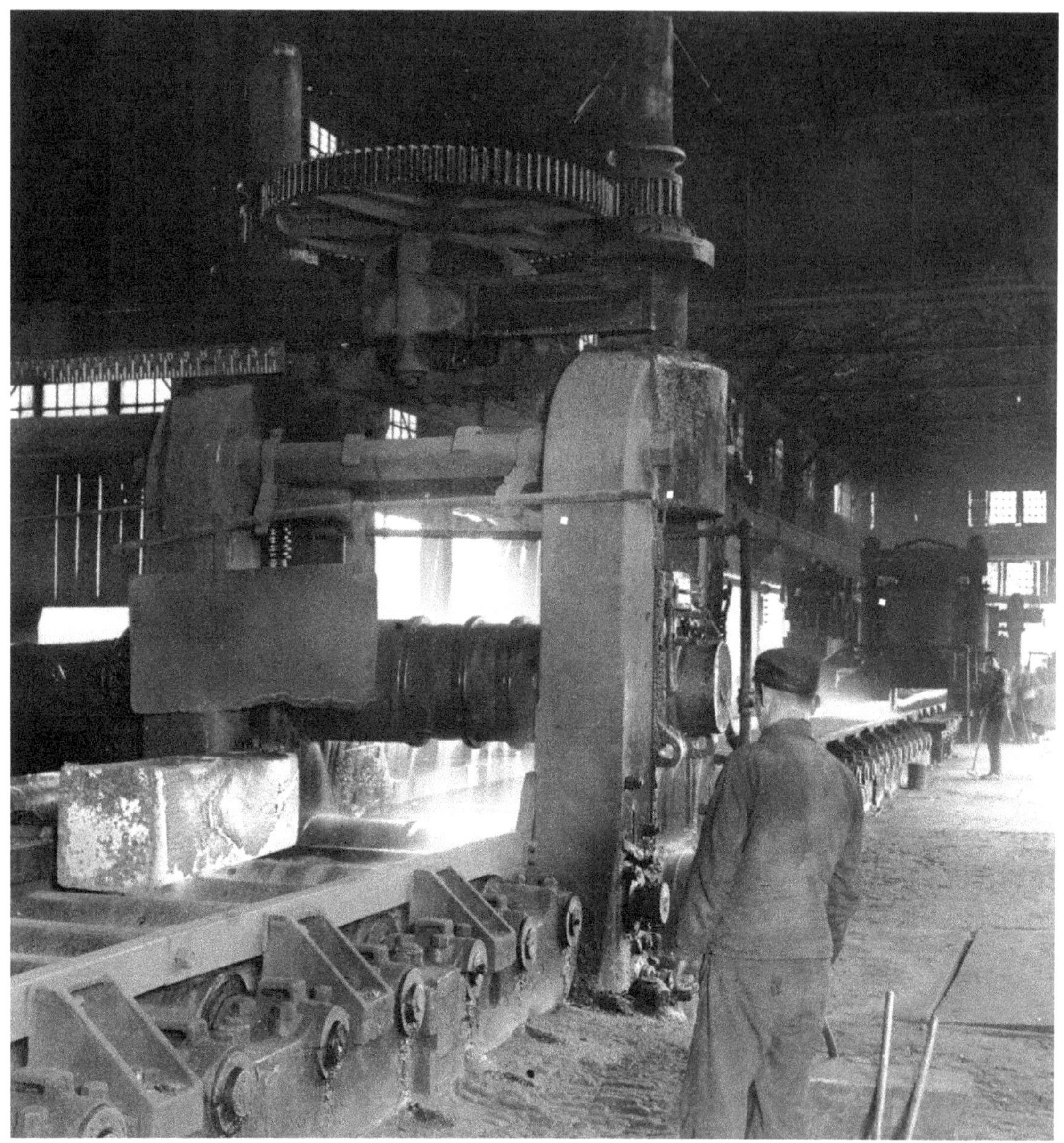

White-hot ingots of steel roll down the line in a Homestead steel mill. In the final steps of the process, each ingot is stretched to a length of 75 feet.

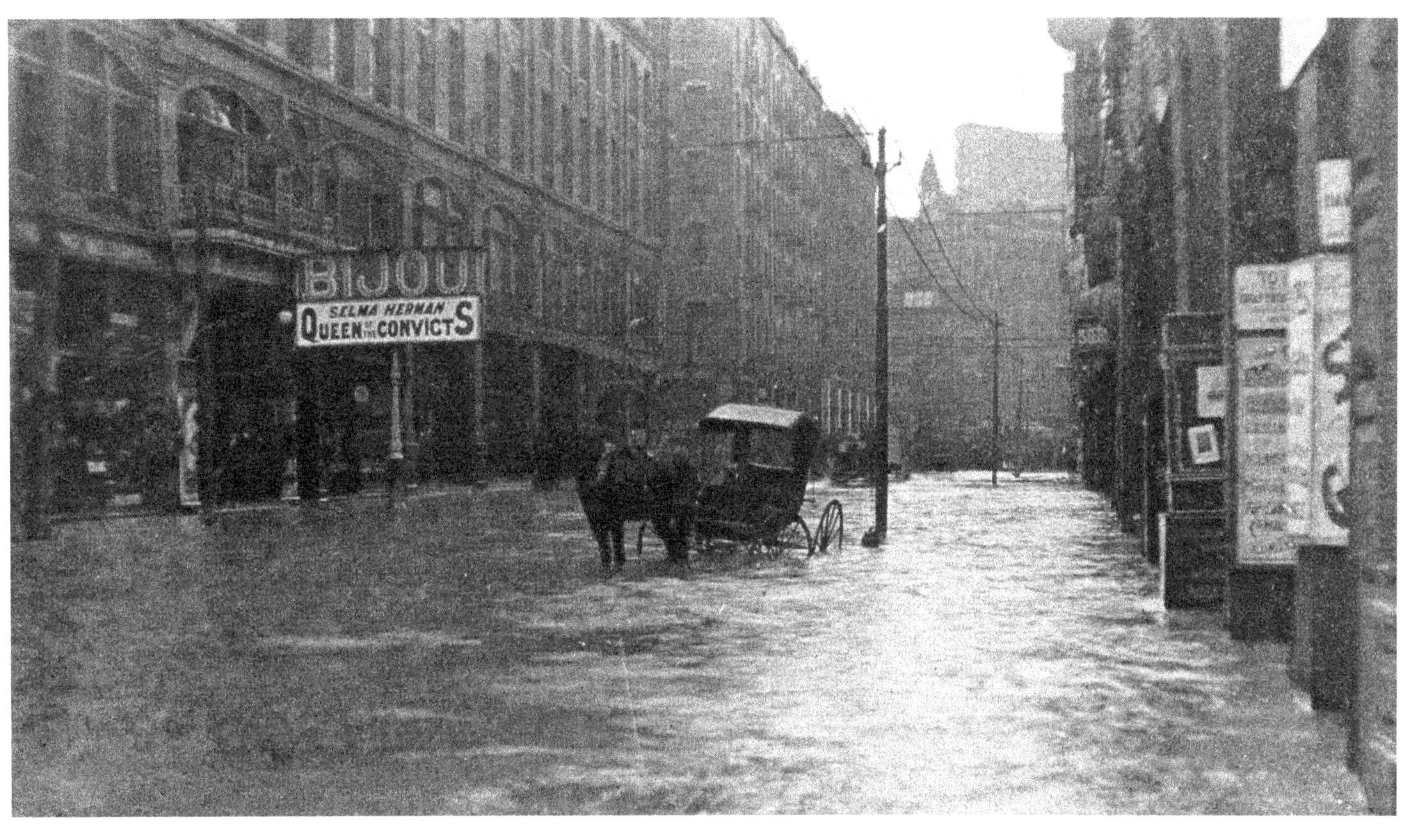

A lone horse and carriage passes the Bijou Theatre on Penn Street in Pittsburgh during a destructive flood that struck the city in March of 1907.

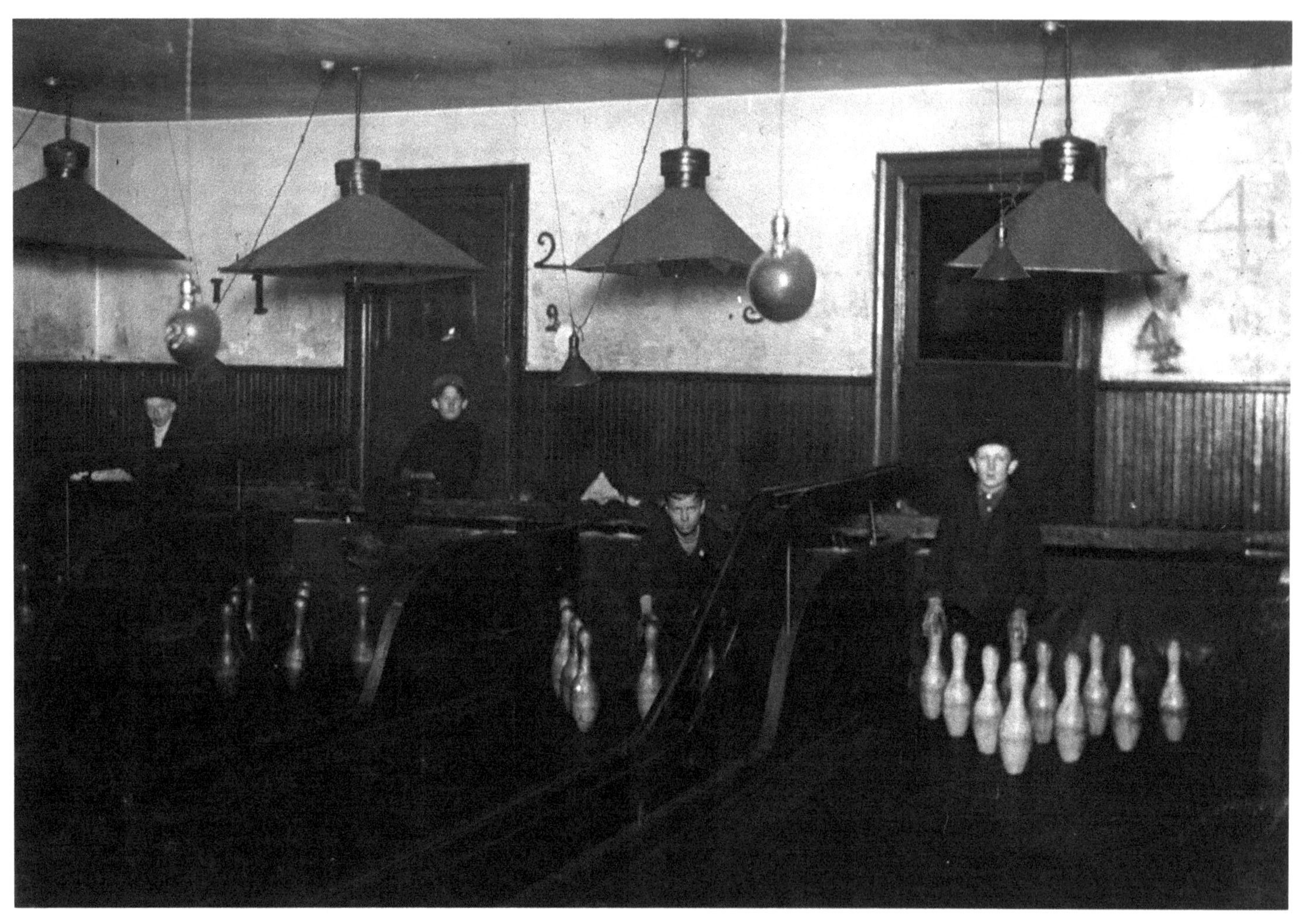

Pin boys work late into the night at a bowling alley in Pittsburgh, 1908. This image is by Lewis W. Hine, who traveled the country as an investigative photographer for the National Child Labor Committee.

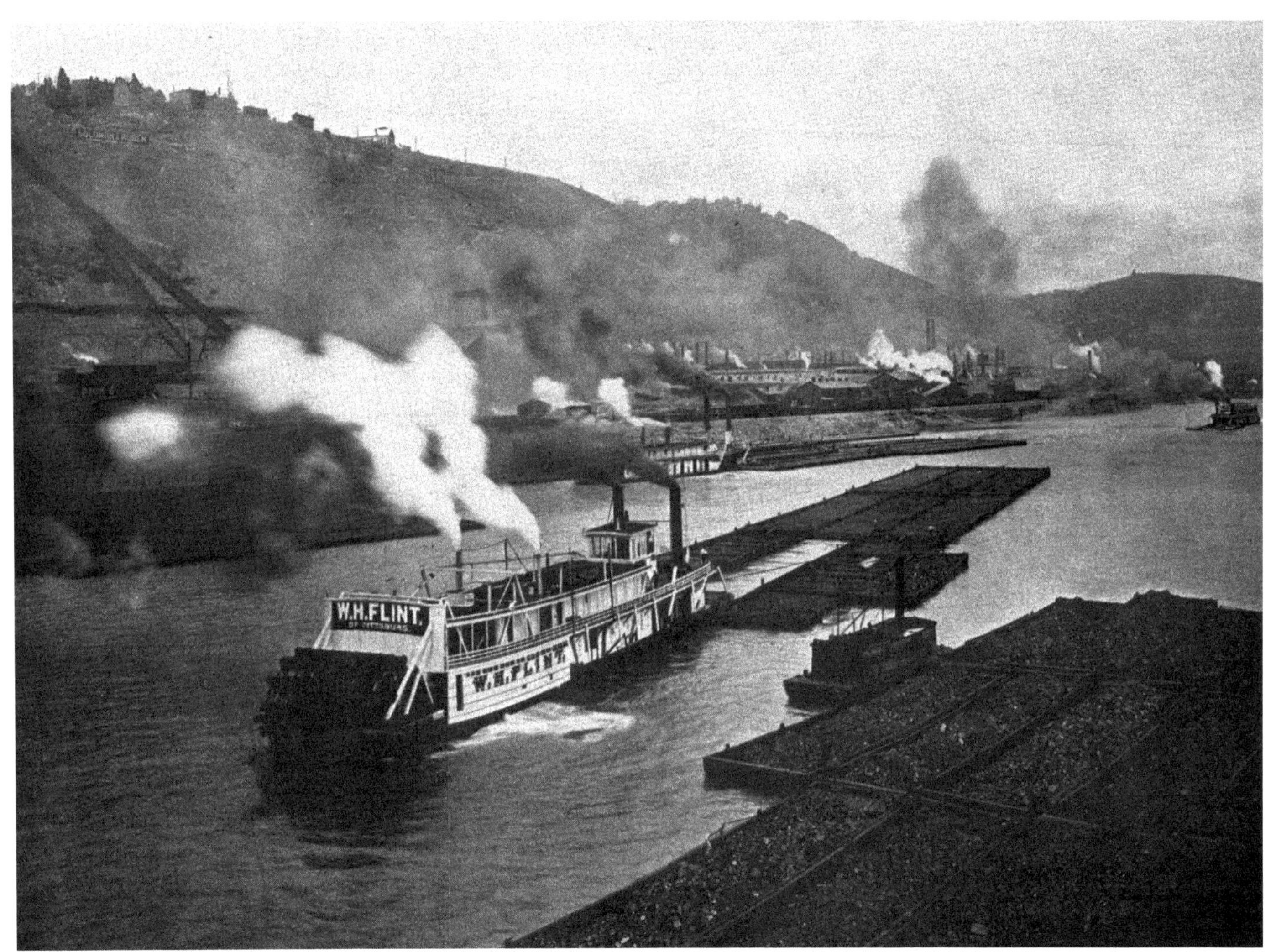

A steam-powered coal barge is maneuvered with a full load along the Ohio River near Pittsburgh in 1908.

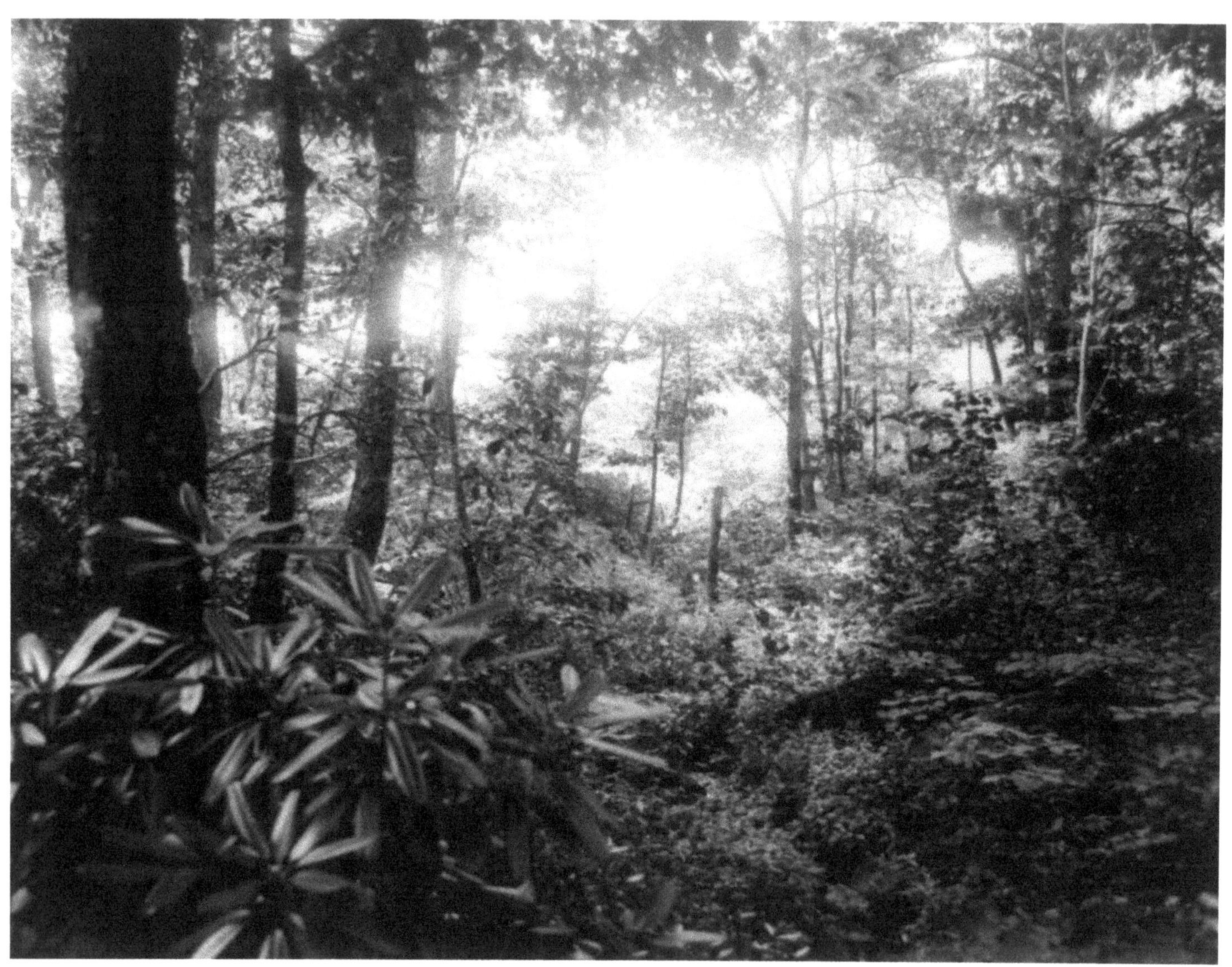

The wooded intersection of Braddock's Road and White Oak Level Road near McKeesport, circa 1908. Braddock's Road is the route along which British general Edward Braddock led a failed effort to take the French Fort Duquesne and lost his life during the Battle of Monongahela in July 1755.

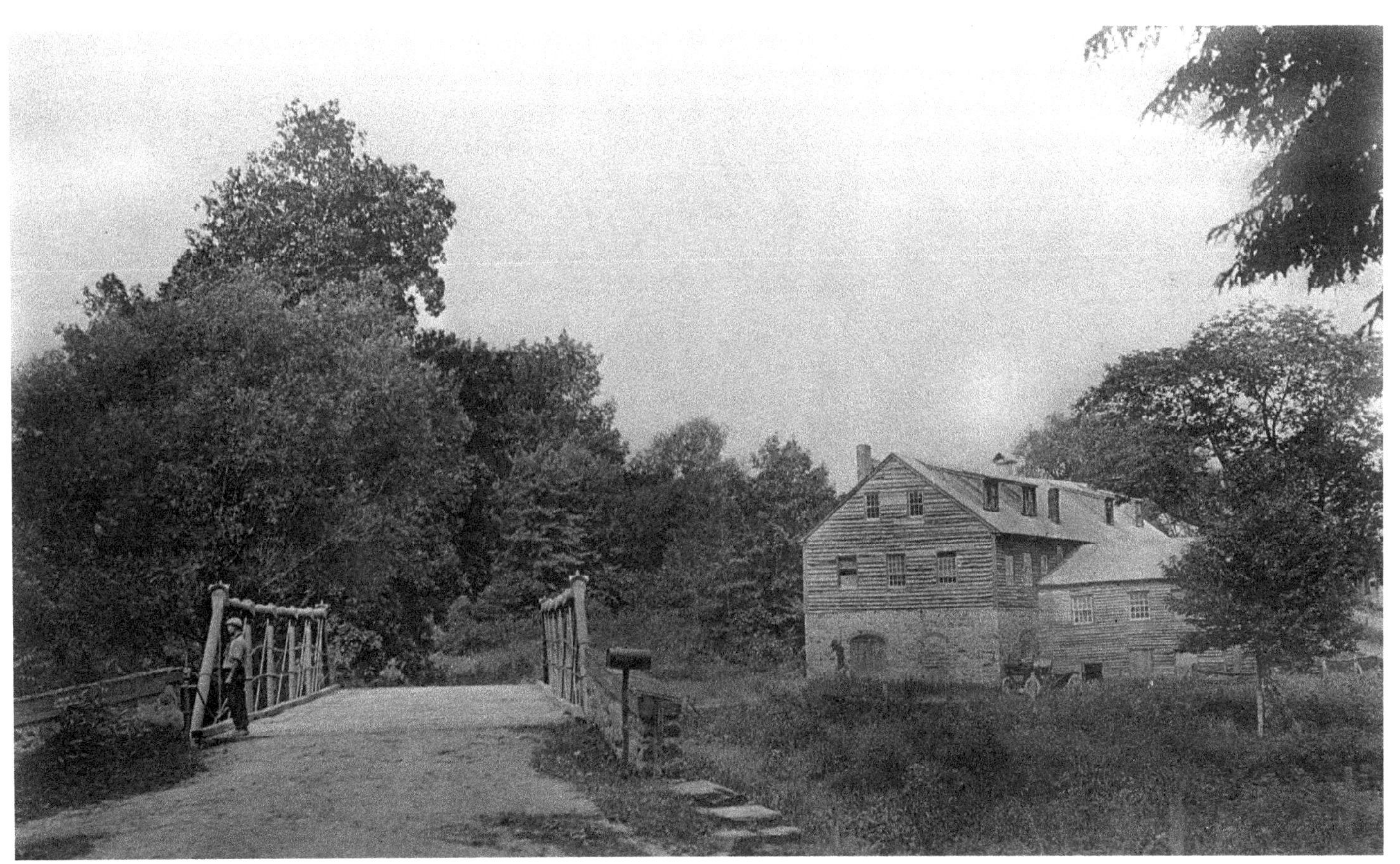

The William Henry family, originally of Lancaster, were among the country's leading gun manufacturers when they built a large new factory near Belfast, Northampton County. The company, which produced weapons for all American conflicts from the American Revolution through the Civil War, went out of business in the late 1800s. The factory and homestead, seen here circa 1910, are now part of the Pennsylvania Longrifle Museum in Jacobsburg.

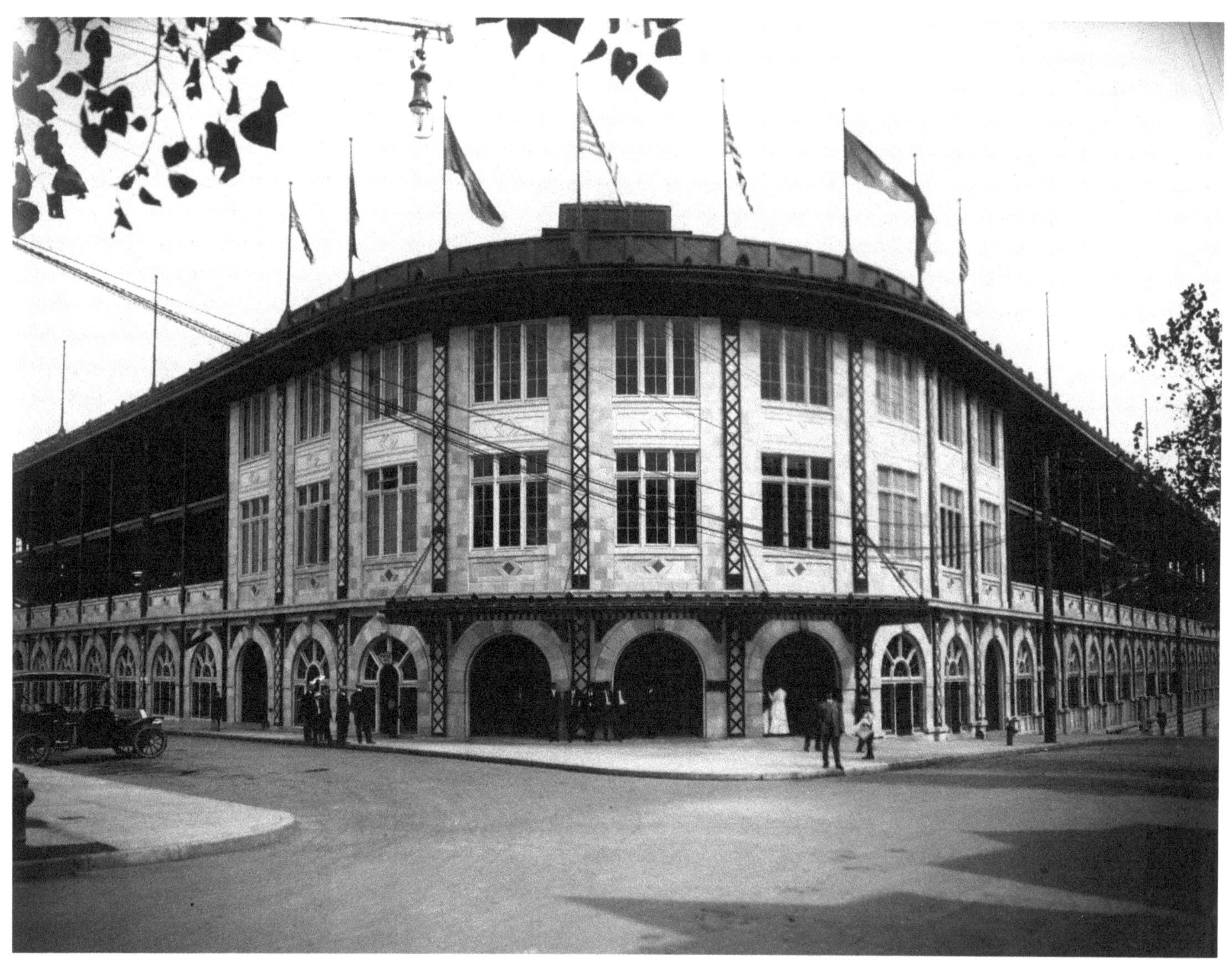

The main entrance to Forbes Field, longtime home to the Pittsburgh Pirates and the Pittsburgh Steelers, circa 1909. The Pirates lost the first baseball game played at Forbes Field, in 1907, but went on to win three World Series before the last game was played there in 1970.

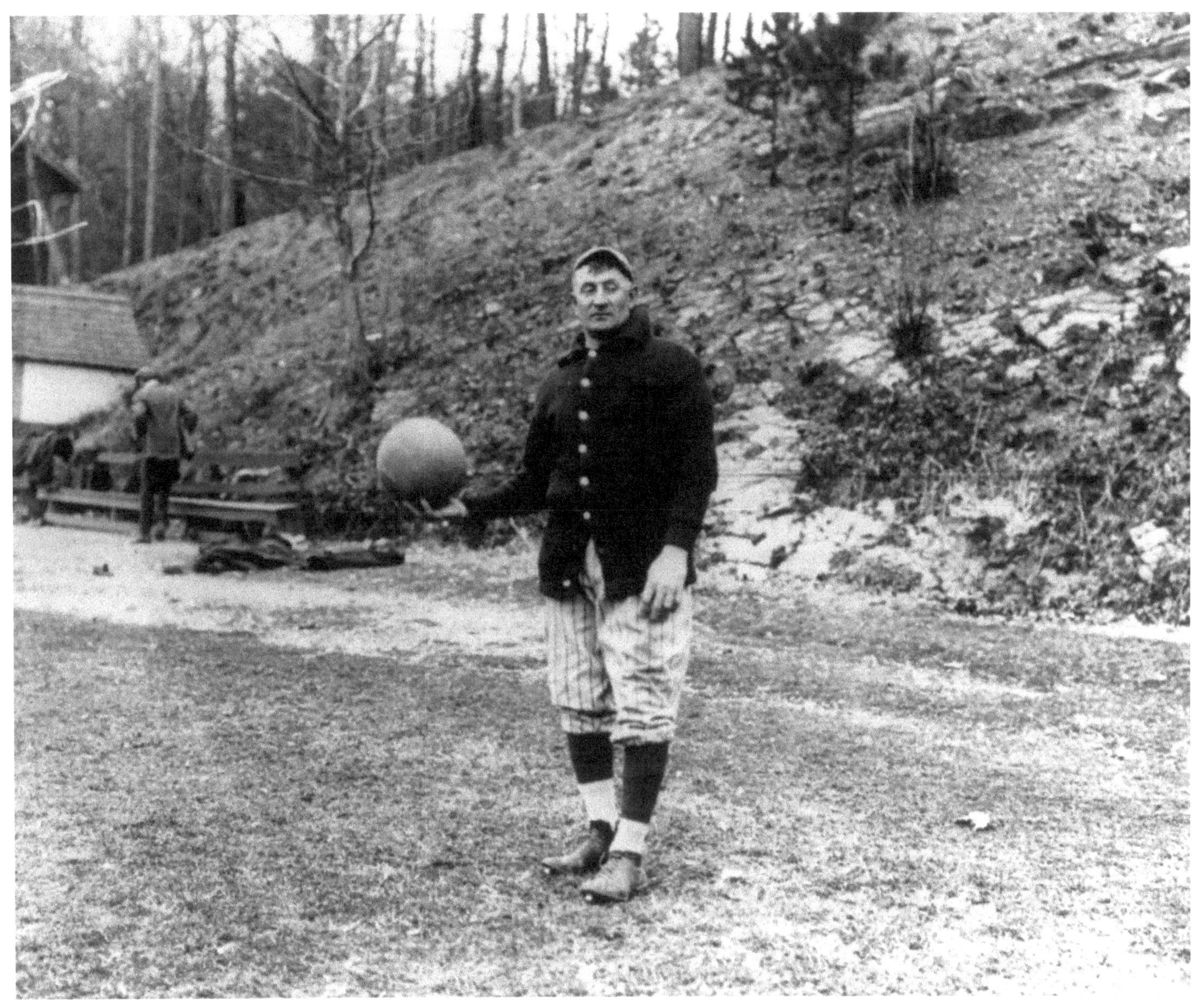

Considered by many to be the greatest shortstop in baseball history, Pittsburgh Pirate John Peter "Honus" Wagner (nicknamed the "Flying Dutchman") poses with a medicine ball, circa 1910. Wagner was among the first five inductees to the Baseball Hall of Fame in 1936.

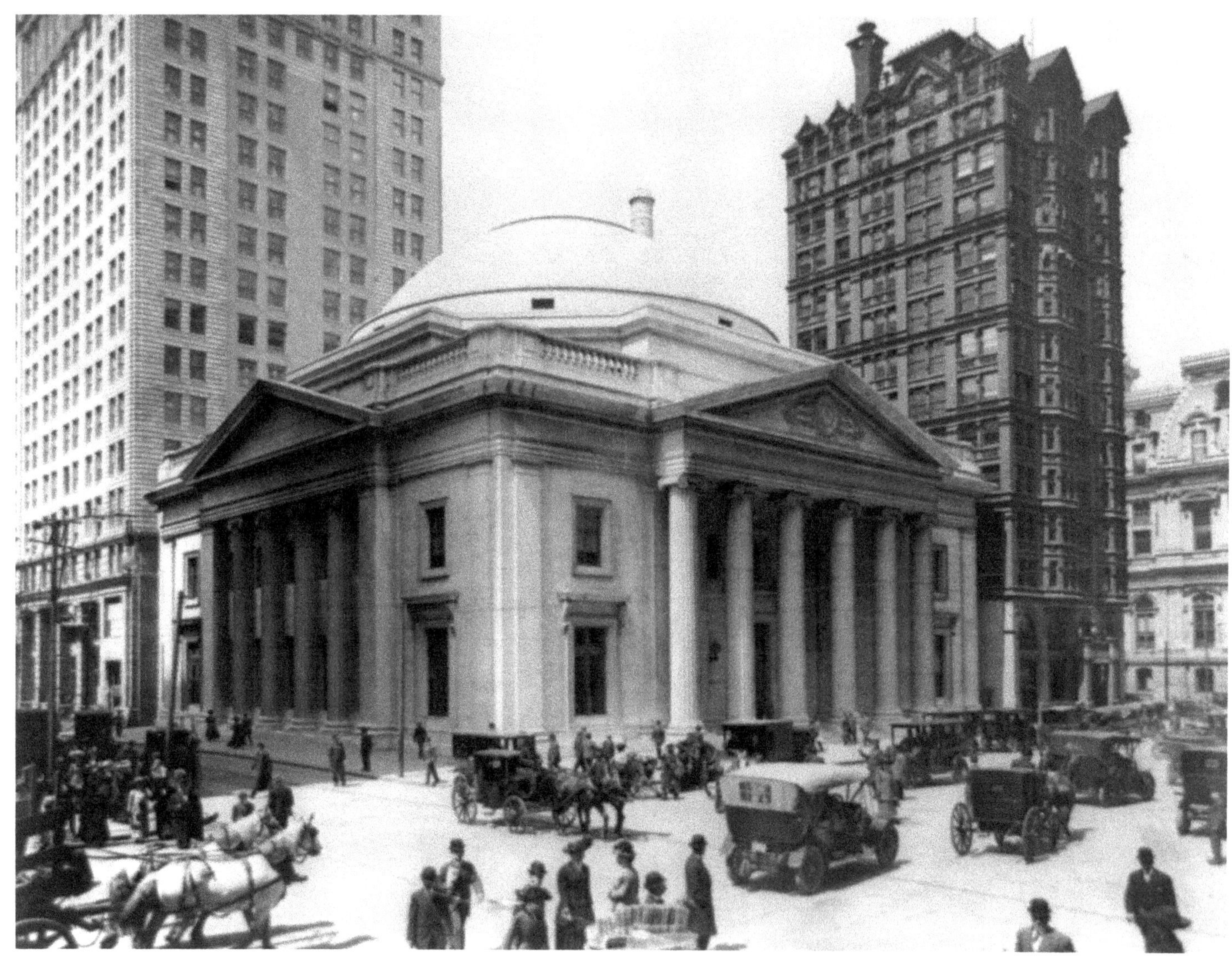

The neoclassically designed Girard Trust Building on South Broad Street in Philadelphia, circa 1910. Following the addition of a 300-room tower next to the original domed building, the former bank building is now home to the Ritz Carlton Hotel.

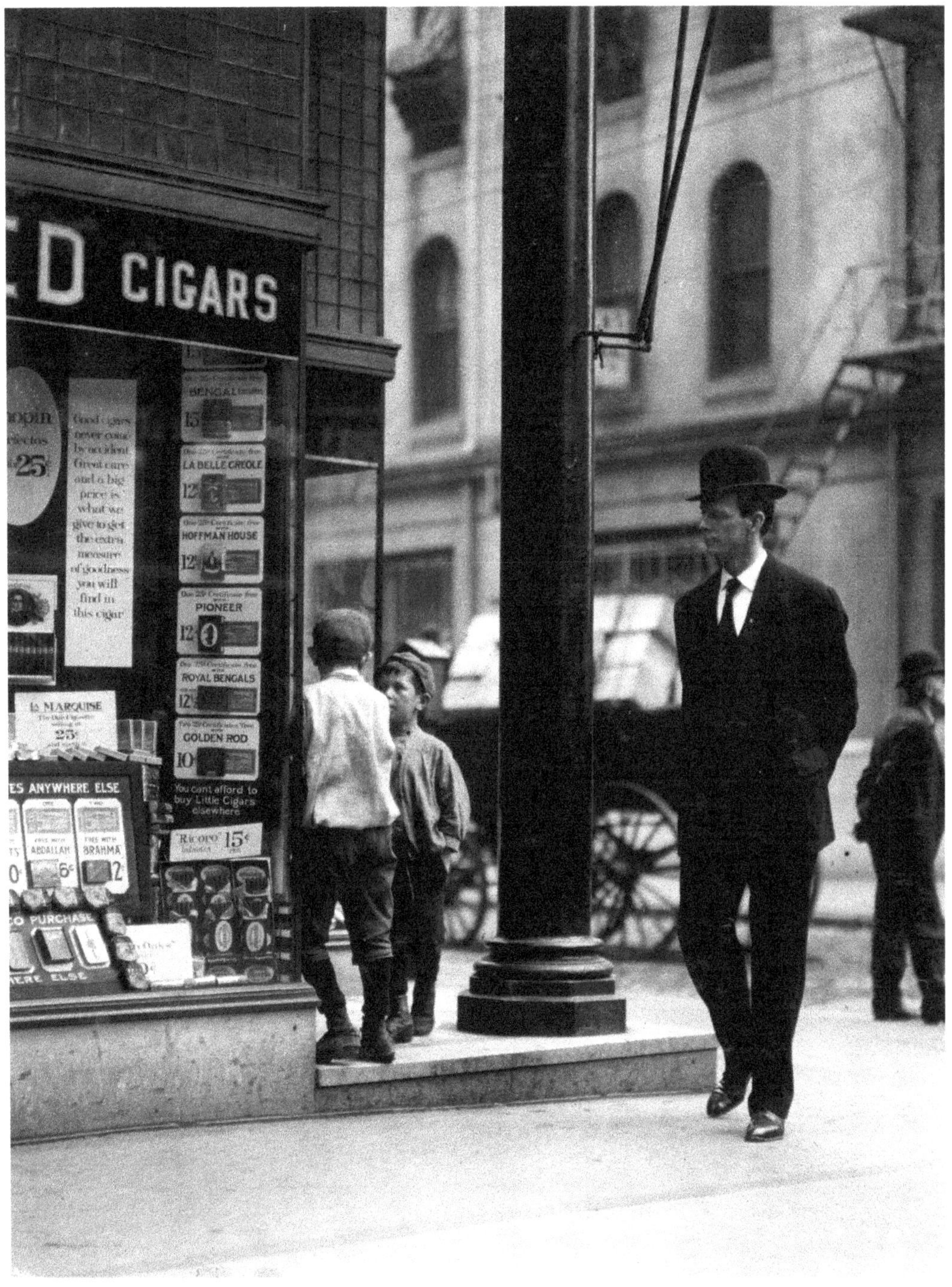

Two newsboys wait in front of a corner cigar store in Philadelphia, hoping to get tobacco coupons from sympathetic customers.

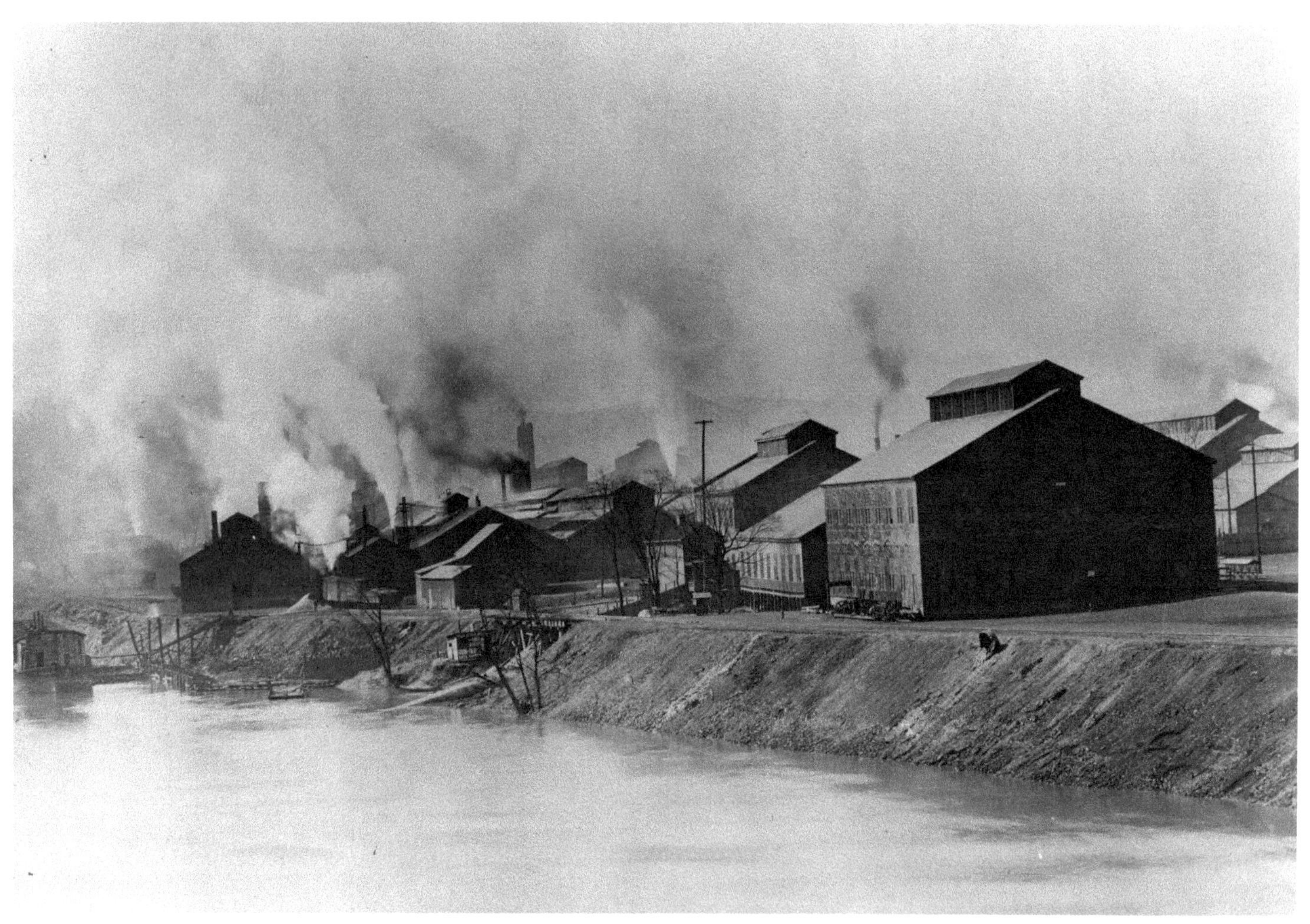

Wire mills, manufacturers of wire cable, in Donora, Washington County, circa 1910. The smoke seen here foretells of a fatal level of pollution reached in the town October 30-31, 1948, when 19 people died within a period of 24 hours.

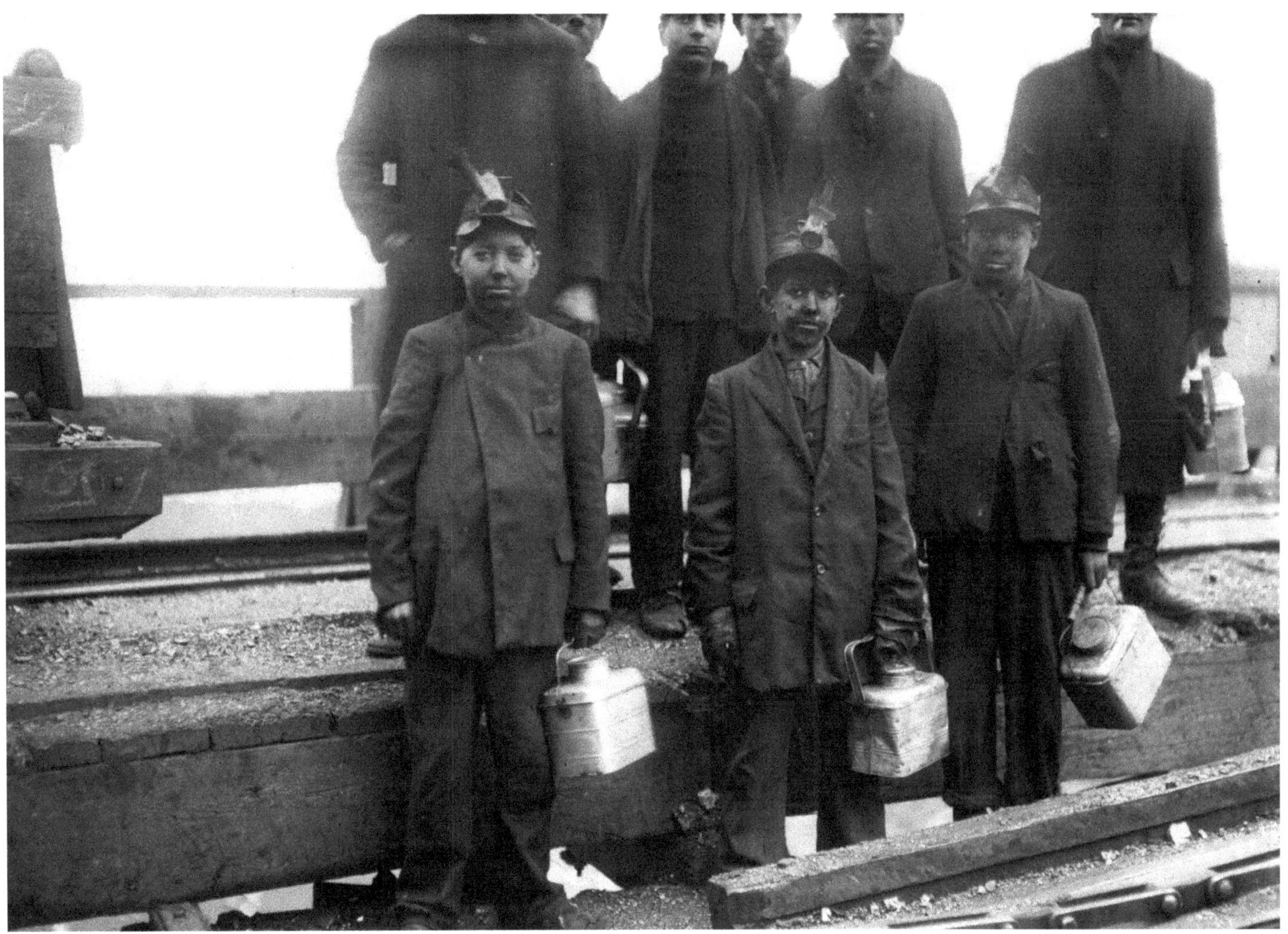

Young boys outside Shaft No. 6 of the Pennsylvania Coal Company mine in South Pittston, Luzerne County, December 1910. Through photographs like this one, investigative photographer and social documentarian Lewis W. Hine hoped to expose the use of young children in dangerous industries such as coal mining.

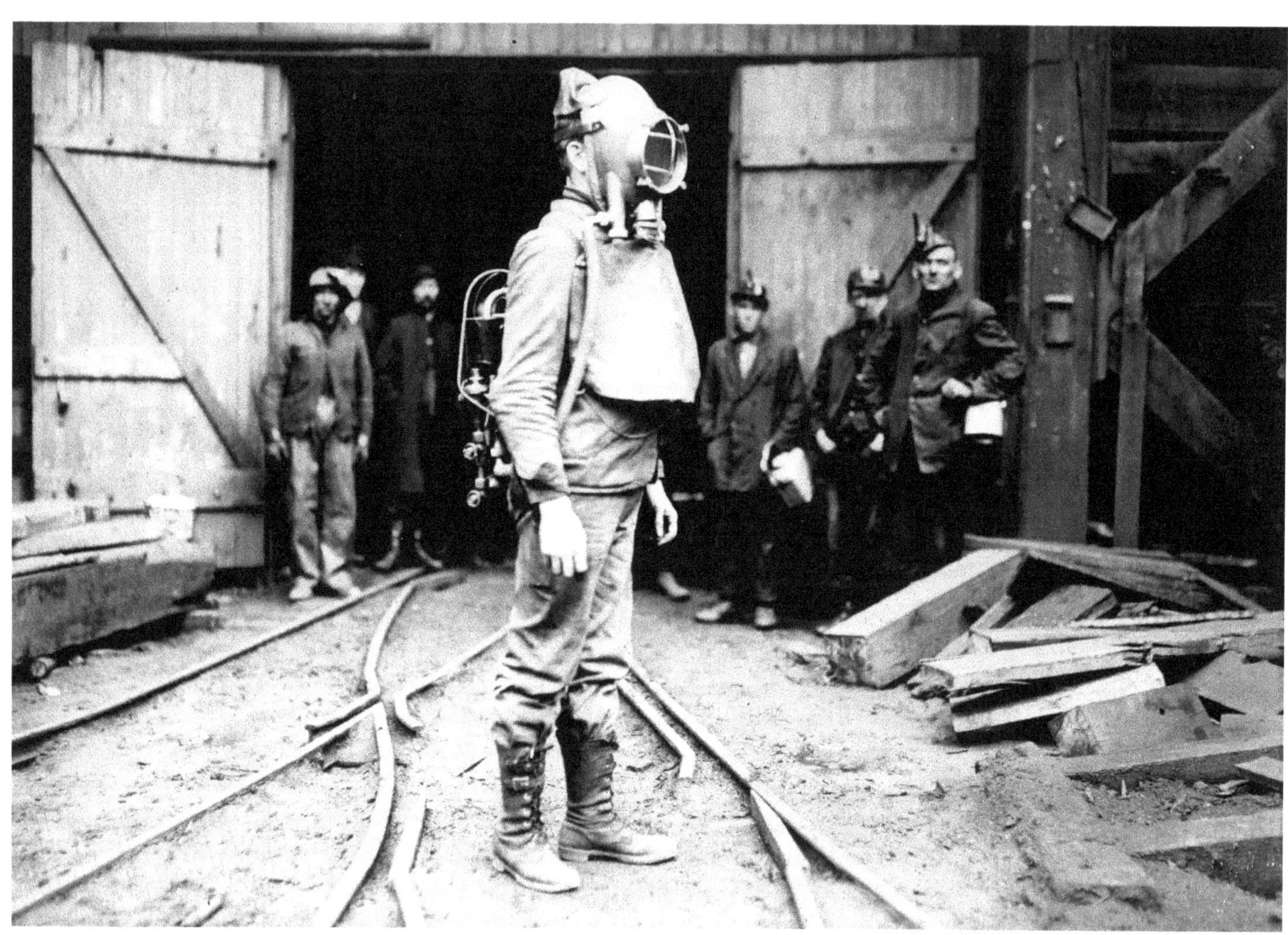

The high danger in coal mining is evidenced by the presence of a "First Aid to the Injured" worker, fully outfitted in a Draeger Oxygen Helmet designed to aid breathing in toxic environments. This photo was taken at the Avondale Shaft, D. L. W. Colliery in Luzerne County, the site of a particularly deadly mine fire in 1869.

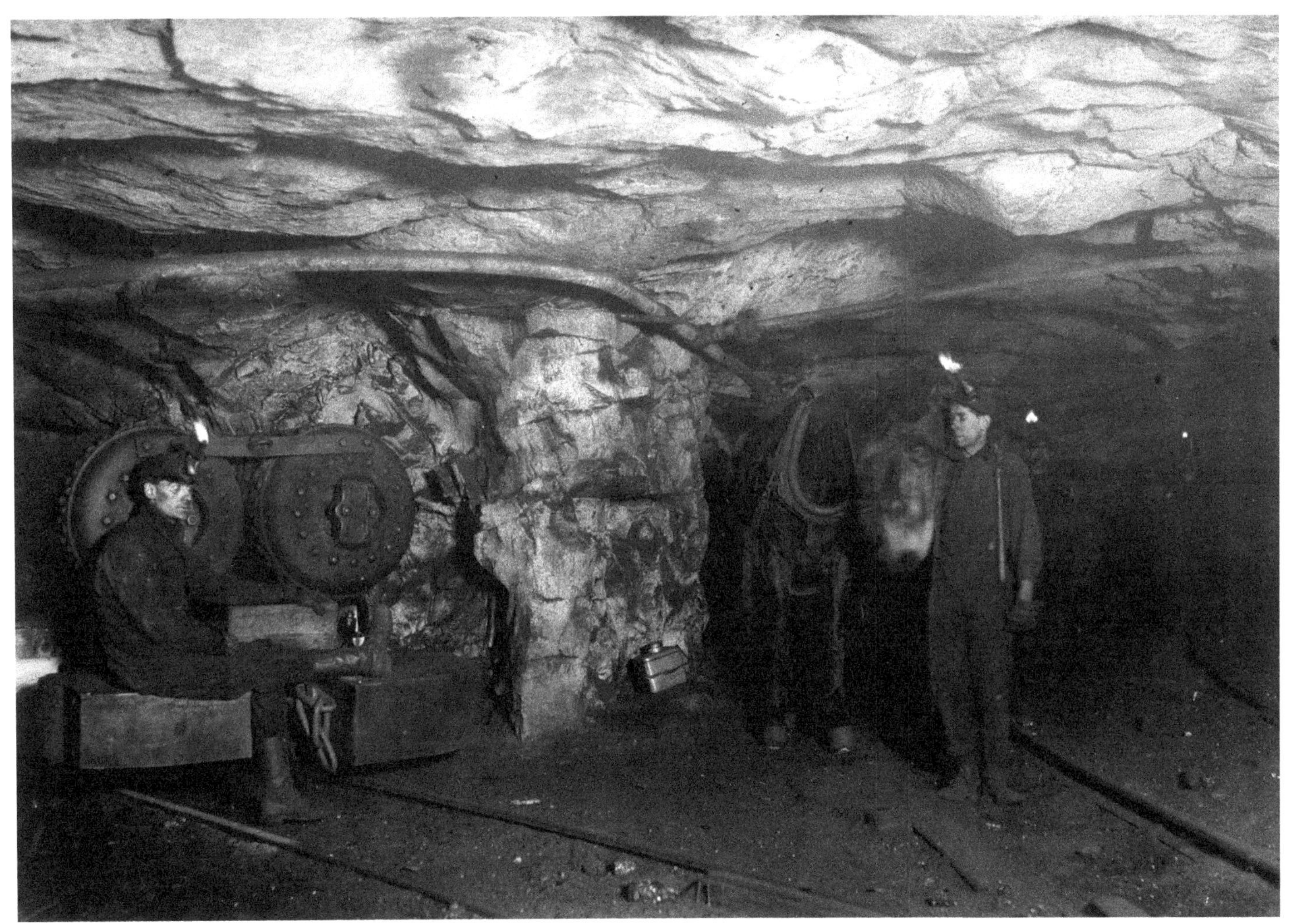

Mules and children worked side by side with motorized trucks and men in many coal mines, including Shaft No. 6 in South Pittston on this day in January 1911.

Following Spread: A view north over the Delaware River at Dingmans Ferry, Pike County.

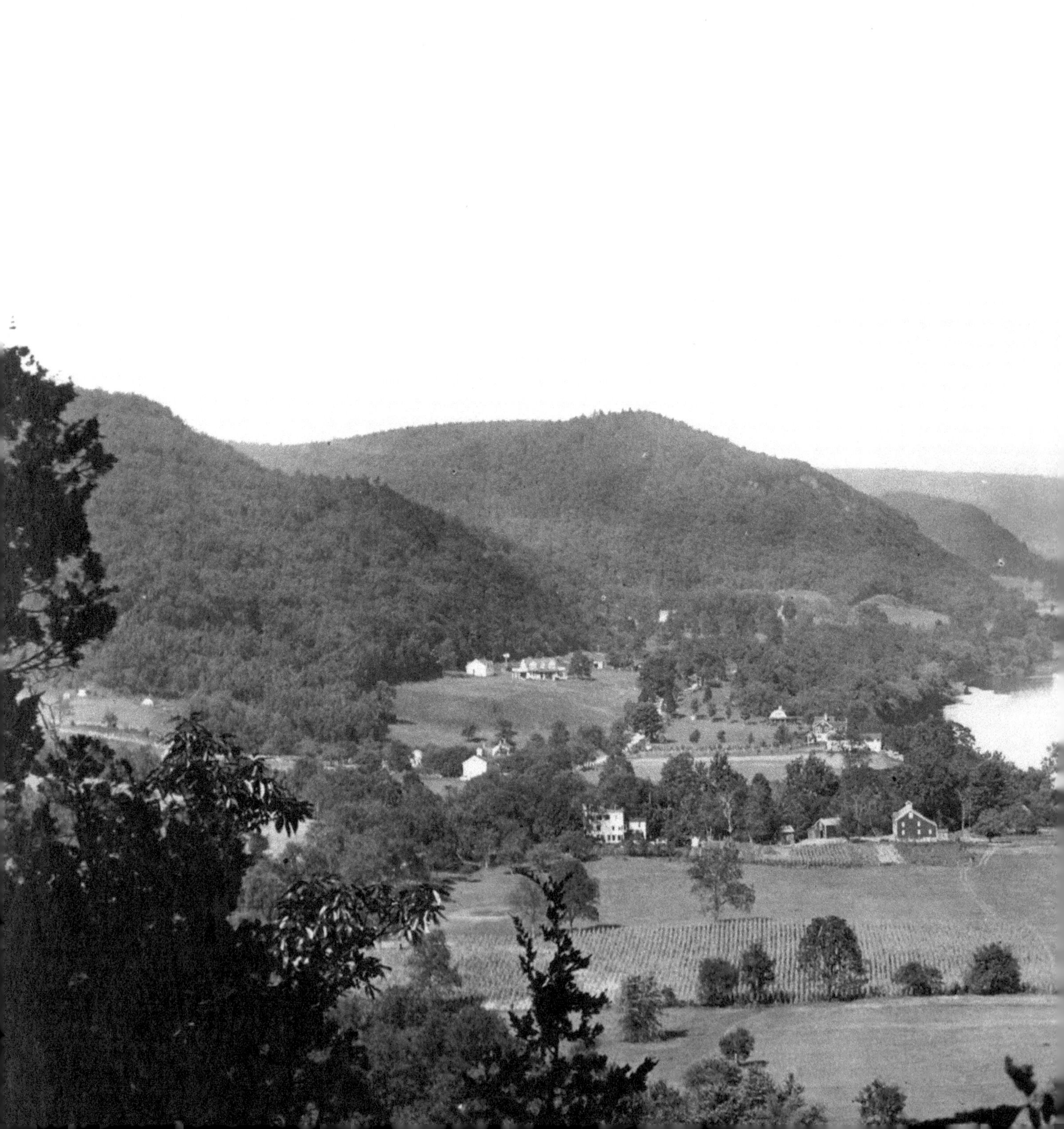

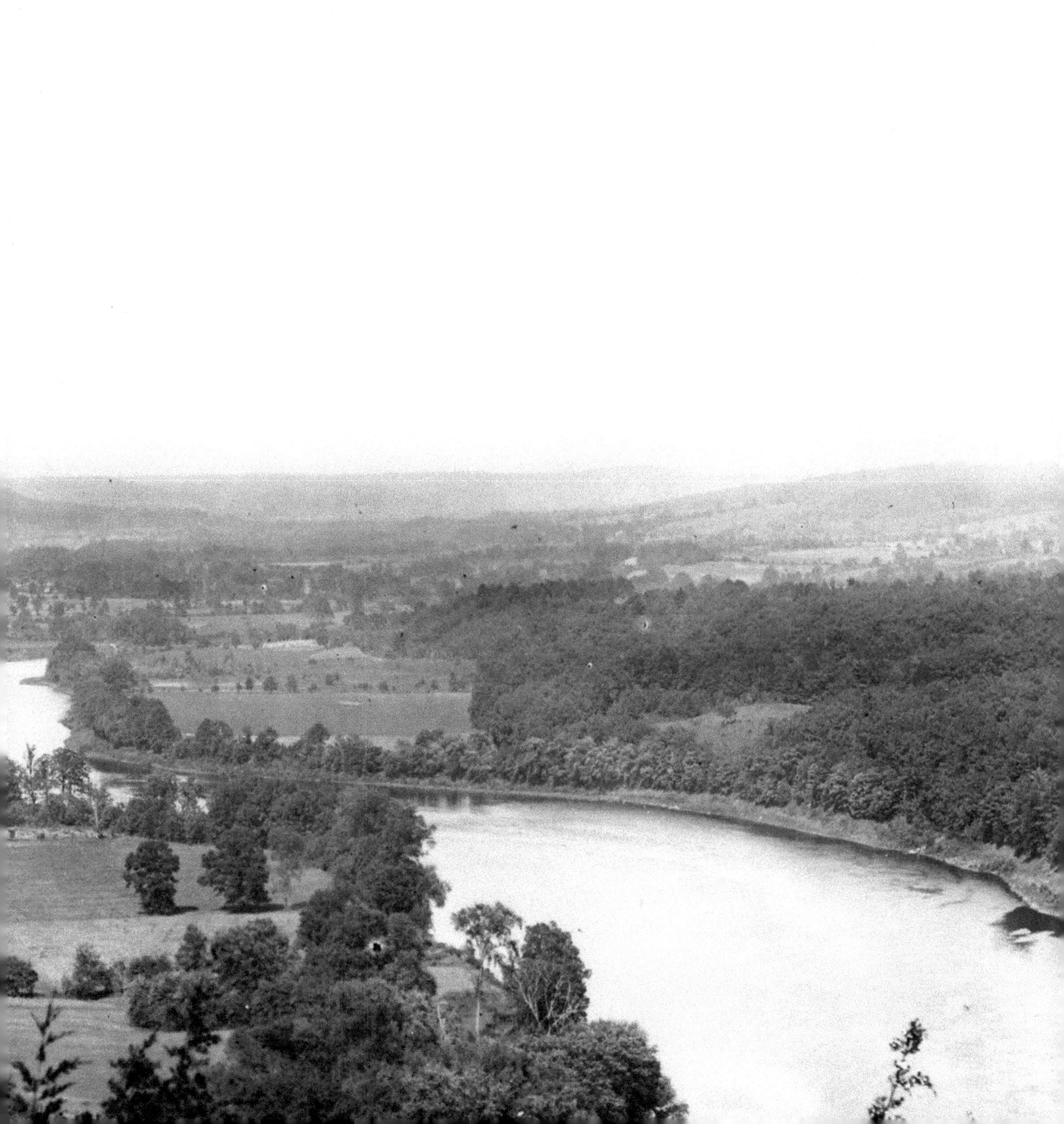

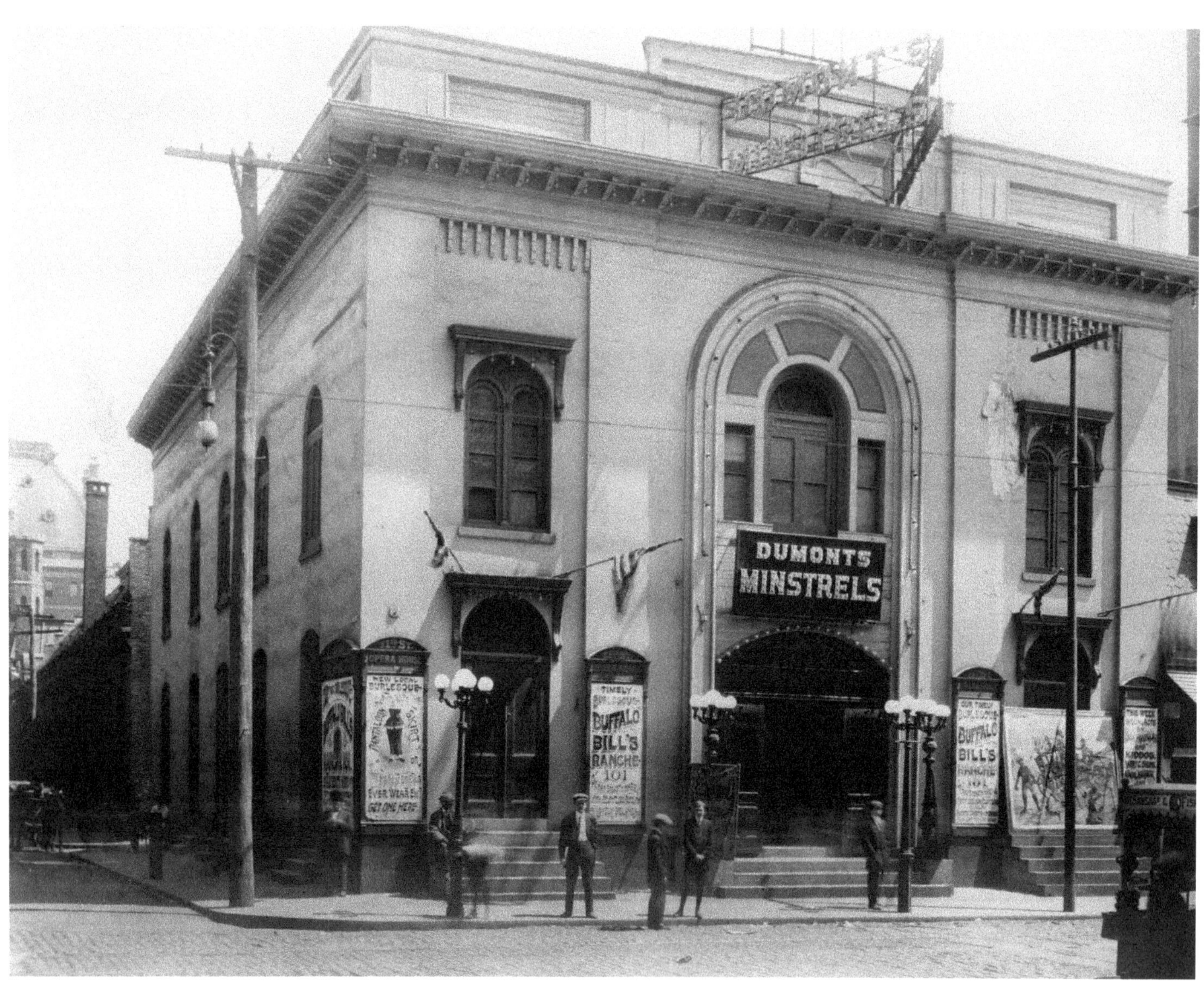

One of several minstrel and burlesque houses in Philadelphia, Dumont's Opera House was located on North Eleventh Street near Ranstead Street.

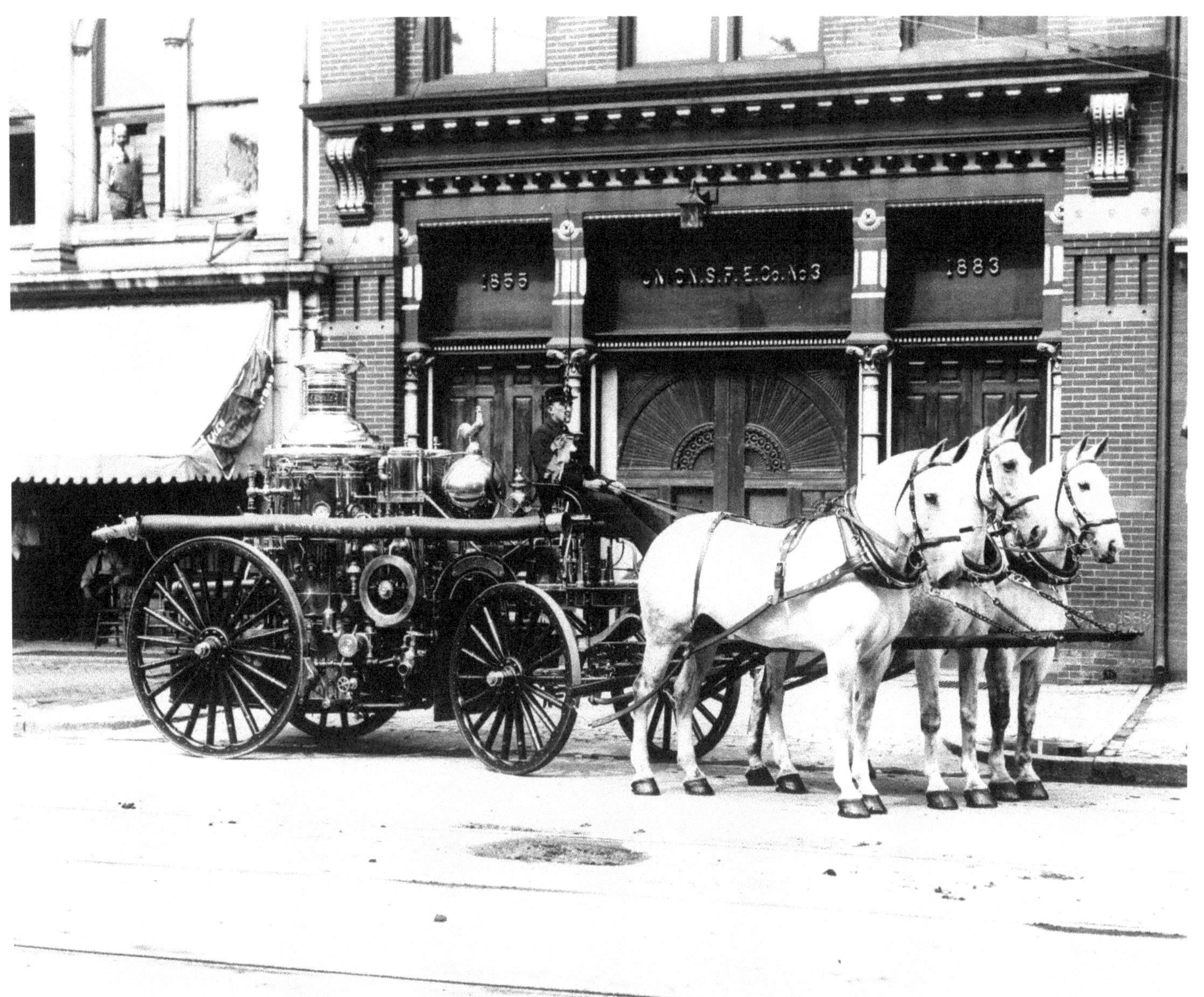

Union Engine No. 3 poses in front of a York firehouse, circa 1911. The first fire-fighting unit in York was the volunteer Sun Fire Brigade, organized in 1771.

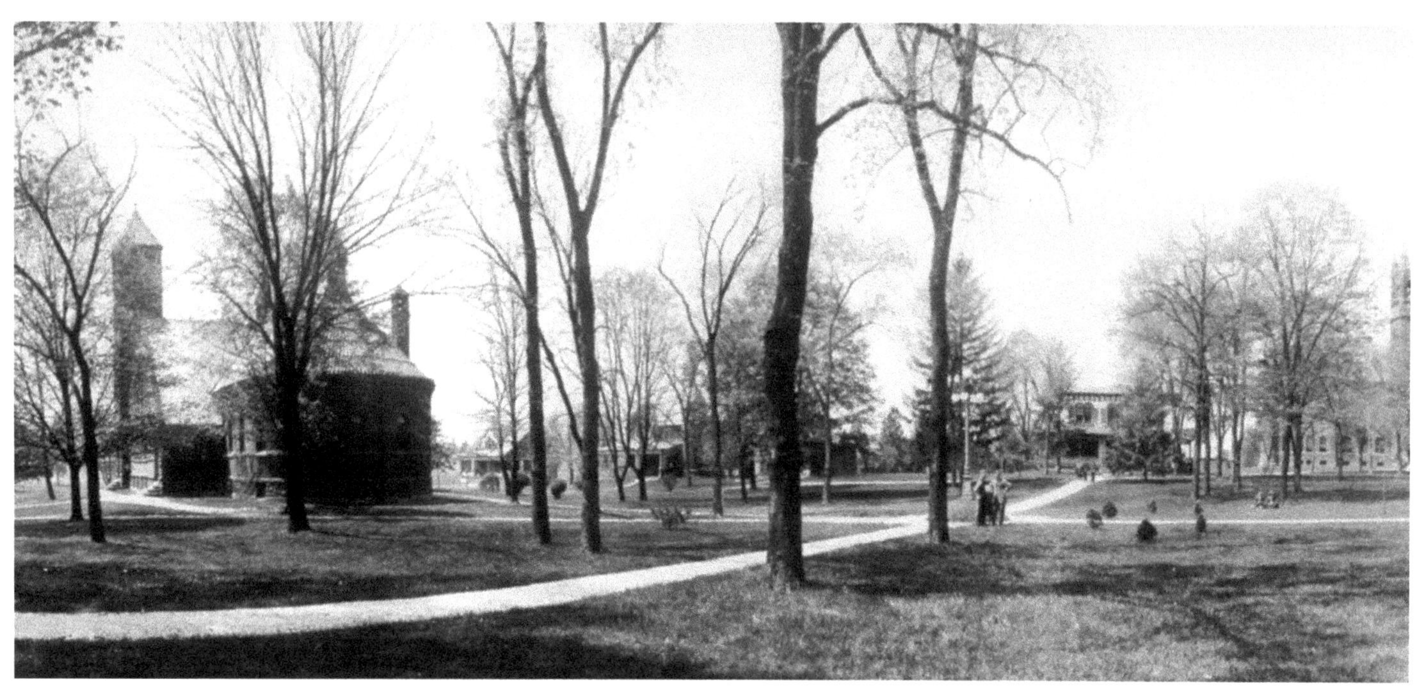

The campus of Pennsylvania College in Gettysburg in 1913, with the Brua Chapel at left. Founded in 1832, the school was renamed Gettysburg College in 1921.

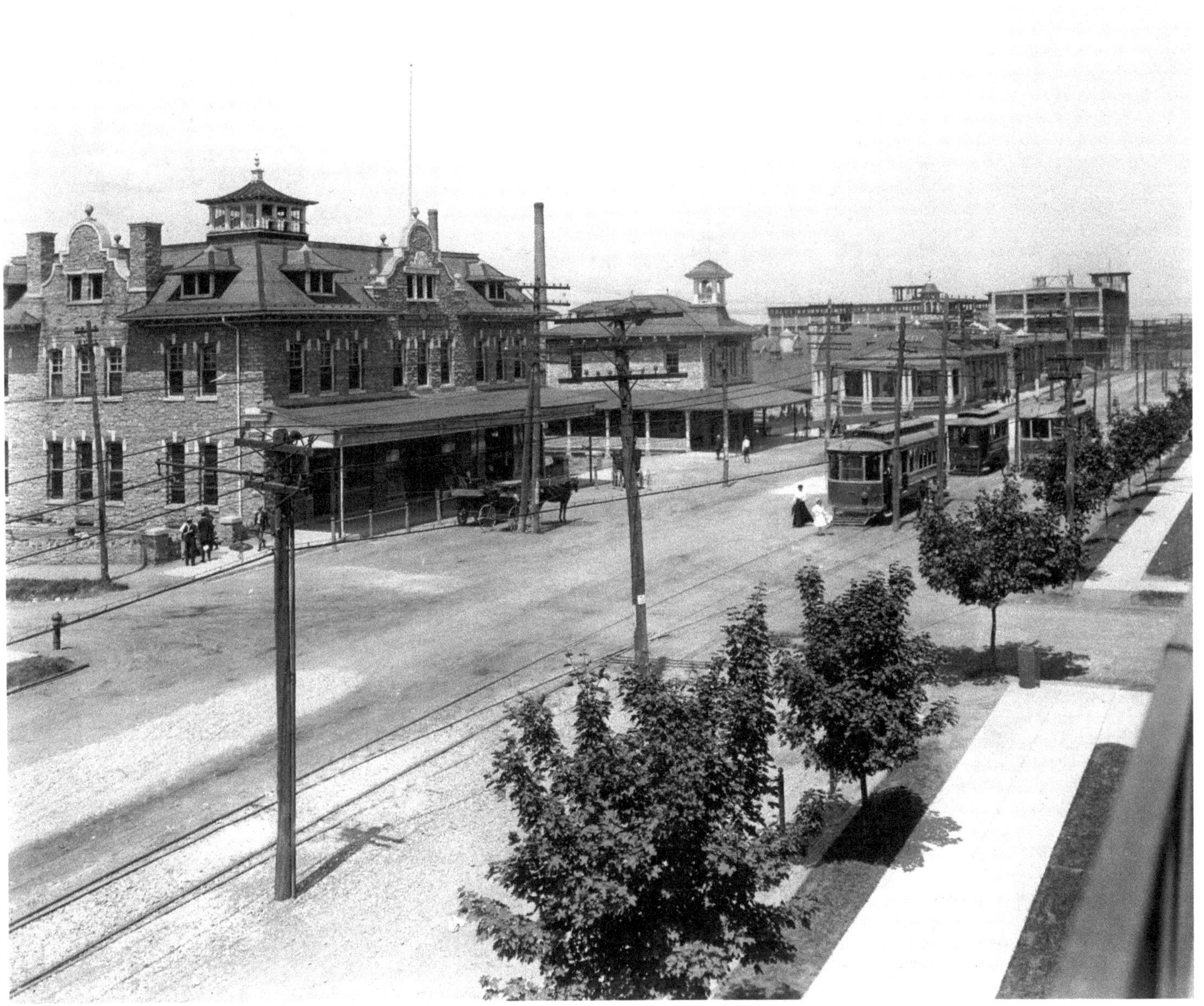

With the Hershey chocolate factory opening in Derry Township in 1905, a company town developed by Milton Hershey grew up around it. Viewed circa 1913, trolley-lined Chocolate Avenue features Cocoa House—home to the local YMCA and other organizations—at far left, along with the Volunteer Fire House, the Hershey Cafe, and the chocolate factory at the far end of the street.

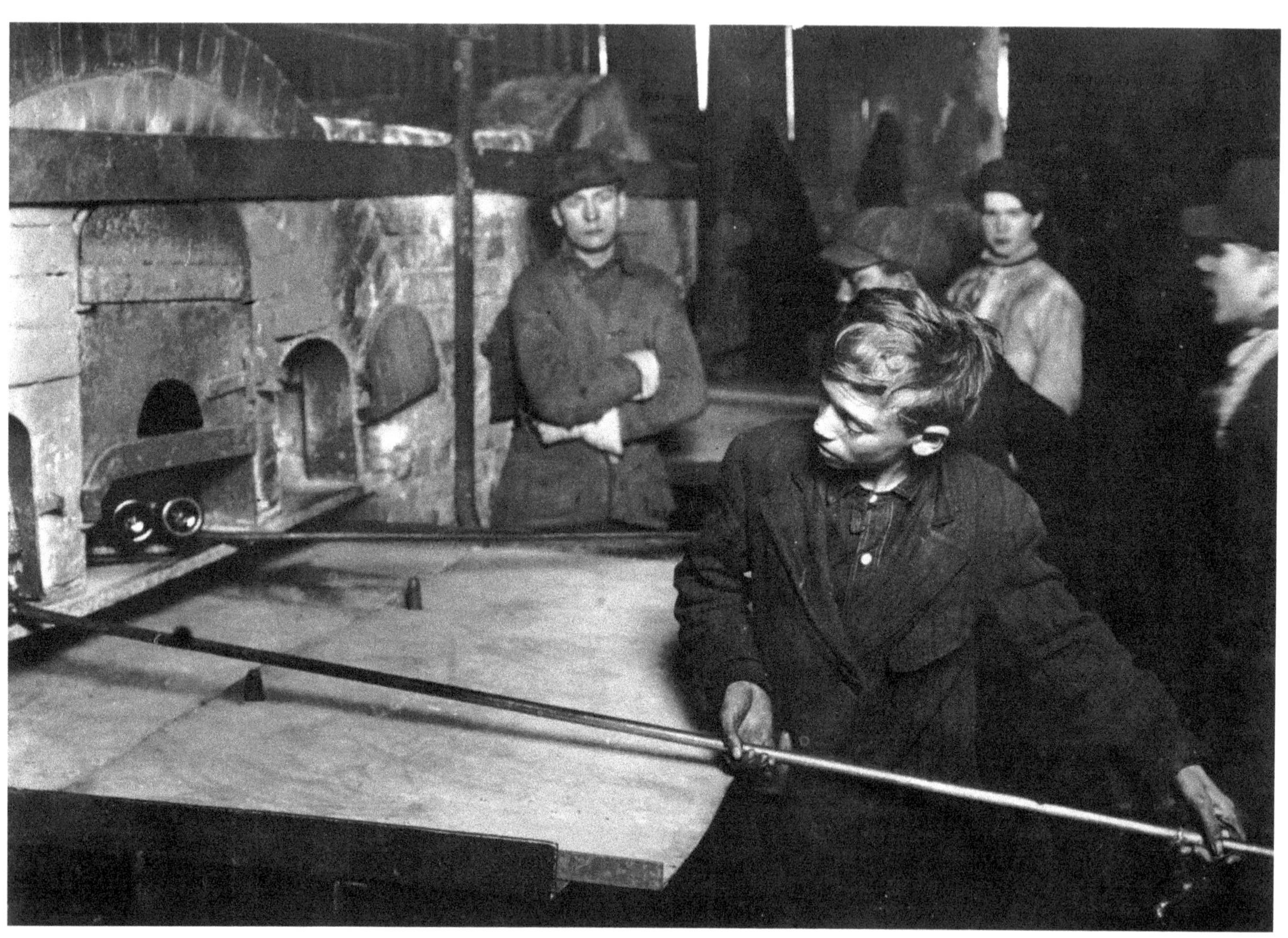

This Lewis W. Hine photograph shows young boys preparing molten glass for the blowers at the Wormser's Glass Works in Pittsburgh.

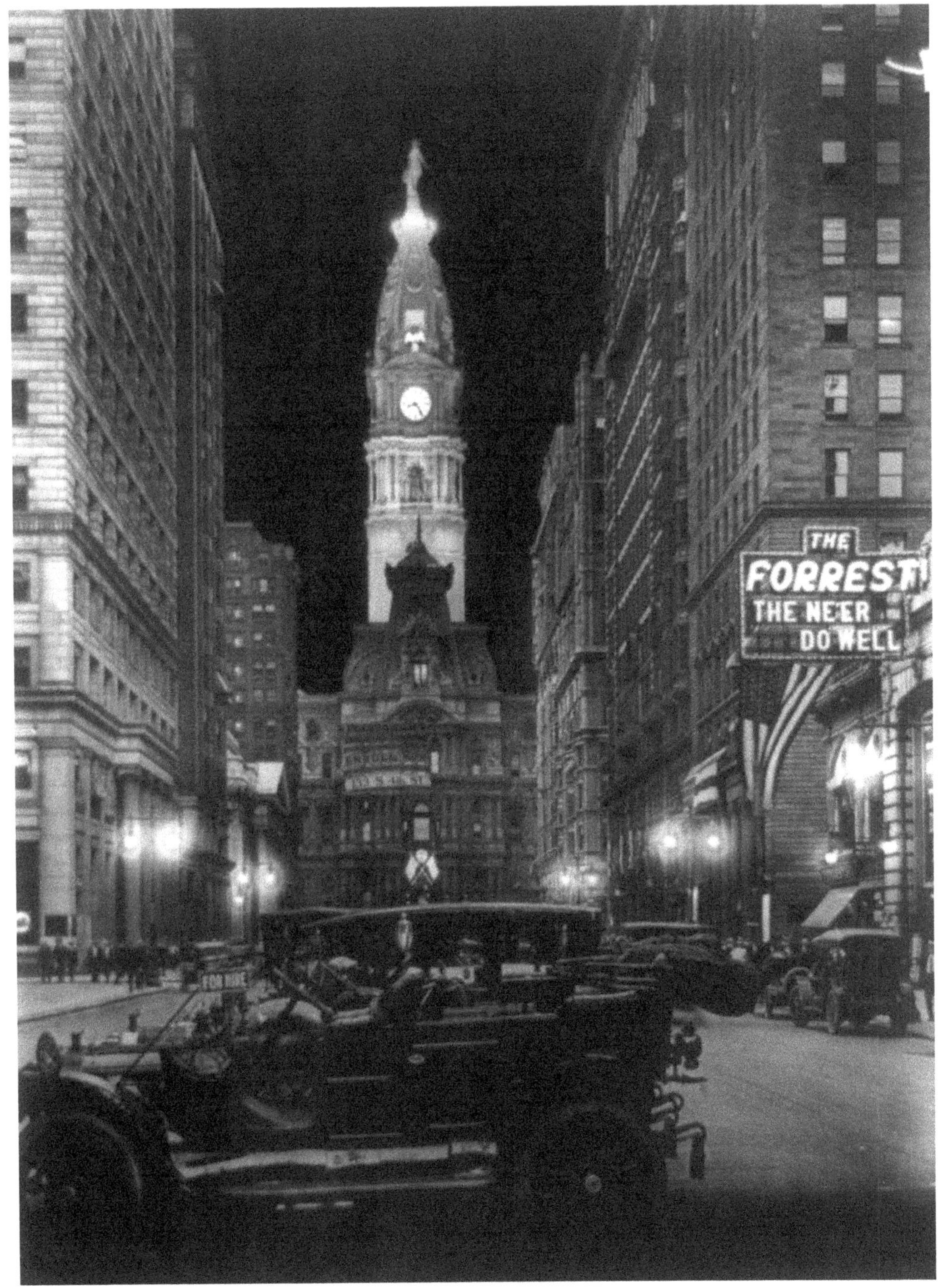

The scene at night, viewed north on Broad Street toward Philadelphia's City Hall, 1916. The City Hall tower, built in the 1890s, remains the world's tallest masonry structure bearing a statue (of city founder William Penn).

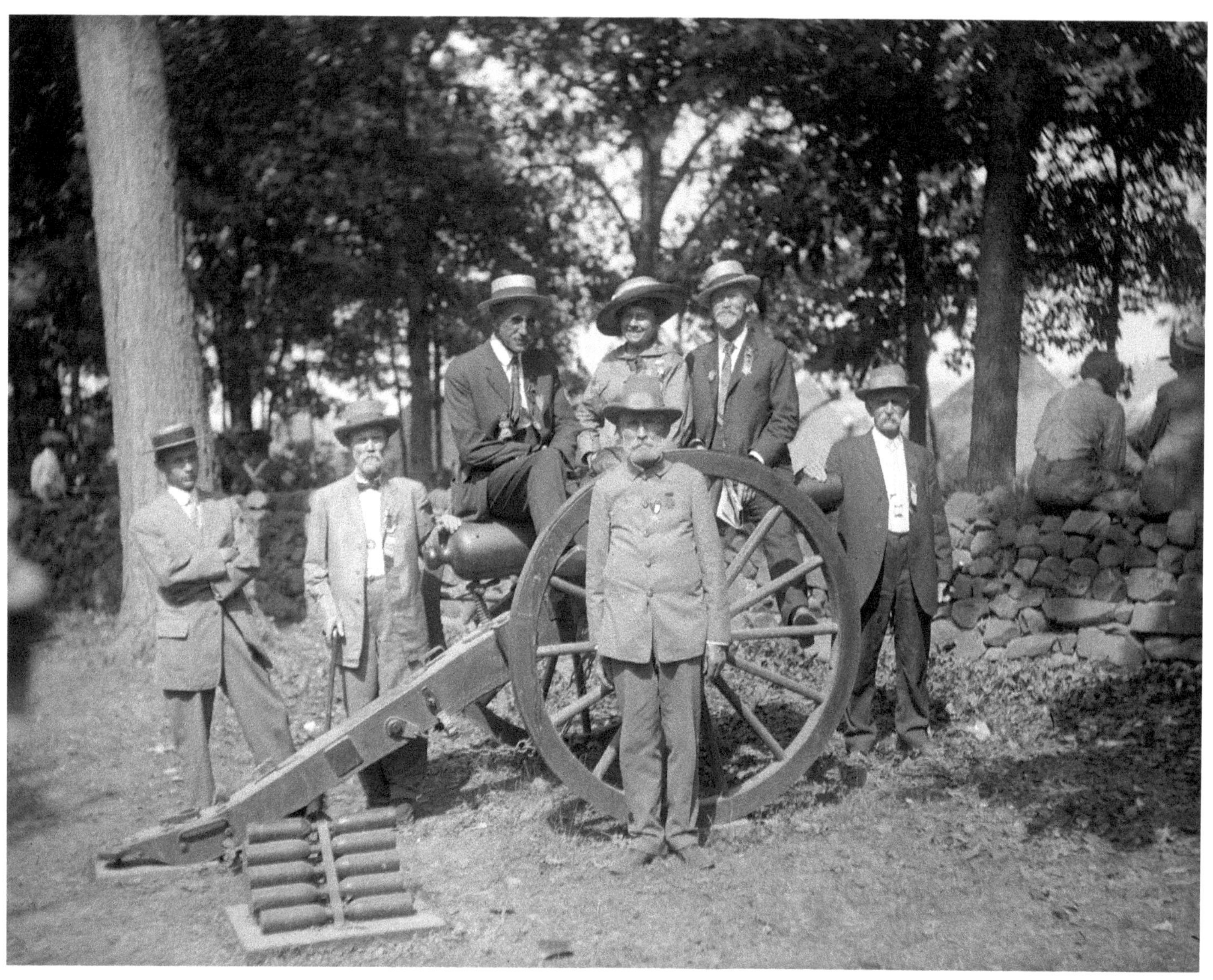

During the time of the First World War, members of the Grand Army of the Republic, an organization of Union veterans of the Civil War, gathered for a reunion in Gettysburg. The woman at center is perhaps a member of the auxiliary Woman's Relief Corps.

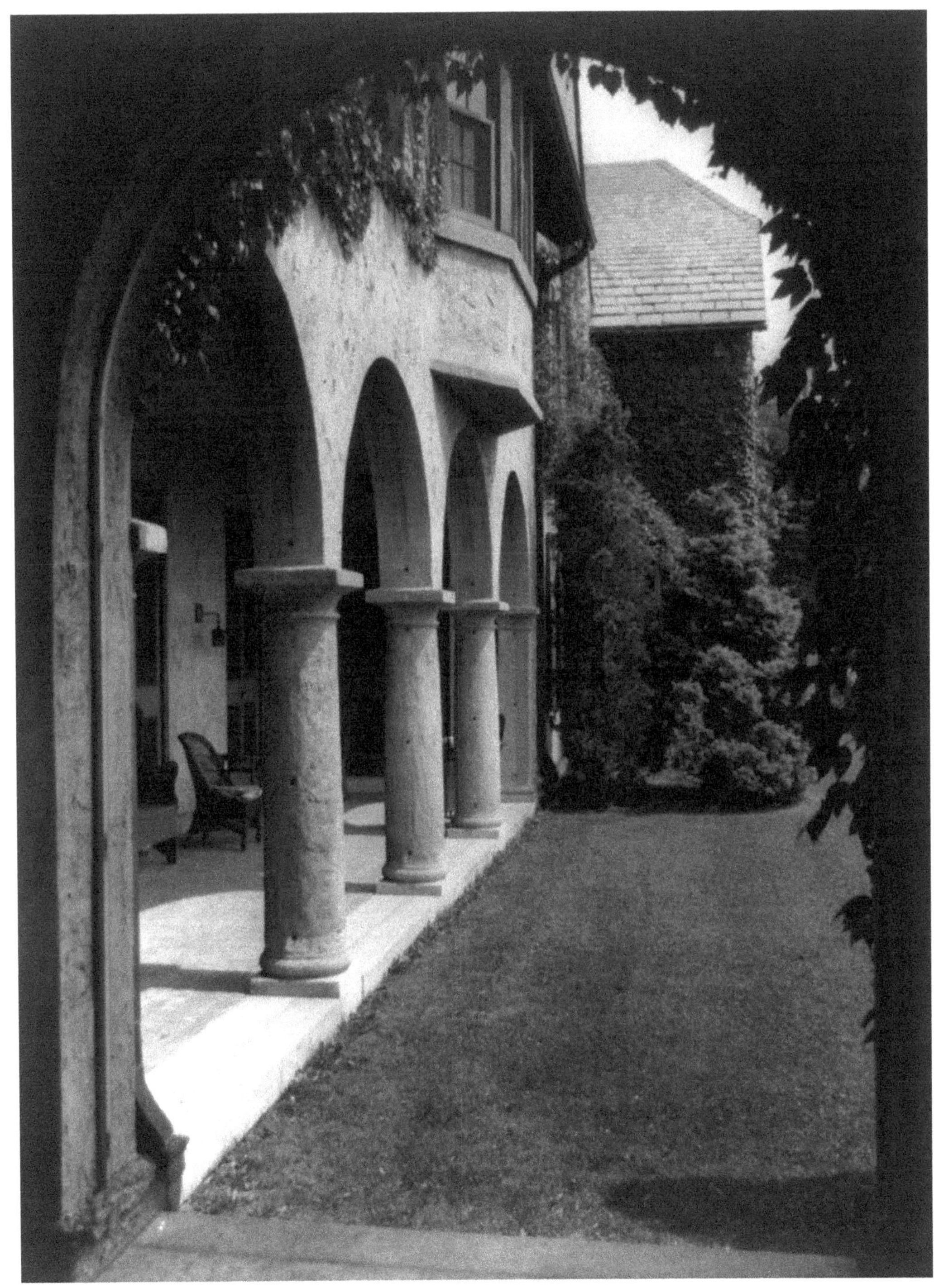

The grand side entrance to Allgates, the home of Horatio Gates Lloyd in Haverford, Delaware County. Built by Wilson Eyre in 1910, the 75-acre estate was known for its remarkable gardens.

Sightseers cross a wooden bridge at one of eight dramatic falls in Bushkill Falls, circa 1919. The combined "Niagara of Pennsylvania" along Bushkill Falls Creek remains a major tourist attraction.

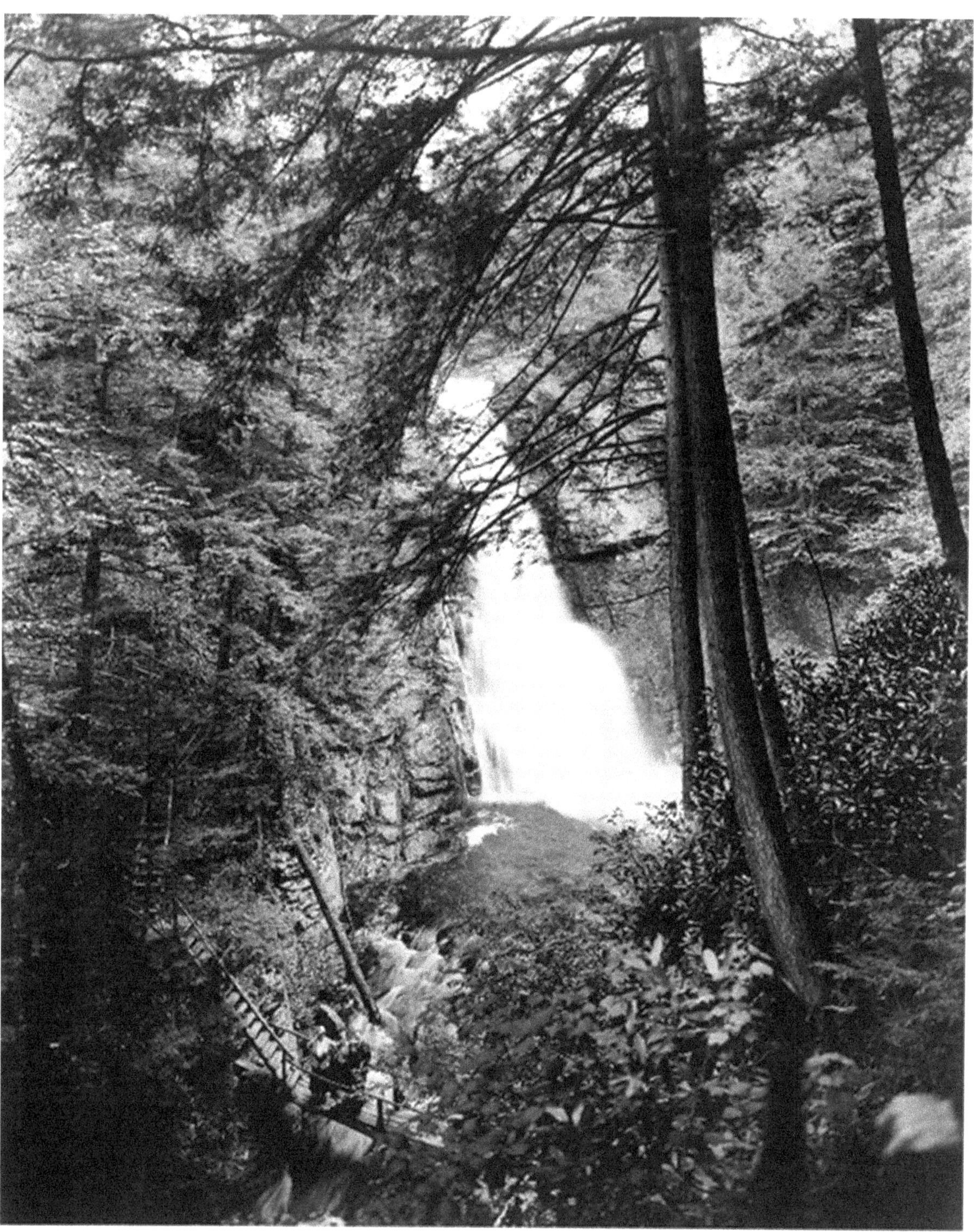

Peaks and Valleys

(1920–1949)

The years between the world wars marked a shift in the long-term successes of Pennsylvania's industries. High demand for Pennsylvania iron, steel, and coal during the wars was balanced by sharp reductions in postwar production. The closely allied coal, railroad, and steel manufacturers shared the challenges of aging factories, ongoing labor strife, and improved technology and competition from other states.

Yet as some areas began to see decline, others experienced new successes. In Pittsburgh, the commercial radio industry was launched when KDKA began broadcasting on November 2, 1920, and within five years, on the opposite side of the state, the Atwater Kent Manufacturing Company of Philadelphia was producing more radios than any firm in the country. The rise of the automobile led to a temporary demand for steel that was countered by the discovery of an affordable way to extract and manufacture aluminum, patented and implemented by Pittsburgh's Aluminum Company of America (ALCOA). Railroads, once essential to the movement of goods throughout the state, were less economically relevant, as newly paved roads and the country's first high-speed turnpike were developed in the 1930s and 1940s. Finally, labor relations were stabilized following the intervention of the federal government, only for jobs and opportunities to slowly slip away.

World War II offered the state another opportunity to revive its greatest manufacturing industries. A remarkable 1.25 million Pennsylvanians served on the battlefronts, while at home thousands of businesses ran 24-hour work cycles to fulfill demand for the tools of war, including trucks, tanks, ships, and airplanes. Civilian defense brigades and bond drives supported the national war effort. At the war's end, peace inspired a vision of Pennsylvania's secure economic future where all citizens reached their highest potential. The reality, however, was more complex and included instability, economic disparity, and conflict.

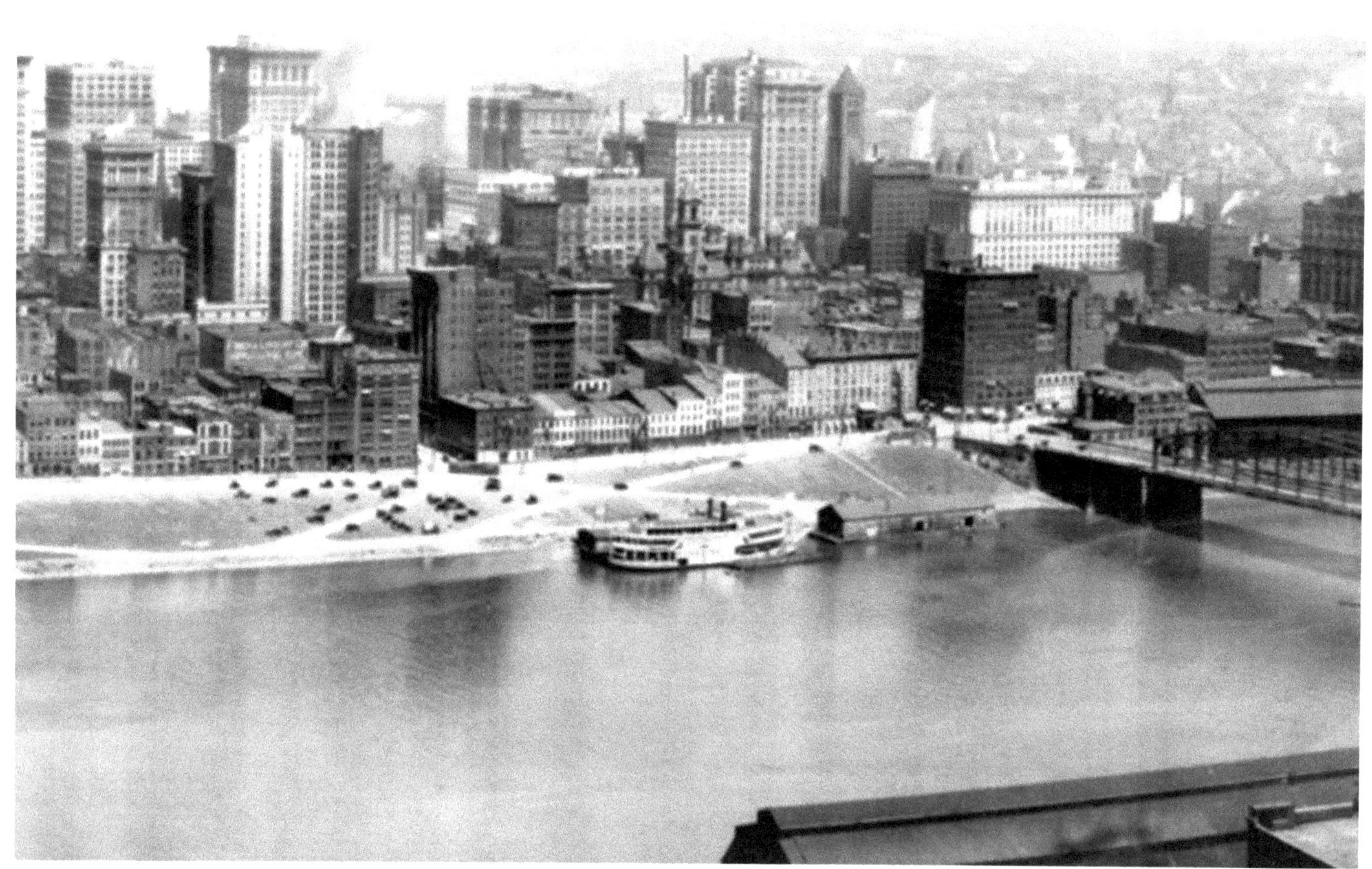

A view north across the Monongahela River shows the downtown Pittsburgh skyline, circa 1920.

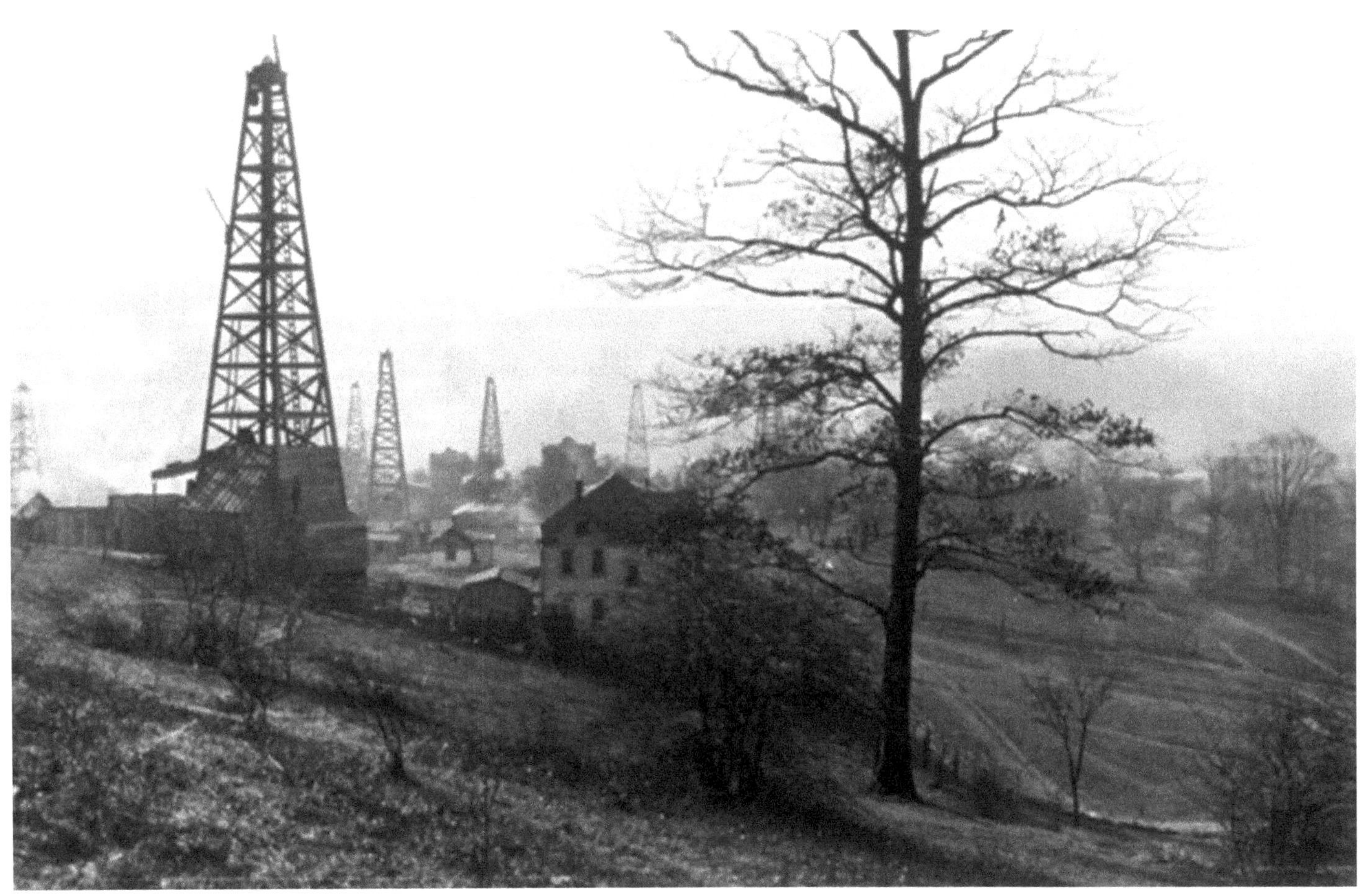

Following the discovery of an extensive natural gas vein in the Snake Hollow section of McKeesport in 1918, more than $1 million in gas was extracted within the first few years, and the northwestern region of the state experienced a tremendous economic boom.

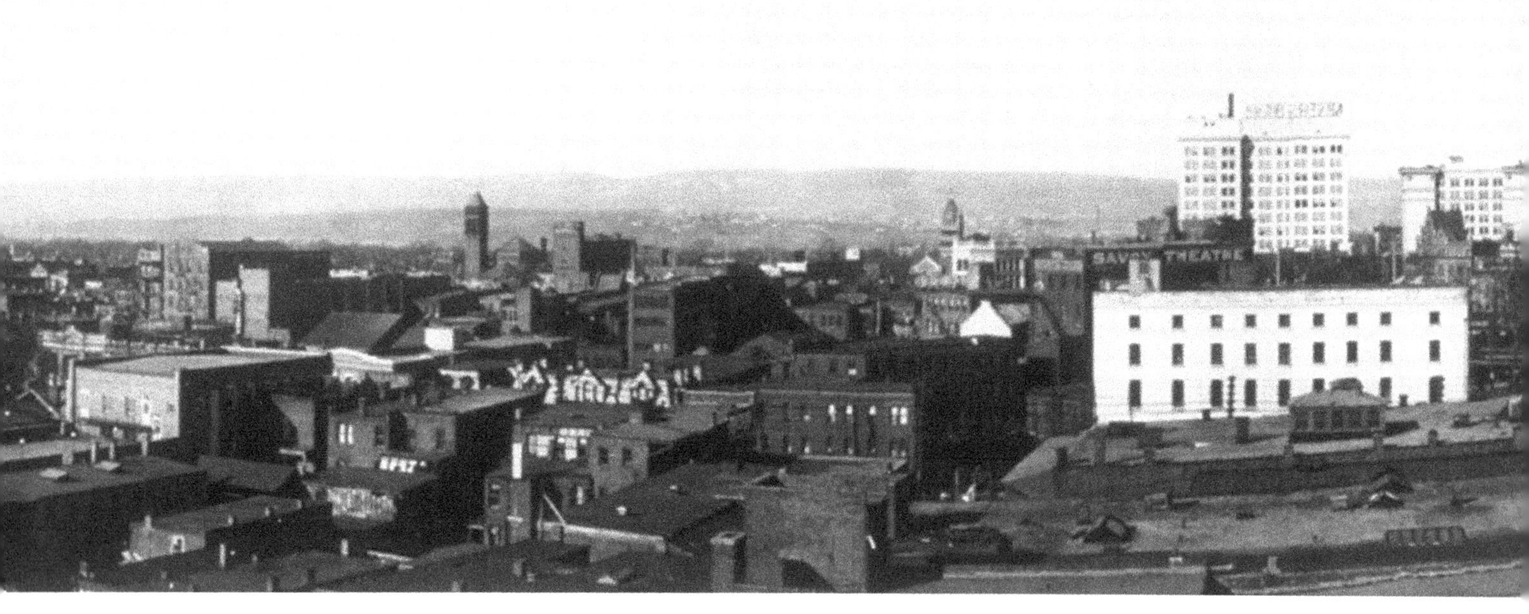

The city of Wilkes-Barre, county seat of Luzerne County, as seen from the Redington Hotel in 1921.

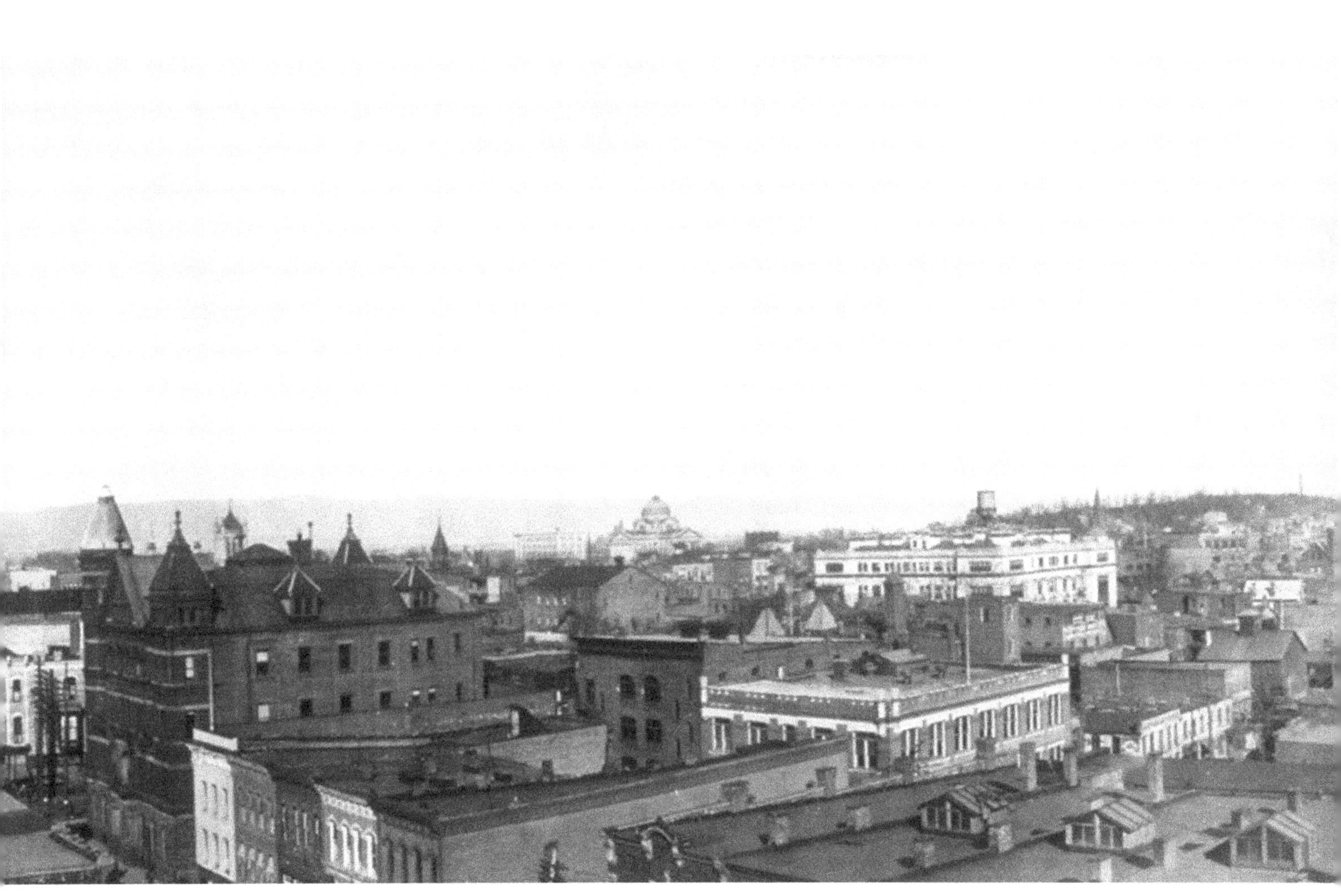

Philadelphia's second Episcopal church, St. Peter's, was established in 1761 to serve the growing numbers of residents living along what was then the southern boundary of the city near South Street. Notable burials in the churchyard include artist Charles Willson Peale and naval hero Stephen Decatur, whose monument rises above all others in this view from 1920.

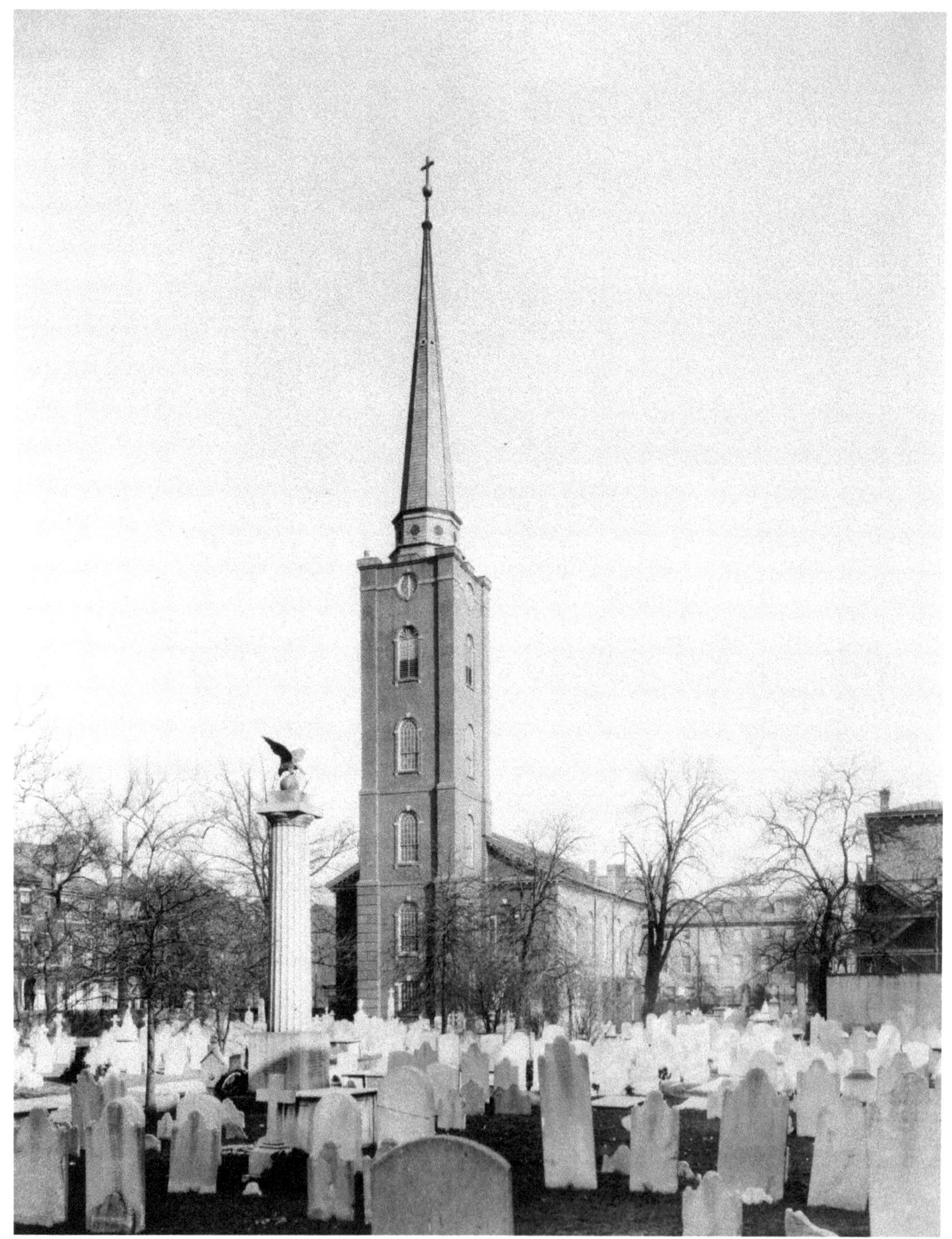

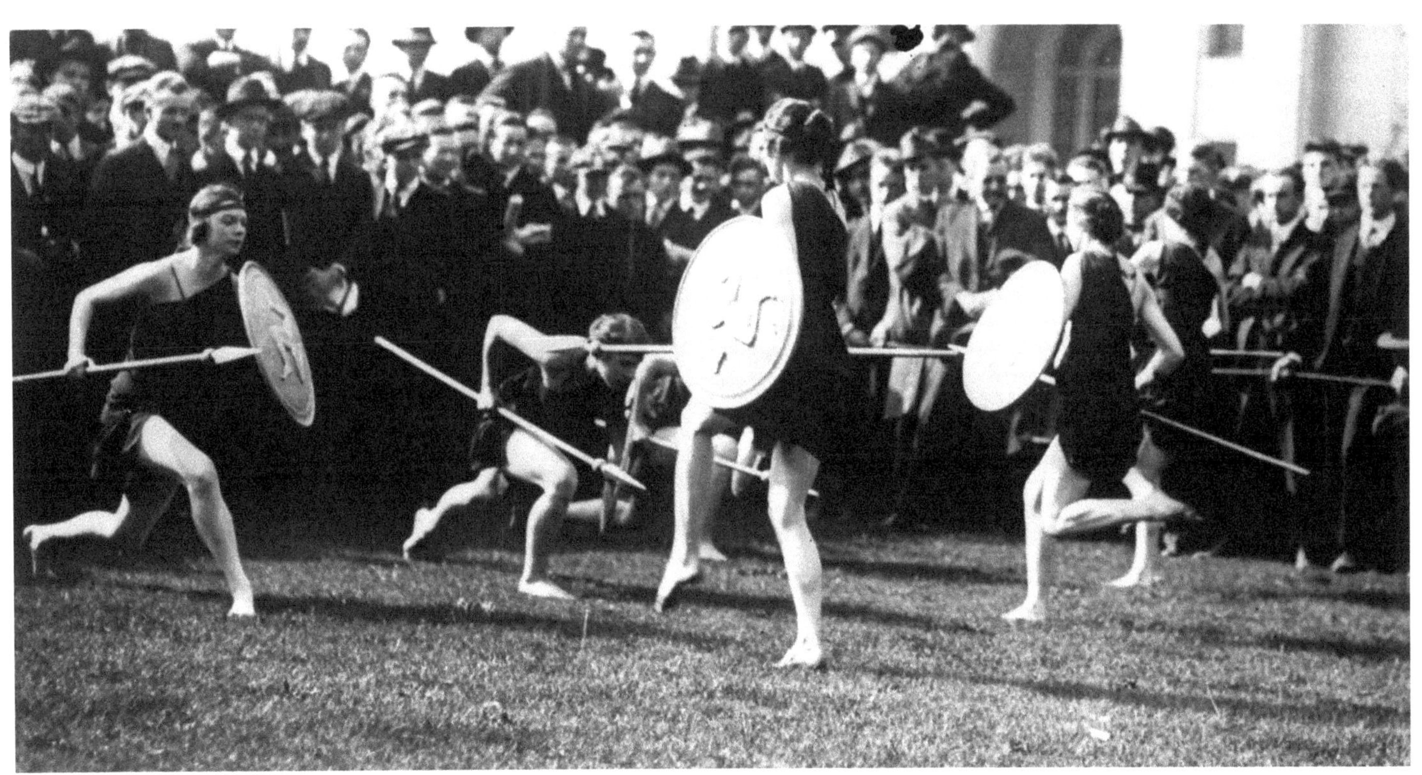

In a performance for the Carnegie Institute of Technology in Pittsburgh, circa 1920, the Marion Morgan Dancers exhibit Morgan's trademark use of free-flowing togas and bare feet in unique modern dance interpretations of classic works of ballet. Morgan went on to choreograph dance sequences for Hollywood.

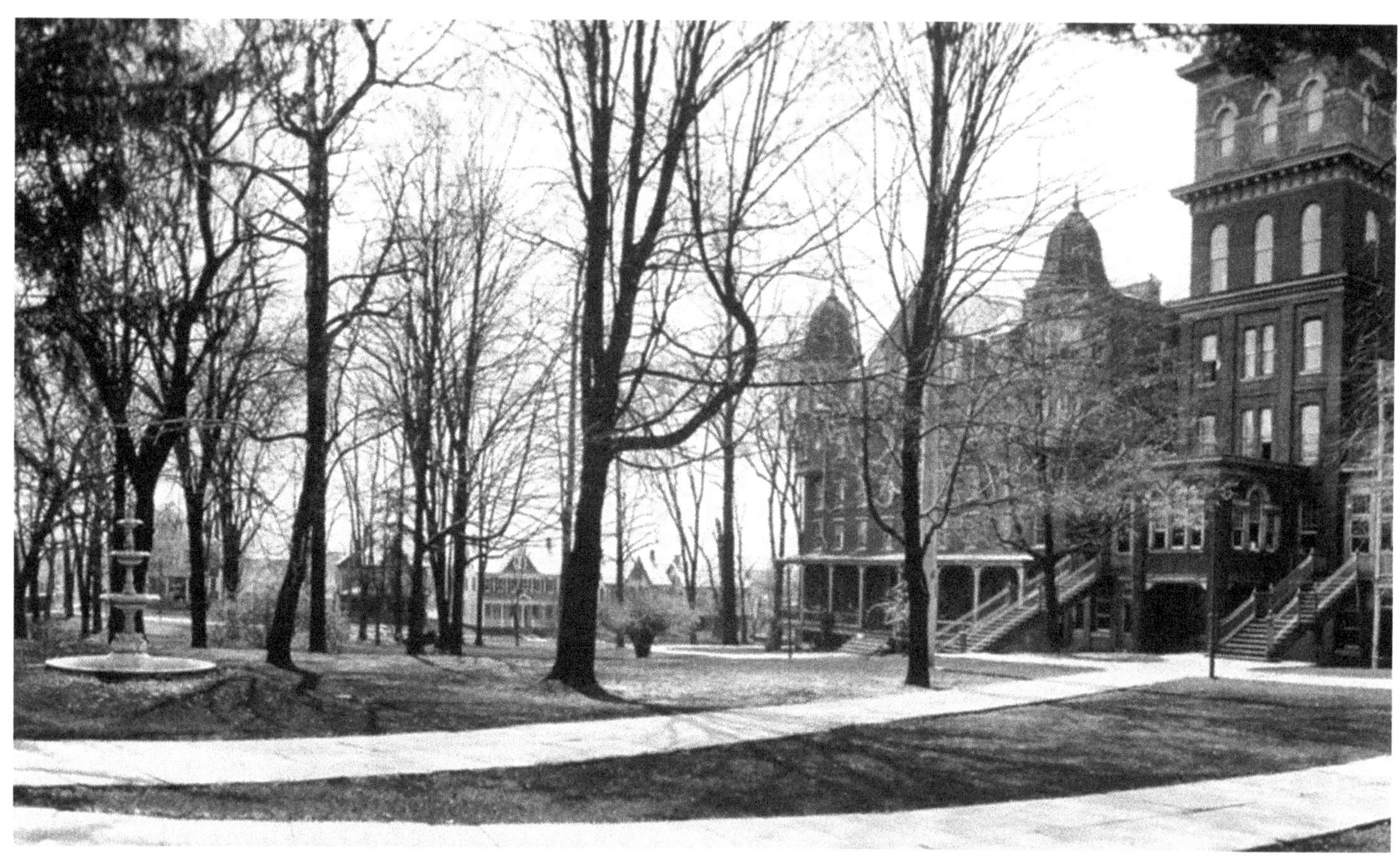

Established in 1855, the Lancaster County Normal School, the first "normal school" in Pennsylvania, prepared high school graduates to be teachers. The school was called the Millersville State Normal School when this photograph was taken, circa 1921, and now serves a broader educational purpose as Millersville University.

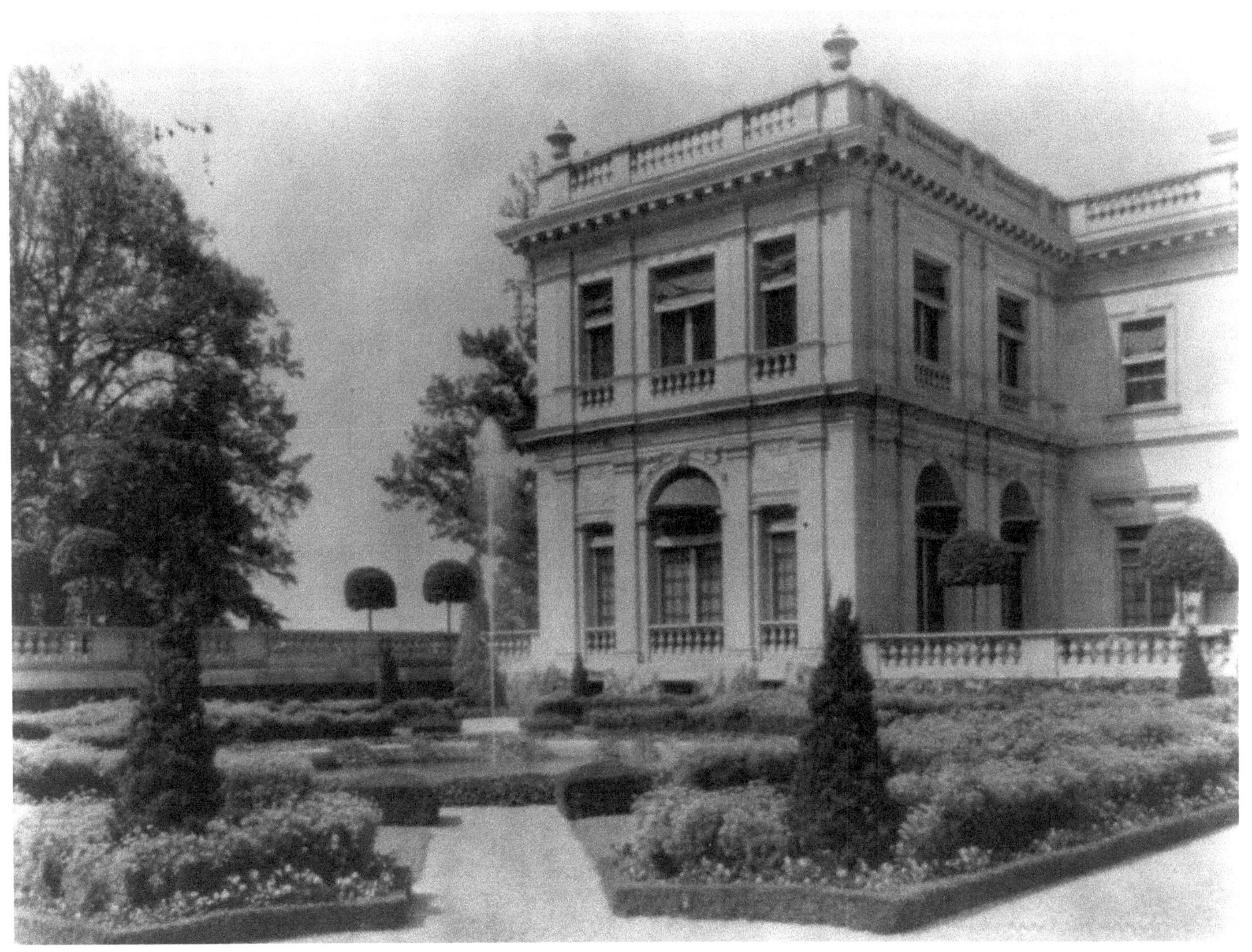

Featuring a remarkable 150 rooms, 28 bathrooms, and 3 elevators, Whitemarsh Hall in Montgomery County was one of the country's most extravagant private homes. Designed by classical architect Horace Trumbauer for banker Edward Stotesbury, the estate was completed in 1920 at a cost of over $3 million. It was demolished in April of 1980.

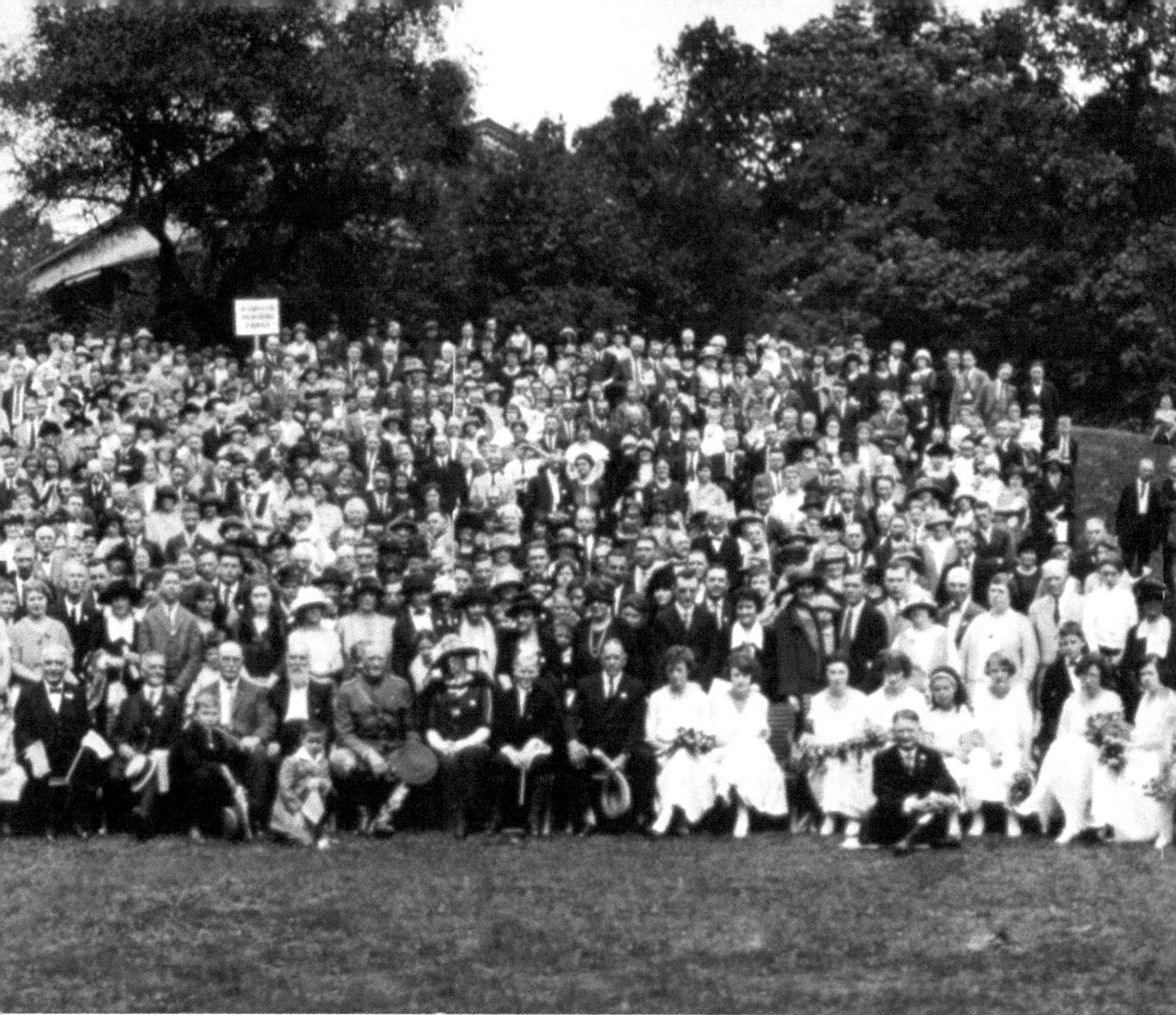

Attended by the 110th United States Infantry Band, a Pershing family reunion is captured in Idlewild Park, Westmoreland County, on September 8, 1923. The family's most famous member, General John J. Pershing, appears to be the man in uniform at left in the front row.

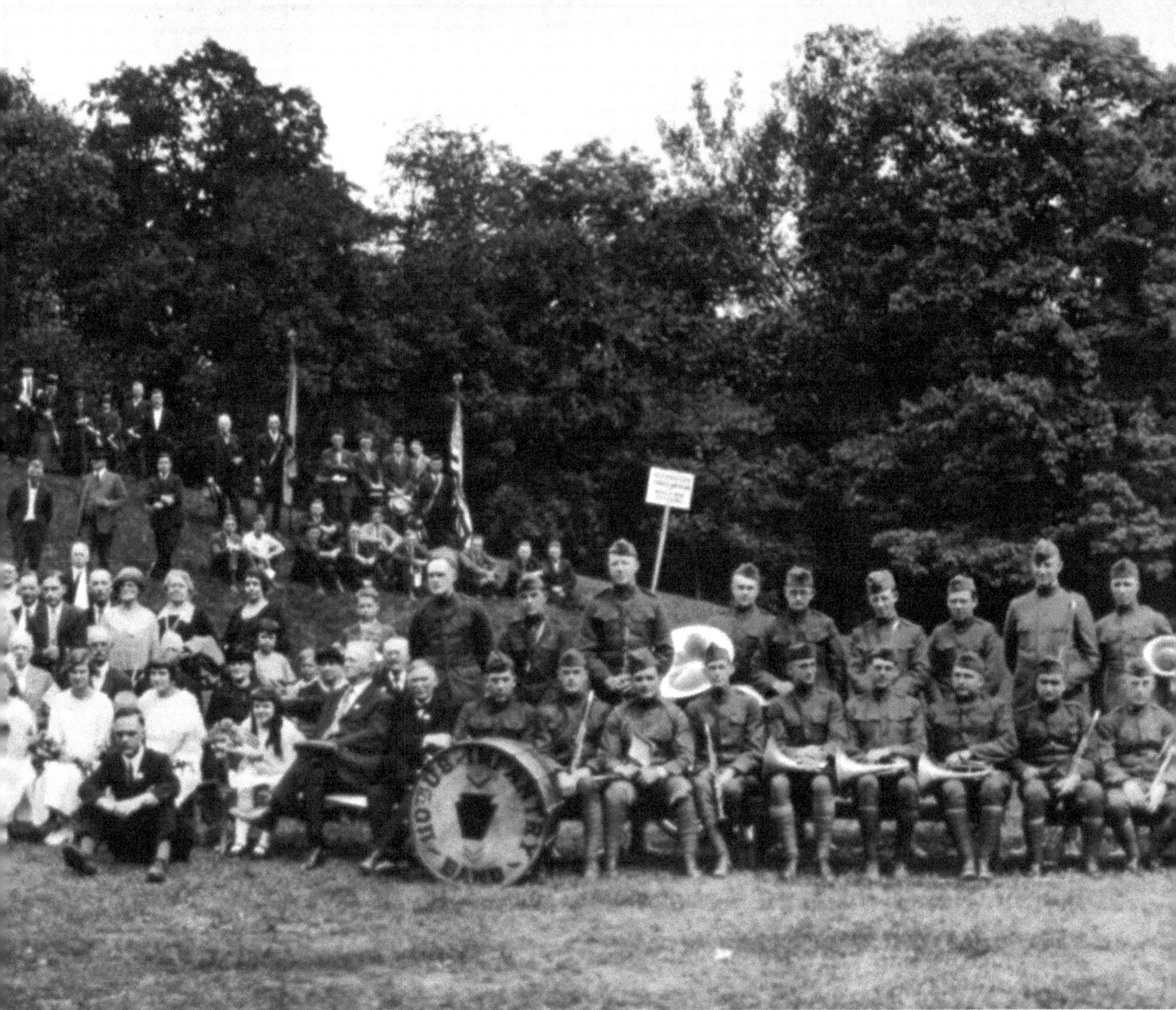
INFANTRY
BAND

Stanley Harris, manager of the Washington Senators, shakes hands with opposing manager and baseball icon Connie Mack of the Philadelphia Athletics in 1924, the year the Senators went on to win the World Series. Mack served a remarkable 49 years as the A's manager, 1901–1950.

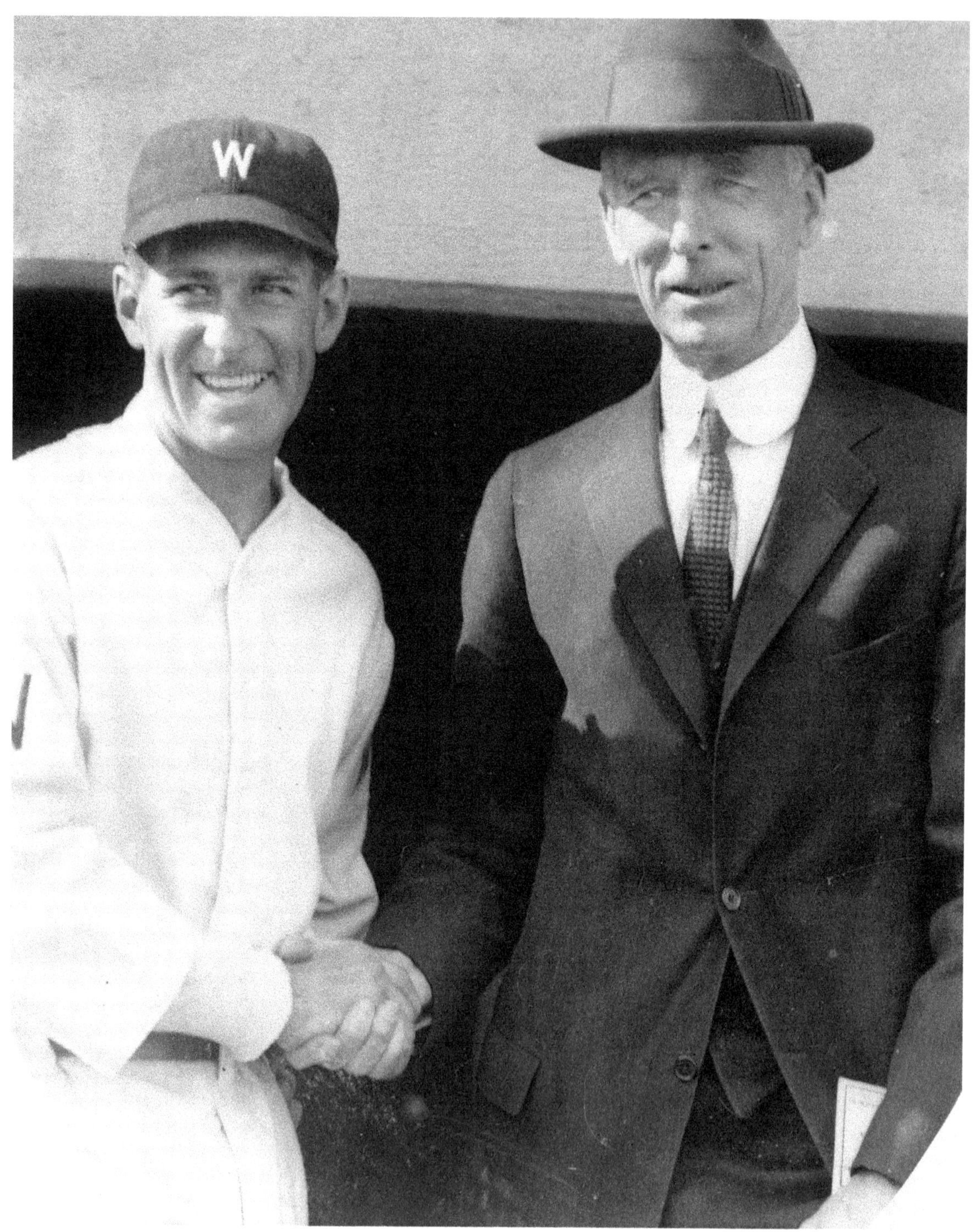

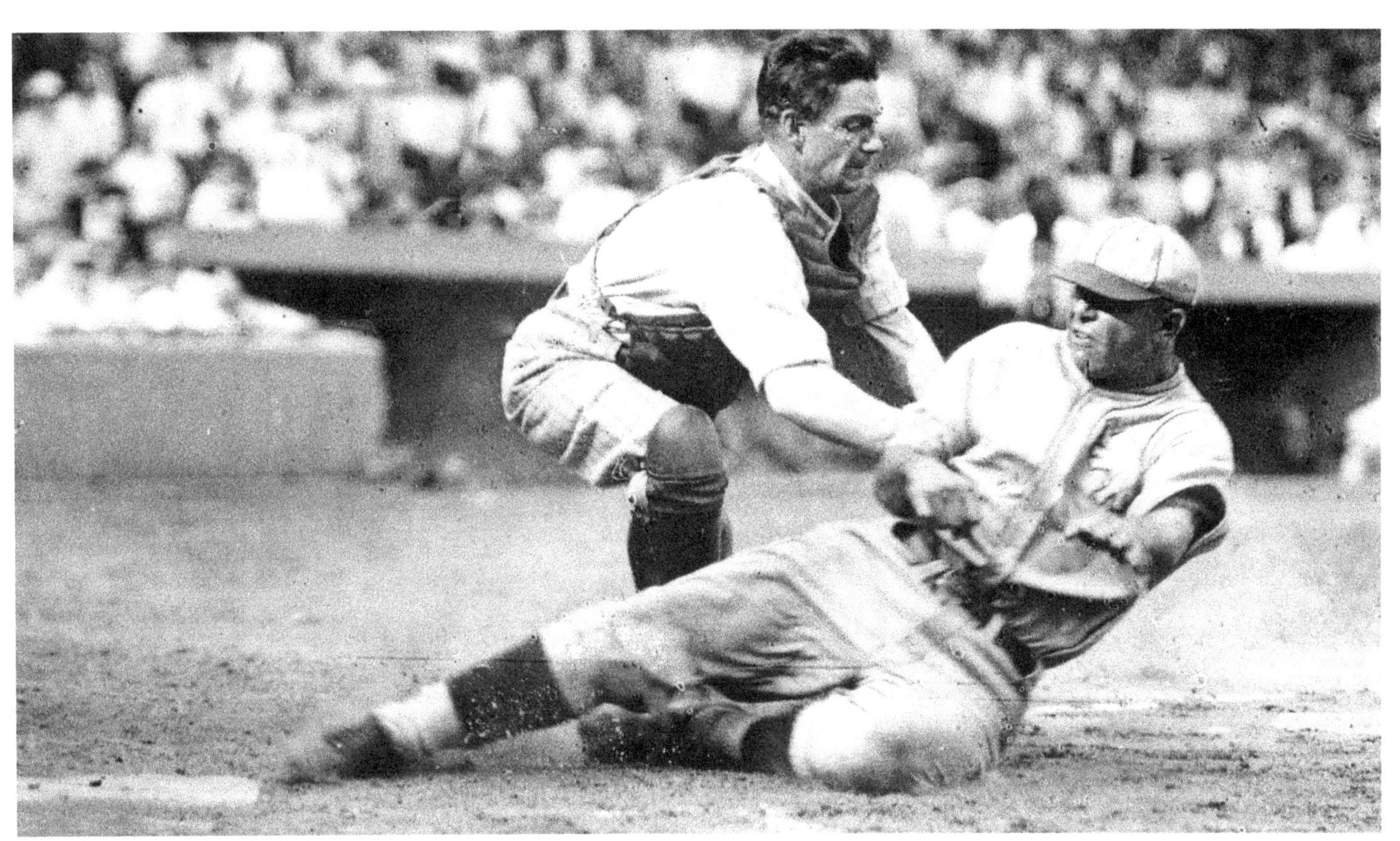

Outfielder Bing Miller of the Philadelphia Athletics is tagged out at home plate by Herold "Muddy" Ruel of the Washington Senators.

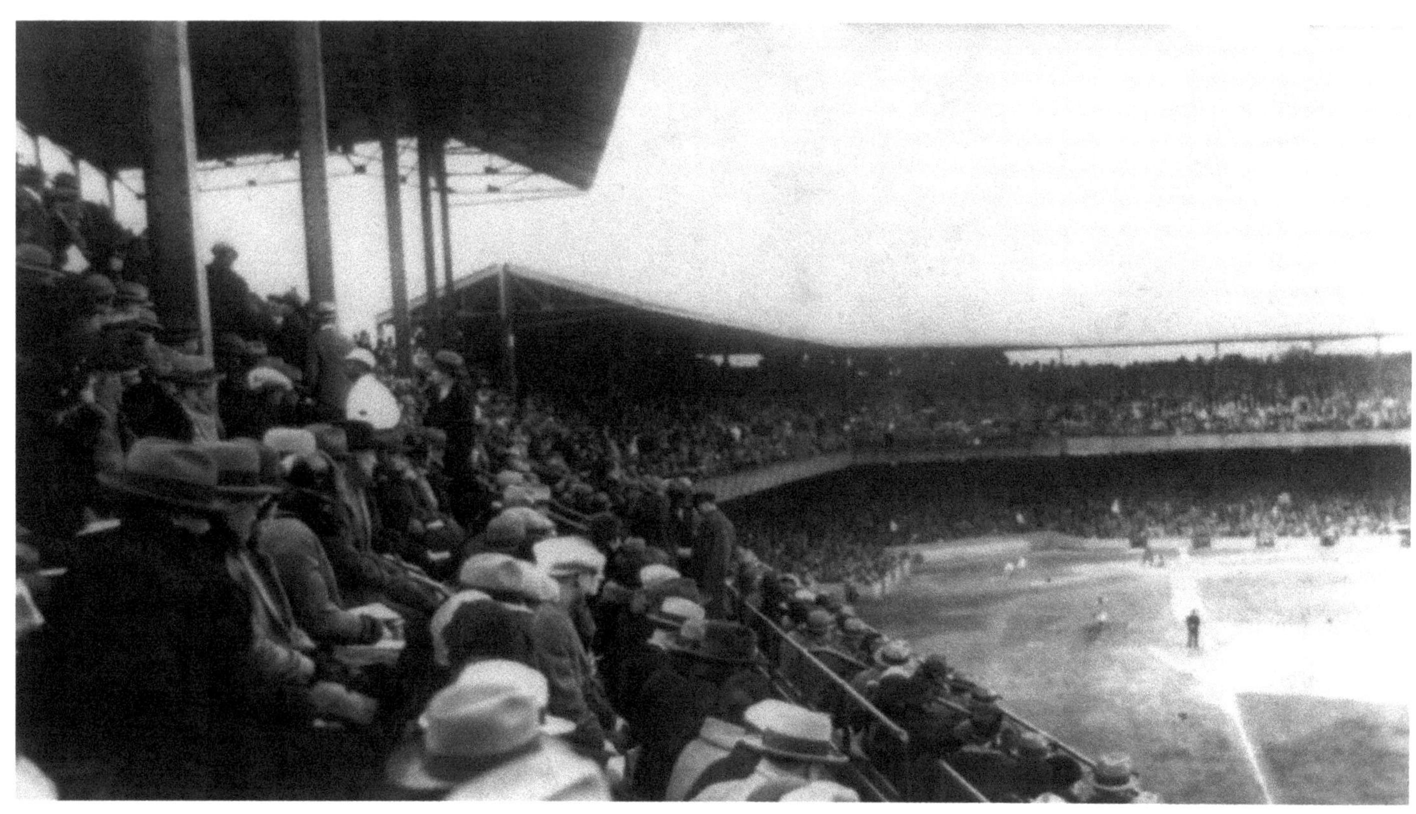

In 1925, the champion Washington Senators were themselves defeated by the Pittsburgh Pirates in seven games during the World Series. Here, spectators watch the two pennant winners at play at Forbes Field in Pittsburgh.

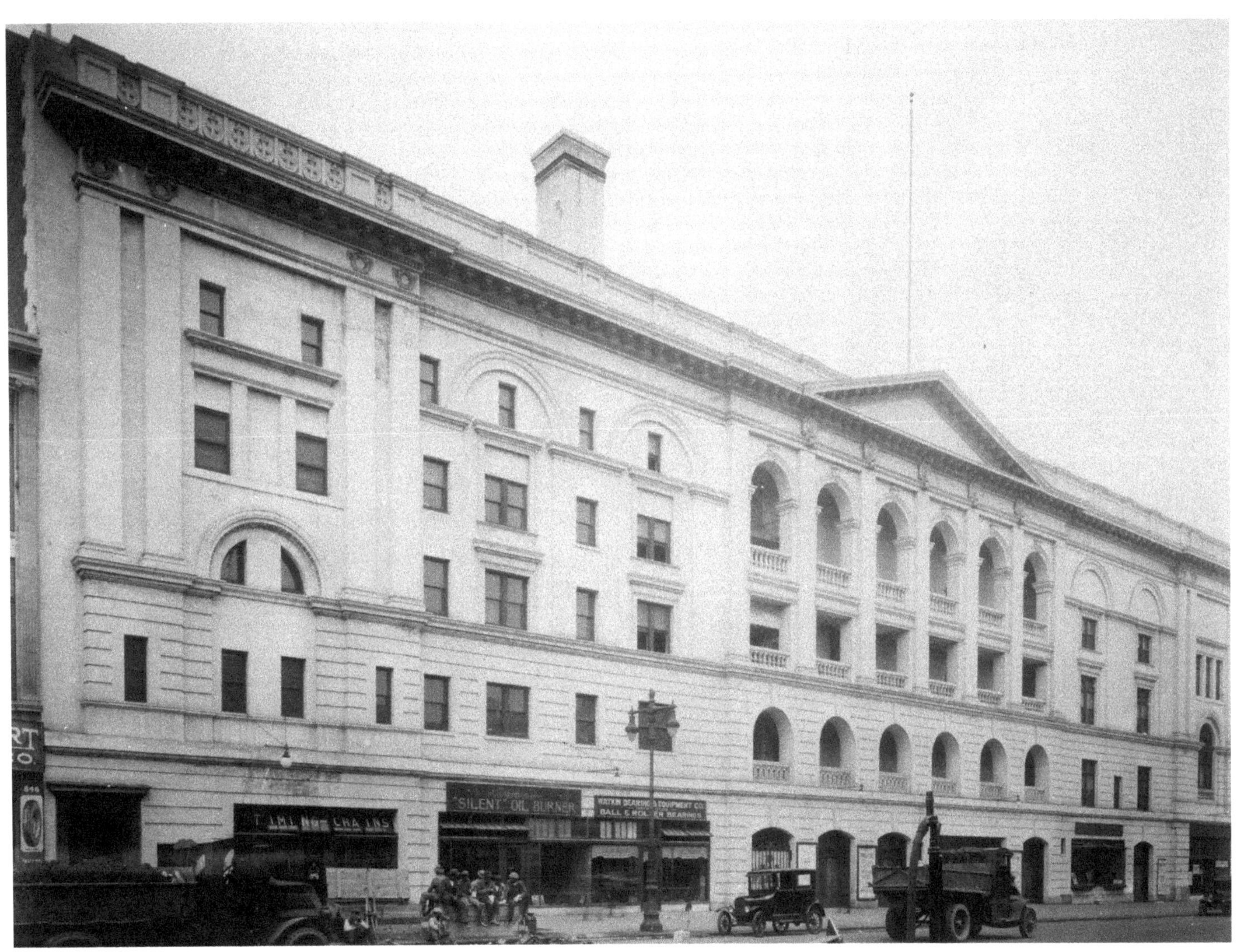

Oscar Hammerstein's Philadelphia Opera House, also known as the Metropolitan Opera House, opened on North Broad Street in 1908 to great acclaim. Within four years, Hammerstein sold his interest in the opera house to millionaire Edward T. Stotesbury. Seen here circa 1925, the building has been used as a church since 1948.

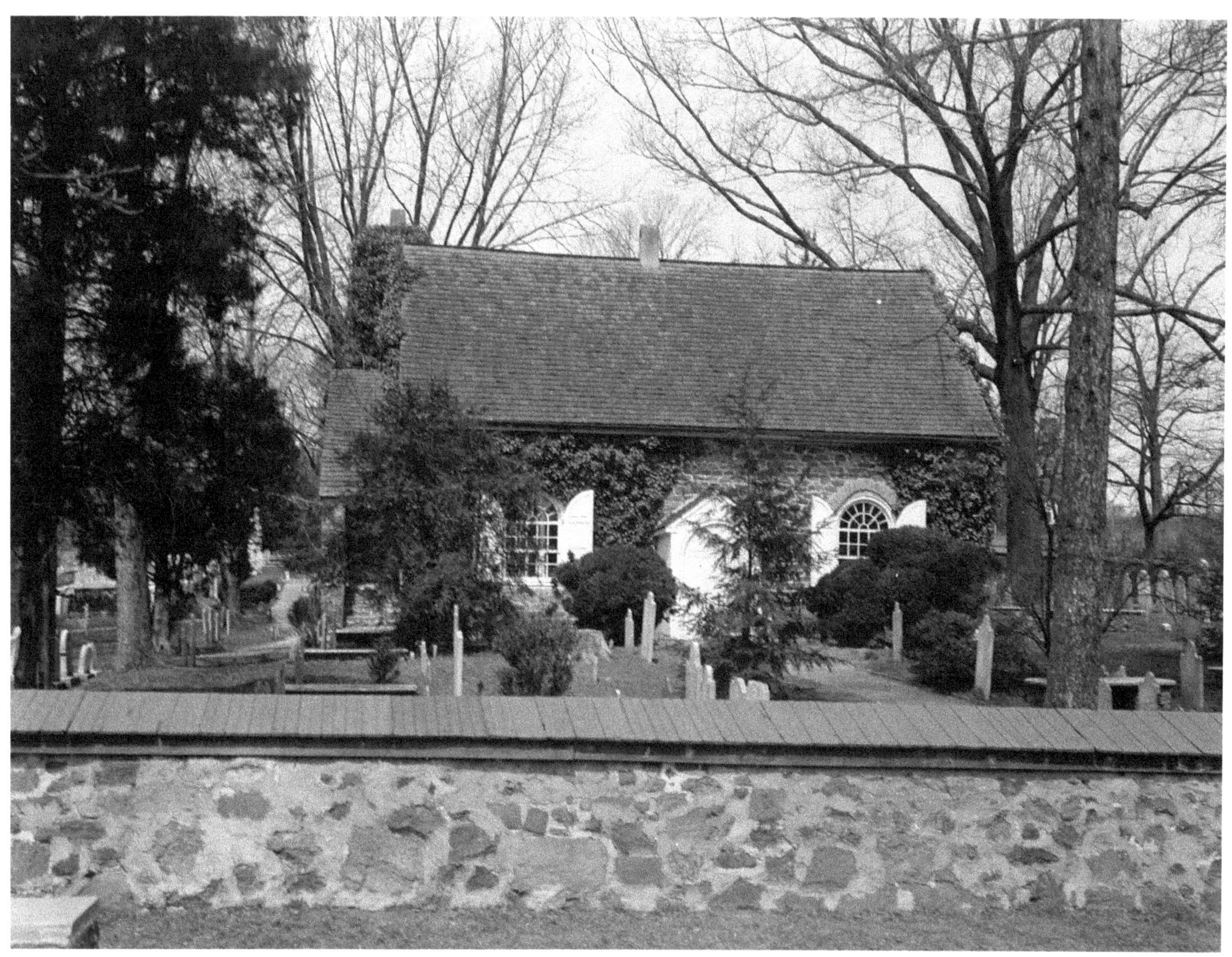

St. David's Episcopal Church in Wayne, Delaware County, was built in 1715 and is seen here in 1925. One of the earliest non-Quaker churches in the state, St. David's would bear witness to the rapid development of the town of Wayne in the 1890s into one of the string of bedroom communities along the Main Line.

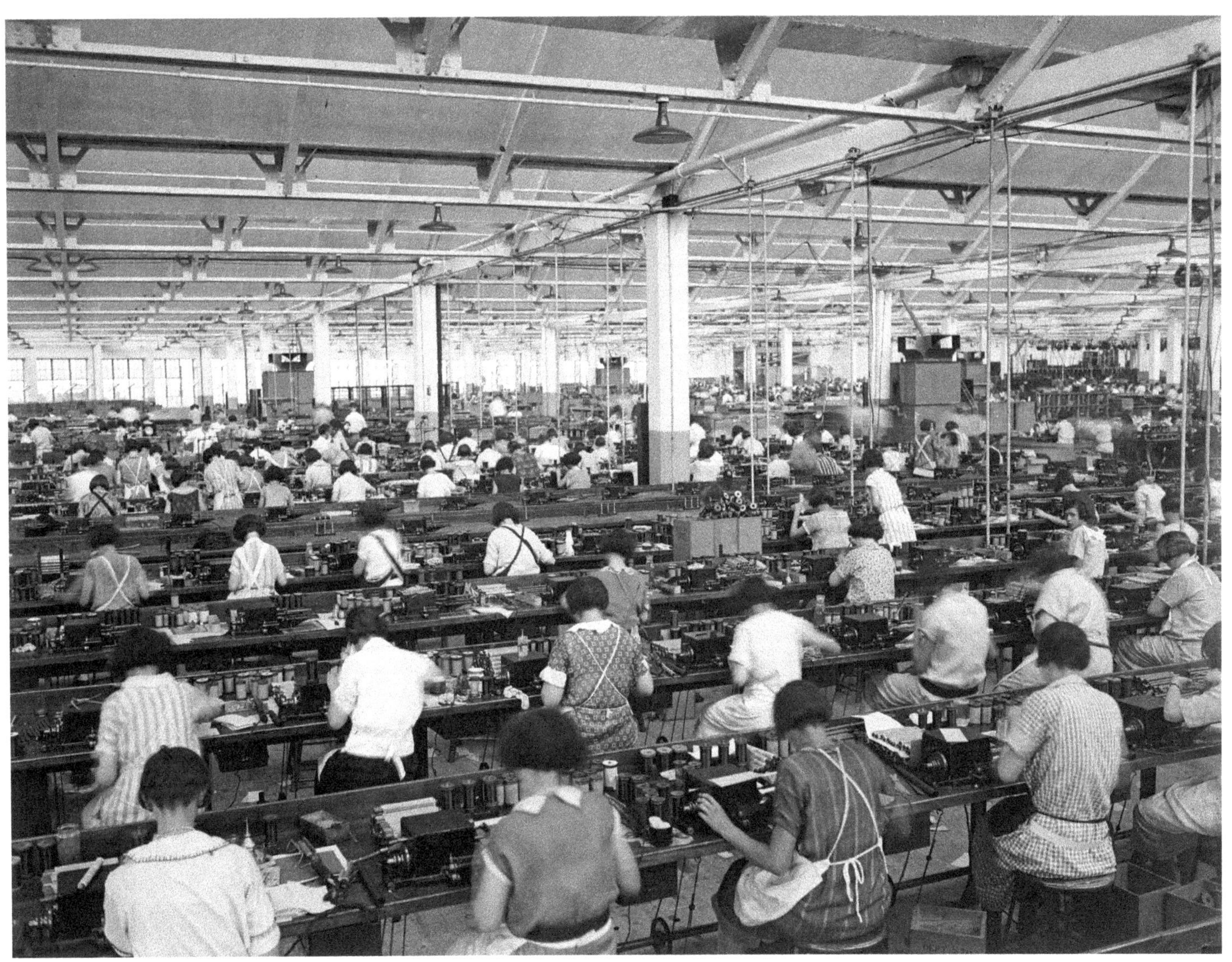

Workers labor at the Atwater Kent Manufacturing Company factory on Wissahickon Avenue in Philadelphia. Originally a manufacturer of small electronic parts, the company was the single largest producer of radios in the country by 1925 and within five years employed more than 12,000 people.

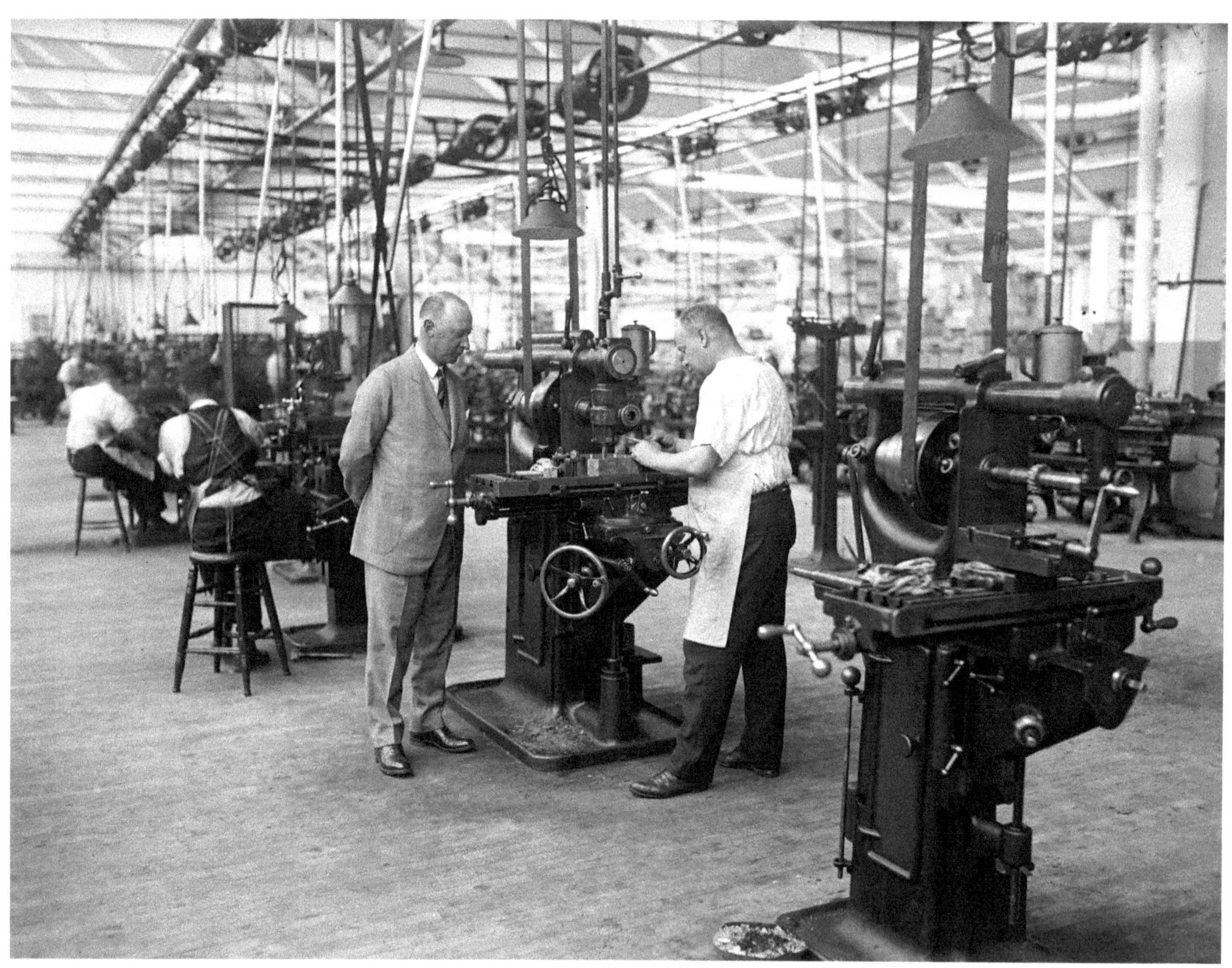

A. Atwater Kent, founder and owner of the radio manufacturing company, visits a tool room in his Philadelphia factory. In 1929, Kent shifted the company's production from small tabletop radios to large floor models. However, the advent of the Great Depression resulted in the failure of the company, which closed in 1936.

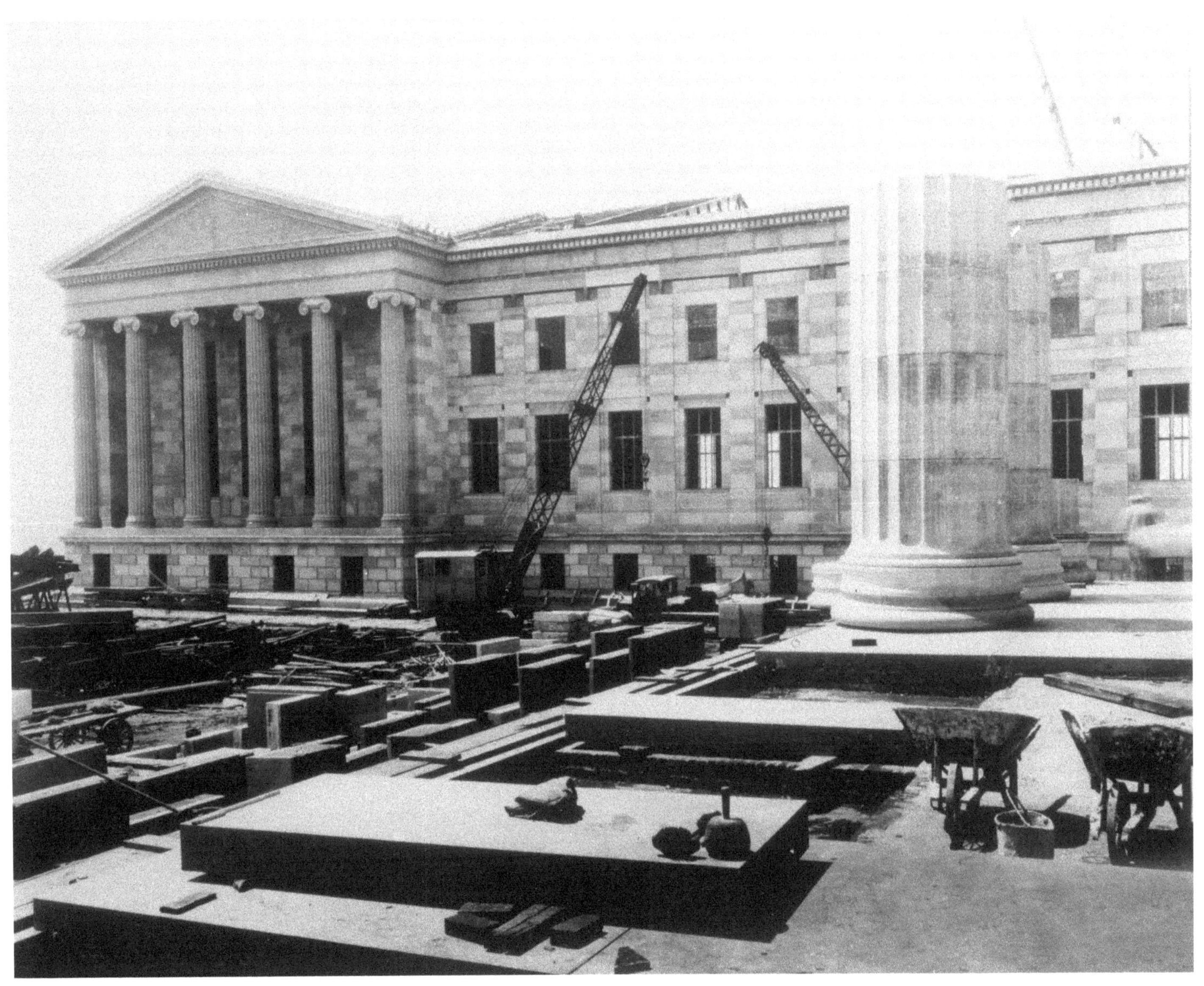

Completion of the Philadelphia Museum of Art was still two years away when this photo was taken in June of 1926. Designed by Horace Trumbauer and the architectural firm of Zantzinger, Borie and Medary, the Greek-revival building stood on ten acres of reclaimed land that was once the site of the Fairmount Reservoir.

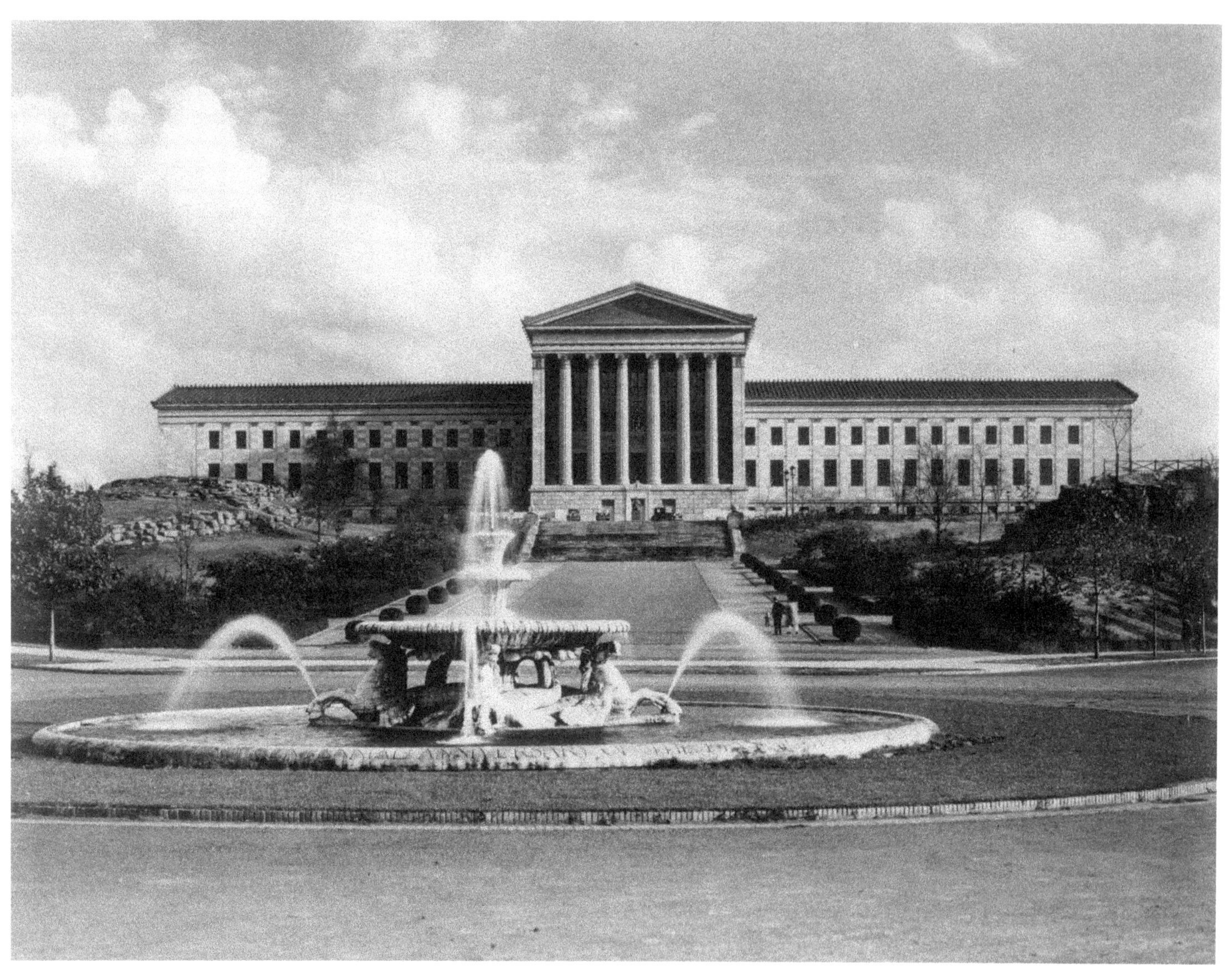

The newly completed Philadelphia Museum of Art on Benjamin Franklin Parkway in Fairmount Park in 1928. The "Fountain of the Sea Horses," a replica of Bernini's original in the Borghese Gardens in Rome, is seen in the foreground.

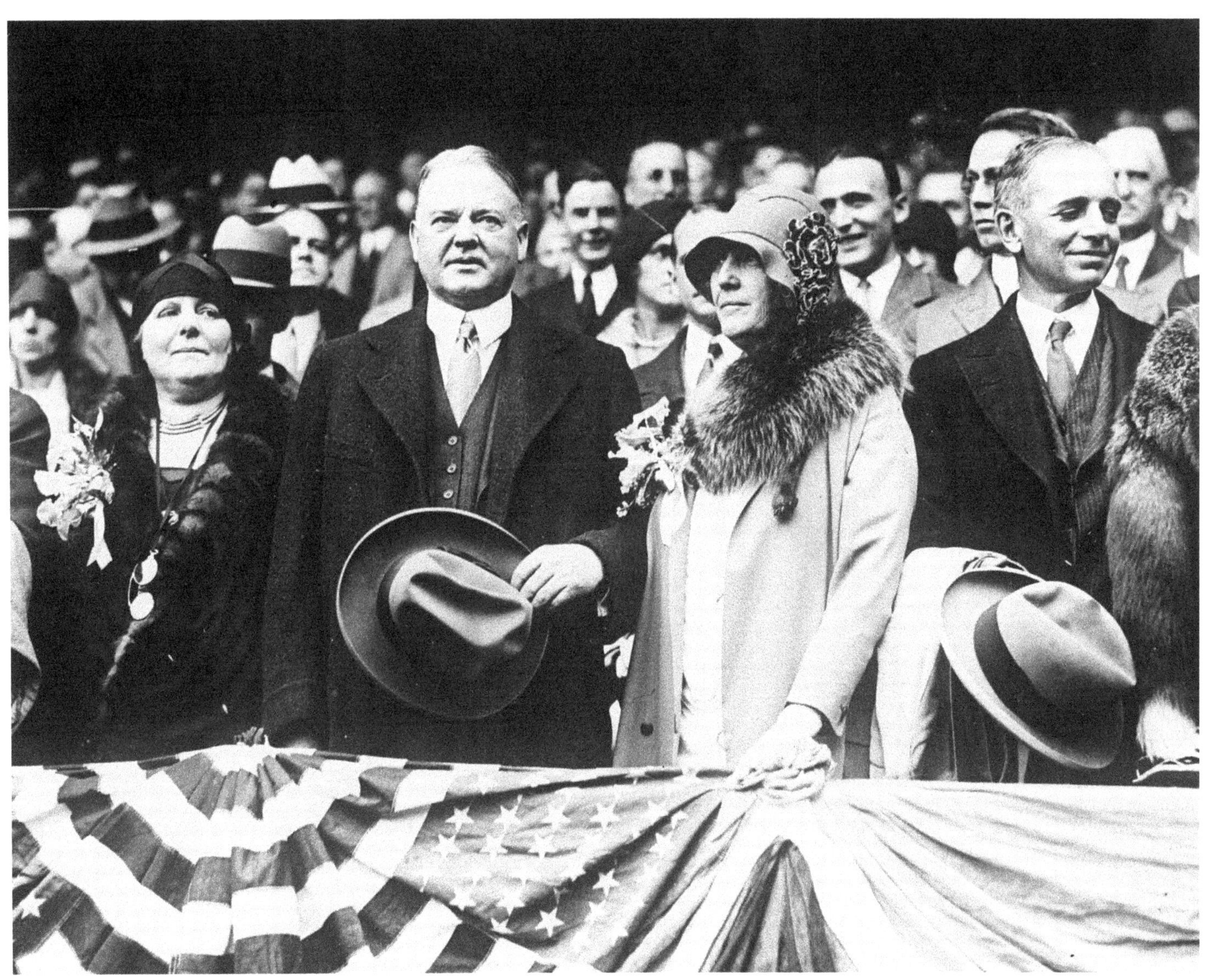

President and Mrs. Herbert Hoover attend the World Series at Shibe Park in Philadelphia, October 1929. The Philadelphia Athletics defeated the Chicago Cubs in five games to win the Series for the fourth time.

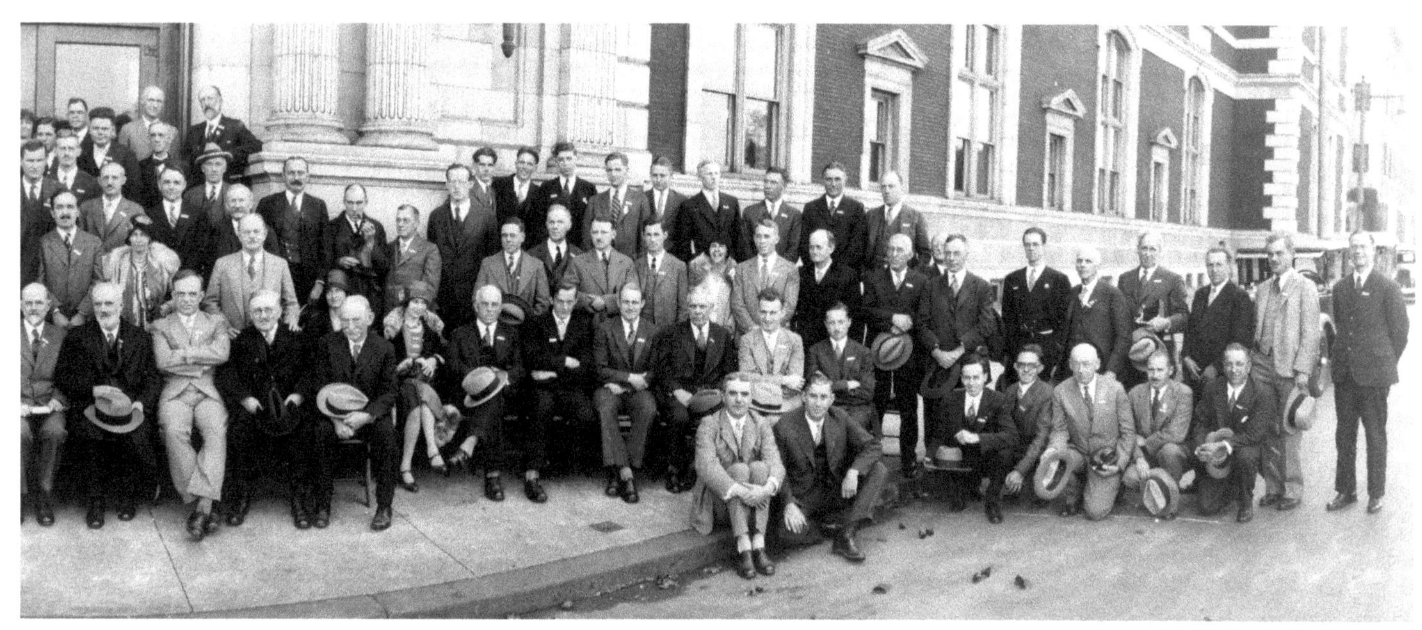

Participants at the forty-seventh meeting of the American Ornithologists' Union pose in front of the Academy of Natural Sciences in Philadelphia, October 1929. Founded in 1812 and home to the world's first assembled dinosaur fossil skeleton, the academy remains one of the finest natural history museums in the country.

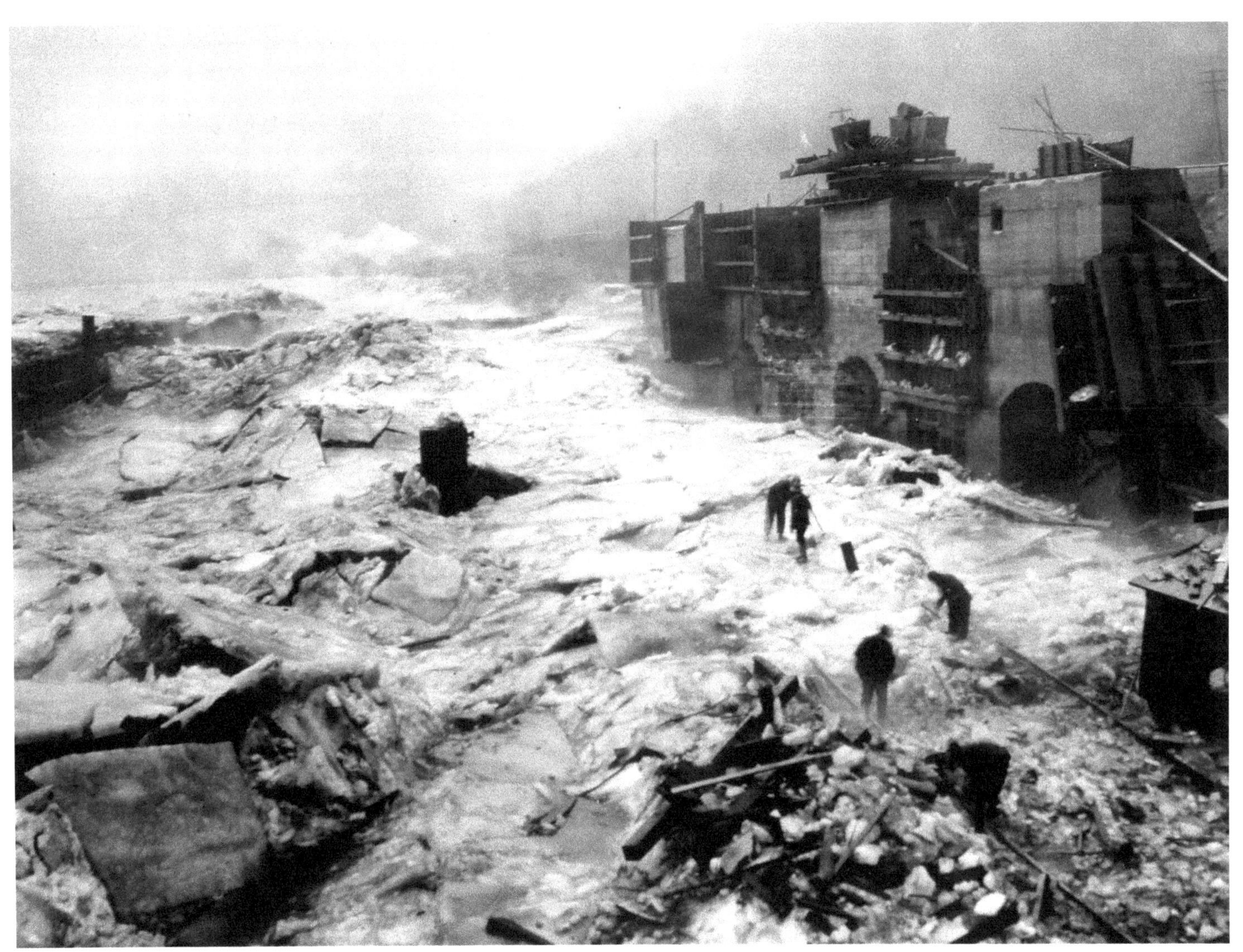

Workers struggle to clear an iced-over coffer dam at Lock and Dam Number 8 along the Allegheny River in Kittanning, Armstrong County, on December 16, 1929.

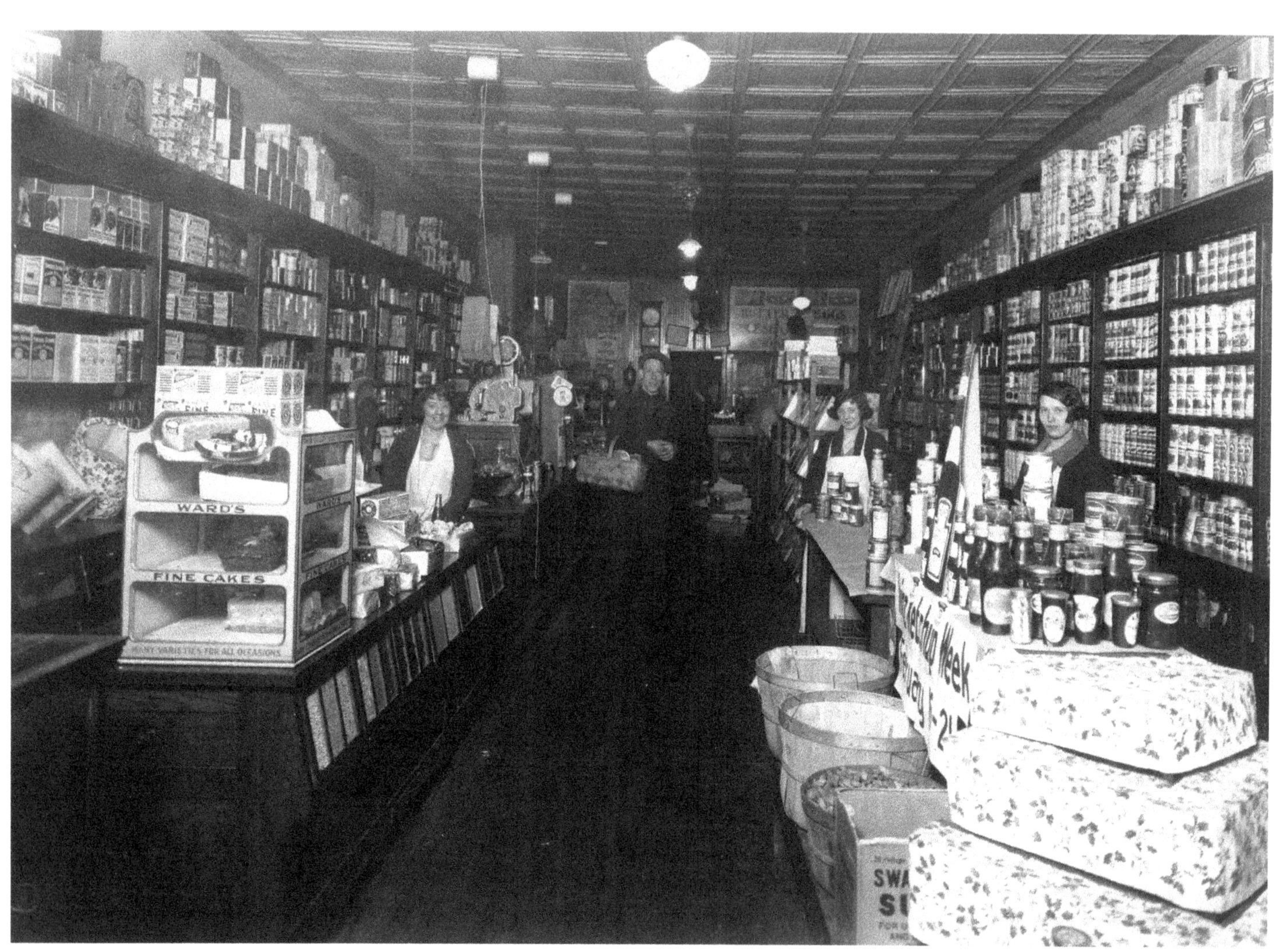

Clerks await customers inside Chantler's General Store in Tarentum, Allegheny County, circa 1930.

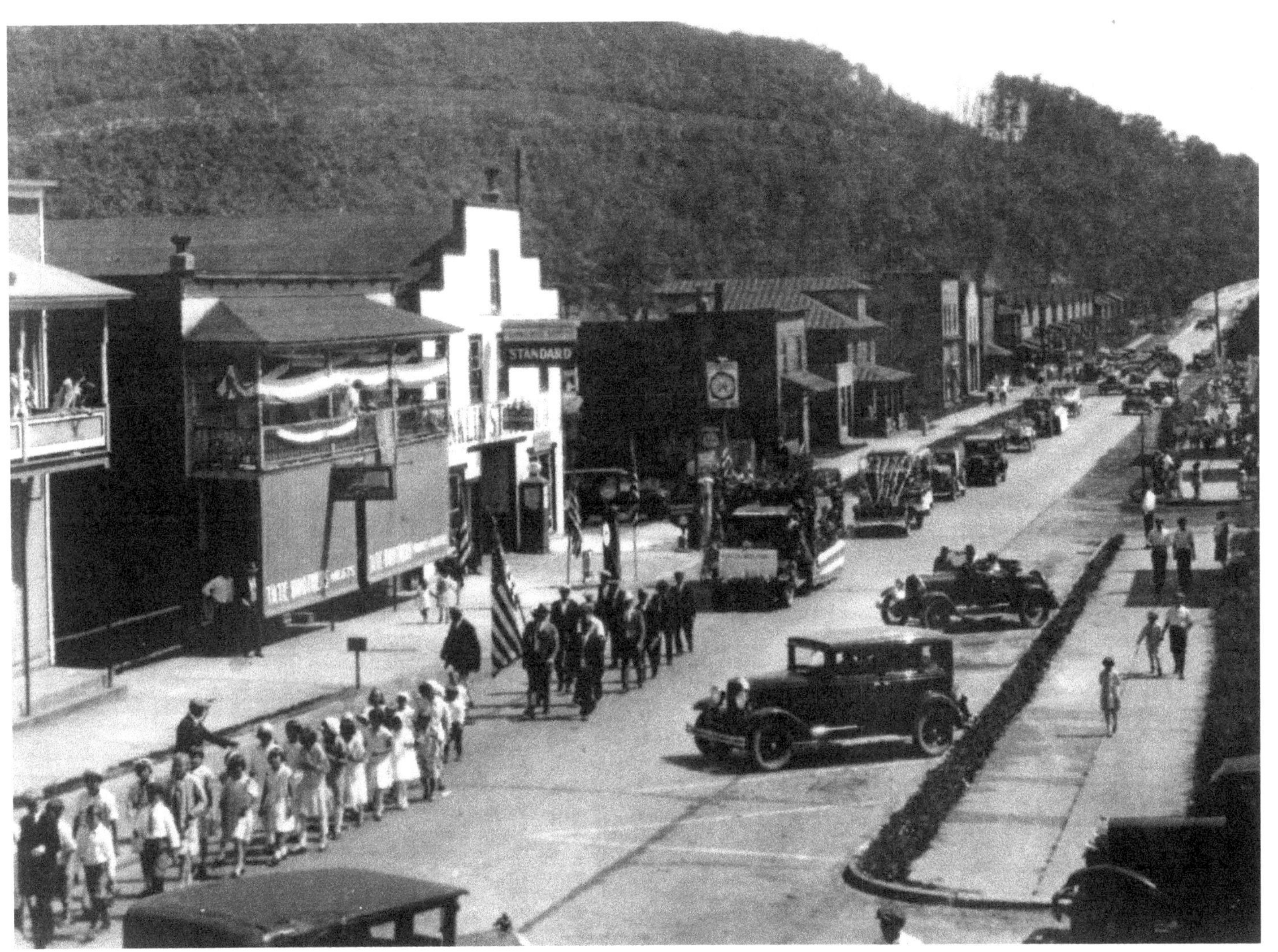

Townspeople in a Fourth of July parade in 1930 march down Franklin Street in Clymer, Indiana County.

Curious pedestrians walk across the George Westinghouse Bridge on opening day in 1932. The bridge, which carries Route 30 over the Turtle Creek Valley, was at one time the longest concrete arch in the world.

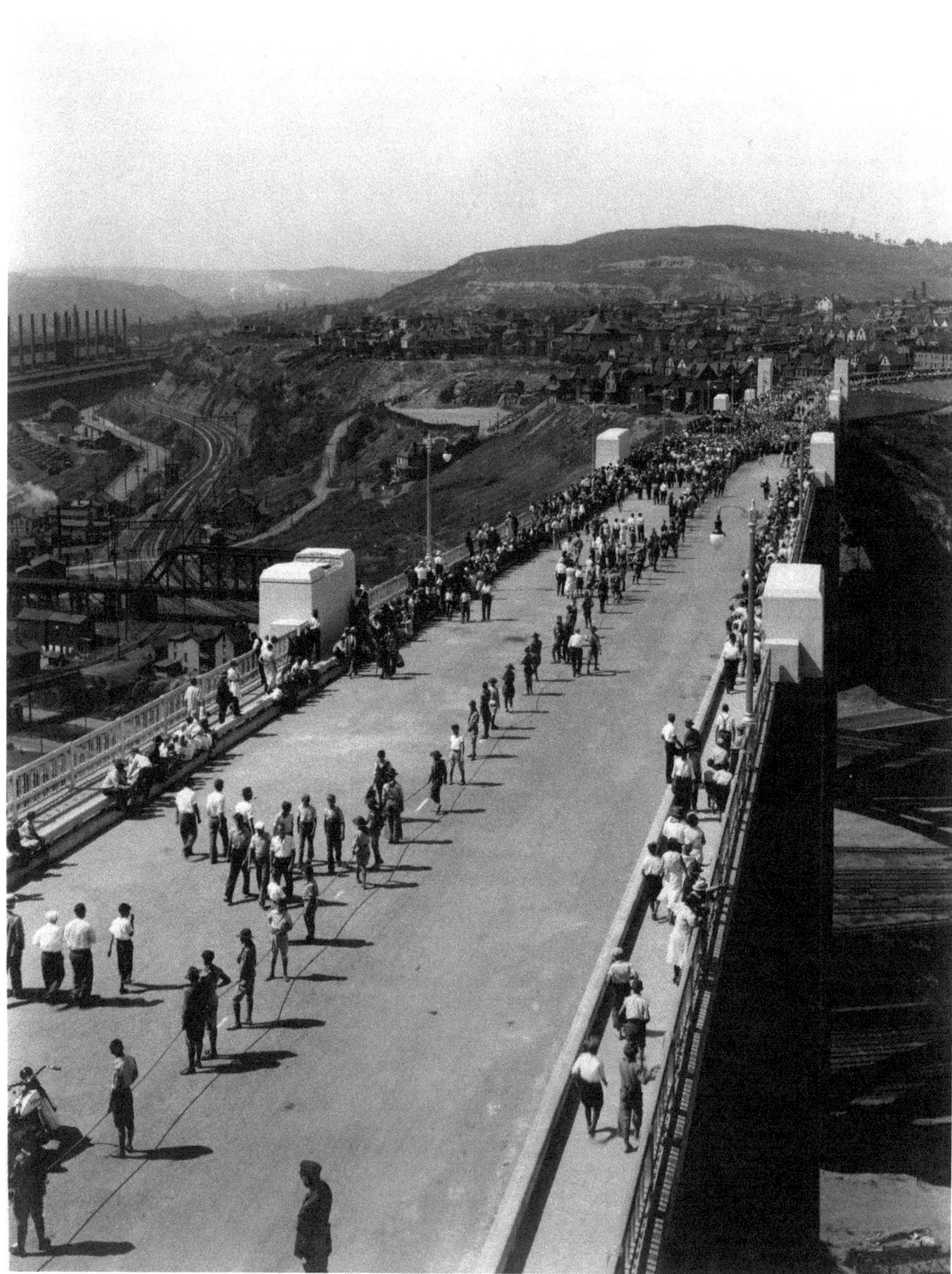

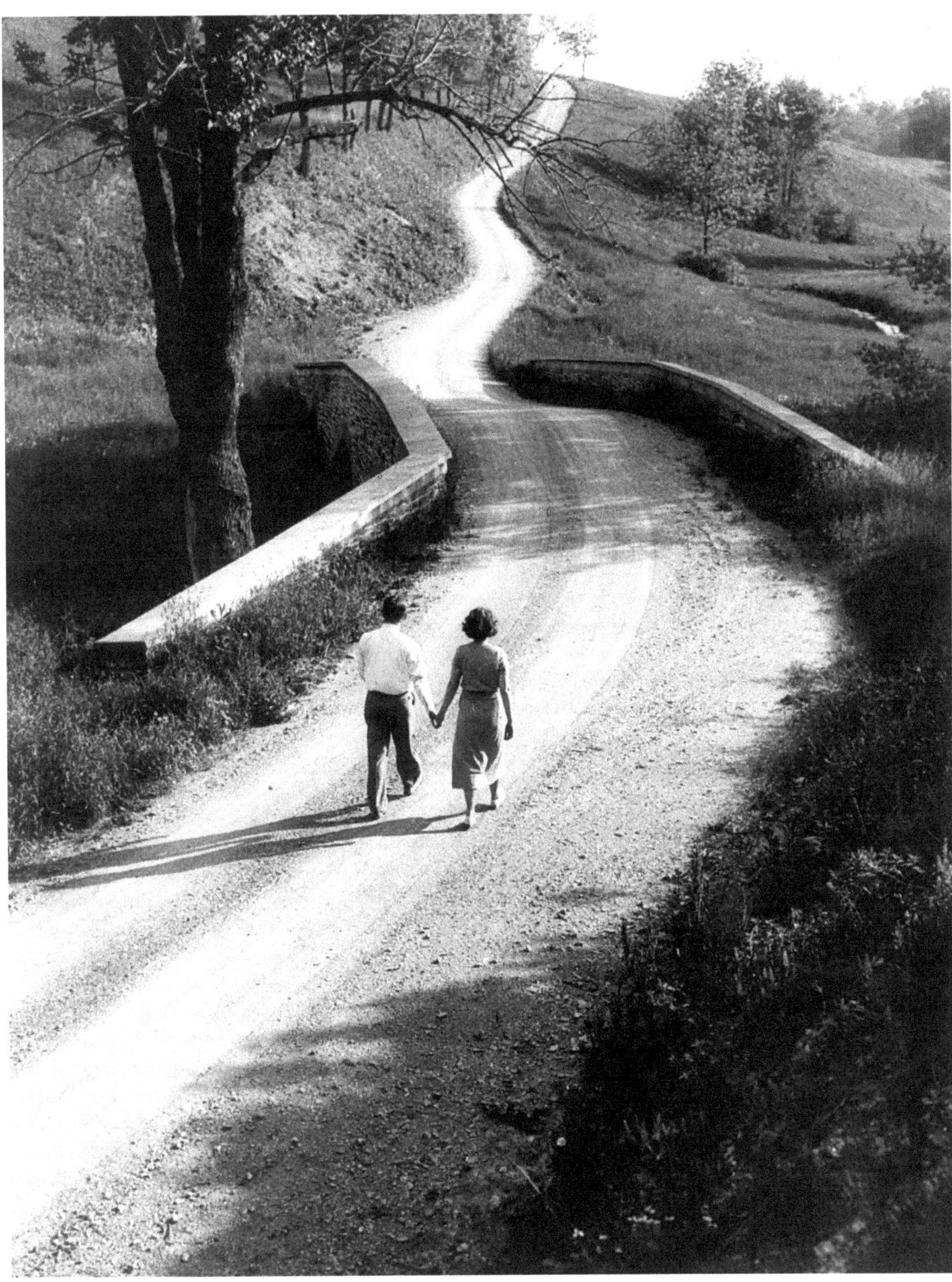

A couple enjoys a lovely stroll along a country road somewhere in Pennsylvania, circa early 1930s.

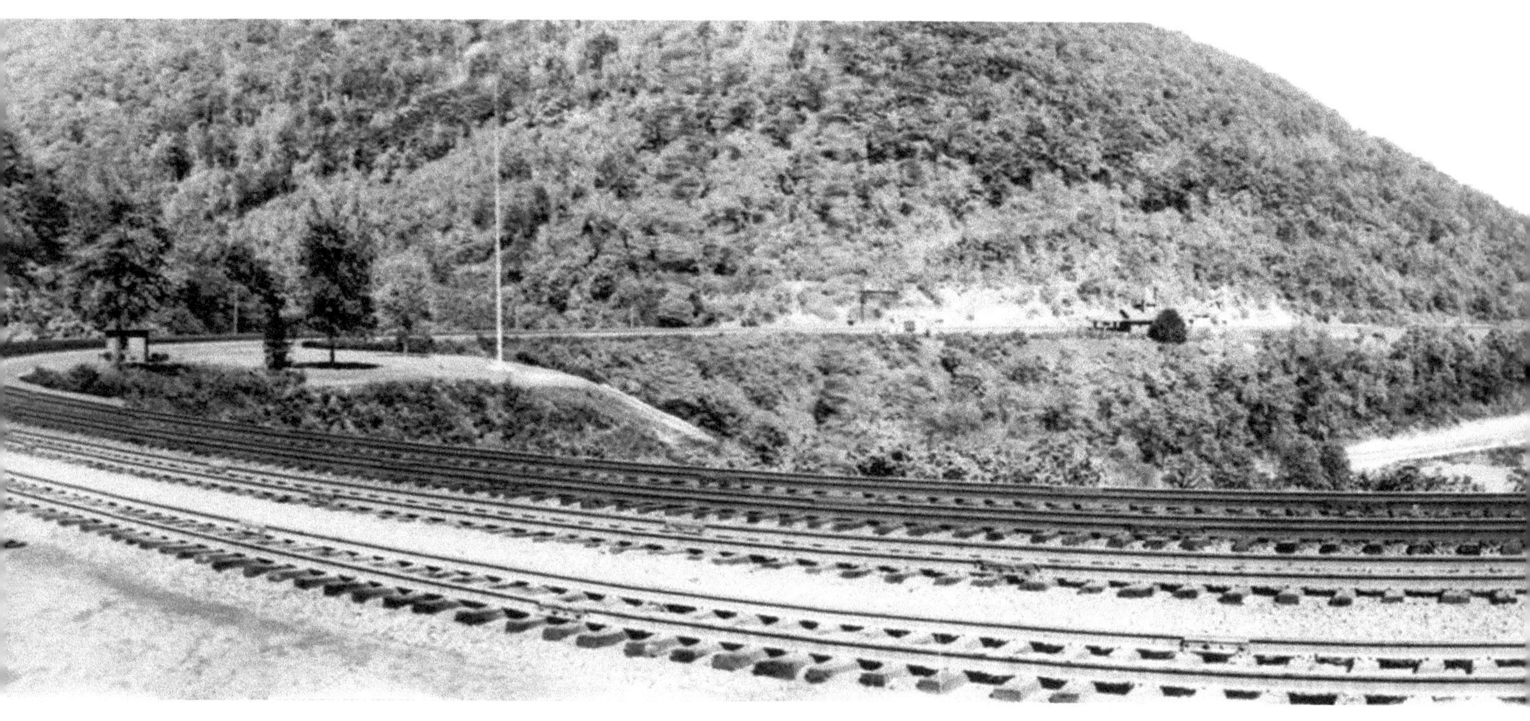

The Horseshoe Curve at Altoona, October 12, 1934. This remarkable feat of engineering has been in continuous use since it opened on February 15, 1854. Designed to ensure safe and efficient passage of trains through the Allegheny Mountains, the Horseshoe Curve was made a National Historic Landmark in 1992.

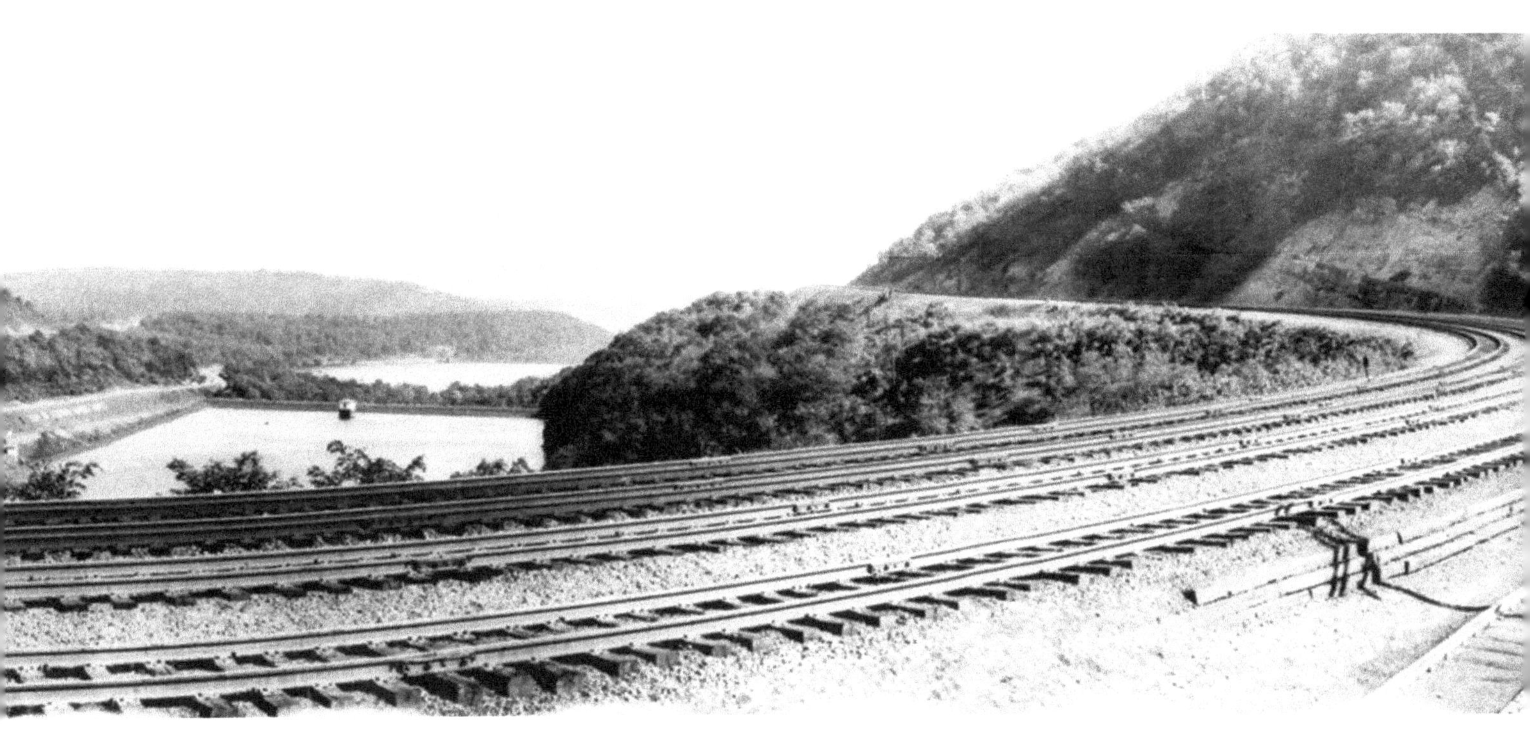

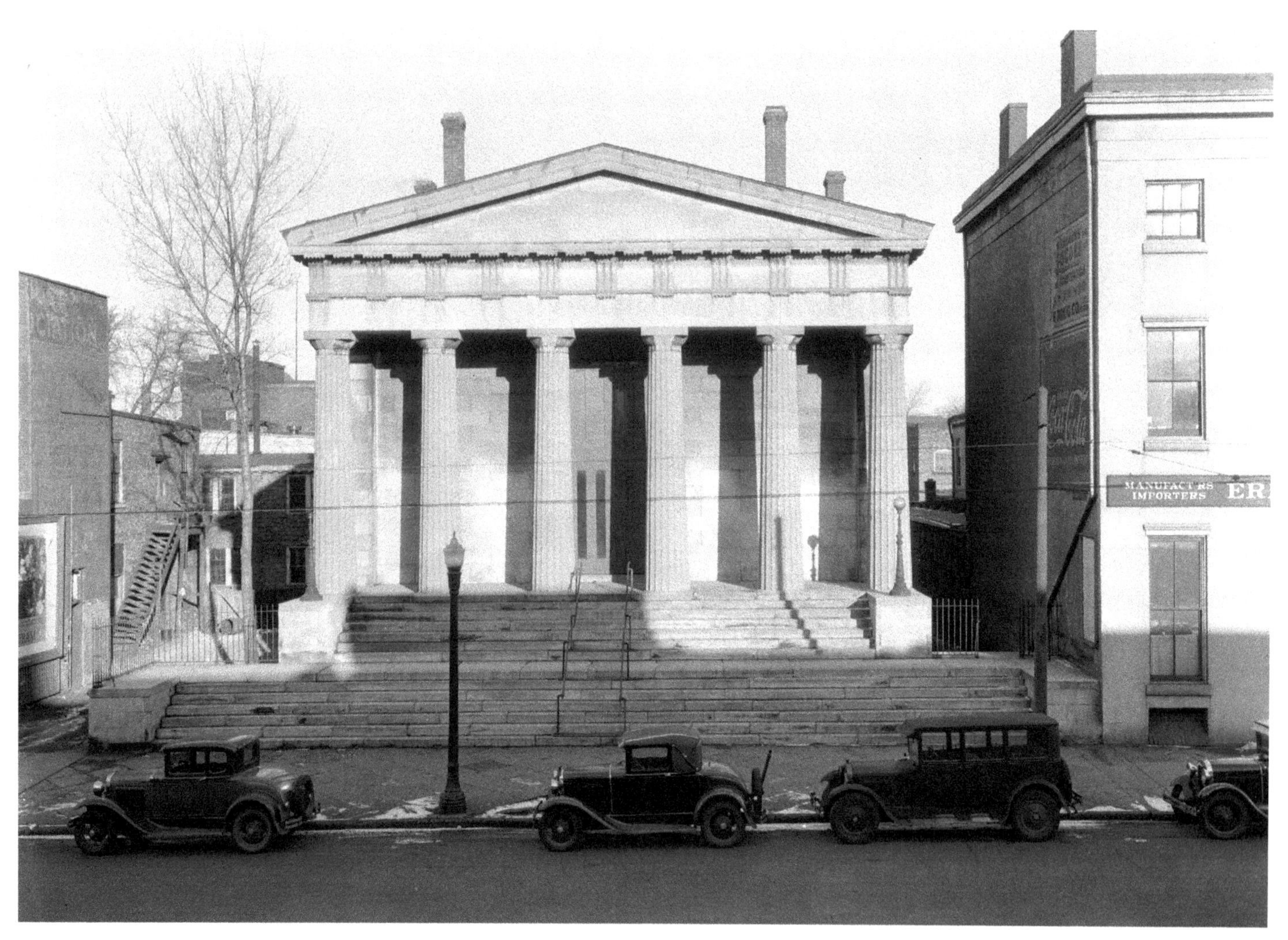

Currently home to the Erie Art Museum, the Old United States Customs House is seen here on January 21, 1935.

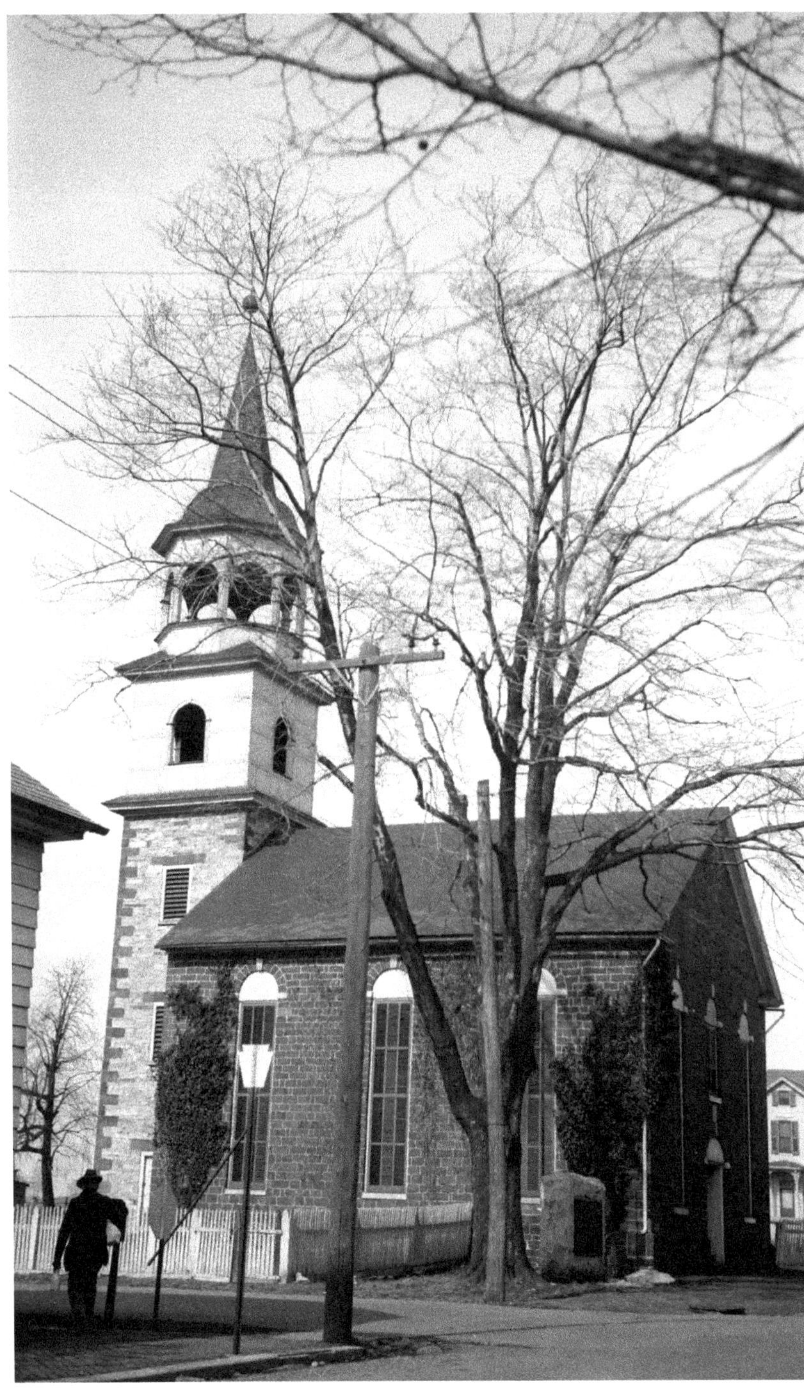

St. Peter's United Lutheran Church on North Union Street in Middletown, Dauphin County. Seen here in March 1935, the structure was built in 1767 and is still home to an active congregation today.

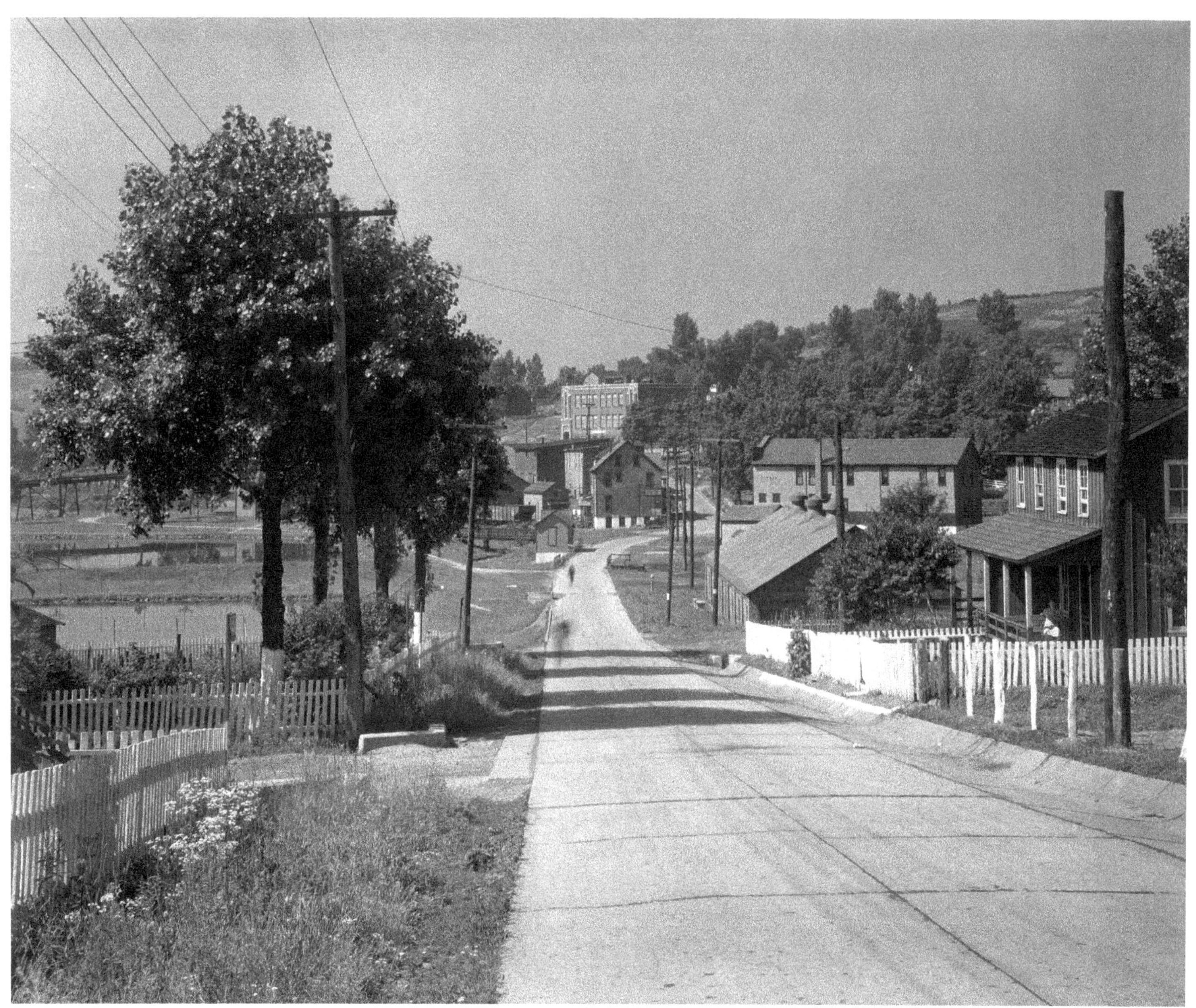

This unidentified mining town in Westmoreland County grew up around one of the several coal mines owned by the H. C. Frick Coke Company. Coke, a product of coal, is essential in the production of steel. In the 1880s, Henry Clay Frick formed an exclusive partnership with Andrew Carnegie in a company which would later become United States Steel. This photograph was taken by Walker Evans, one of several noted photographers employed on federal documentary projects during the New Deal and World War II years.

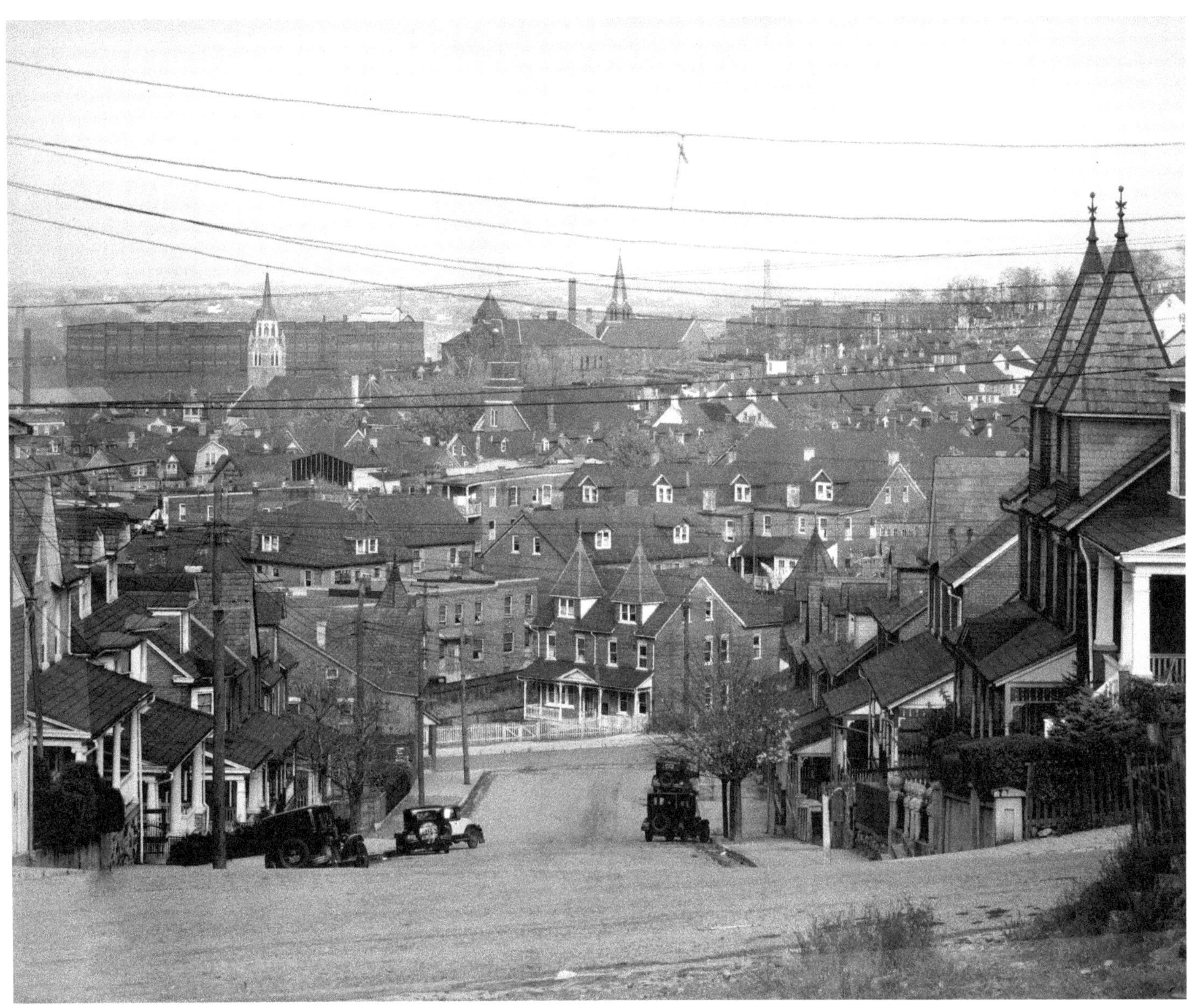

Bethlehem, Pennsylvania, as photographed by Walker Evans in November 1935. The town was founded along the Lehigh River on Christmas Eve 1741 and straddles the boundary between Lehigh and Northampton counties. Created as a Moravian community with all land owned by the church, the town was first opened to non-Moravians in the 1850s.

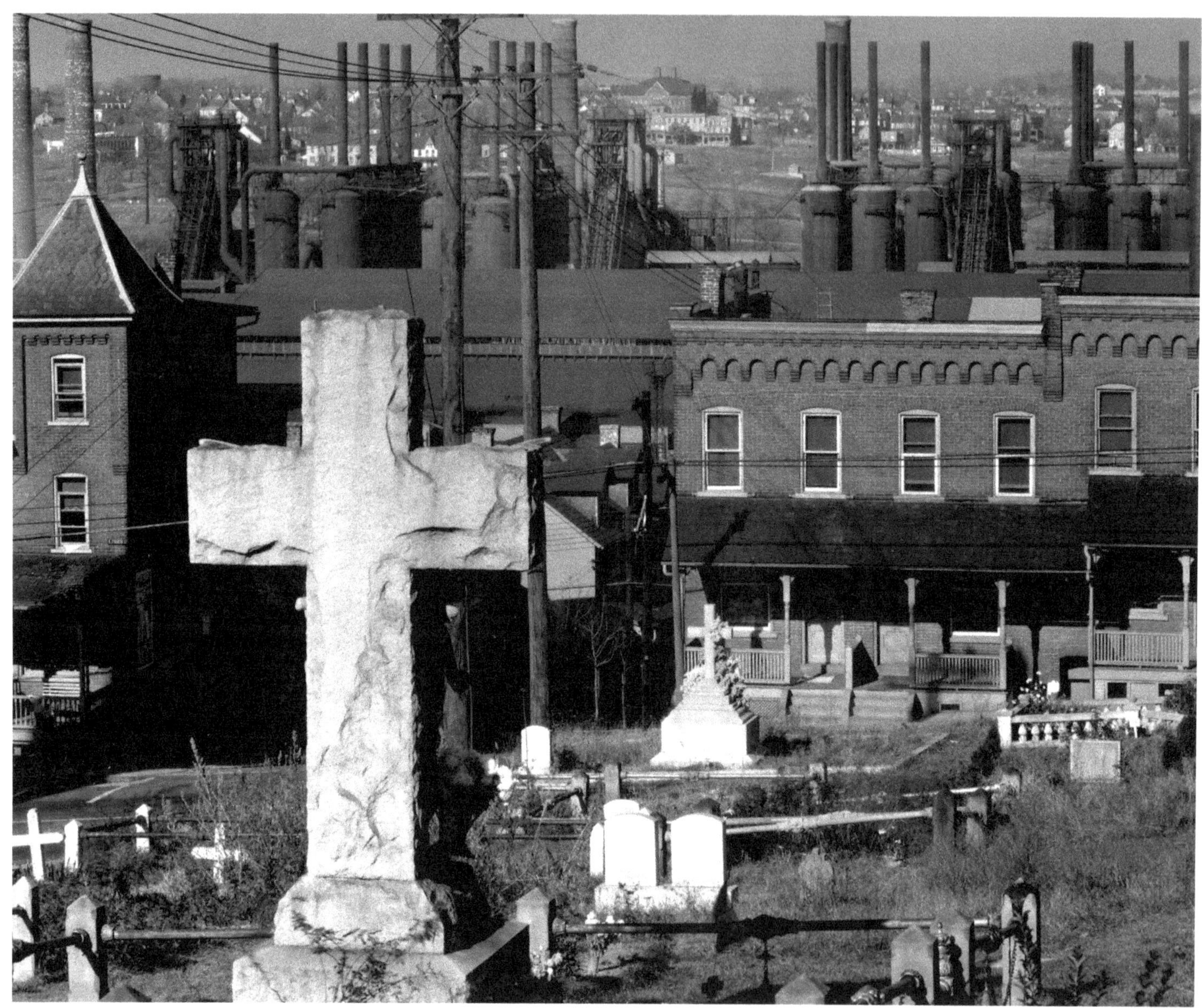

Seen from a neighborhood graveyard in Bethlehem, the stacks of Bethlehem Steel are visible in the distance. The Bethlehem Steel plant, founded in the 1850s and once the second-largest steel manufacturer in the country, closed in 1995.

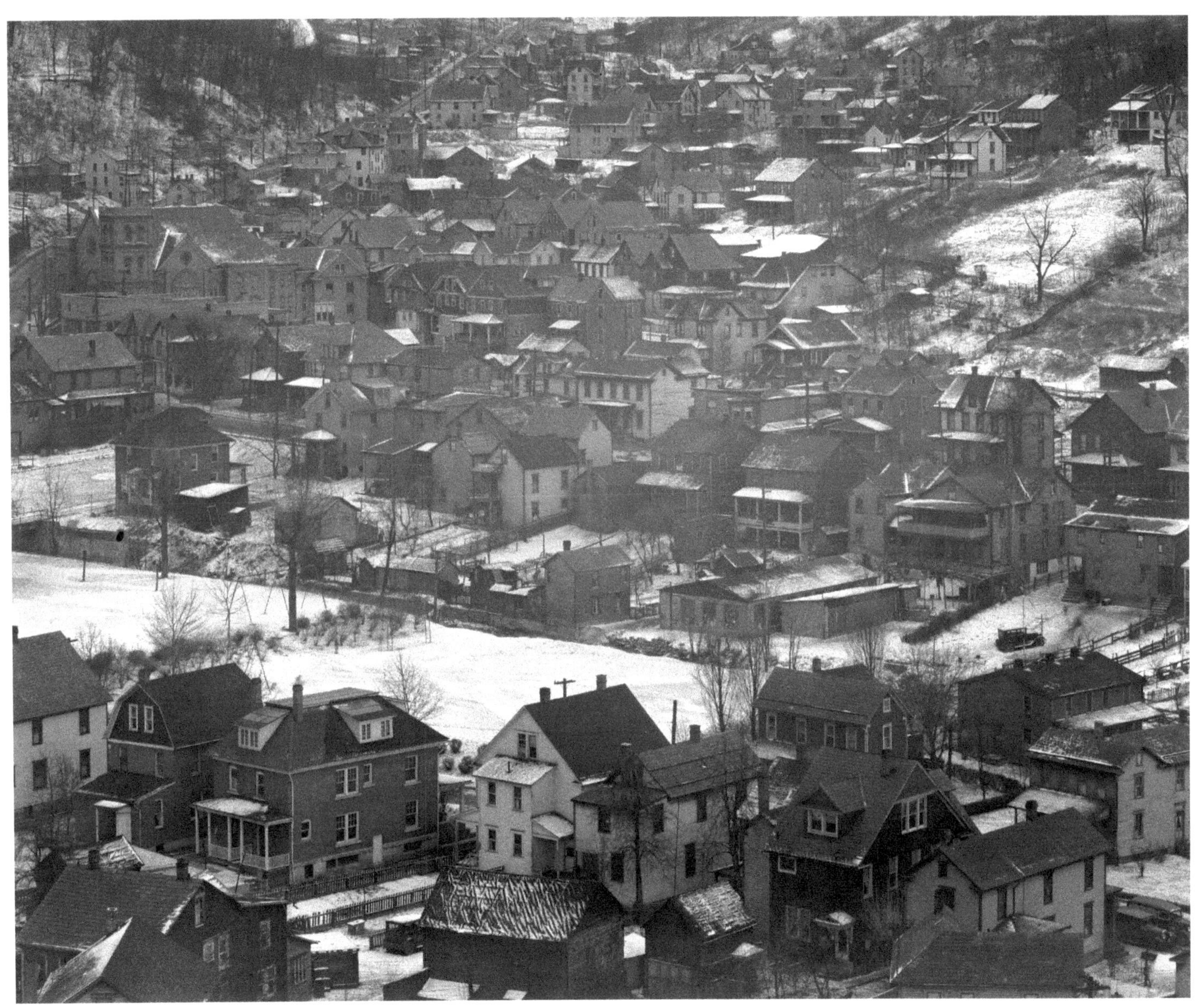

Homes crowd a valley view of Johnstown, Cambria County, as photographed by Walker Evans in November 1935.

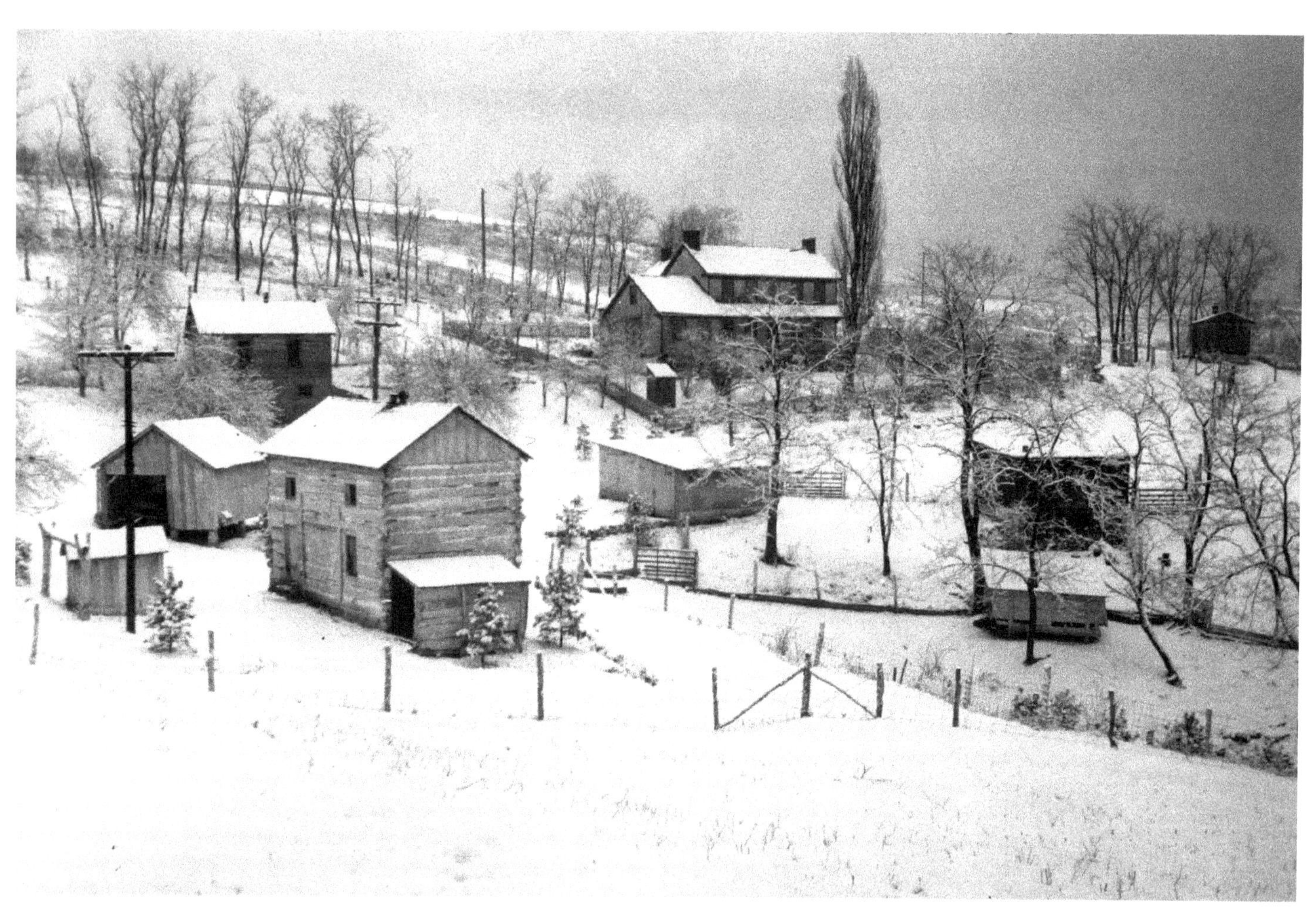

The Miller family homestead in Allegheny County as it appeared in 1937. The original 1840s log house, at lower left, is now a part of the Meadowcroft Museum of Rural Life in Avella, Pennsylvania.

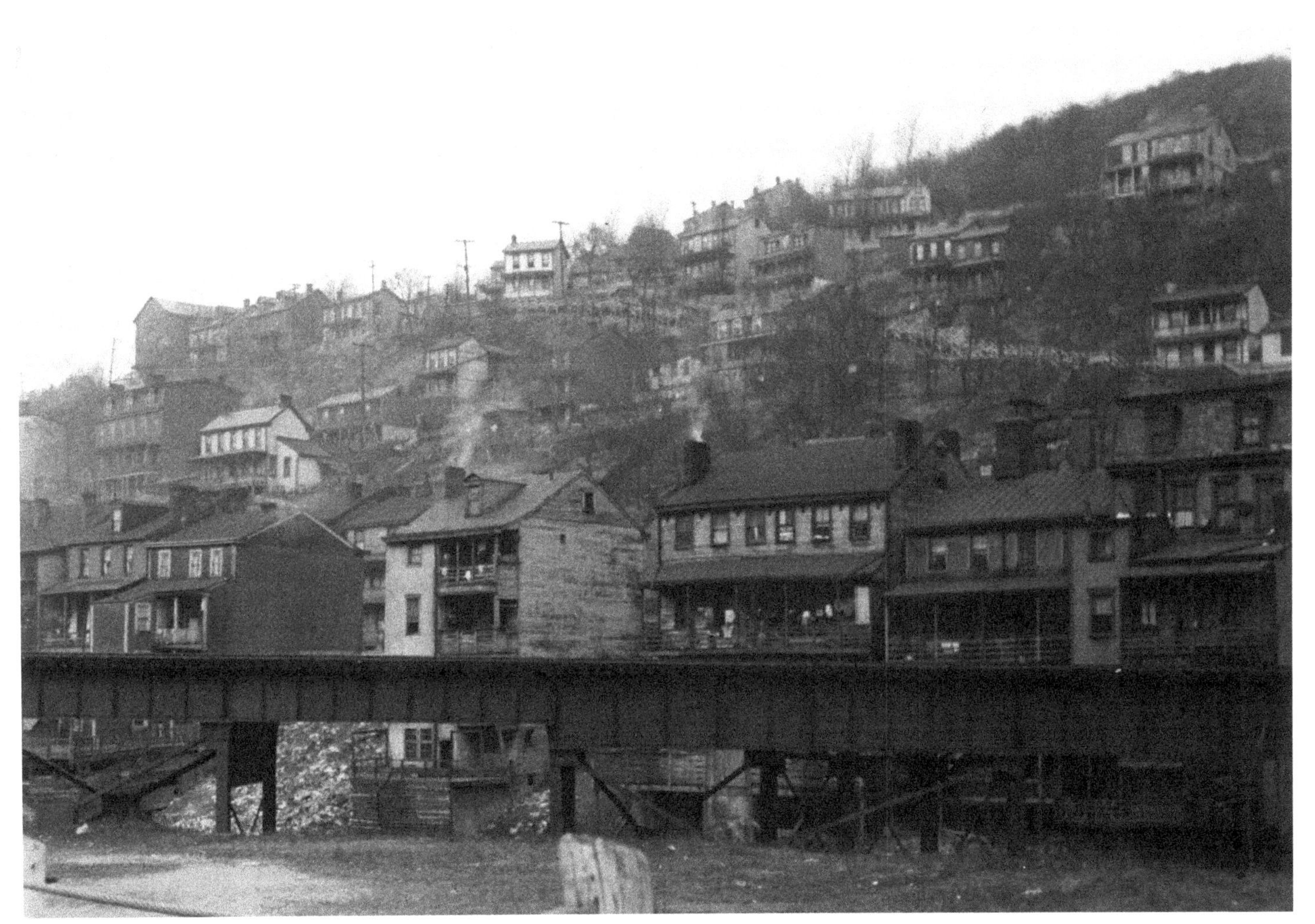

Woodframe homes crowd a hillside in Pittsburgh.

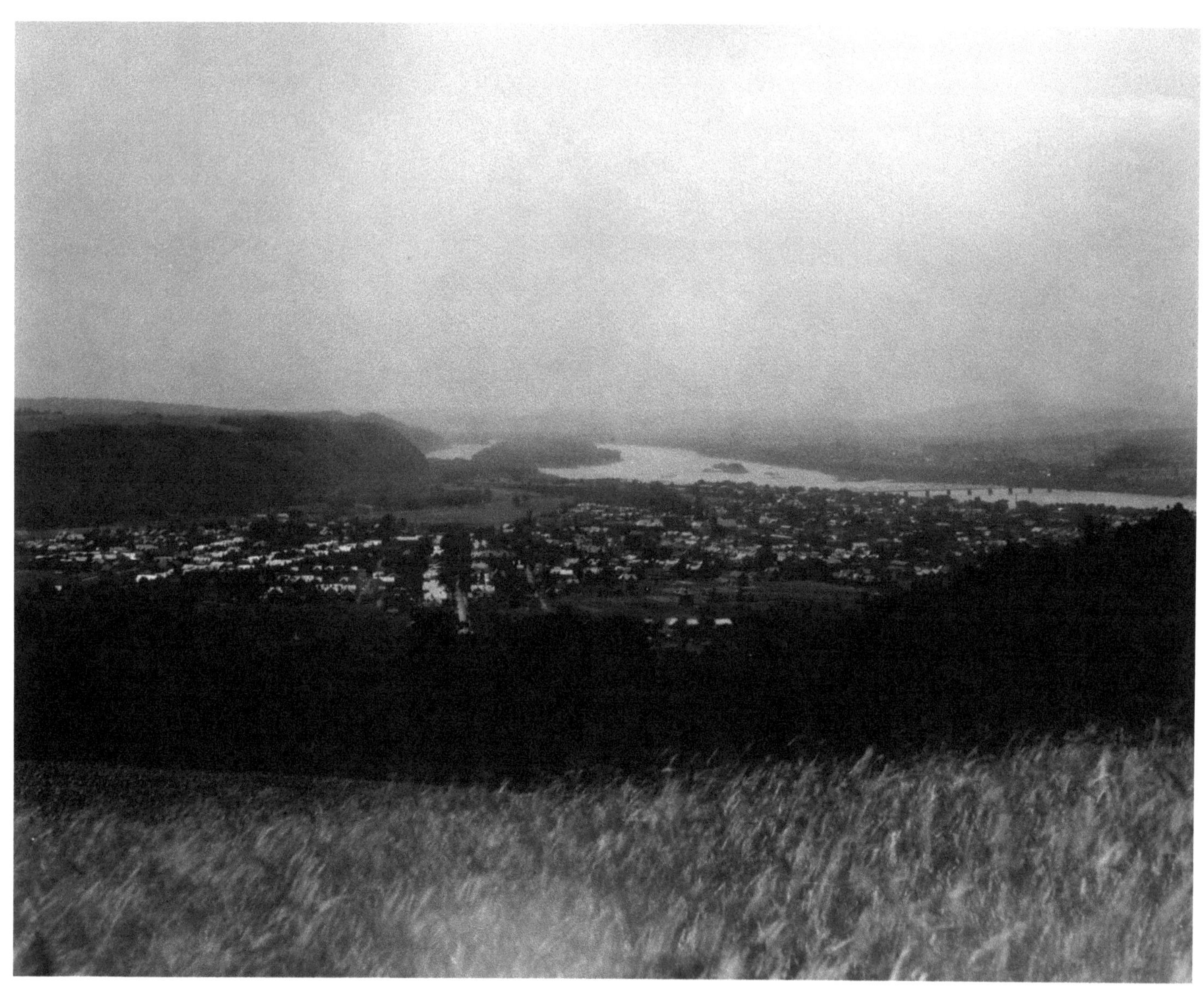

The town of Sunbury and the Susquehanna River rest along the Susquehanna Trail in Northumberland County. The trail, which linked Washington, D.C., with Niagara Falls, New York, was one of several informal auto routes that predated the numbered state road system familiar today.

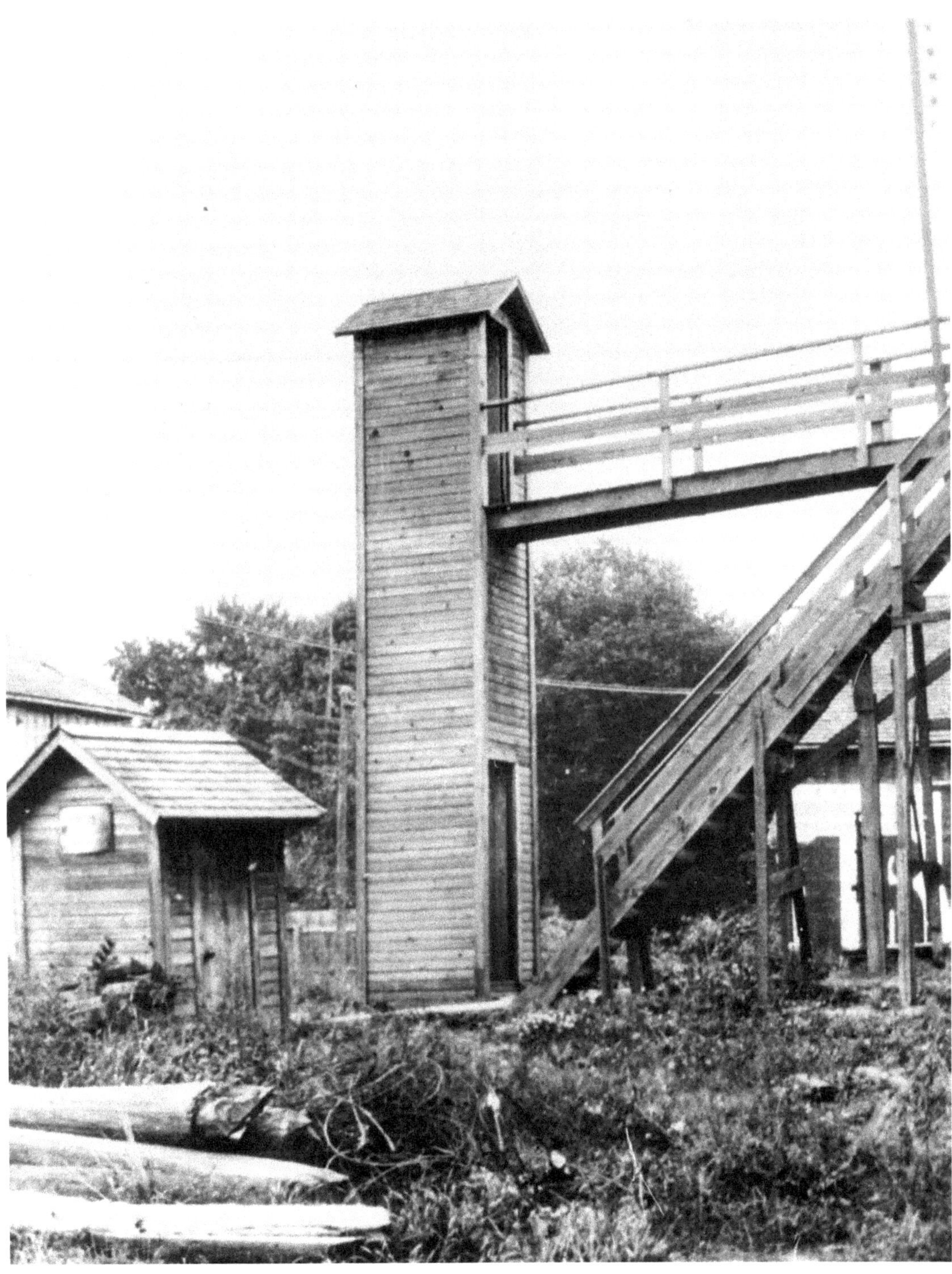

A mysterious double-deck privy looms on a farm in Pennsylvania, circa late 1930s.

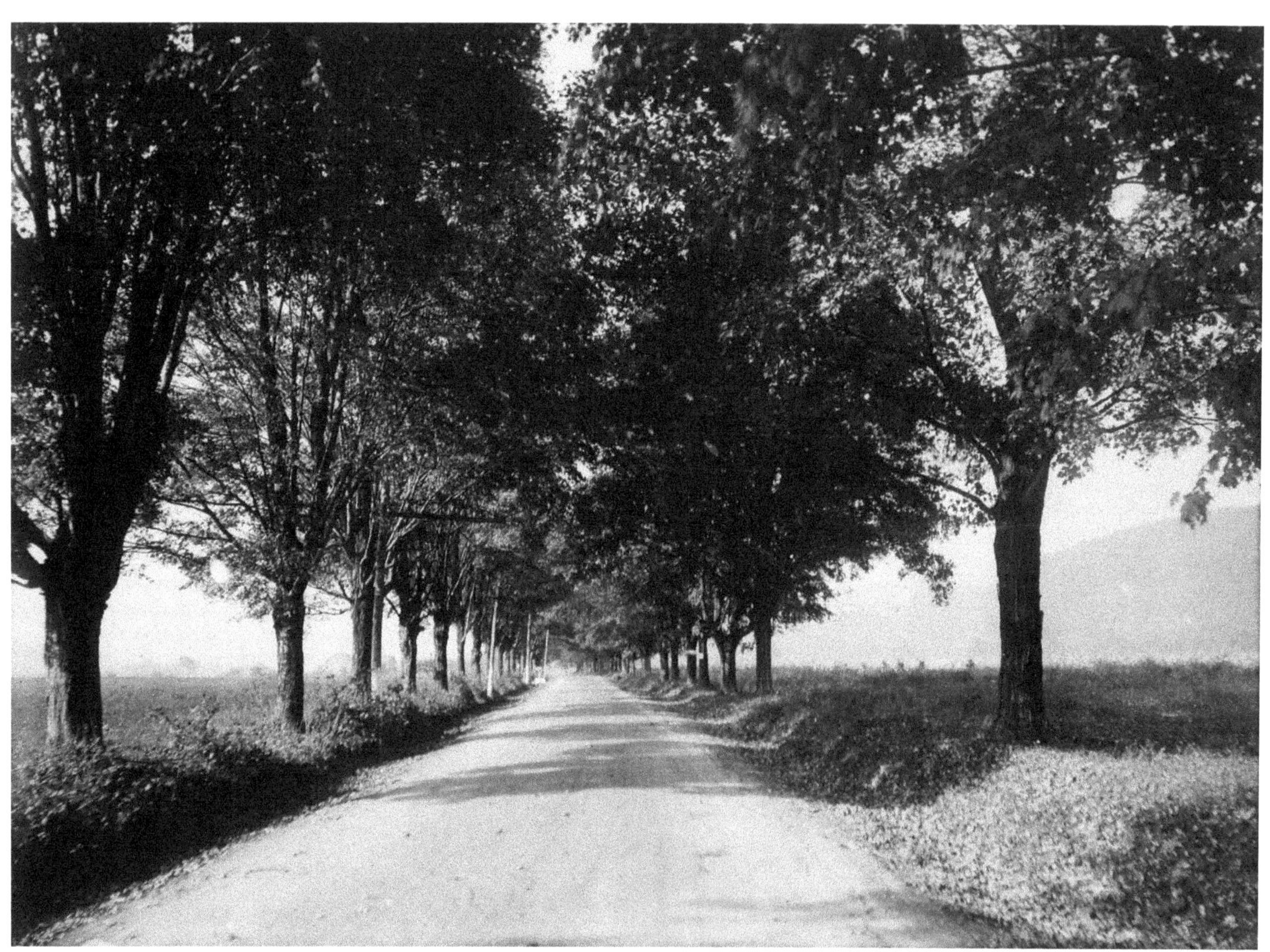

This row of maple trees could be seen near Lycoming Creek on the Susquehanna Trail in the 1930s.

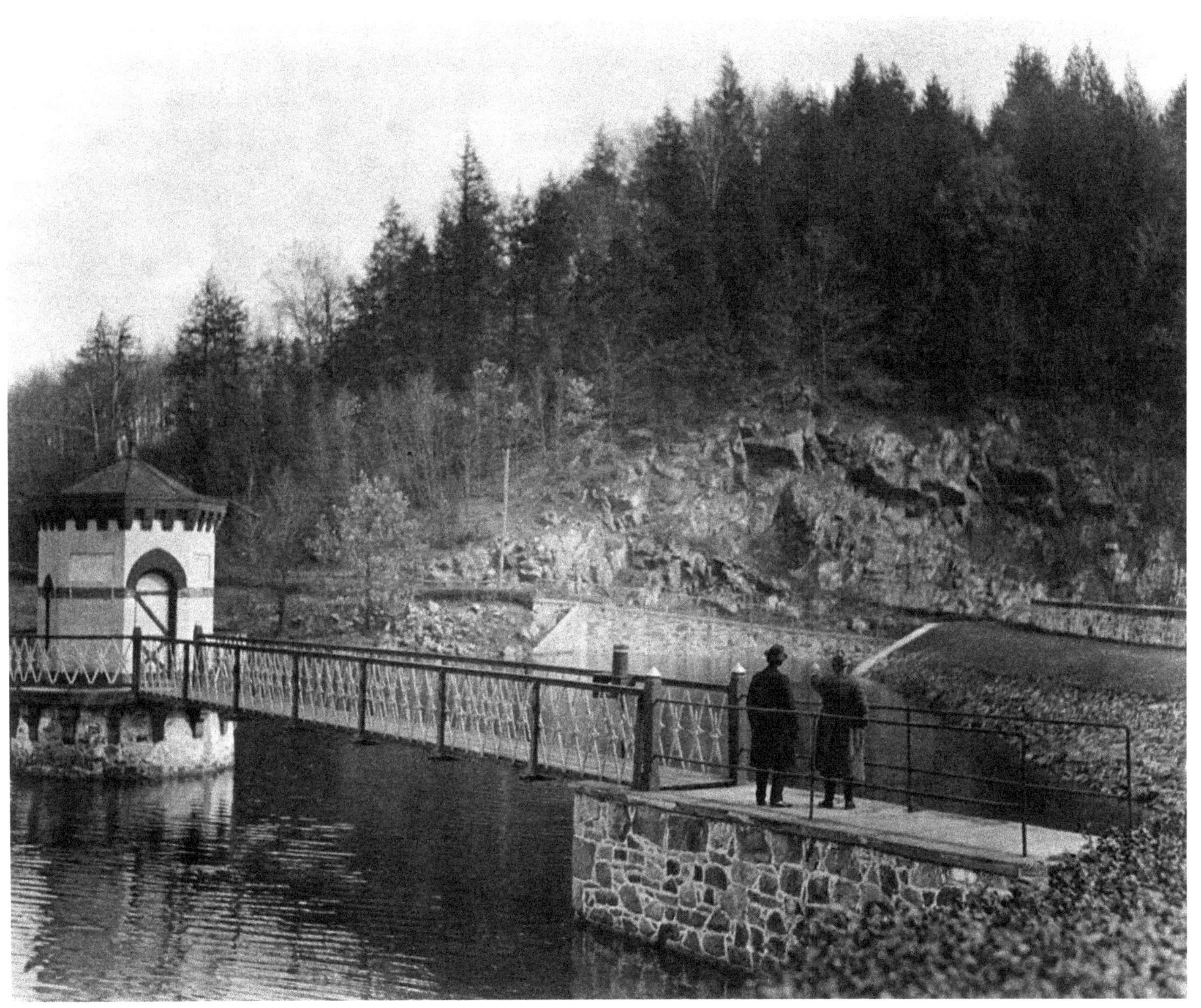

Purchased by the city of Reading in the 1870s to serve the residents' water needs, Antietam Reservoir is still a popular recreation and fishing destination in Berks County.

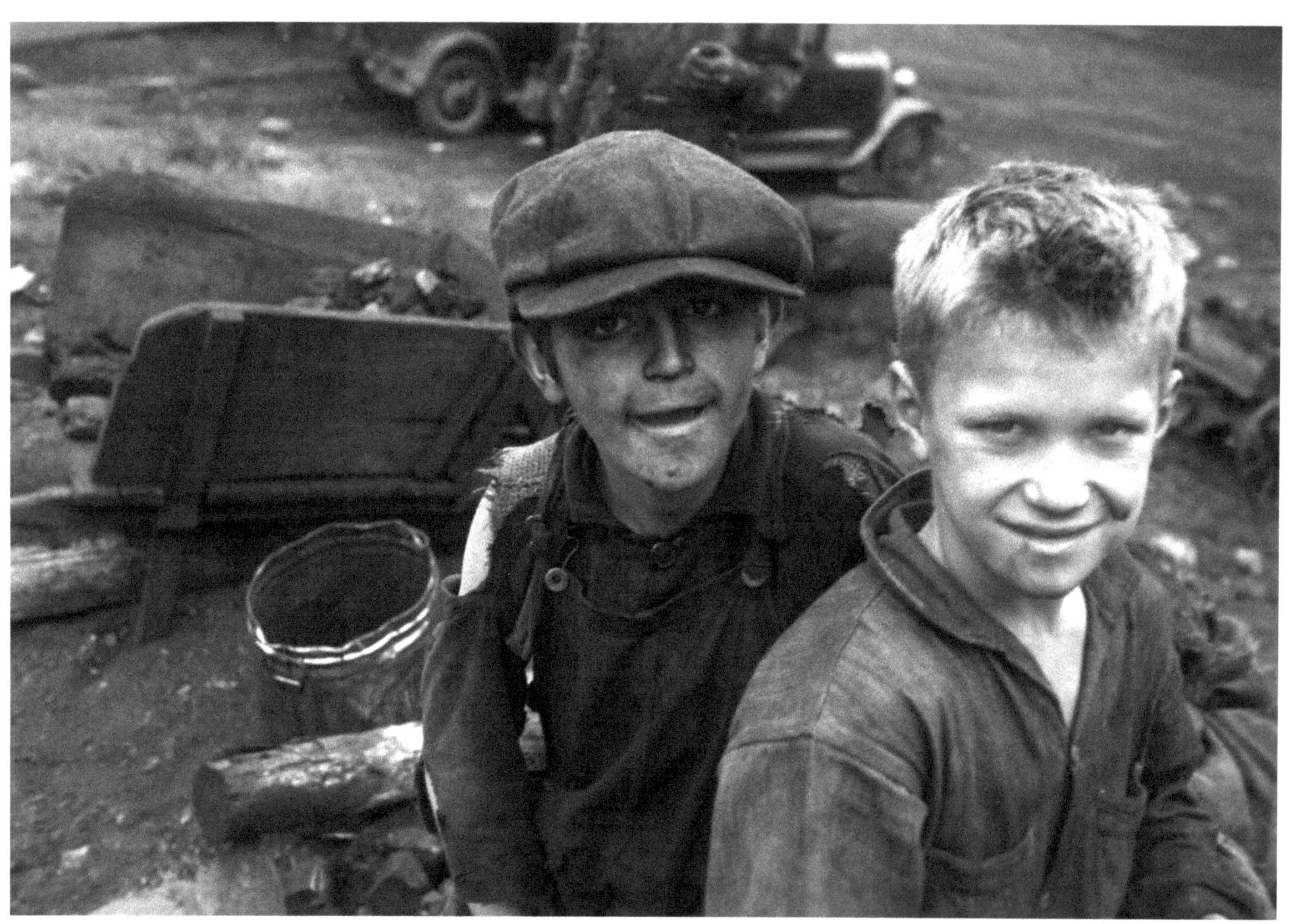

Typical of many coal towns, Nanty Glo, along the Blacklick Creek in Cambria County, grew up around a number of mines at the end of the nineteenth century. These boys, photographed in 1937, worked to retrieve coal scraps from slag piles that resulted from the mining process.

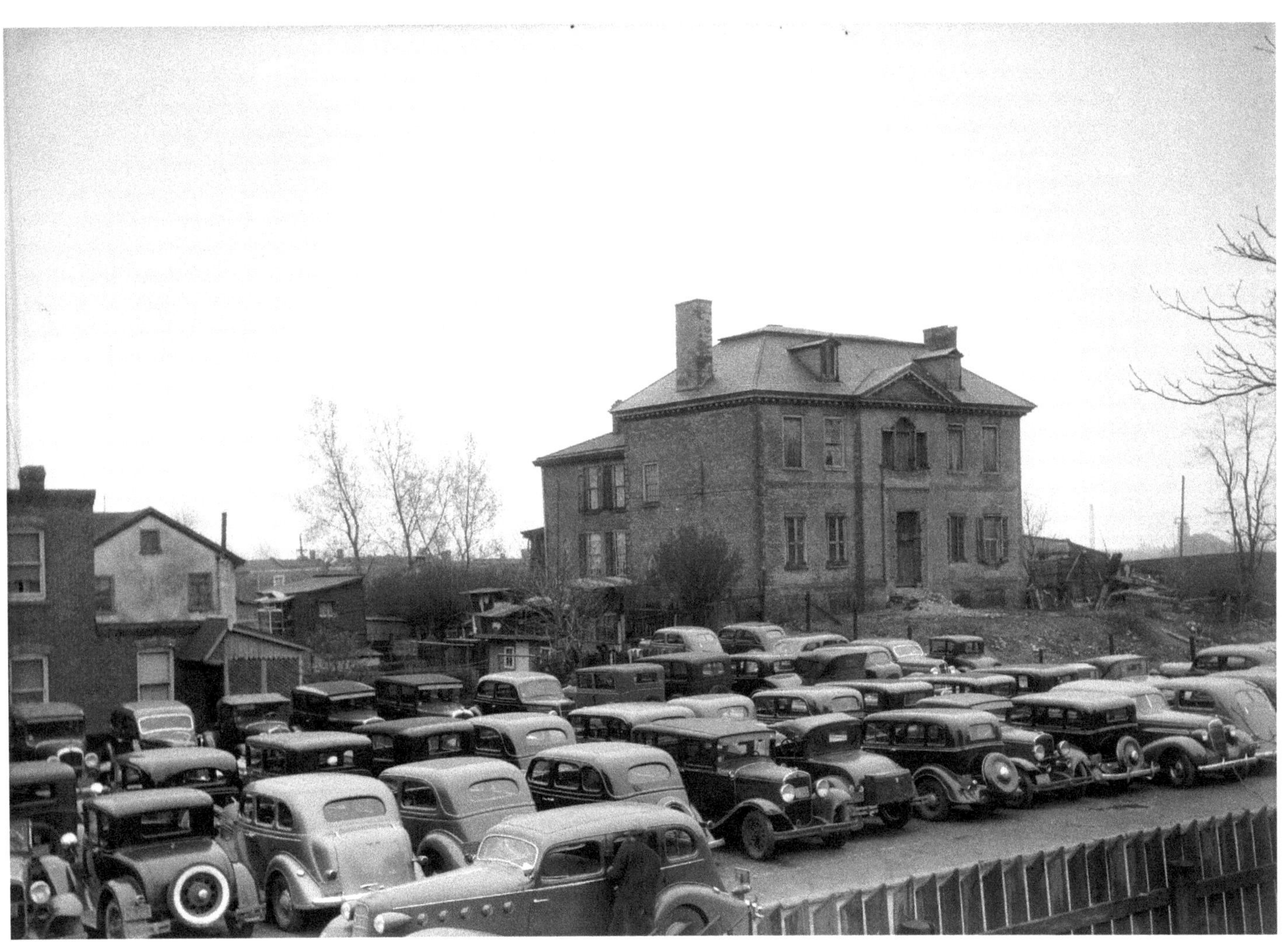

Port Royal, in the Frankford neighborhood of Philadelphia, was built in 1761 by a wealthy immigrant from Bermuda named Edward Stiles. With the grand Georgian home nearing demolition at the time of this photograph in 1937, architectural elements were removed and reconstructed as part of Henry Francis du Pont's home, now the Winterthur Museum and Estate in Delaware.

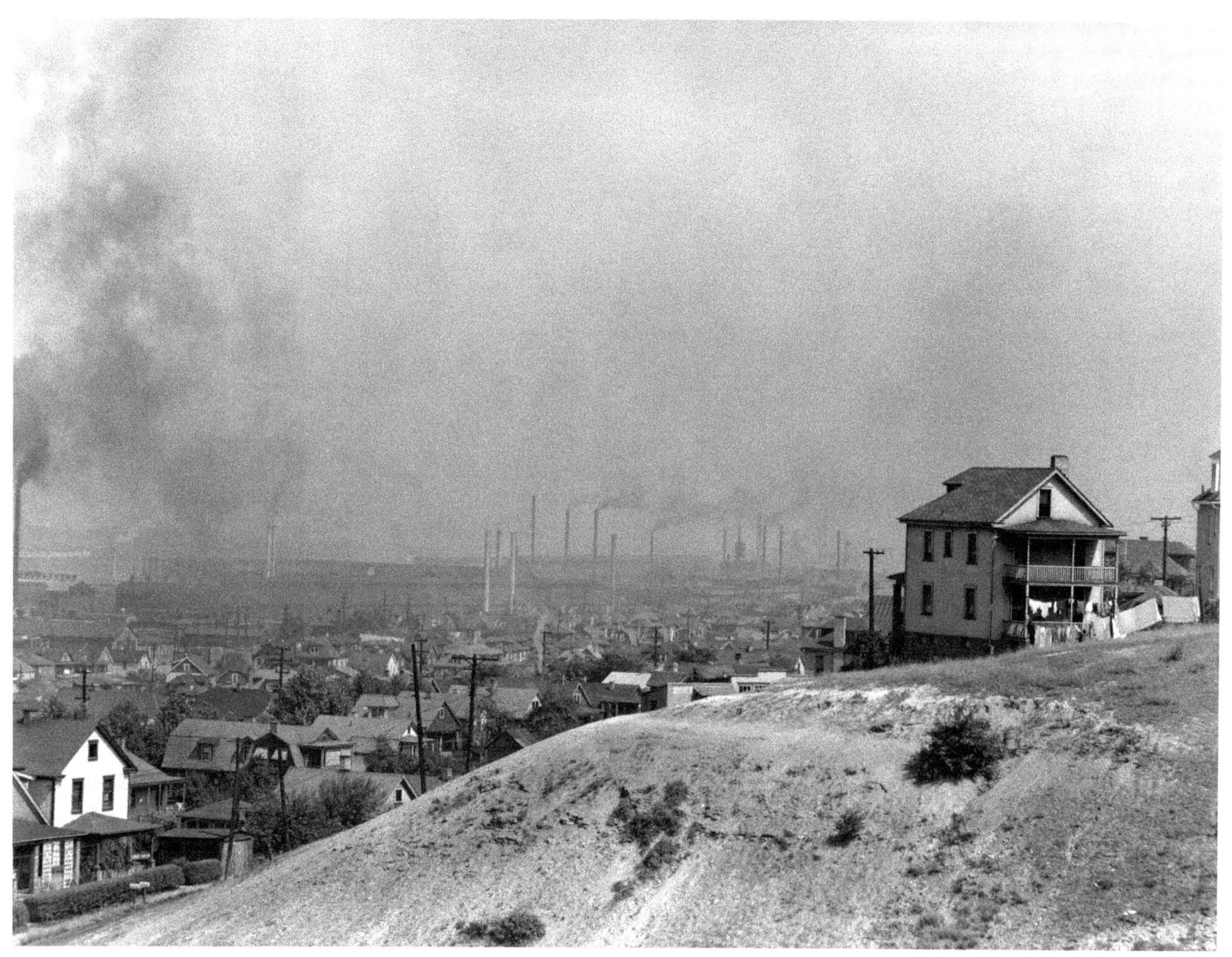

Incorporated in 1905 after the American Bridge Company purchased land from a religious sect, the town of Ambridge is seen here in July 1938. The large smokestacks featured in the photo are representative of the historical importance of steel manufacture to the town.

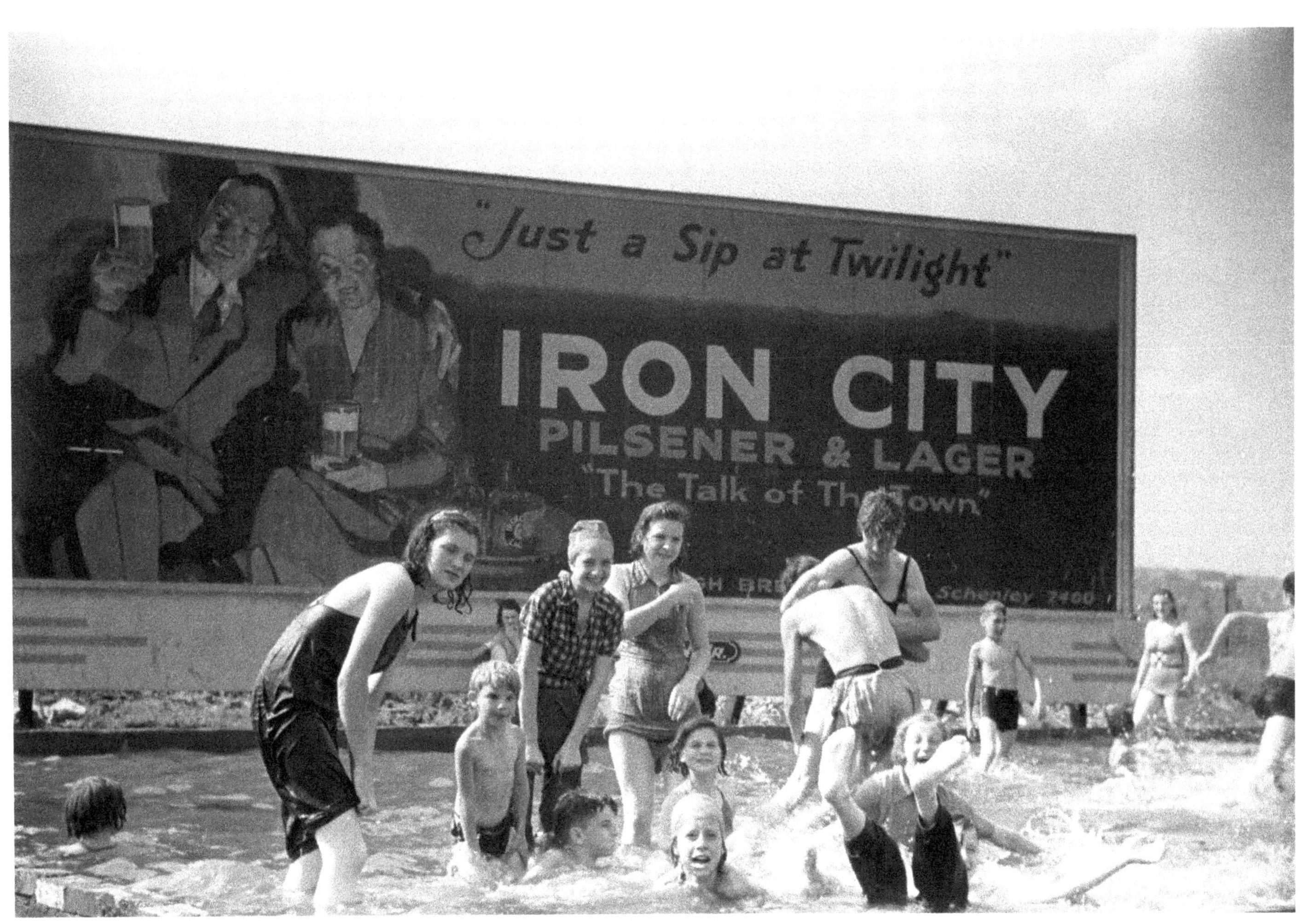

Under the watchful eye of a billboard advertising beer, children of Pittsburgh steelworkers enjoy a swim in a homemade pool, July 1938.

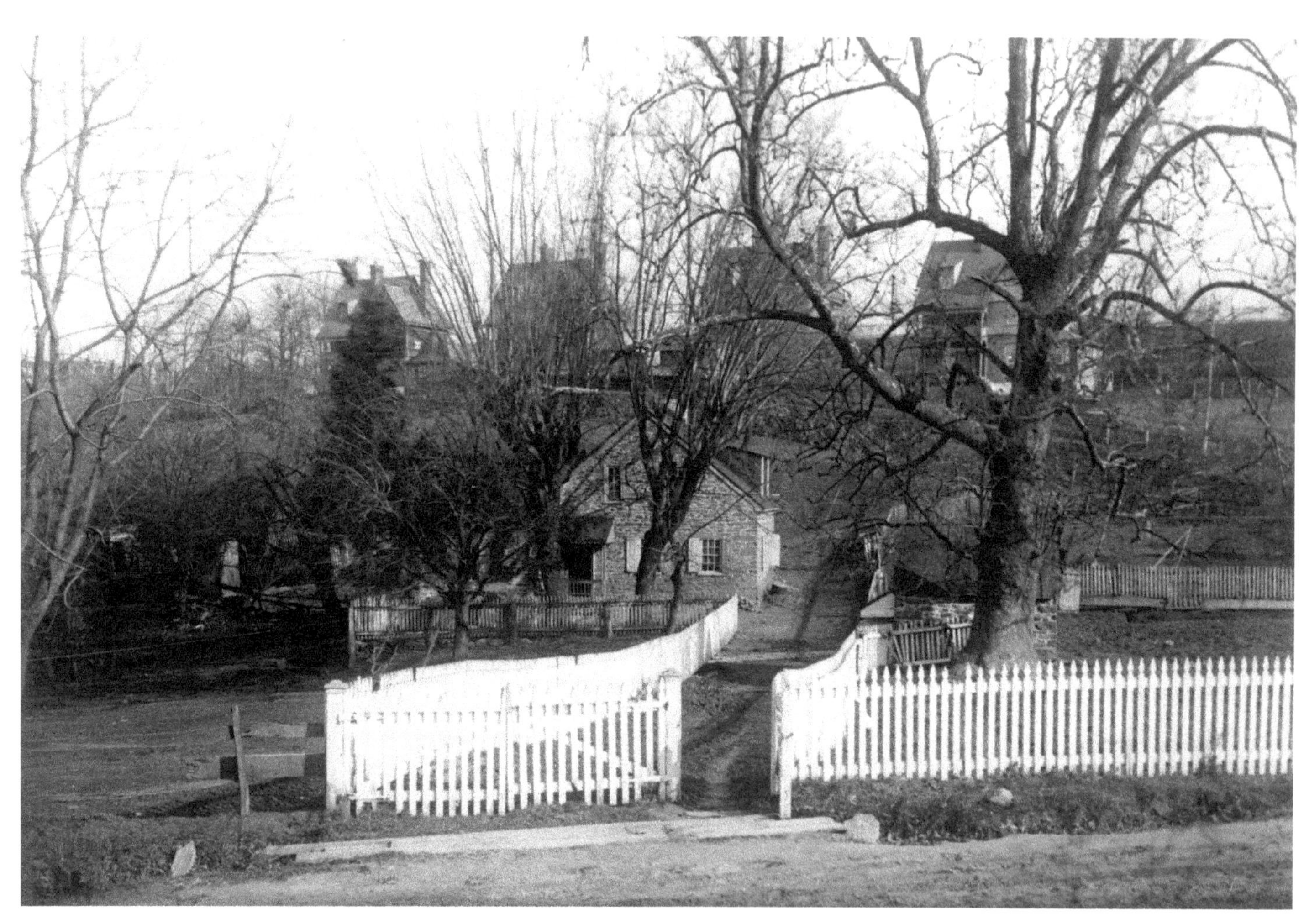

Buttercup Cottage, an old farmhouse along Cresheim Valley Drive in the Chestnut Hill neighborhood of Philadelphia, was used for a time as a retreat for young working women in the 1880s.

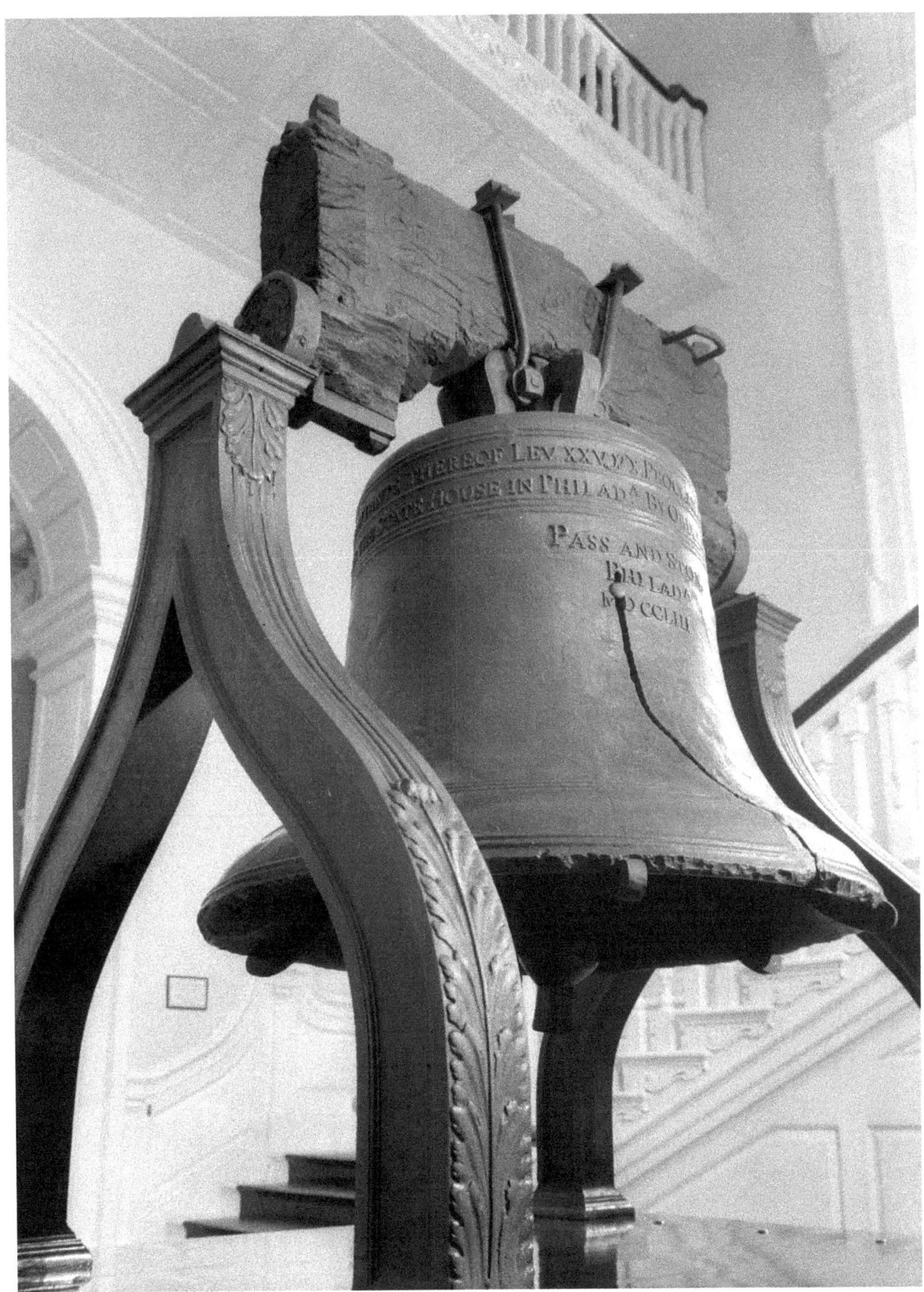

The Liberty Bell on display in the south entrance hall of Independence Hall, circa late 1930s. The bell was moved to a new permanent home across the street at midnight on January 1, 1976, in preparation for the celebration of the nation's Bicentennial.

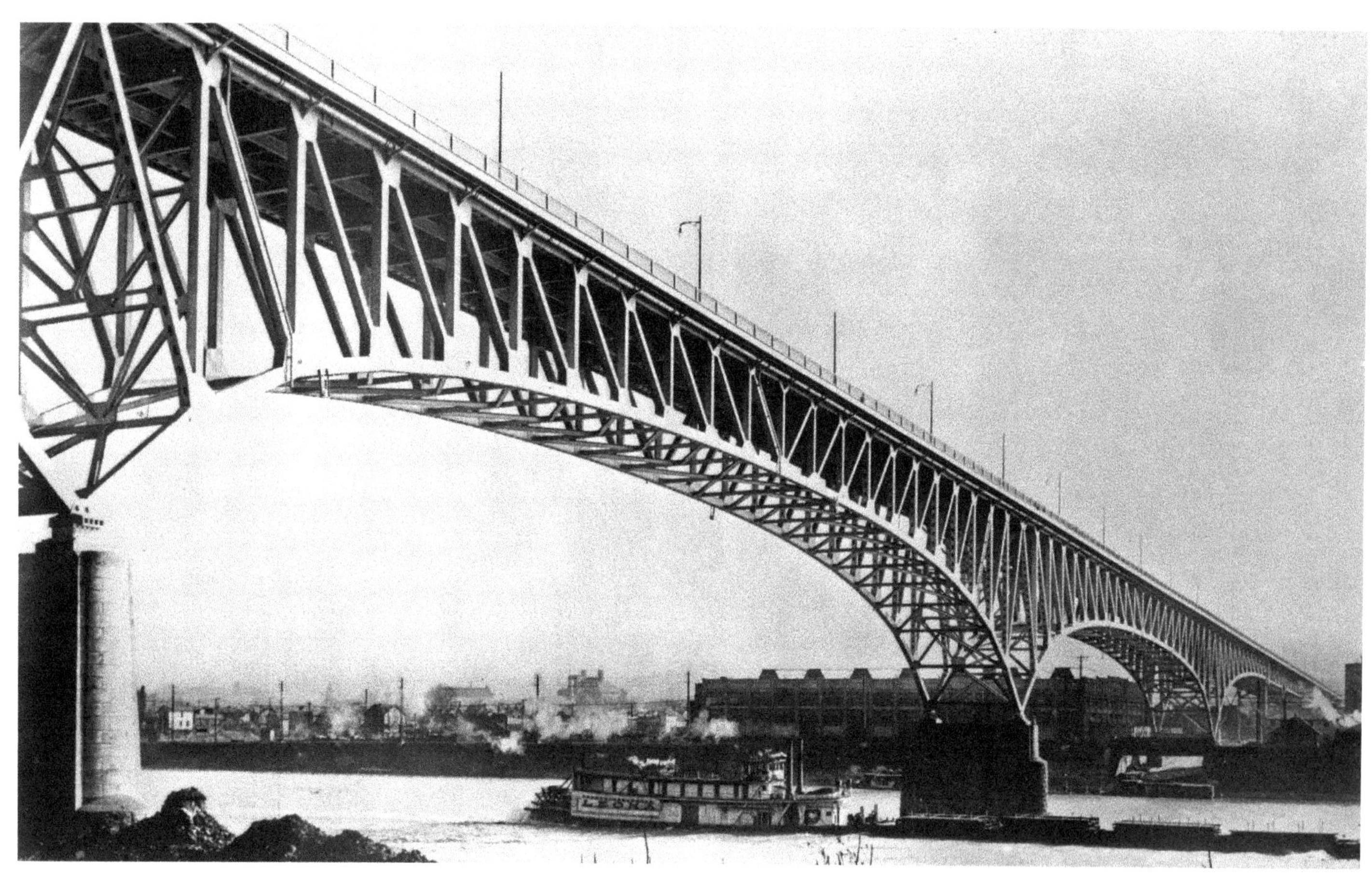

Following the influx of money from New Deal federal programs, many bridges and highways throughout Pennsylvania underwent improvement projects. Seen here in 1939 is one of several updated bridges spanning the Allegheny River in Pittsburgh.

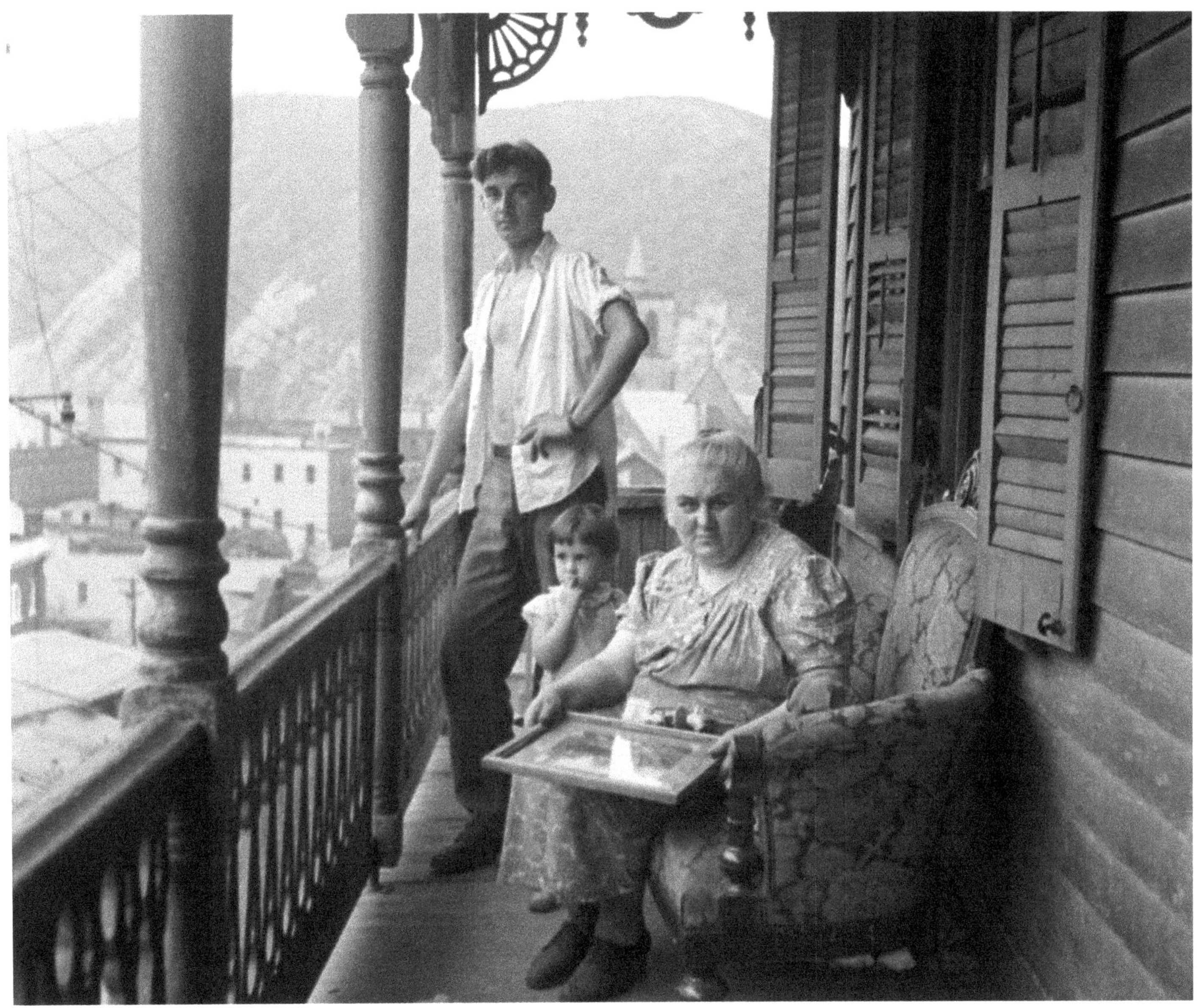

A working family of Polish ethnicity sits on their porch in the town of Mauch Chunk (now Jim Thorpe) in 1940. A center of coal transportation and a significant destination for railroad excursionists in the nineteenth century, Mauch Chunk, as well as many other Pennsylvania mining towns, experienced a difficult economic depression resulting from reductions in coal production following World War II.

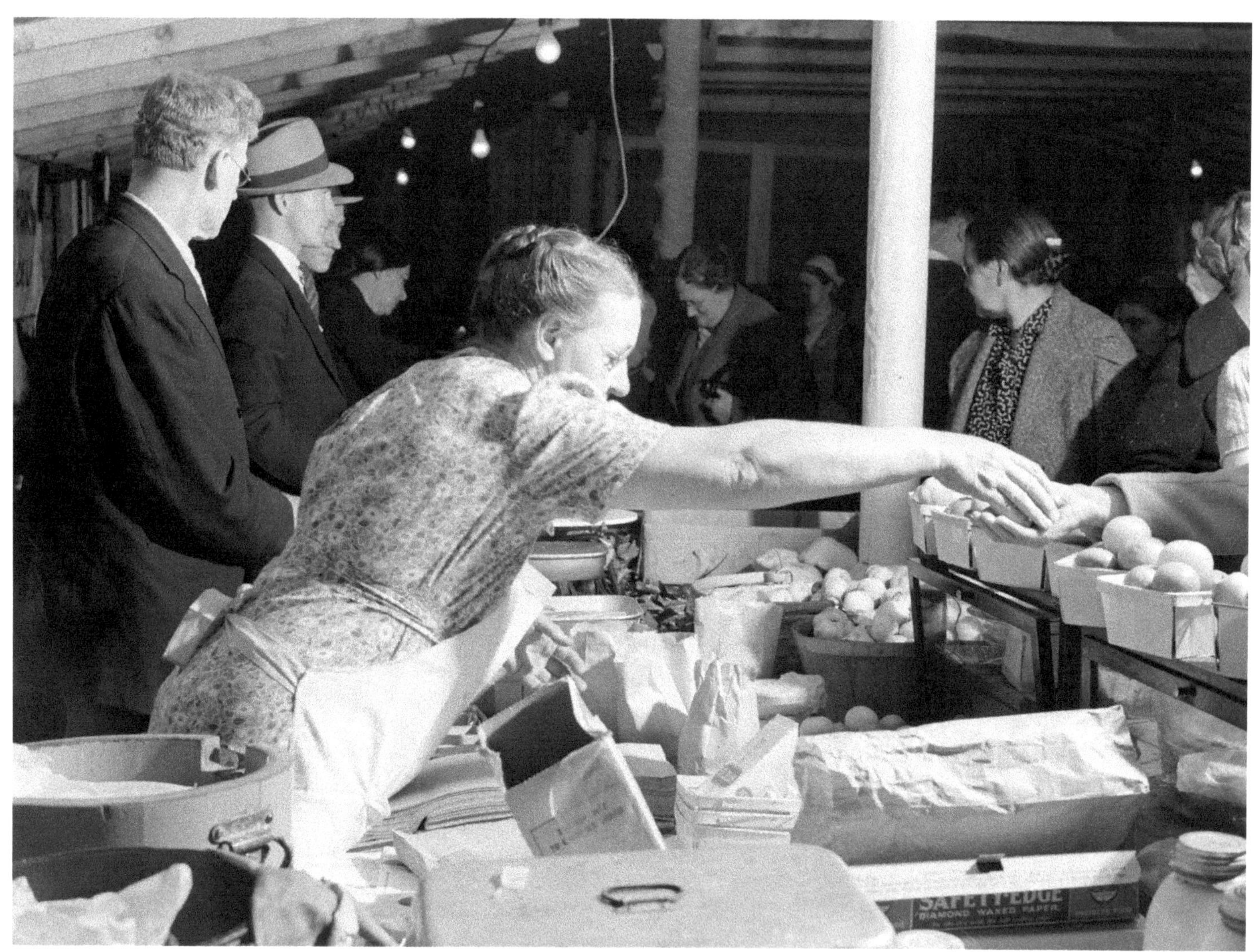

An apron-wearing woman sells vegetables at the Tri-County Farmers Co-op Market in DuBois, Clearfield County, 1940. Markets like this one continue to be staples of the small-farm community throughout the state.

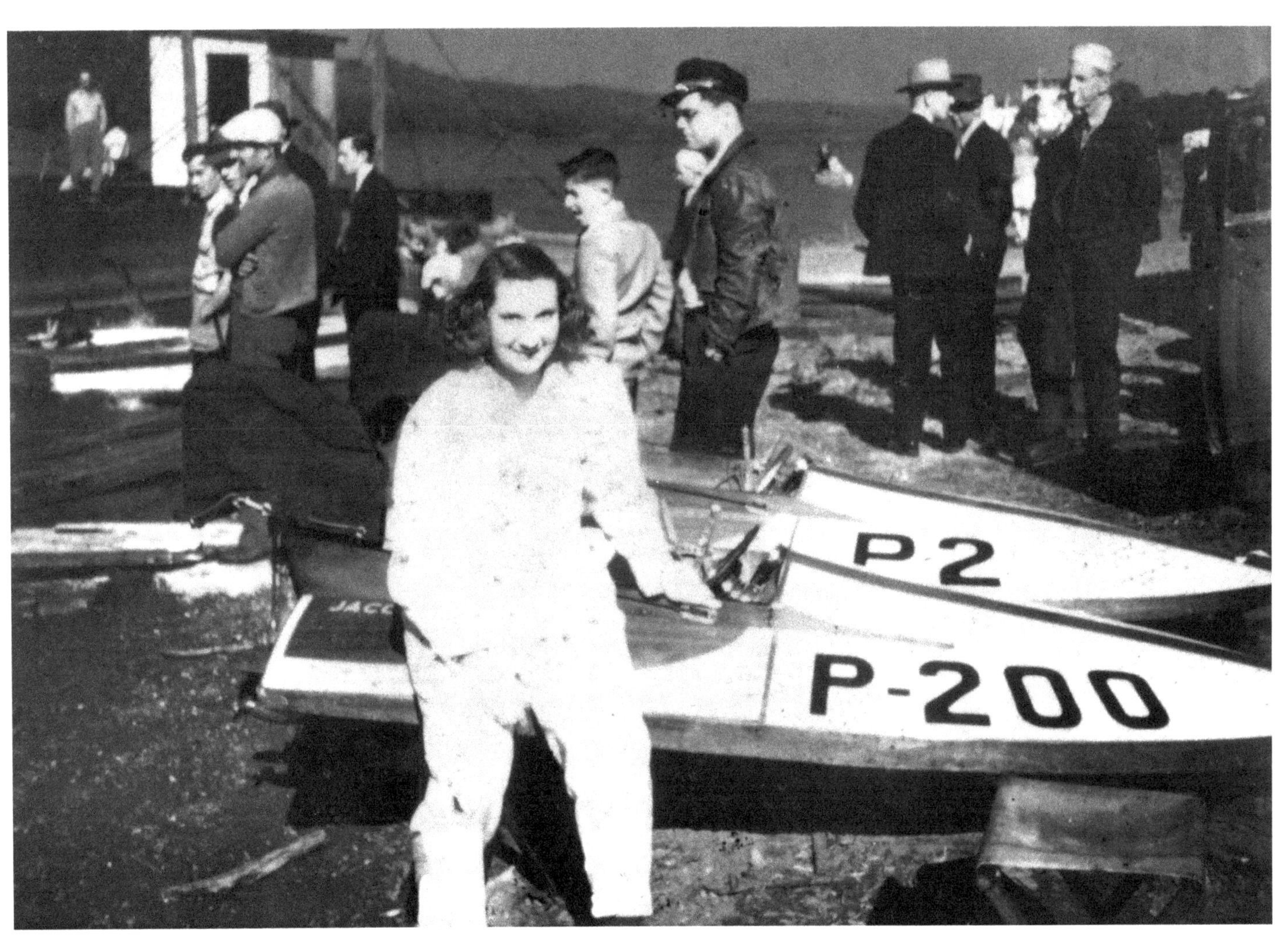

Boat racer Mary Altman proudly poses with her championship P-200 powerboat near Pittsburgh, 1940.

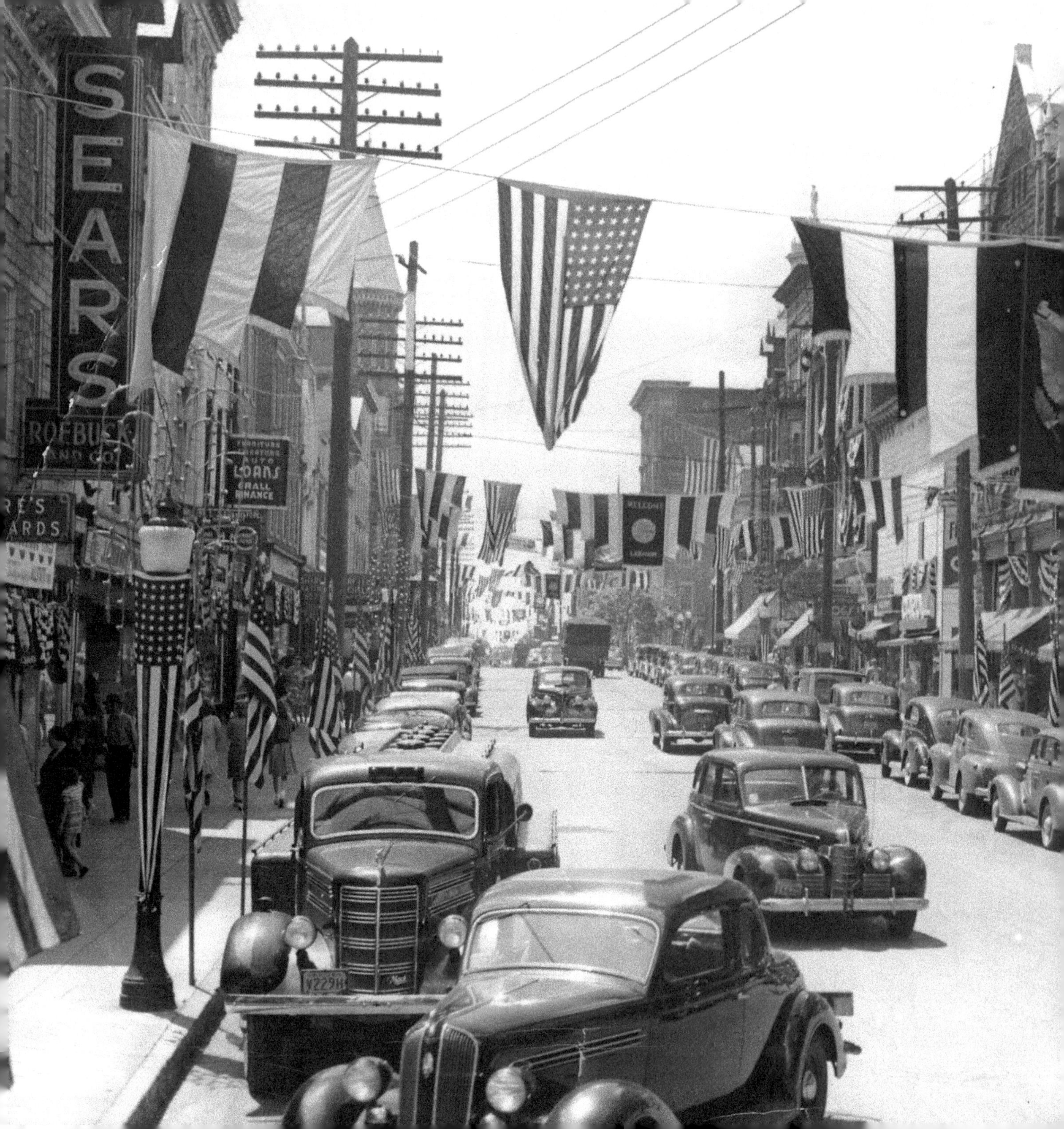
SEARS
ROEBUCK AND CO.
LOANS
SMALL FINANCE

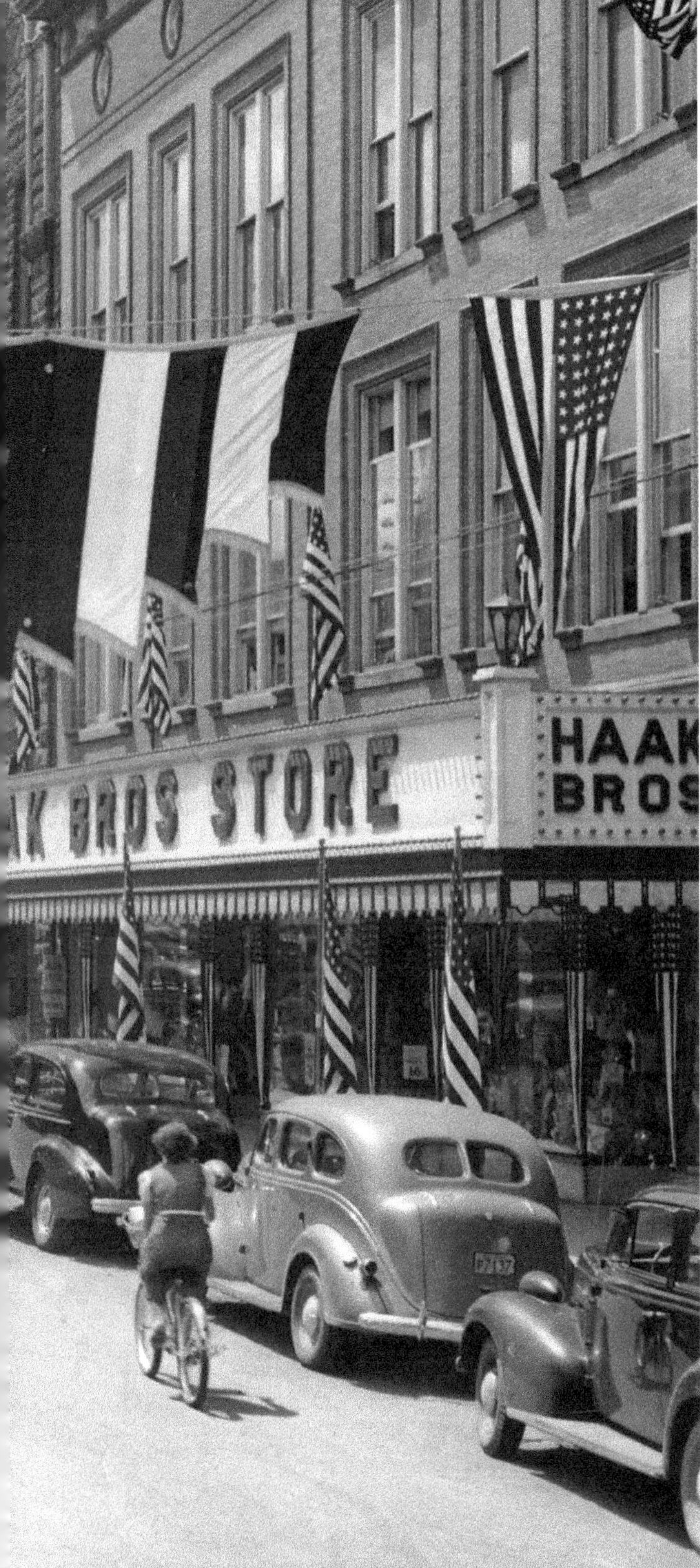

A flag-festooned street in downtown Lebanon as the city celebrates its bicentennial year in 1940.

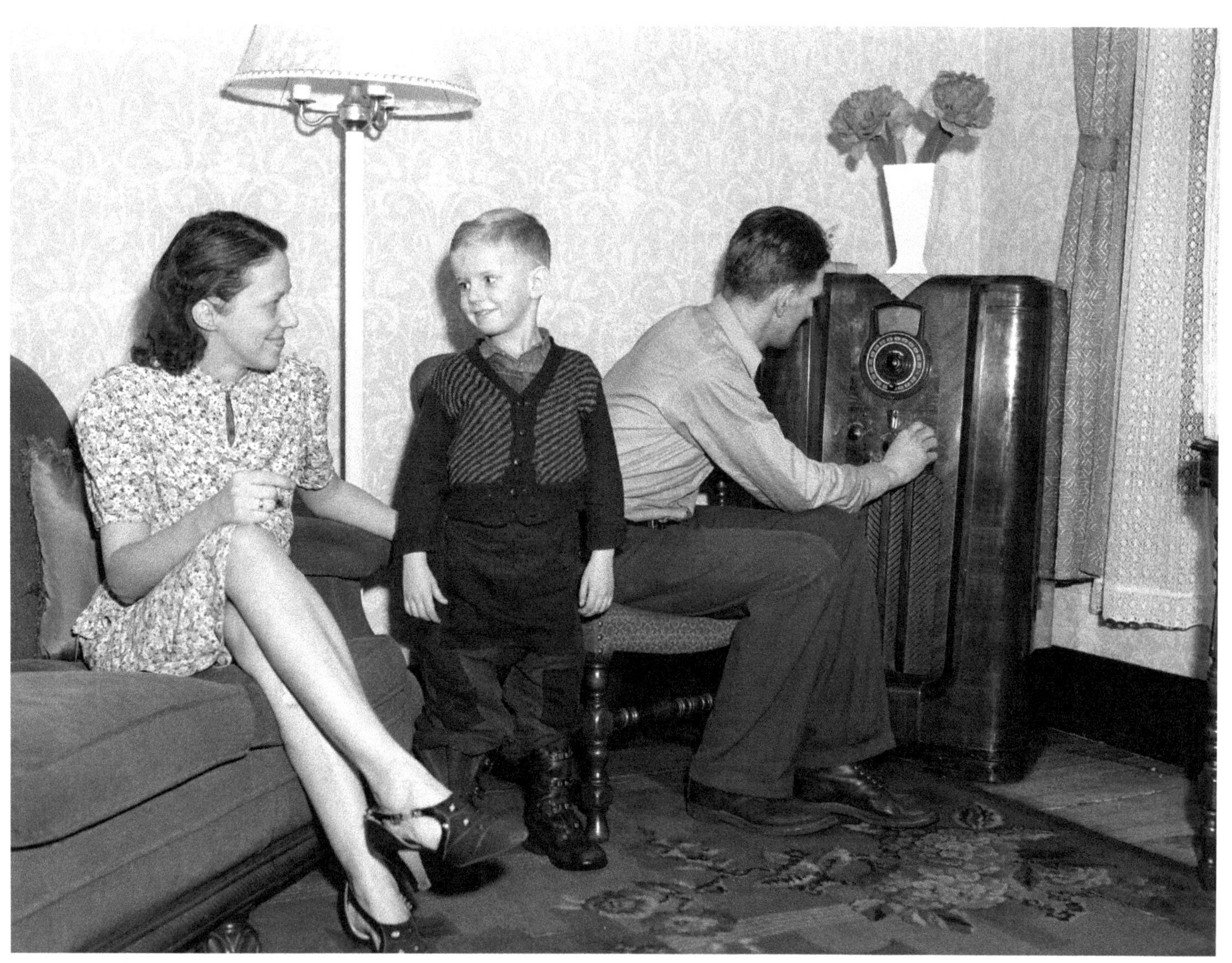

A steelworker and his family in Aliquippa, Beaver County, enjoy time spent listening to the radio in January 1941.

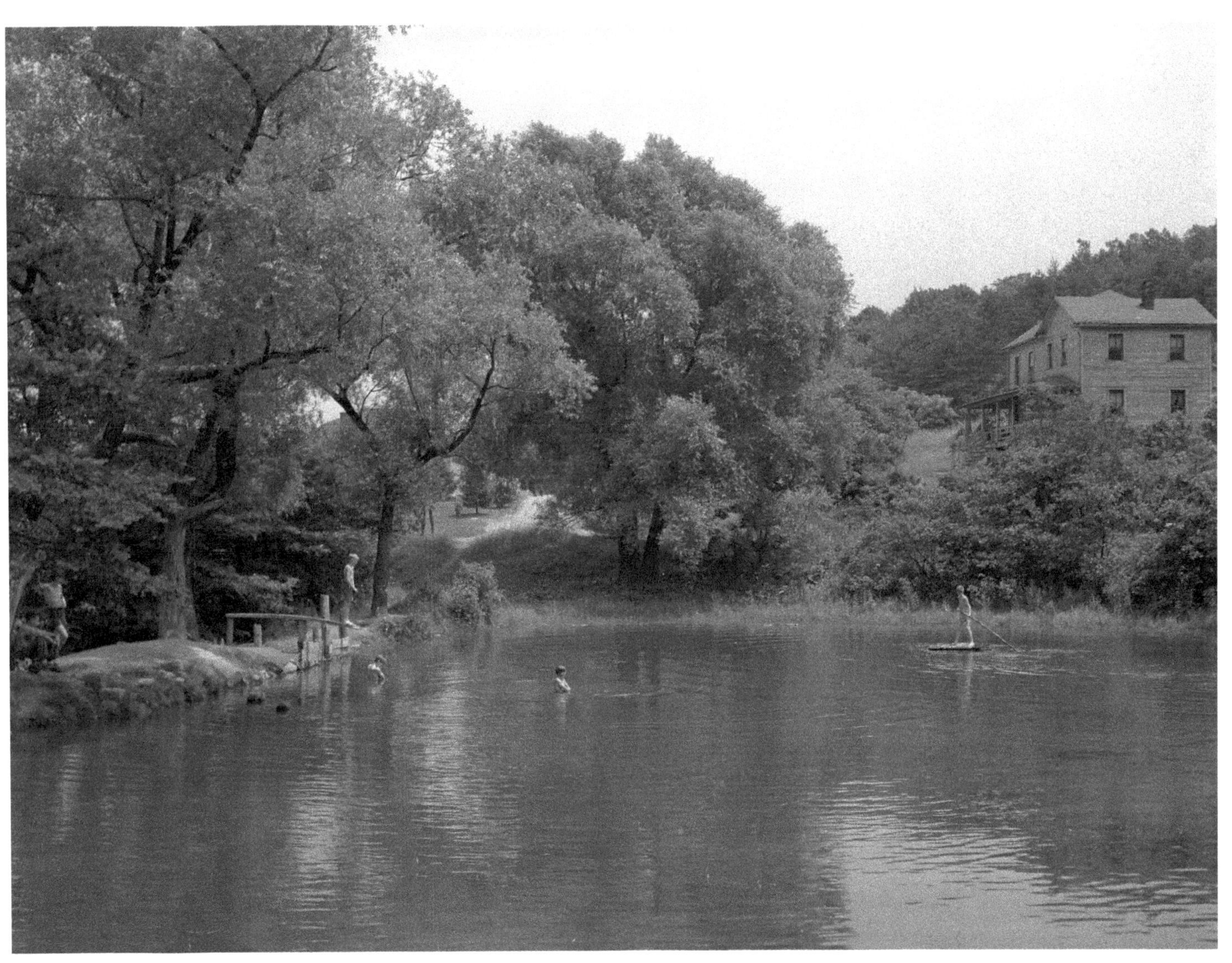

Local children enjoy a swimming hole in Pine Grove Mills, a small town at the center of the state, in July 1941.

In a dramatic explosion of sparks, iron is purified on its way to becoming stainless steel in a Bessemer converter at the Allegheny Ludlum Steel Corporation factory in Brackenridge, Allegheny County, circa 1941.

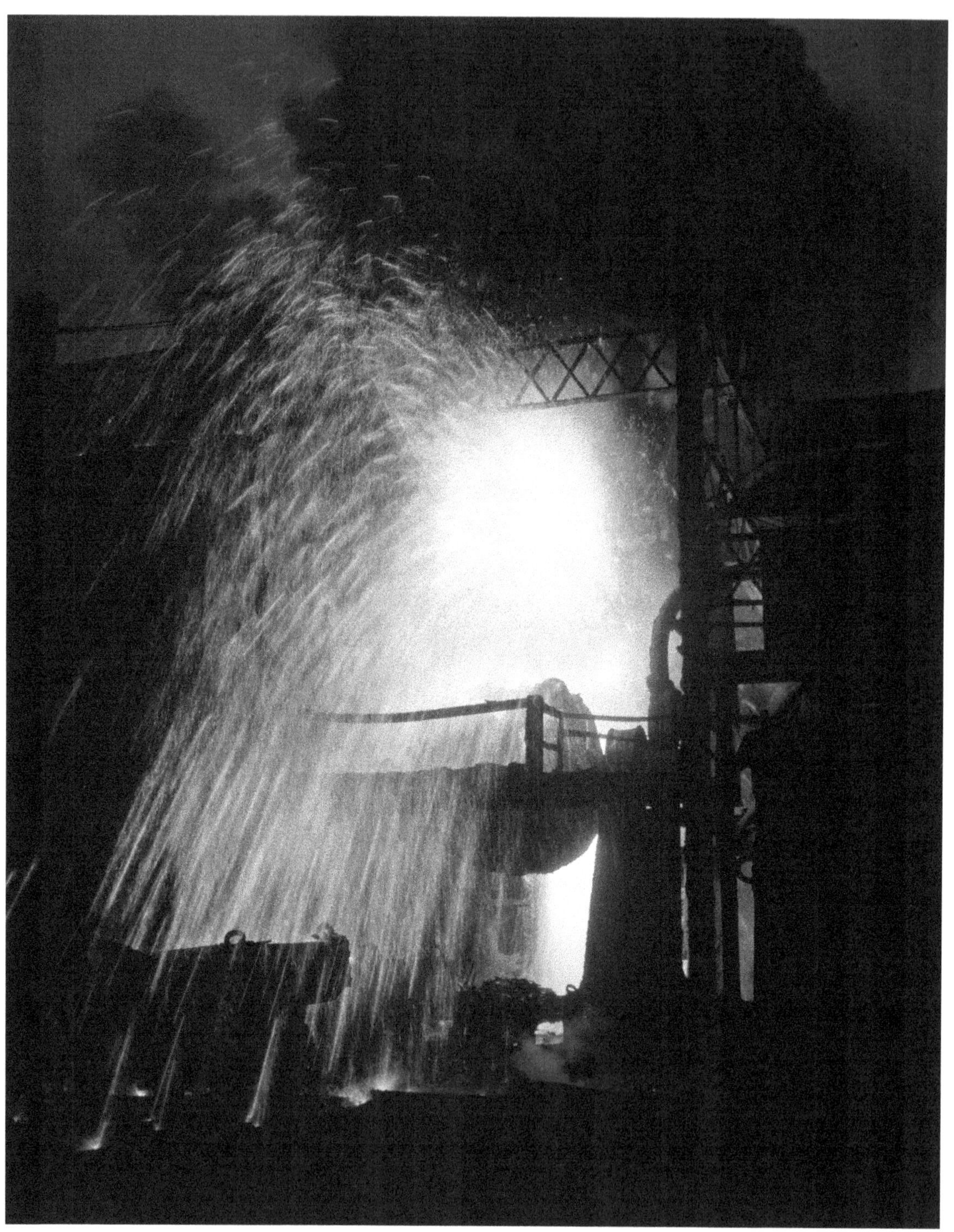

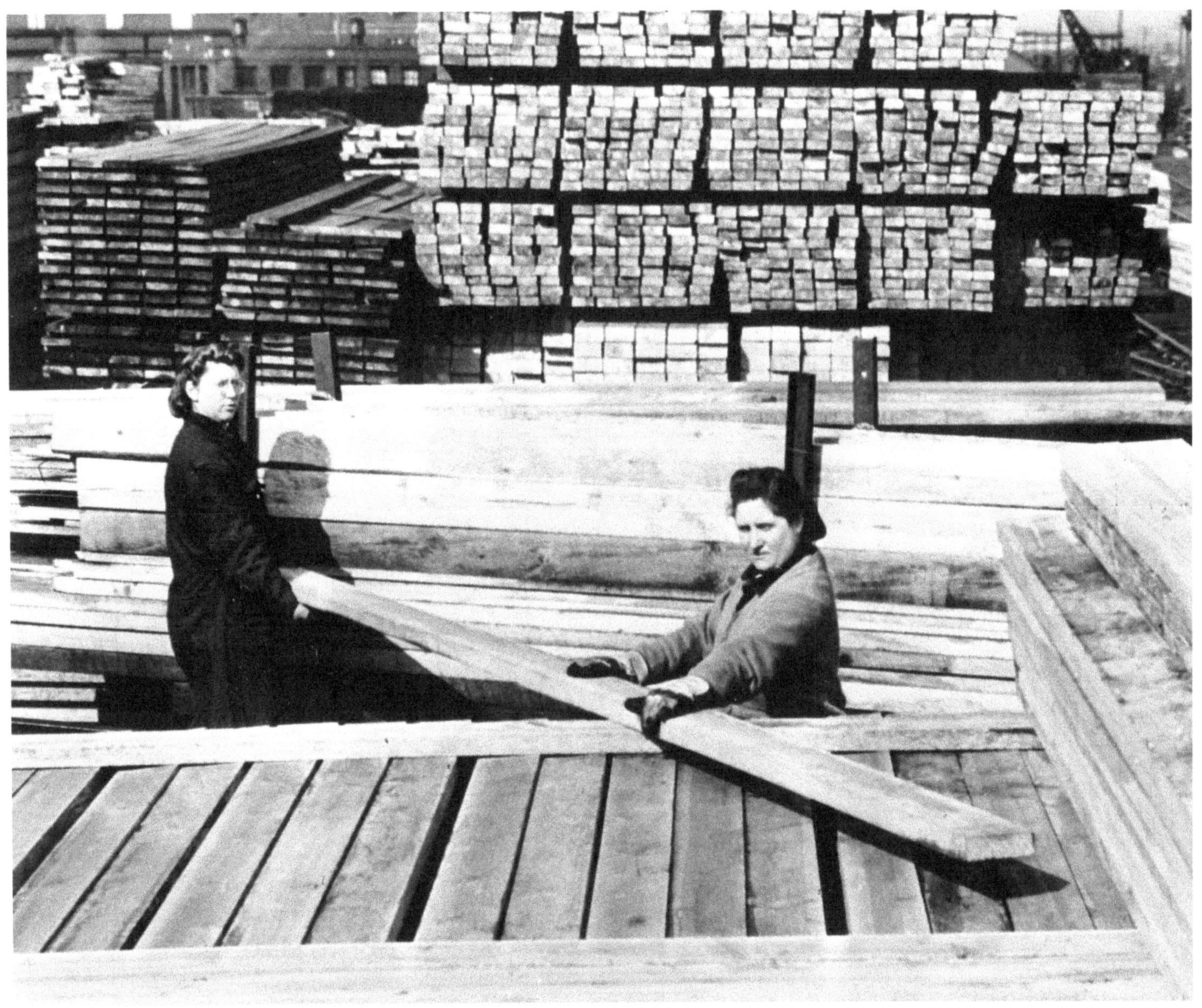

During World War II, women were recruited to work in all levels of industry. Here, two women unload lumber at a railroad yard in Reading.

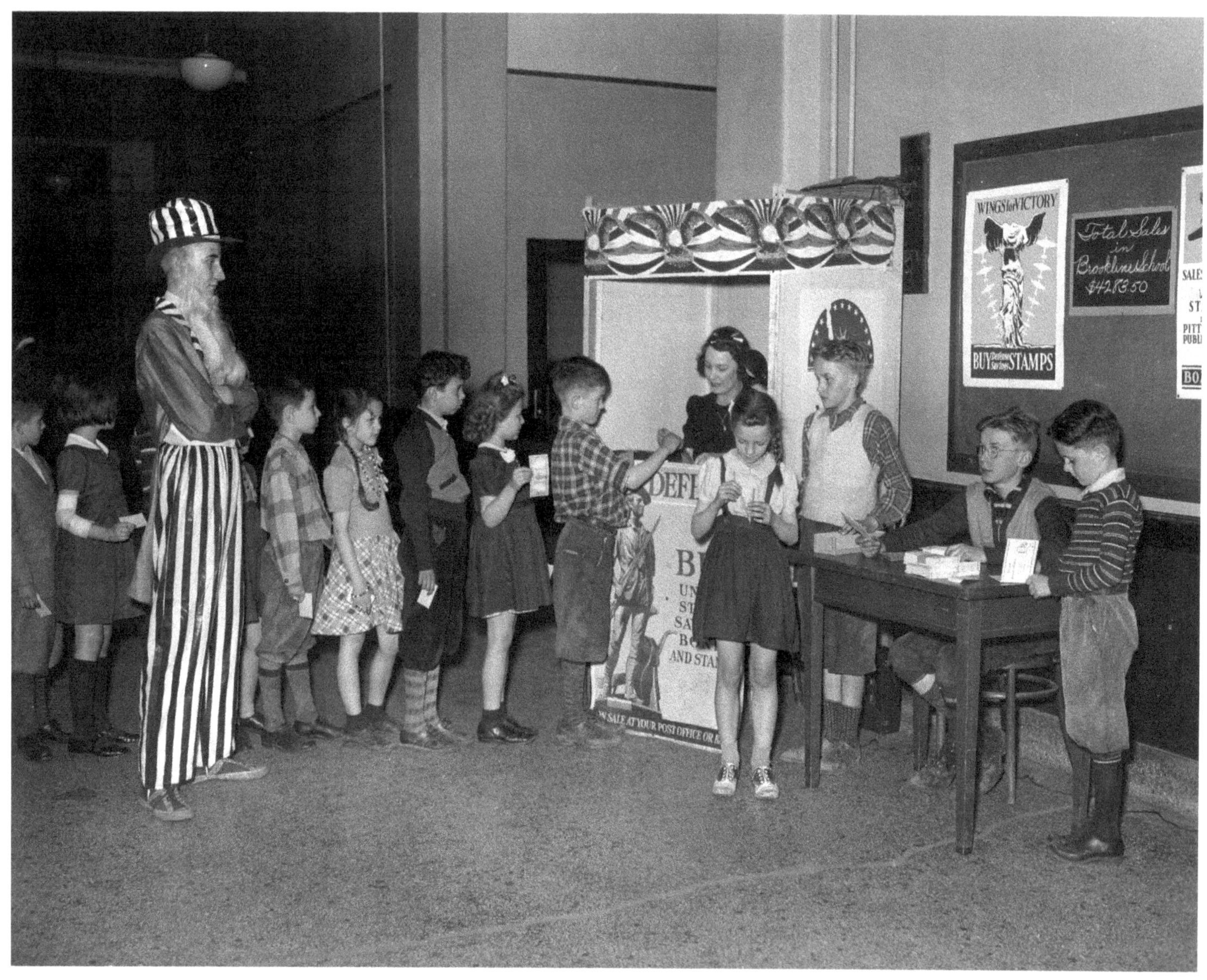

Schoolchildren wait in line to purchase bond stamps at Pittsburgh's Brookline Elementary School.

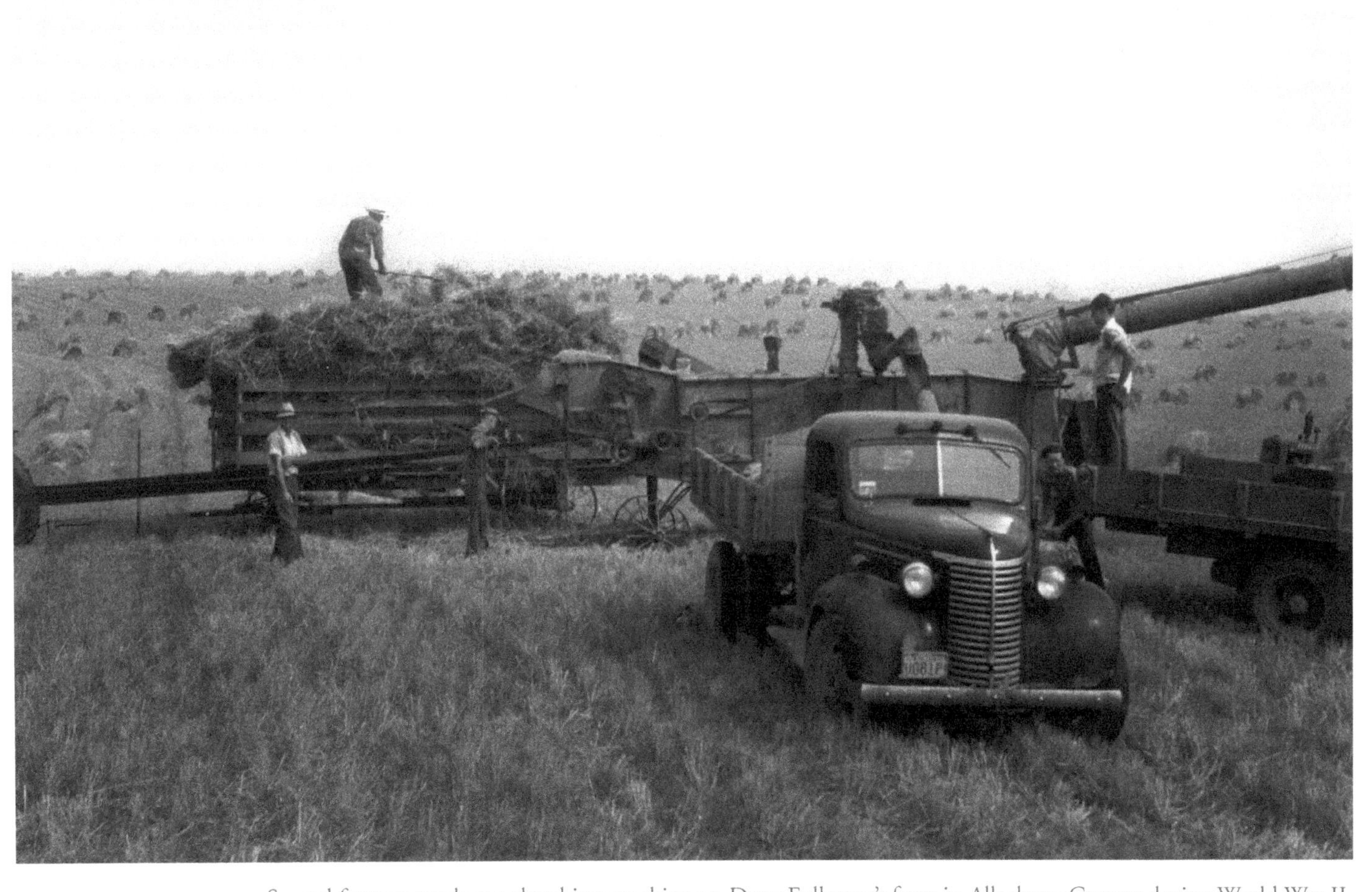

Several farmers work at a threshing machine on Dean Fullerton's farm in Allegheny County during World War II.

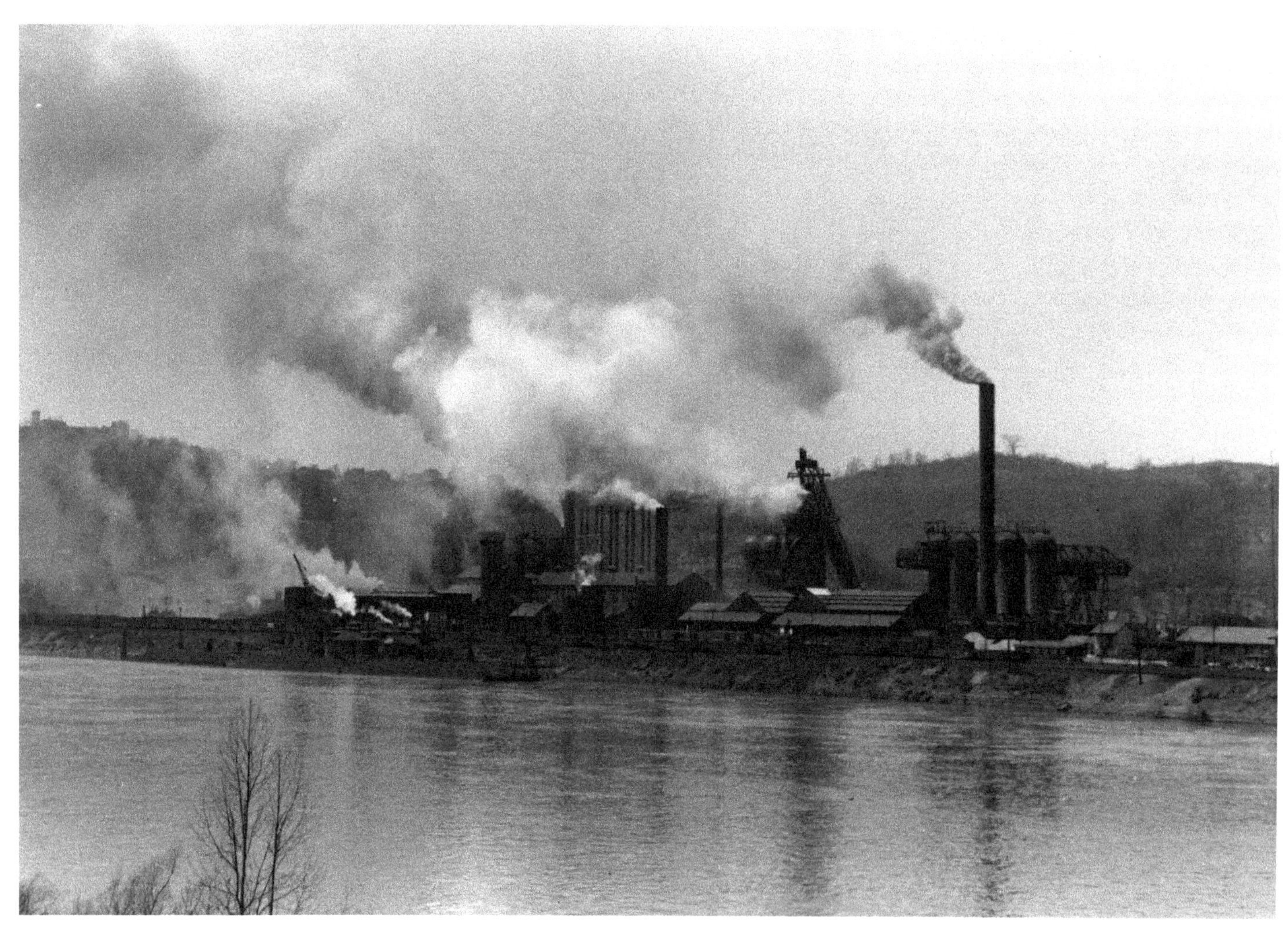

Eliza Furnace, part of the Jones and Laughlin Steel Corporation, along the Monongahela River. Dozens of plants like this one contributed to the infamous smog of Pittsburgh.

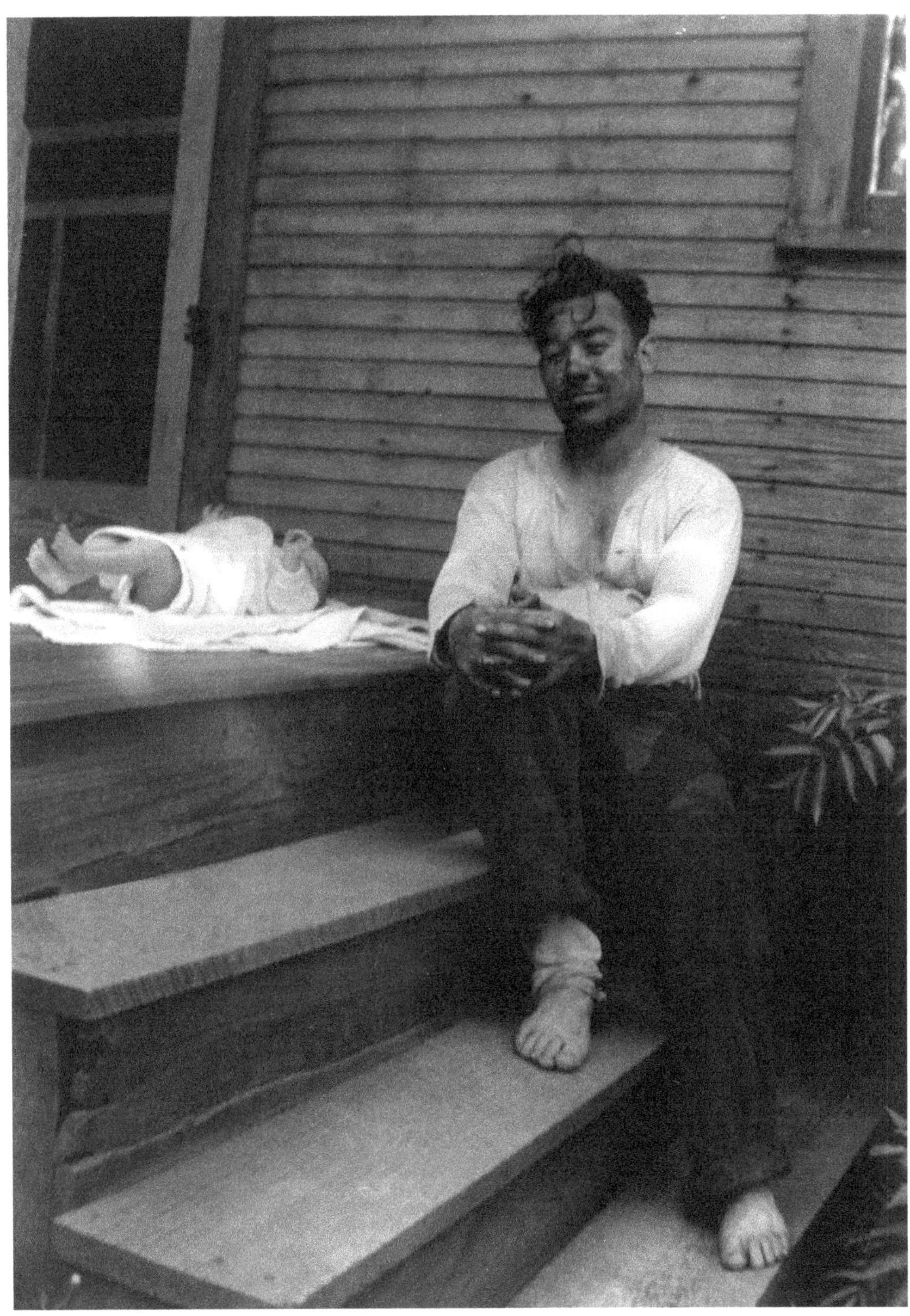

After a hard day's labor in the coal mines near Hendersonville, a miner of Slovakian ethnicity relaxes with his infant son on the porch of his home.

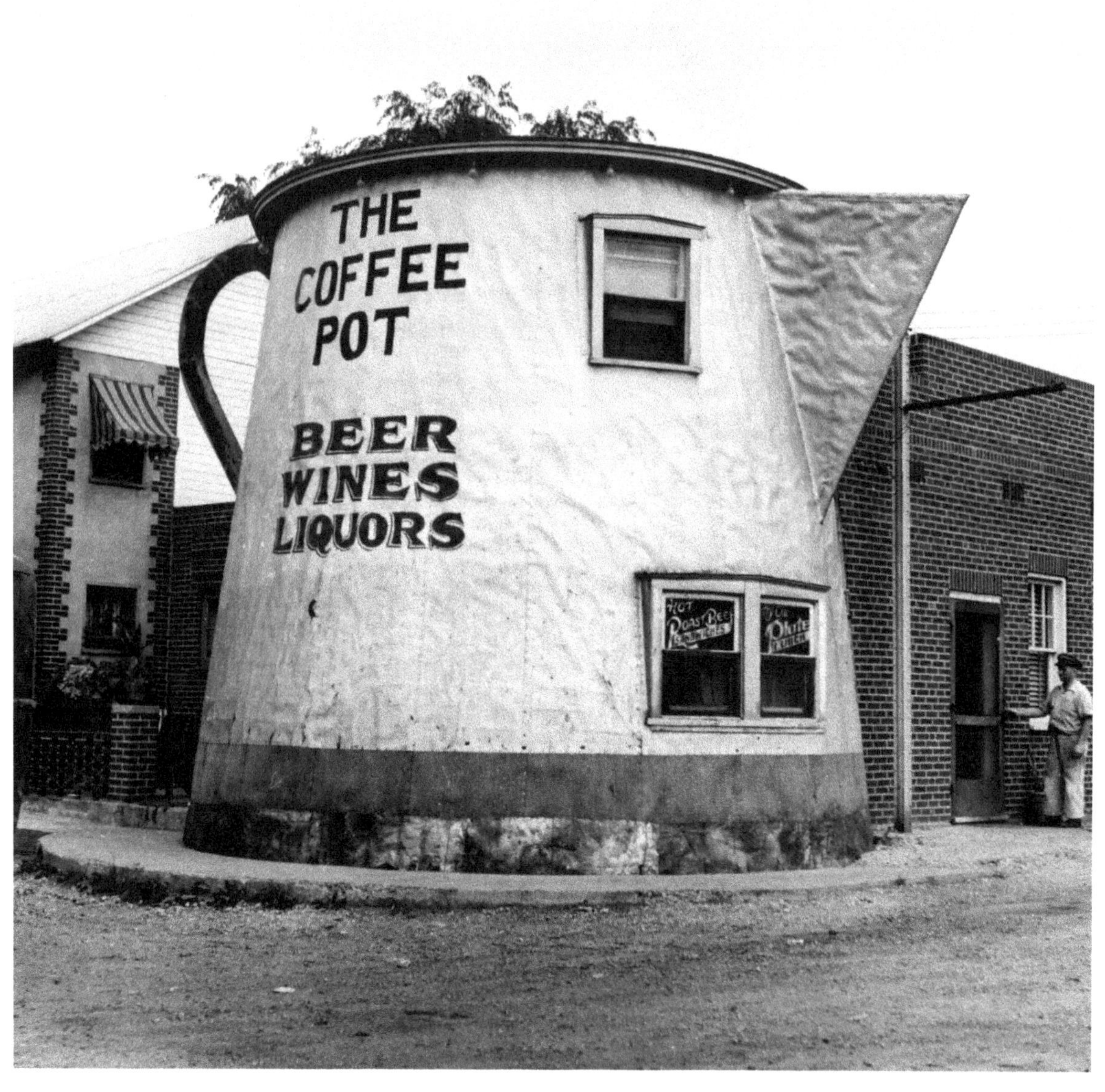

New Bedford's extraordinary Coffee Pot restaurant as it appeared in 1943. Opened in 1927, the unique spot served travelers along the Lincoln Highway (Route 30). Facing demolition in the late 1990s, it was saved by a local preservation group and moved to the nearby Lawrence County fairgrounds in 2004.

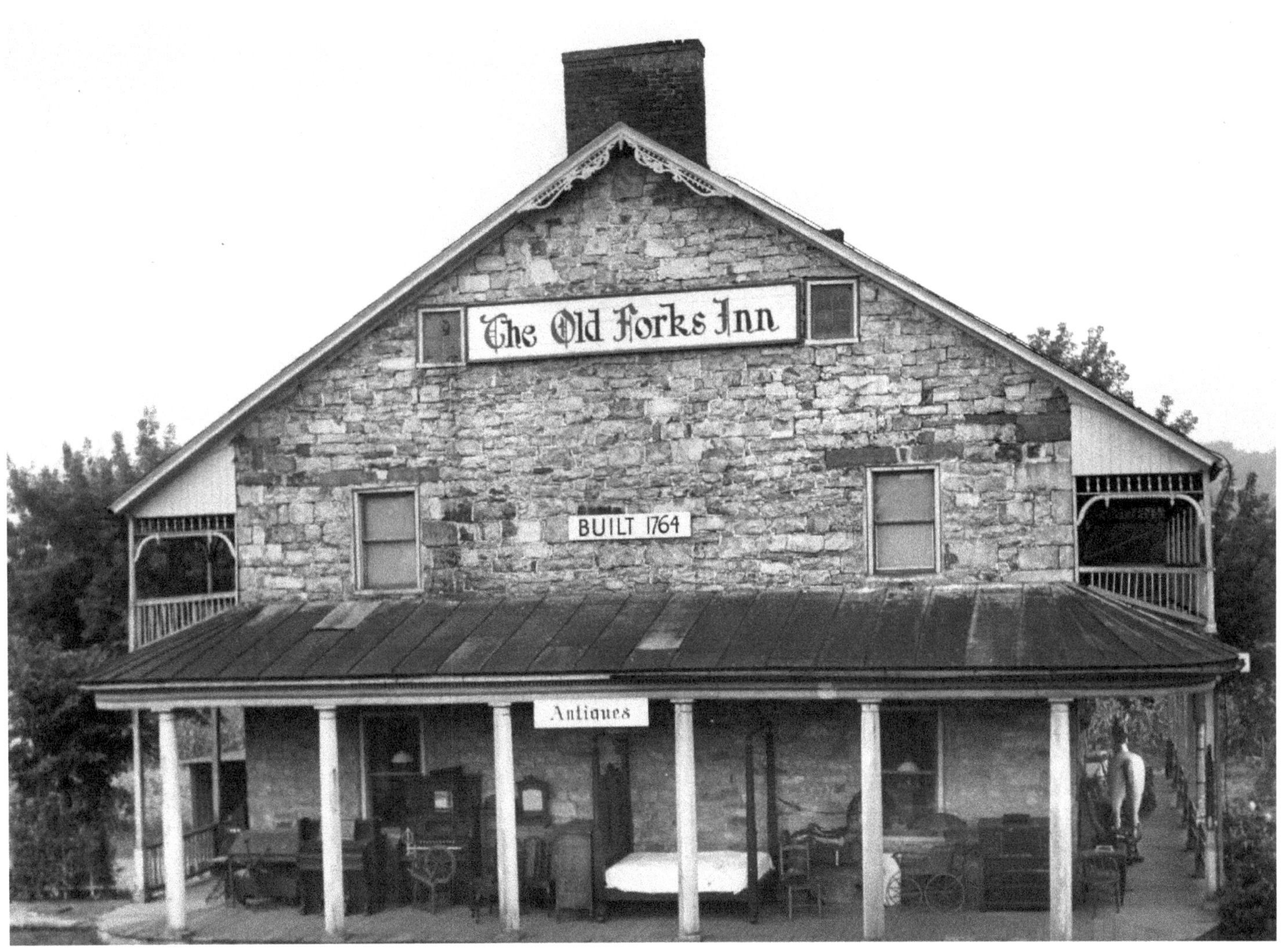

The Old Forks Inn in Bedford as it appeared in 1944. Originally known as the Bonnet Tavern, and recently designated a National Historic Landmark, the eighteenth-century tavern remains a popular bed-and-breakfast and restaurant.

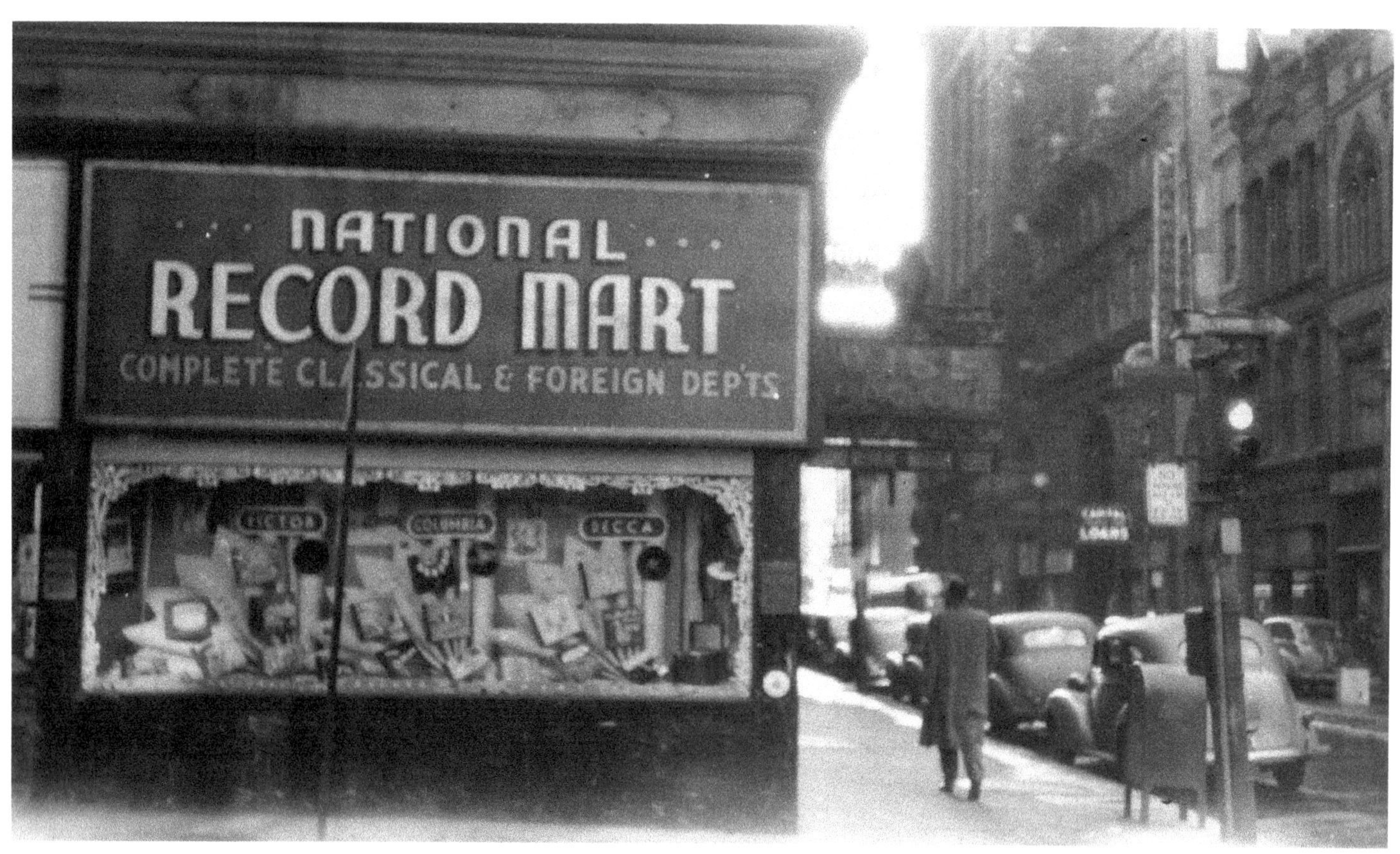

The nation's first music store chain, the National Record Mart was established in Pittsburgh in 1937 as Jitterbug Records. Specializing in prerecorded music, the now defunct company once operated more than 170 stores in 30 states.

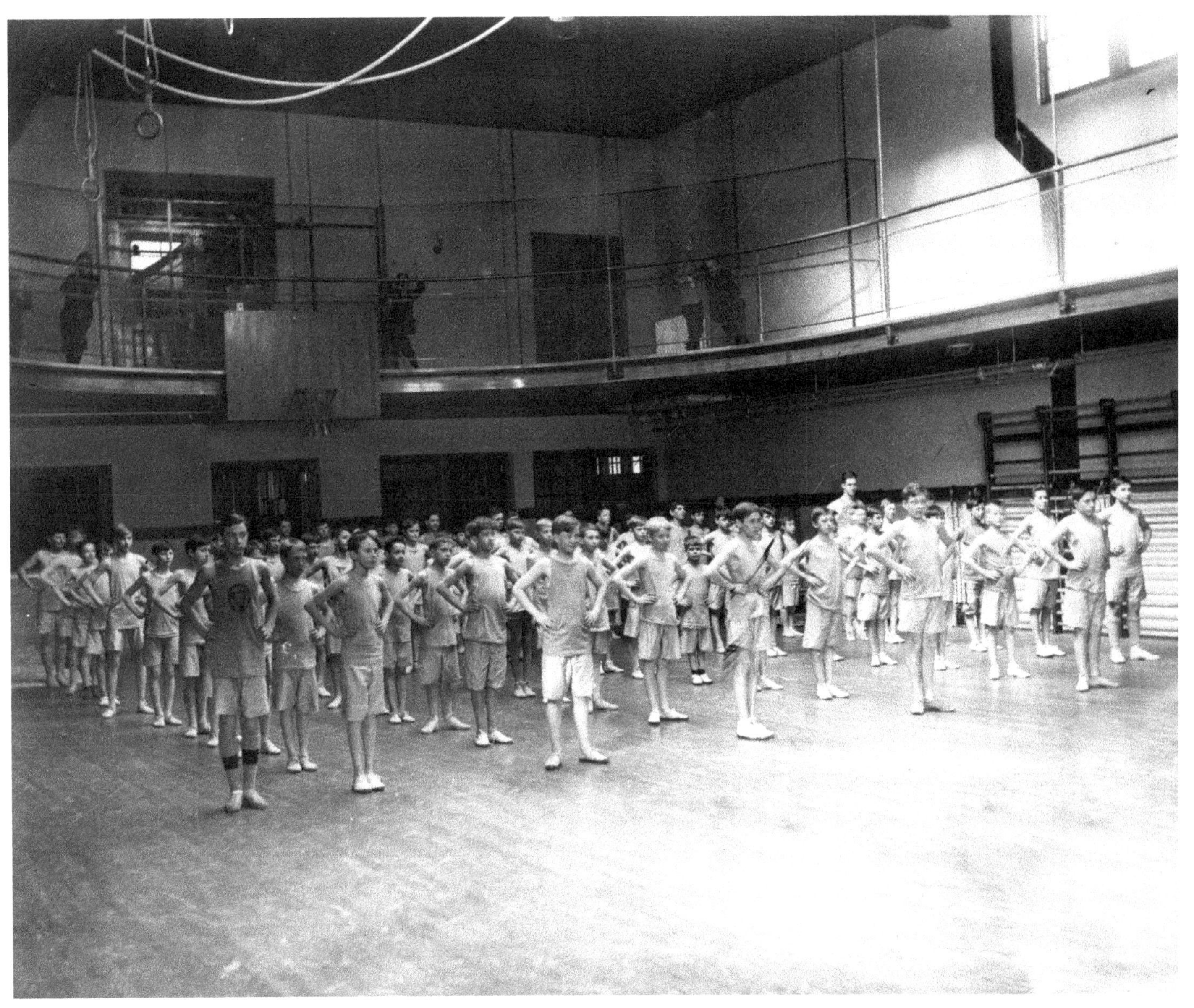

Boys participate in a fitness class at the Young Men's Christian Association in Warren, circa 1945.

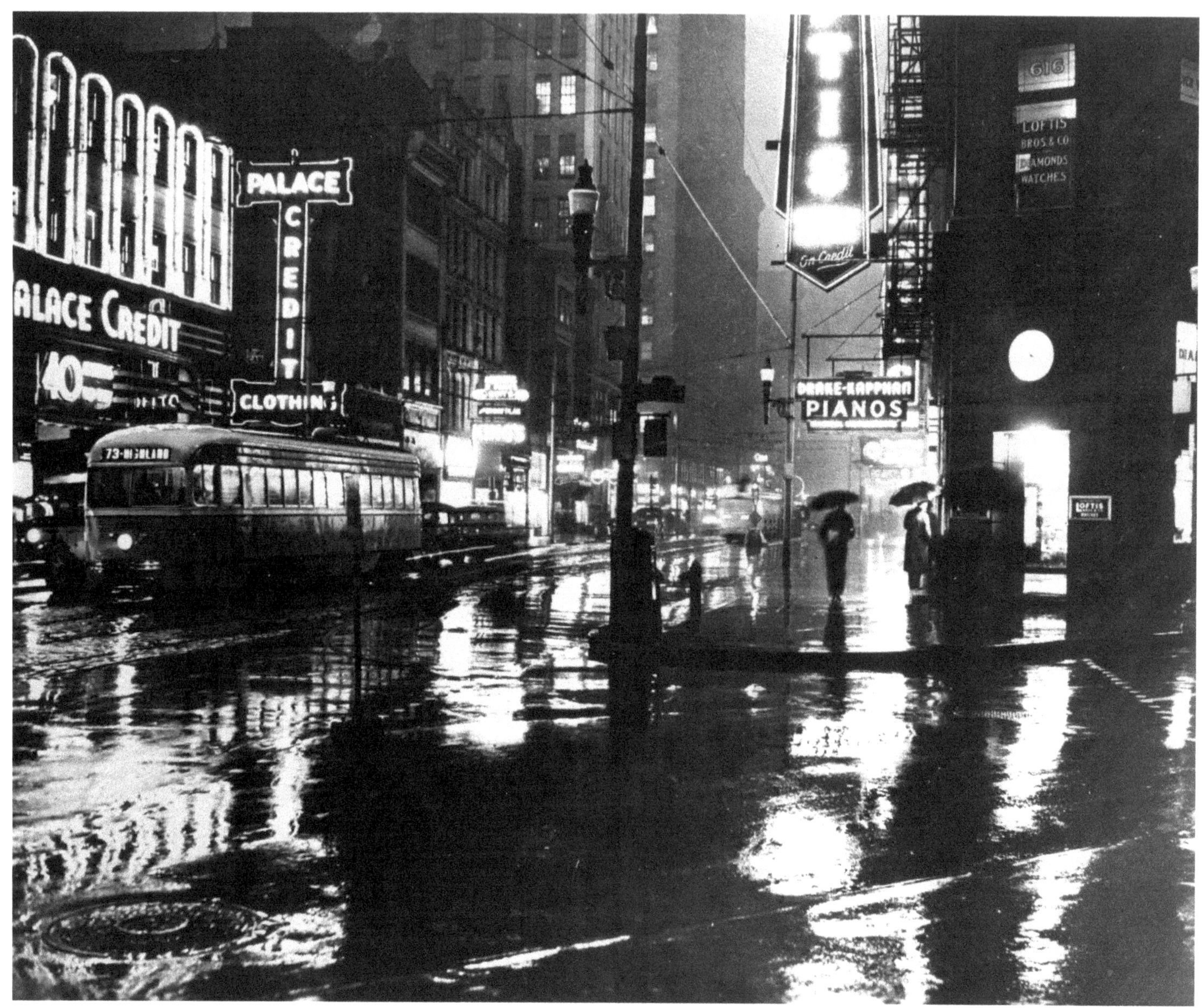

The nighttime appearance of this scene on the streets of Pittsburgh in 1945 is deceptive: the photograph was taken at 9:30 A.M. Mornings like this ultimately resulted in the implementation of "smoke control" policies and a mandatory shift in most homes and businesses from coal heat to natural gas.

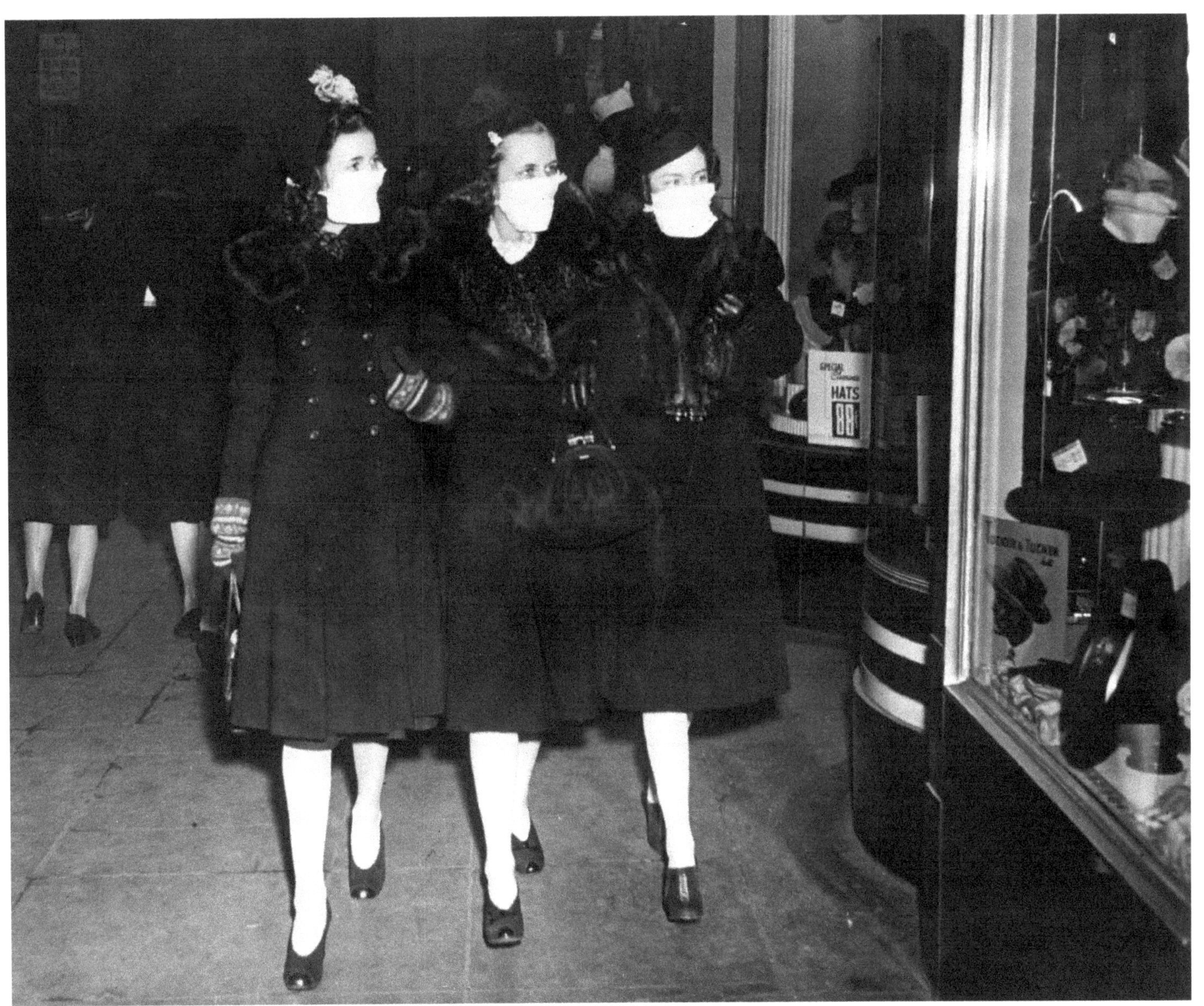

Three women wear surgical masks in response to high levels of pollution and smoke in Pittsburgh in the mid-1940s.

A Gulf service station attendant greets a customer in 1949.

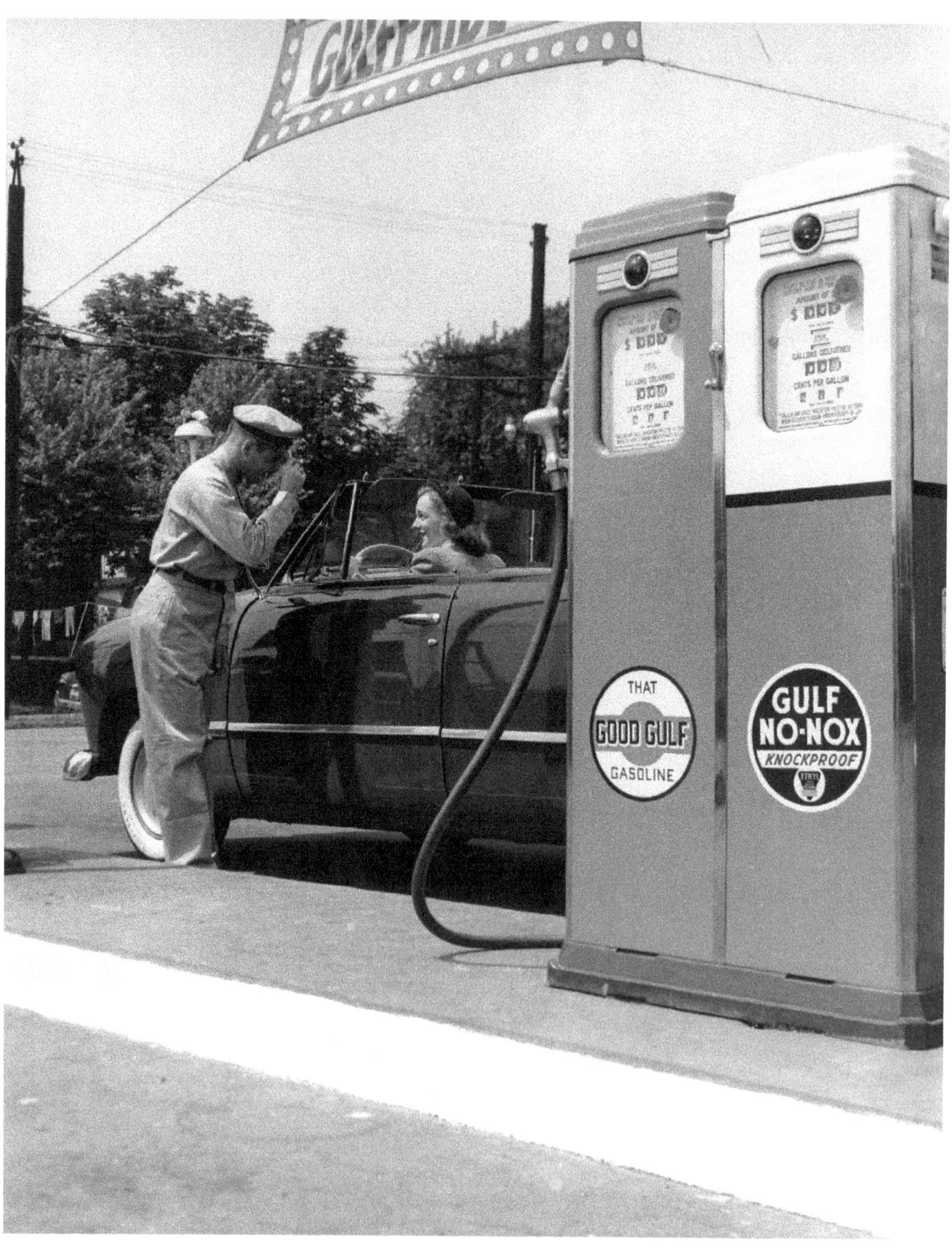

STRENGTH THROUGH CHANGE

(1950–1980)

Pennsylvania experienced the years following World War II as a time of suburbanization, growth of the middle class, and economic innovation. New housing developments crowded around cities as people sought the lawns and picket fences of their dreams. An additional 1,500 miles of interstate highway allowed for easy access to all regions of the state, unintentionally encouraging abandonment of older urban centers. Colleges and universities, long a vital element in the state's cultural and political identity, grew exponentially as thousands of men and women strove to improve their prospects. As traditional industries declined once again in a postwar economy, pioneering steps were taken in the fields of chemical manufacture, food production and processing, and electrical engineering, bringing diversity to Pennsylvania's economy.

But even as new opportunities came to light, conflict and divisiveness presented new challenges. Historically adversarial labor relations became even more so as coal and steel workers initiated strikes in hopes of achieving better quality of life through health care, pensions, and guaranteed career paths. Coal, once the primary fuel source for heating homes, fell victim to growing concerns about occupational safety and air quality. The concurrent rise in nuclear technology led to Pennsylvania building the first commercial nuclear power plant in 1957, and an additional four plants by 1970. However, fears about the safety of nuclear power were realized with the 1979 partial core meltdown of one reactor at Three Mile Island. Railroads, long a well-known state asset, faced the advent of the trucking industry and the subsequent reduction in the need for rail freight.

Ultimately, these decades would test Pennsylvania's ability to evolve, to bring innovative change to an aging infrastructure. Some would fail, such as Bethlehem Steel, the Penn Central Railroad, and much of the anthracite coal industry. Others in the agricultural, medical, and educational industries would succeed in spite of high competition and high costs. Unions, facing stagnant growth among the traditional manufacturing industries, would find new energy within the growing number of white-collar and service-sector workers. Today, public institutions thrive under the careful stewardship of committed and talented leadership, and hundreds of thousands of visitors come from all over the world to enjoy the state's many historical and cultural attractions. Pennsylvania remains a national leader in industry, agriculture, education, and the arts and culture, in a reflection of its storied past, vibrant present, and hopeful future.

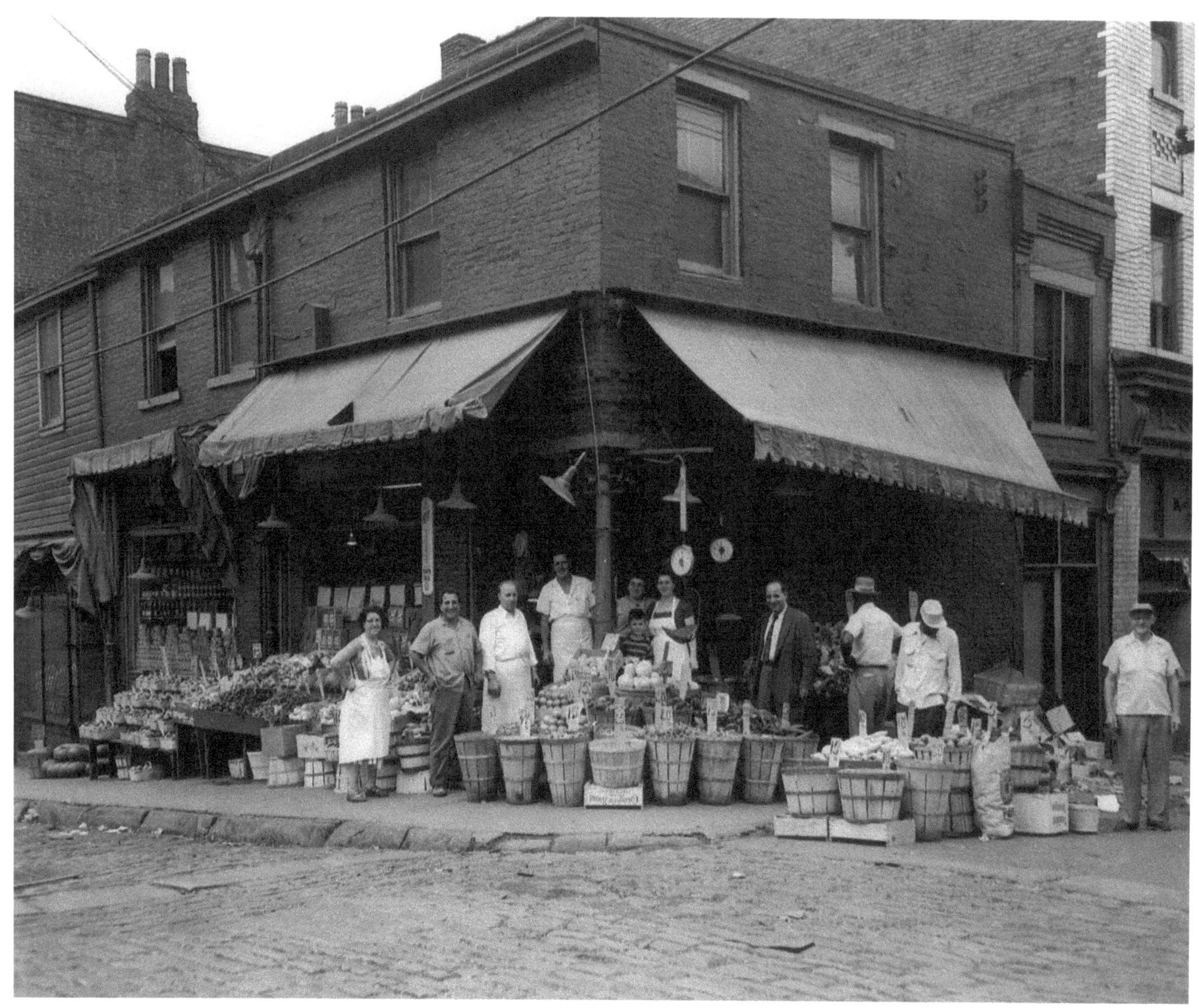

Initially drawn by the possibility of work in the many coal mines, steel factories, and railroads of late-nineteenth-century western Pennsylvania, Italians formed the single largest immigrant group in the region, establishing communities and services such as Marasco's Grocery in the Hill District in Pittsburgh, seen here circa 1950.

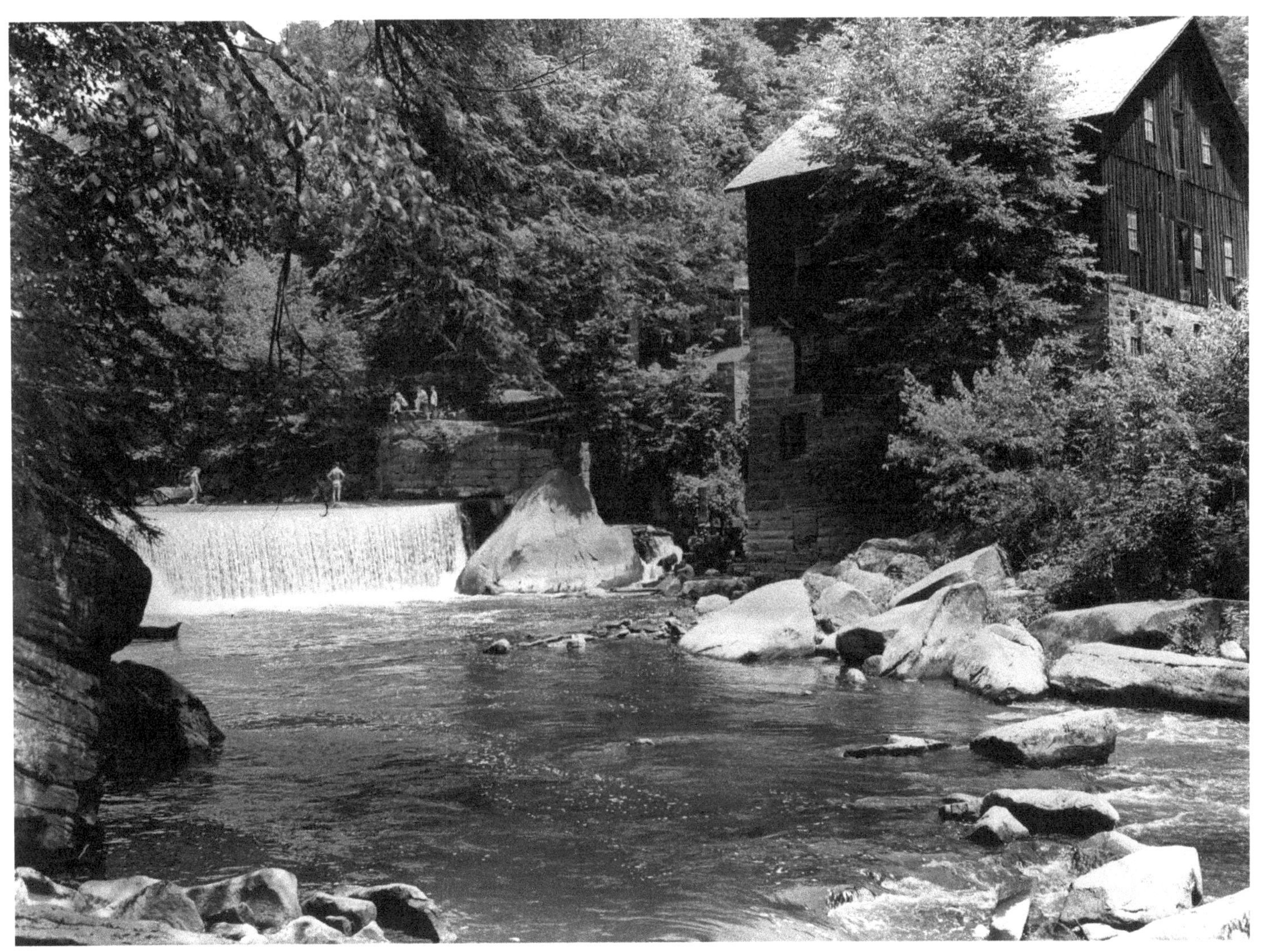

McConnell's Mill State Park, in Lawrence County, no longer permits swimming in Slippery Rock Creek, but in this photo from 1951, visitors enjoy a moment in the mill pond.

A popular destination for school picnics in the 1950s, Kennywood Amusement Park outside Pittsburgh continues to draw thousands of students and families every year. Here, children ride the Racer roller coaster.

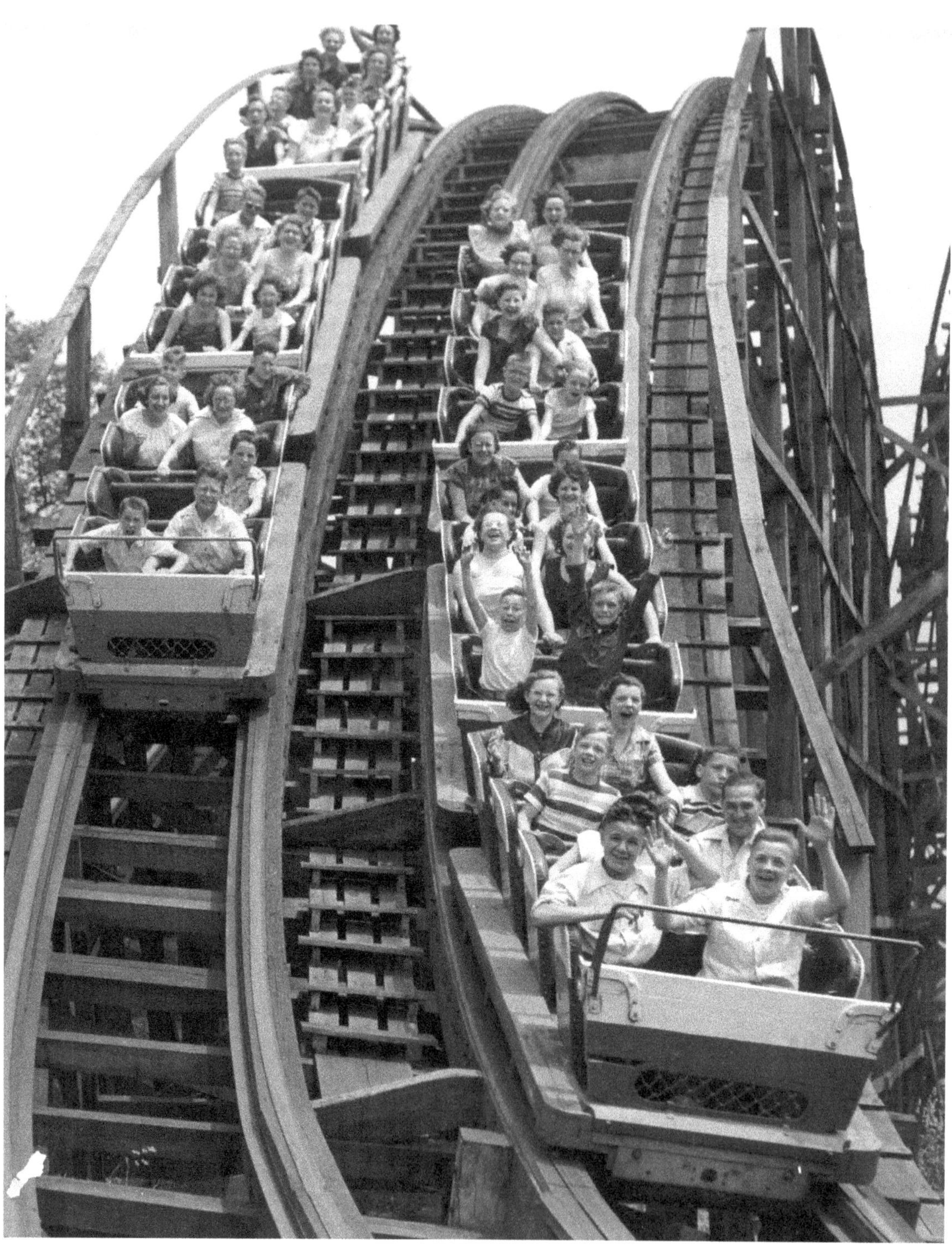

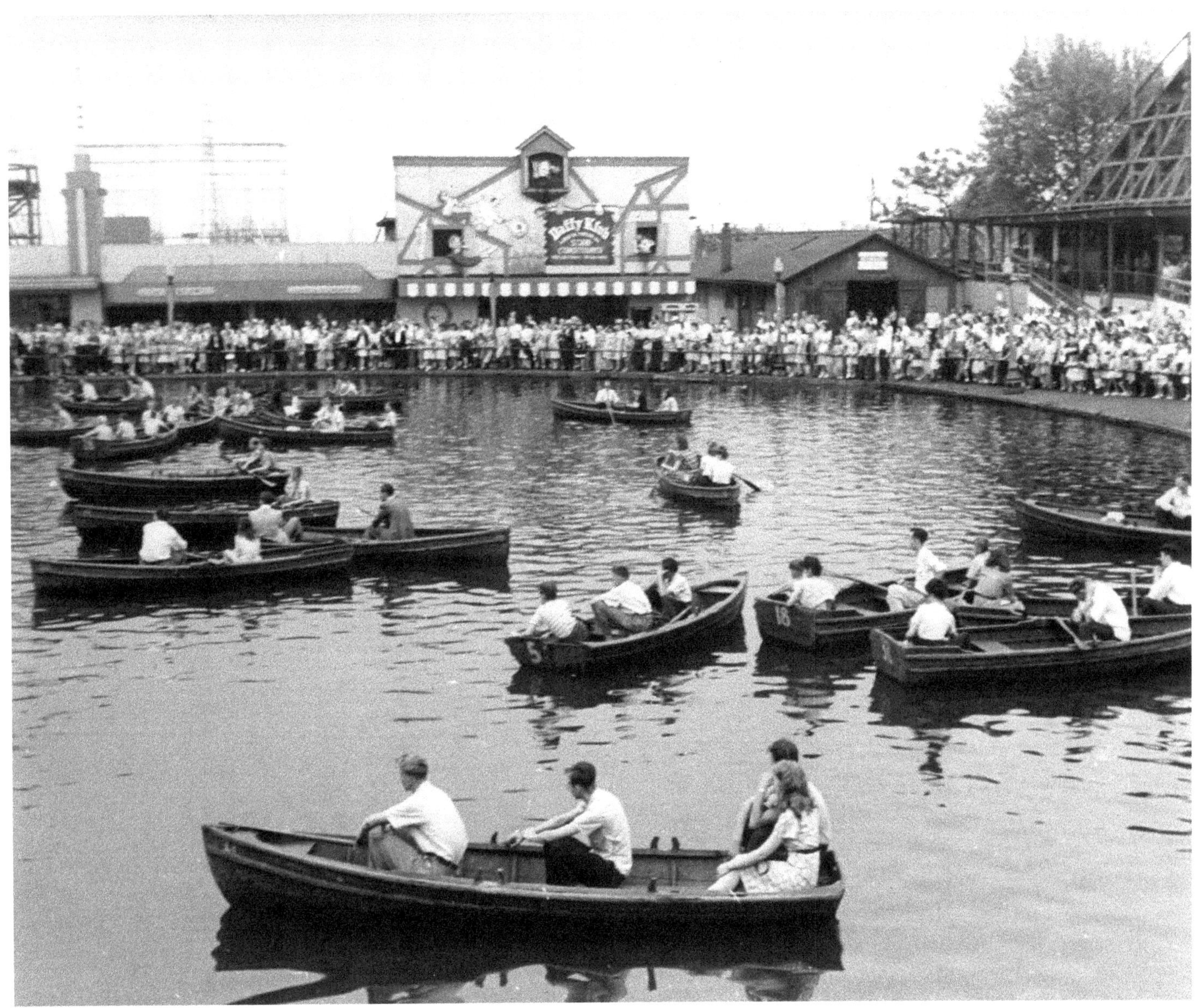

The oldest amusement park in the Pittsburgh area, Kennywood Park featured a casino, a merry-go-round, amusement rides, and a man-made lake for rowboating.

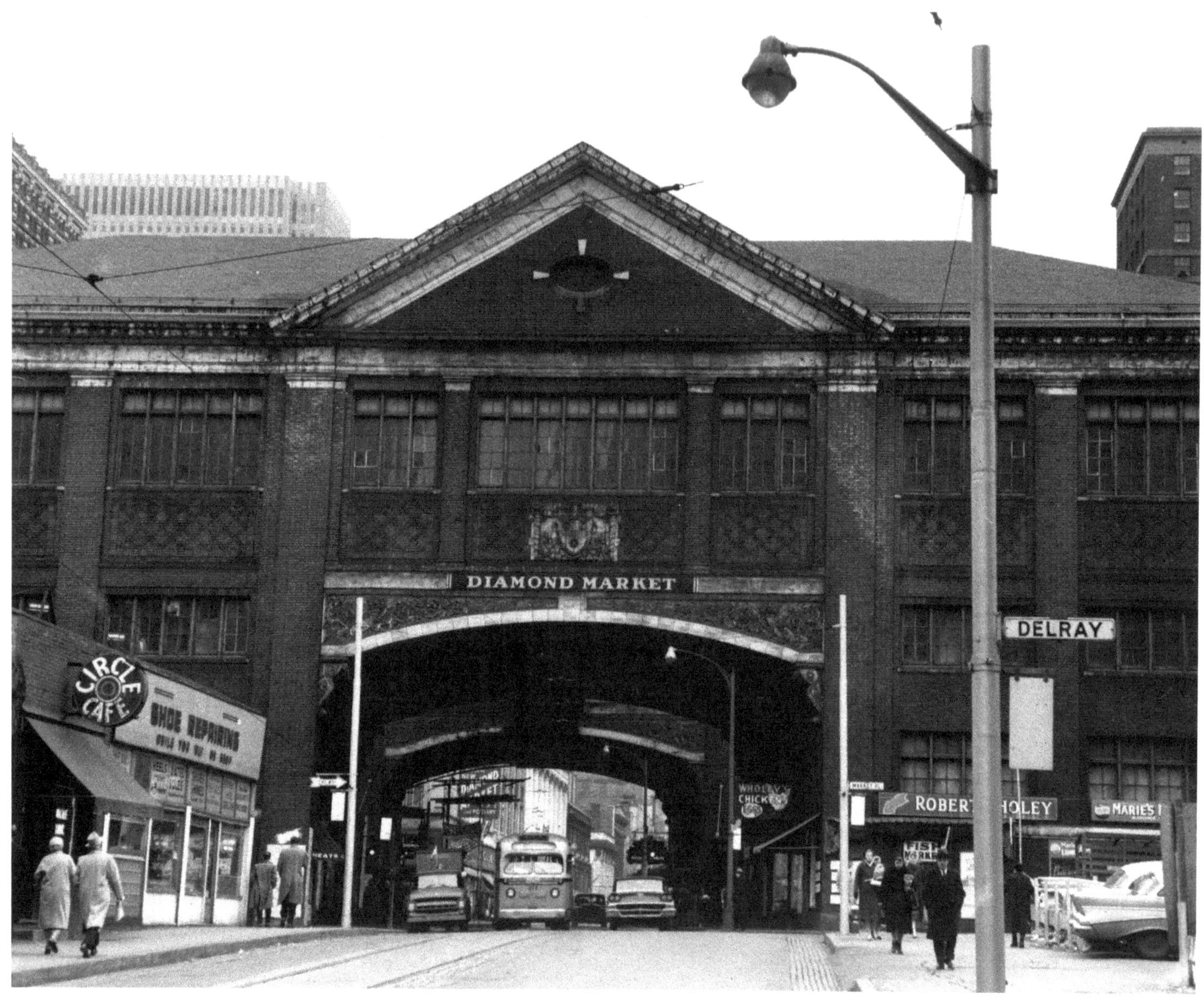

Replaced by the current Market Square farmers' market in the same location, the Diamond Market in Pittsburgh served the local community from 1917 to 1961.

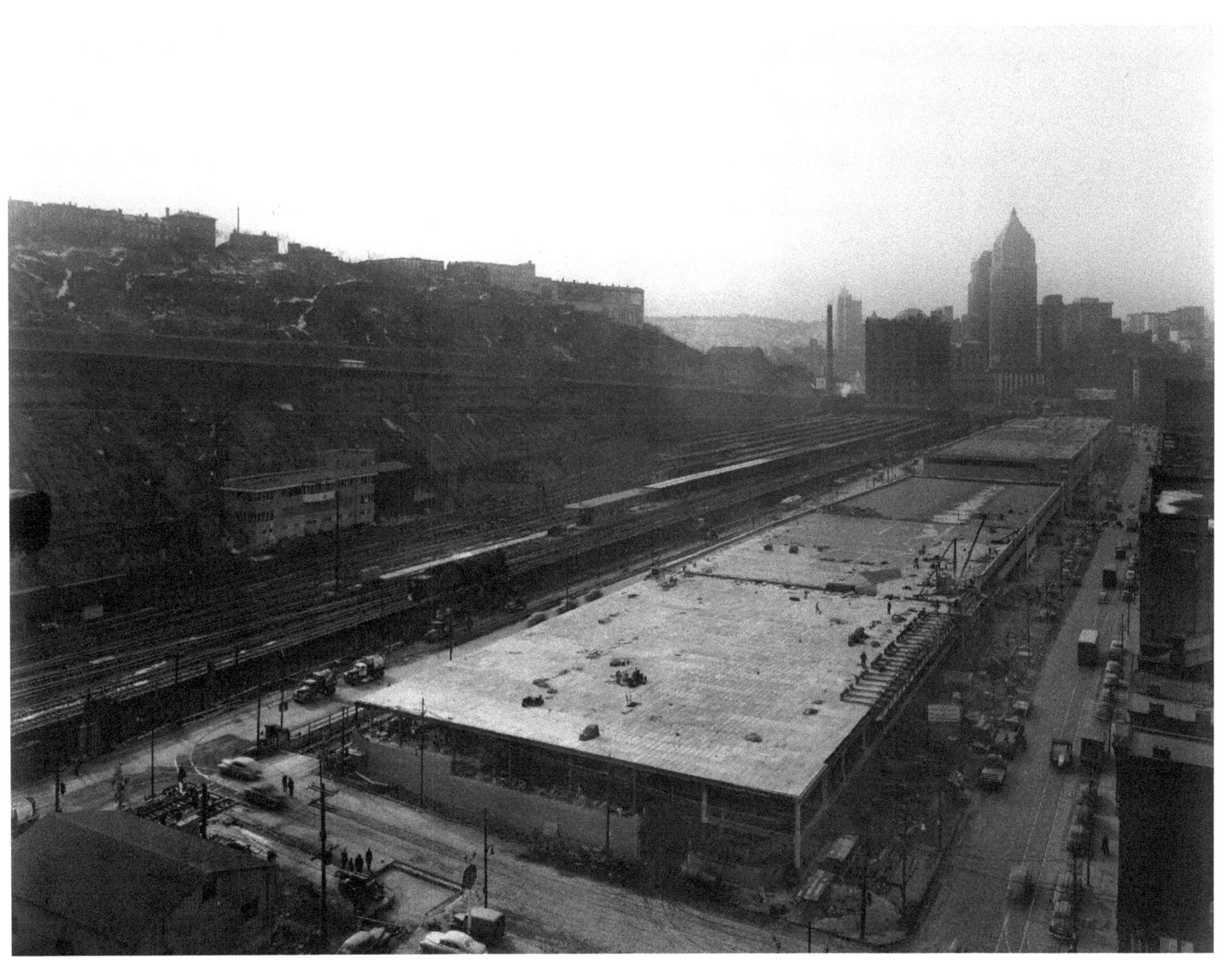

Massive commercial warehouses constructed by the Pennsylvania Railroad in the Strip District of Pittsburgh offered more than half a million square feet of storage. The buildings are still in use as corporate offices.

A view east on Hamilton Street in Allentown toward "The Tower," headquarters of Pennsylvania Power and Light, February 23, 1952. Designed by architect Harvey Corbett and completed in 1928, the art-deco structure was a precursor to similar skyscrapers designed by Corbett for New York City, including Rockefeller Center.

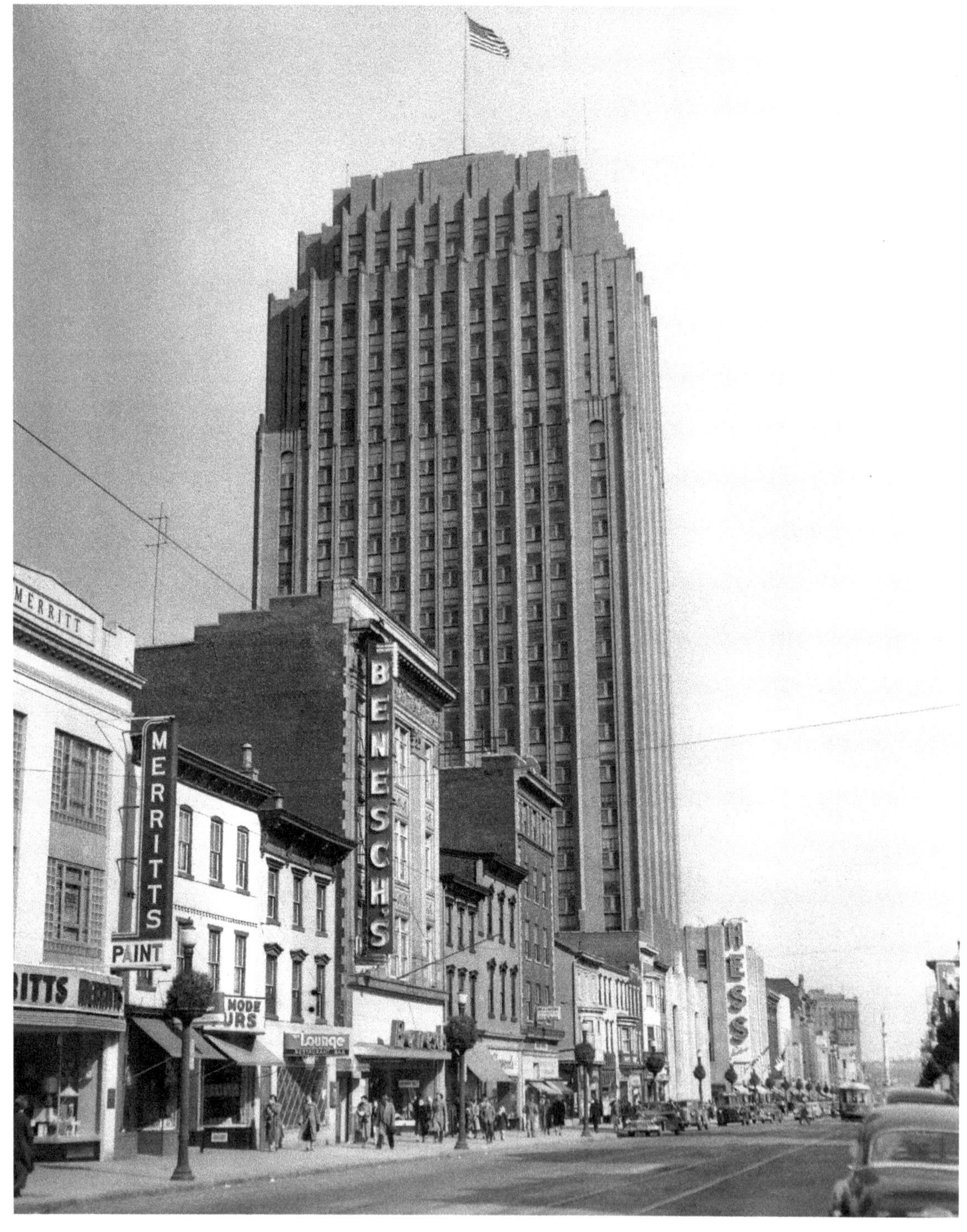

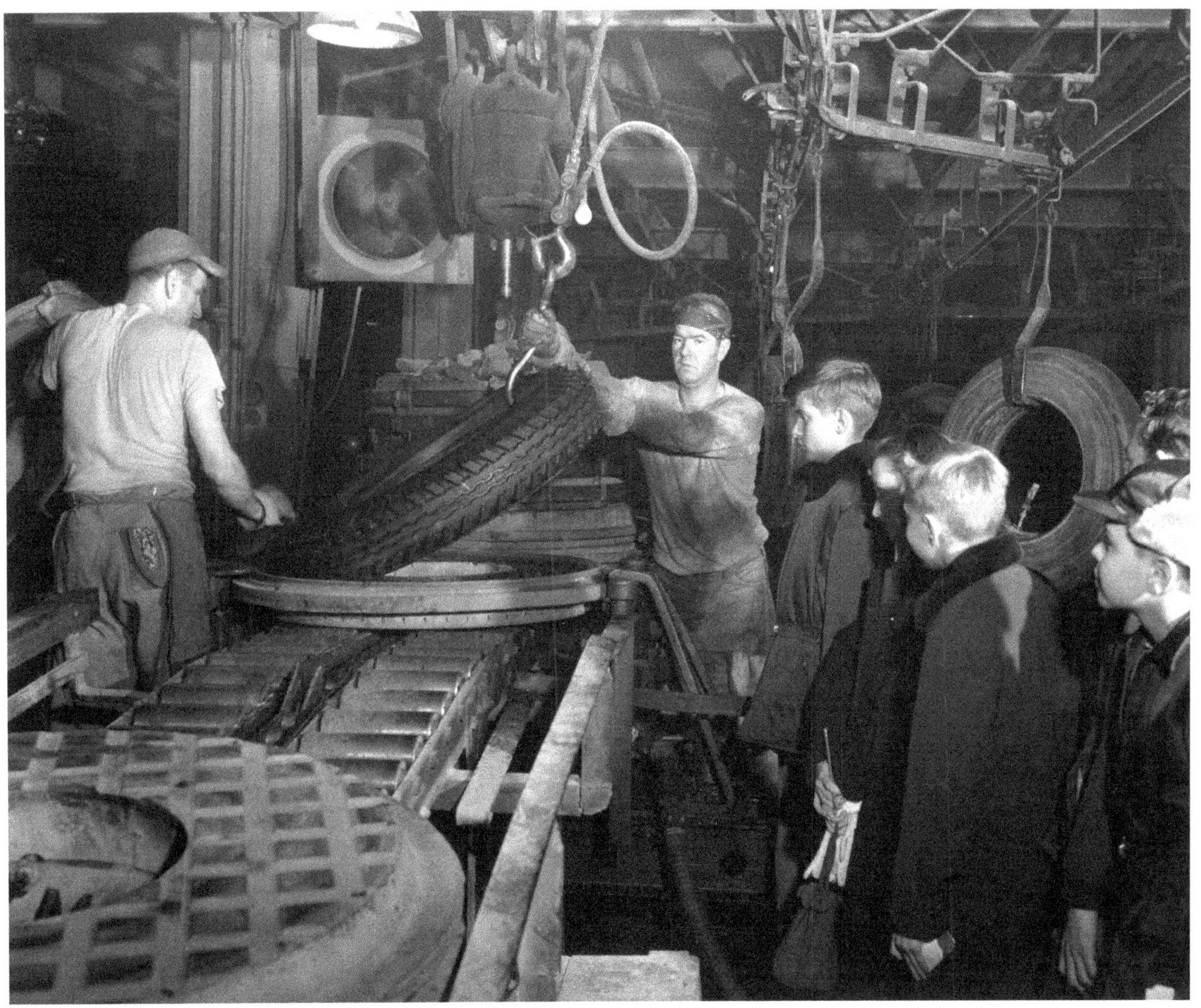

Students from local elementary schools visit the Lee Tire Company in Conshohocken, January 10, 1952. Lee Tires were produced in Conshohocken until 1963; production resumed from 1965 to 1978 under the auspices of Goodyear Tire & Rubber Company.

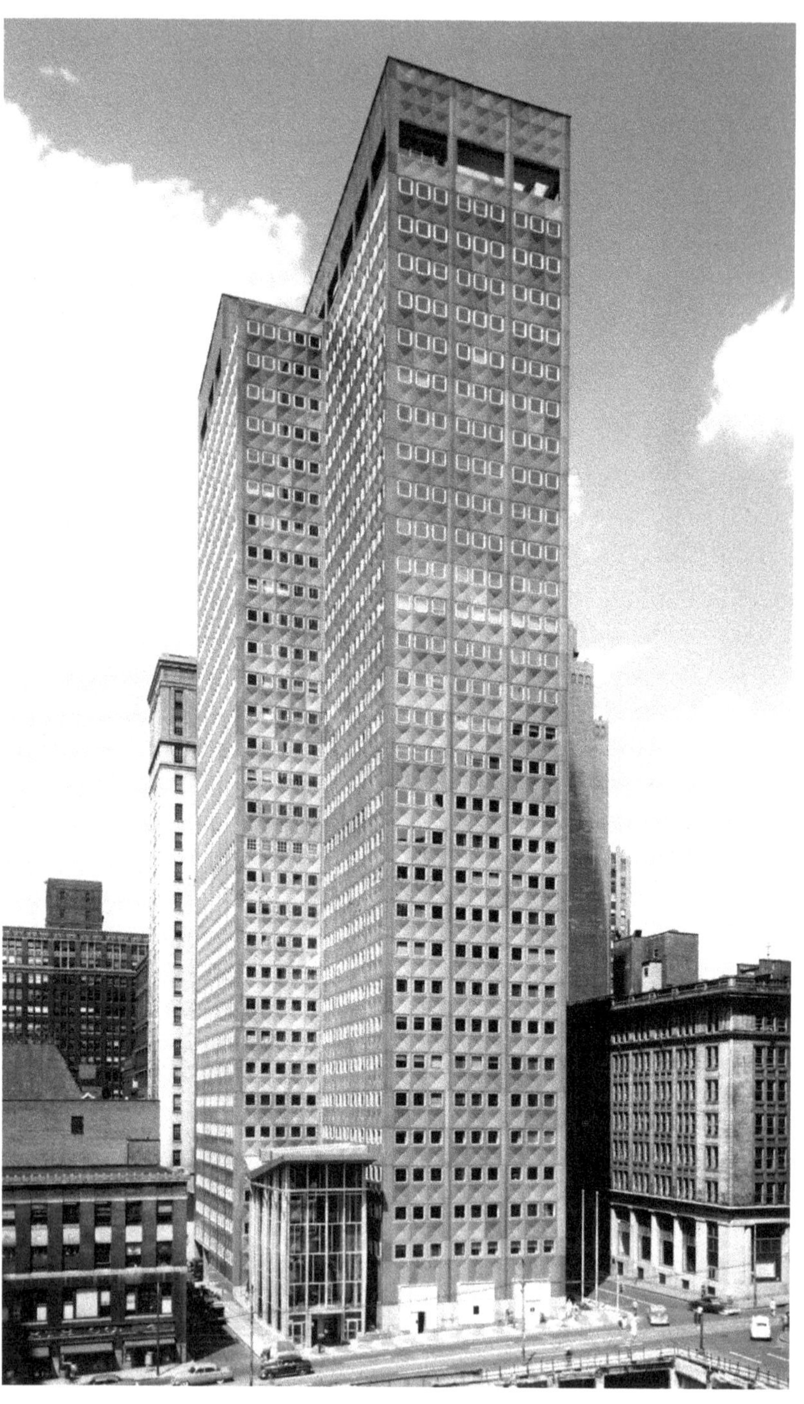

The Alcoa Building in downtown Pittsburgh, as it neared completion in 1953. Designed to fully incorporate the use of aluminum in its structure, from facade to utilities, the building served as headquarters for the Aluminum Company of America (ALCOA) until the late 1990s.

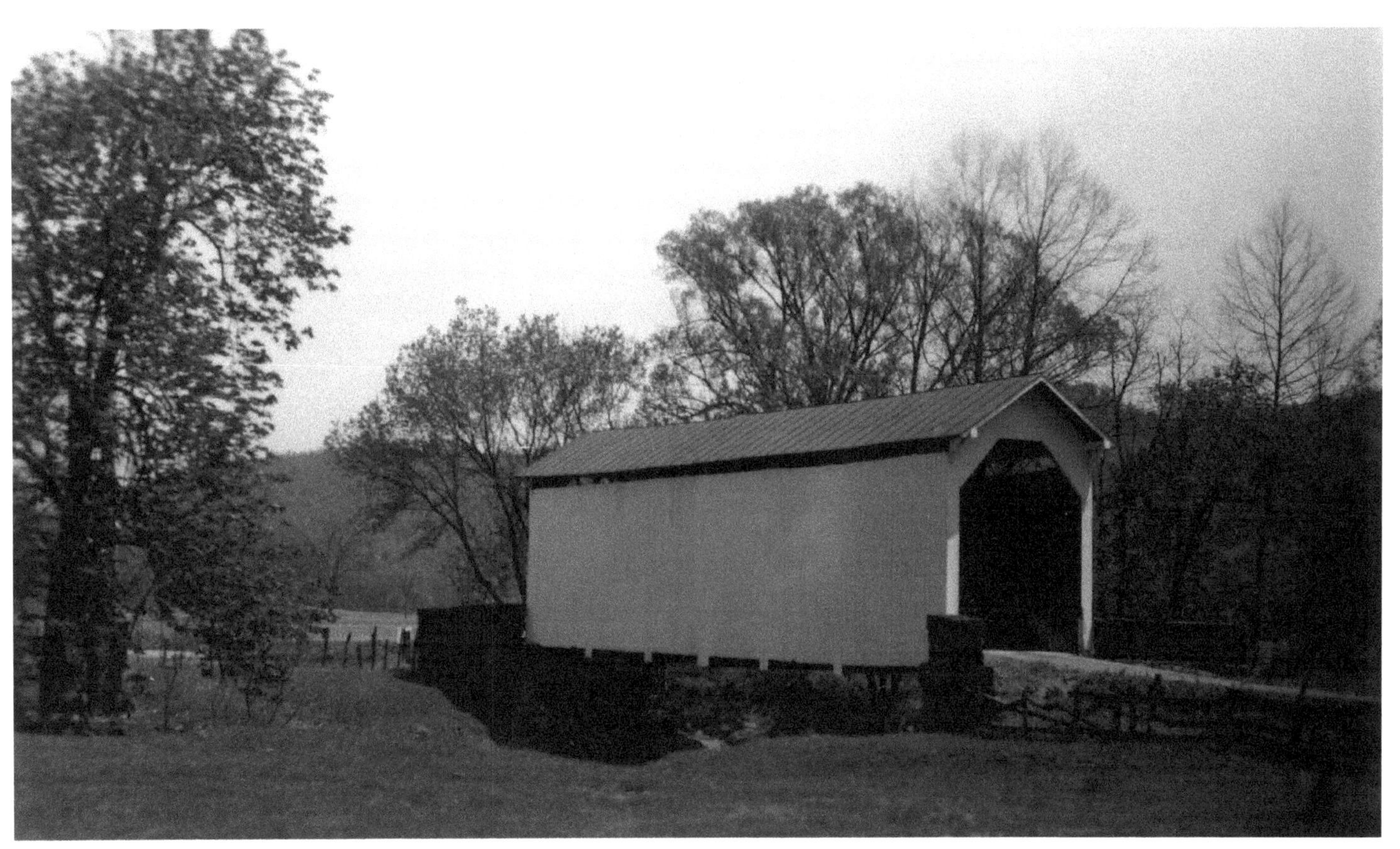

Painted white, this covered bridge over Whiteley Creek in Greene County spans 63 feet.

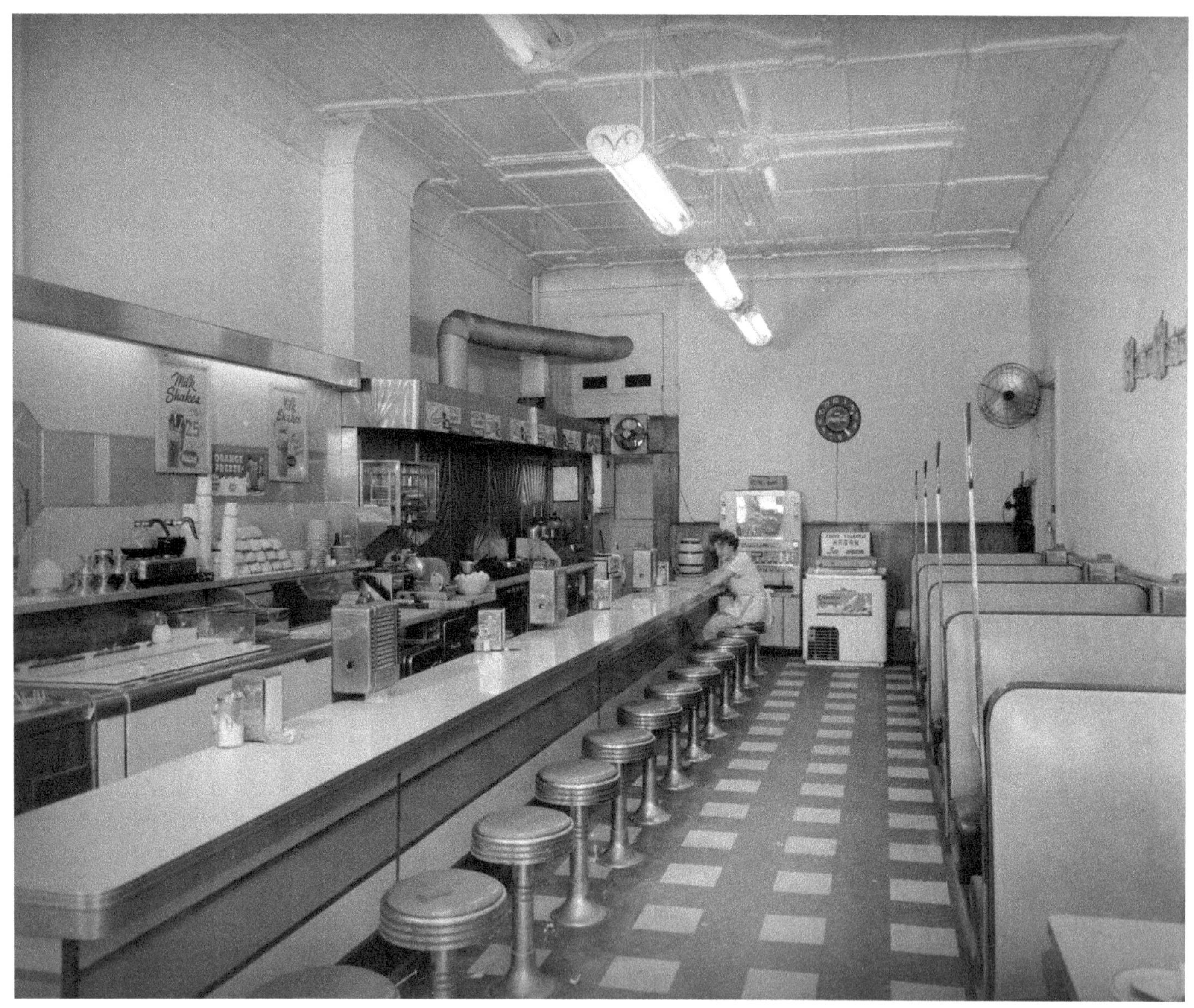

A lone waitress sits at the counter of Hayden's Restaurant on Fifth Street at the heart of the University of Pittsburgh. The restaurant was demolished in the mid-1950s.

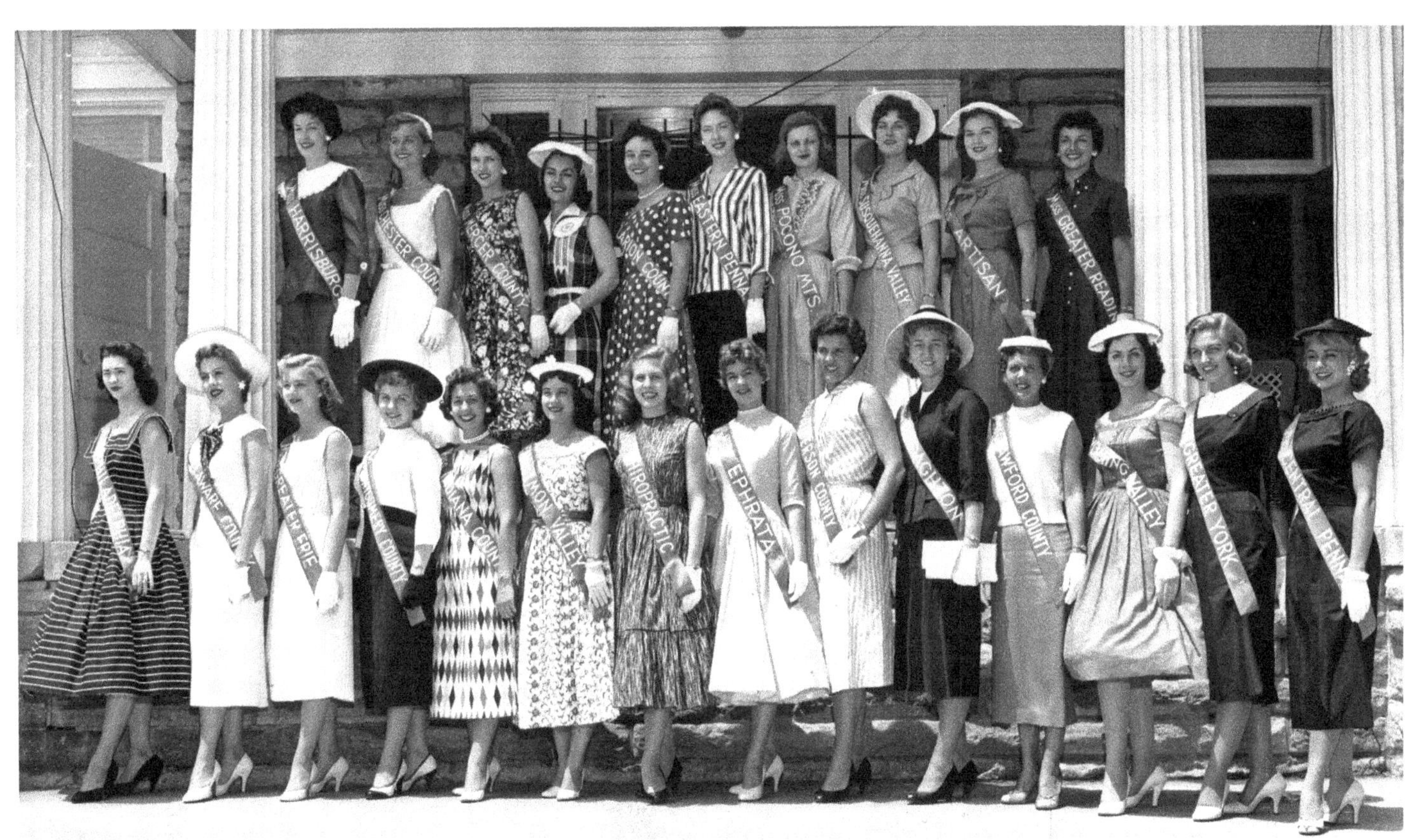

Contestants in the Miss Pennsylvania beauty pageant in 1956, photographed at Longwood Gardens in Kennett Square. Miss Delaware County, Lorna Malcomson Ringler (second from left in the front row), subsequently represented Pennsylvania in the Miss America pageant in Atlantic City.

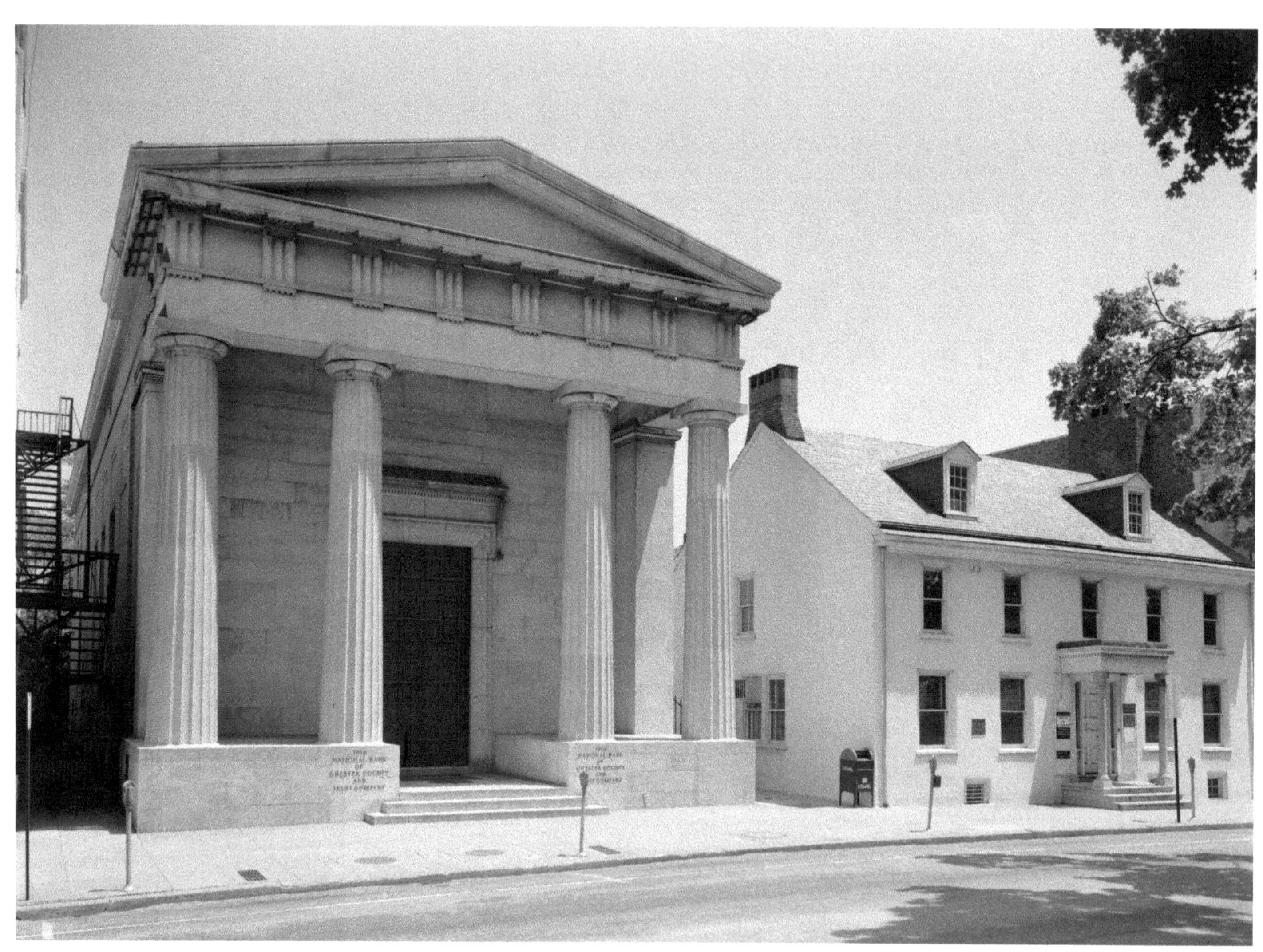

West Chester's Bank of Chester County, located on North High Street. Seen here in June 1958, the 1837 Greek-revival building designed by Thomas Ustick Walter sits at the heart of West Chester's Historic District and remains in use as a bank.

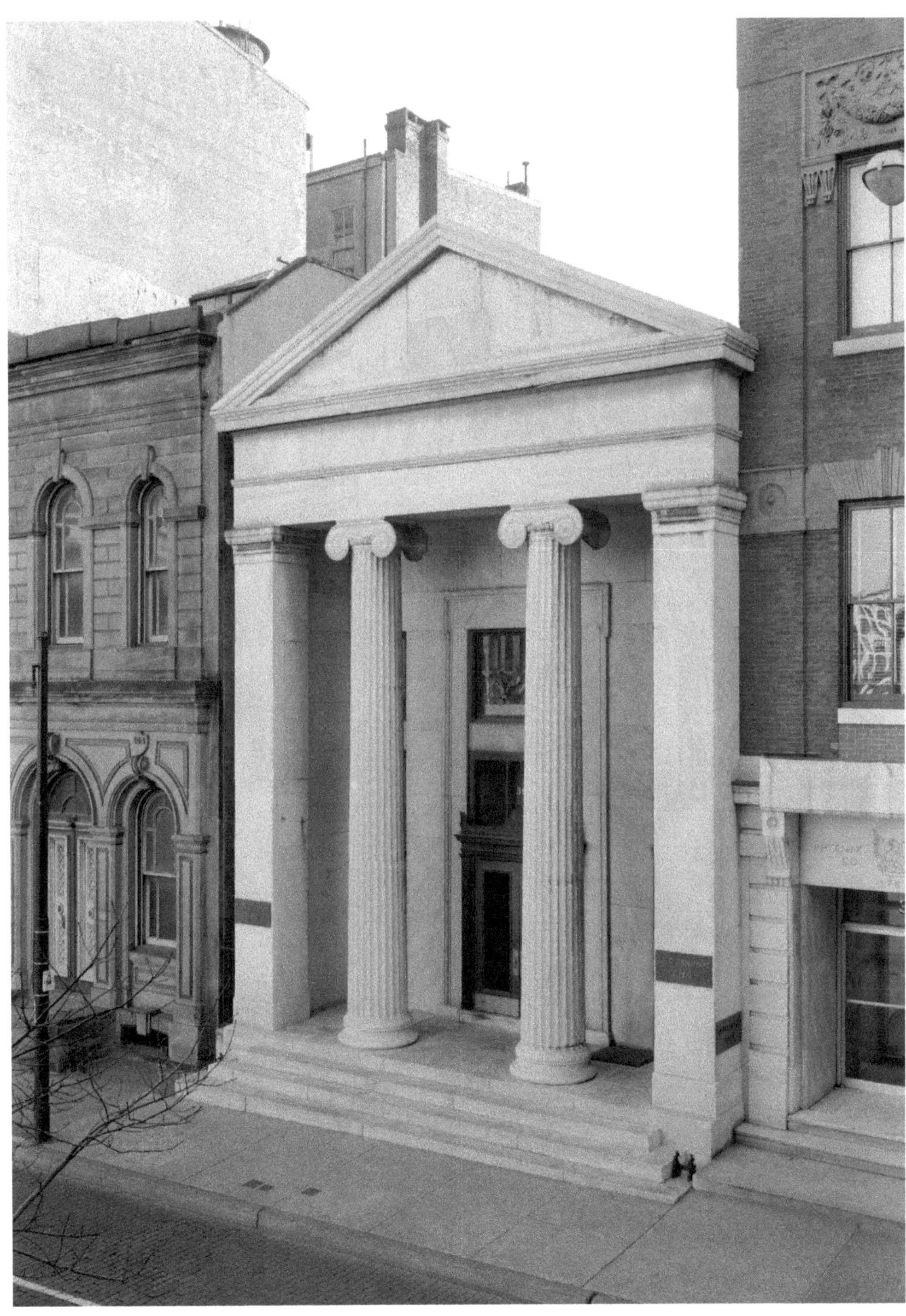

The second home of the Philadelphia Saving Fund Society, at 306 Walnut Street in Philadelphia, as it appeared in 1958. Founded in 1816 and initially located in a building on Sixth Street, the bank charged architect Thomas Ustick Walter with the task of designing and erecting the new building in 1840.

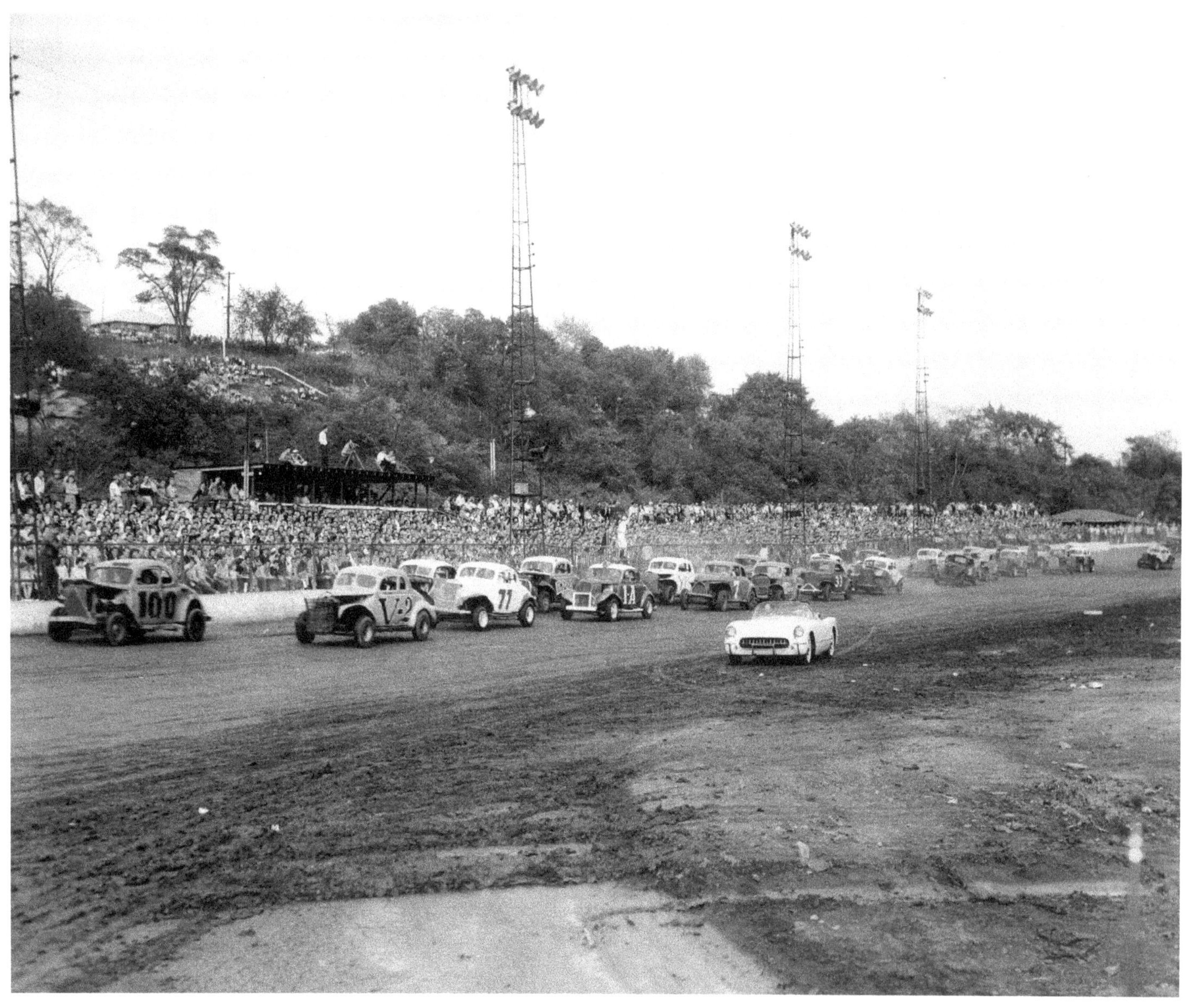

Heidelberg Raceway near Pittsburgh was the home of stock car racing for many years. The raceway closed in 1973.

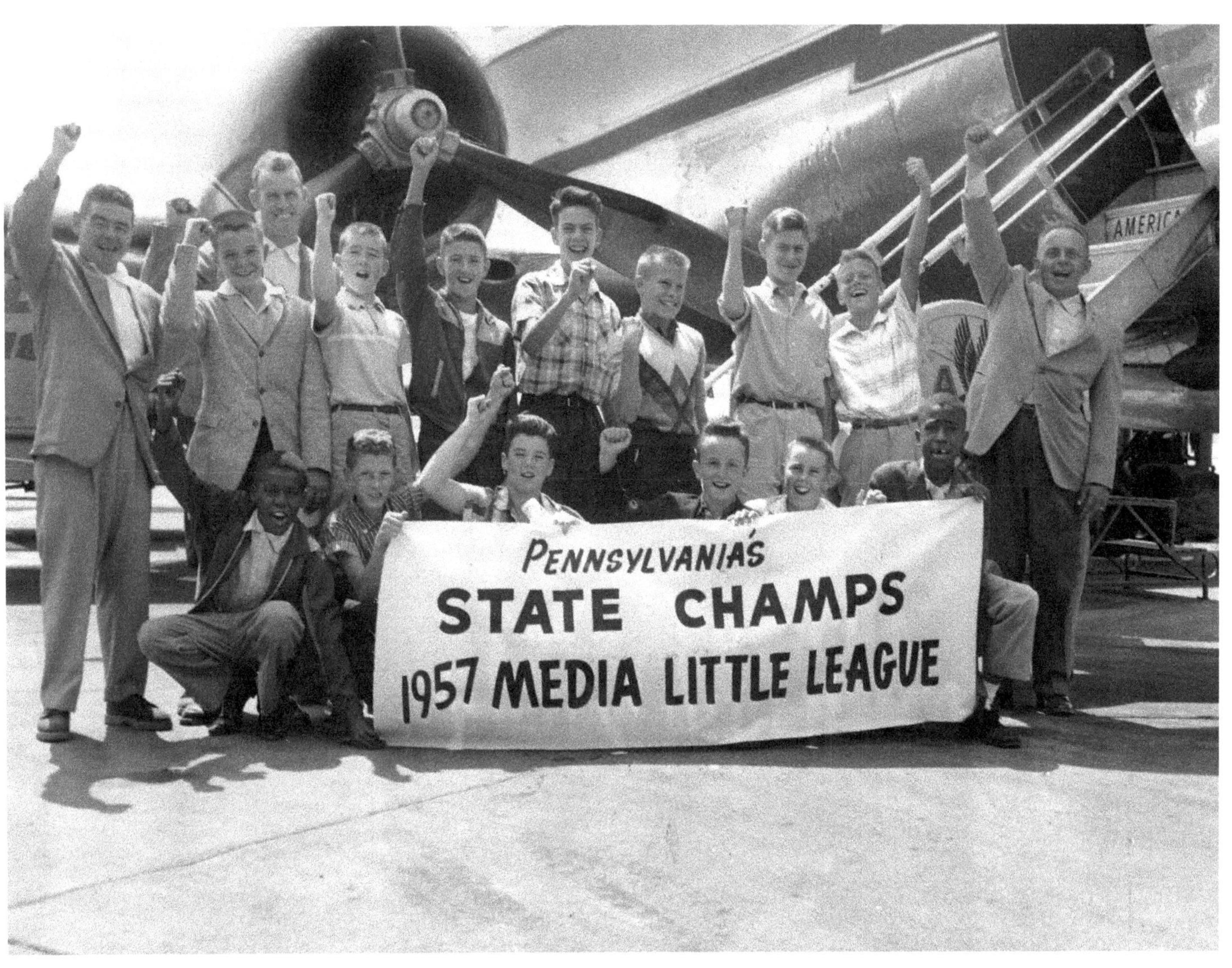

State Little League baseball champions from Media prepare for their flight to New York to compete in the regional contest. They were defeated by the Bridgeport, Connecticut, team, which went on to win the Little League World Series of 1957.

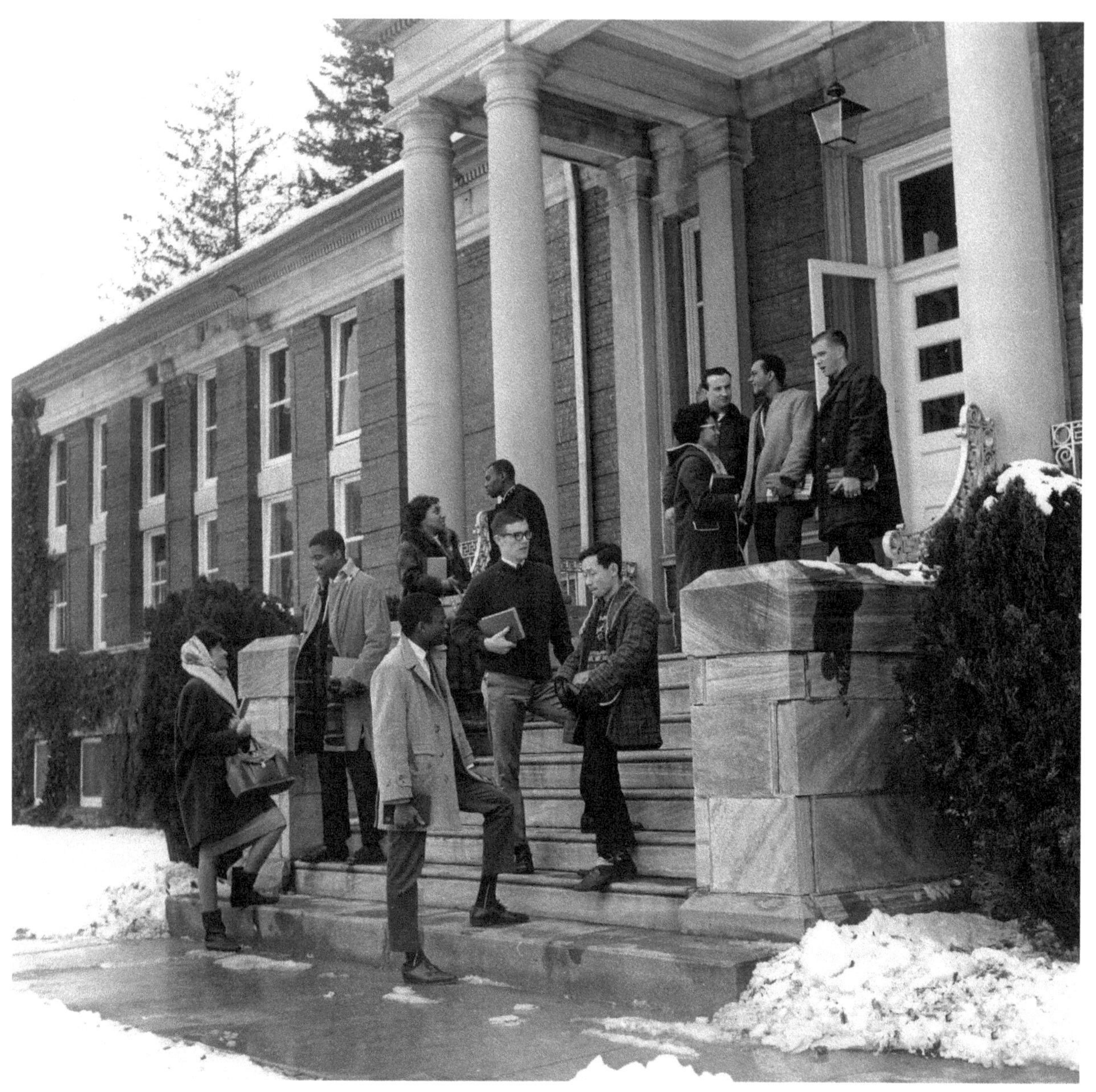

Students at Lincoln University gather on the steps of Vail Hall. Chartered in 1854 for the specific purpose of providing higher education to African American males, the university soon went on to serve an increasingly diverse and international educational community and admitted women for the first time in 1952. Lincoln University includes among its alumni poet Langston Hughes and Supreme Court justice Thurgood Marshall, and today enrolls over 2,000 students.

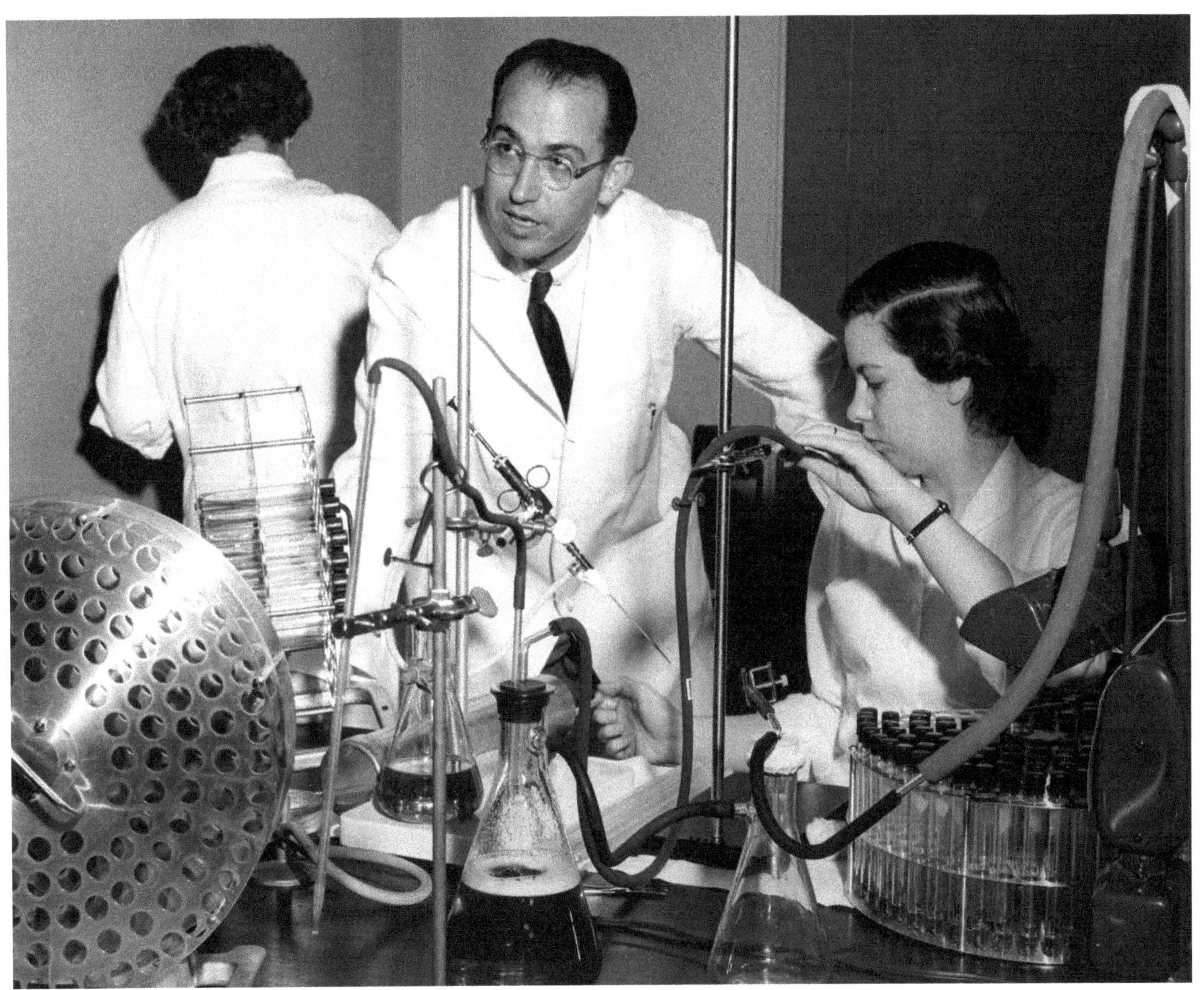

The Virus Research Laboratory of the University of Pittsburgh, with Dr. Jonas E. Salk in residence from 1947 to 1960, was the site of the discovery of the polio vaccination. Here Salk supervises work in the lab.

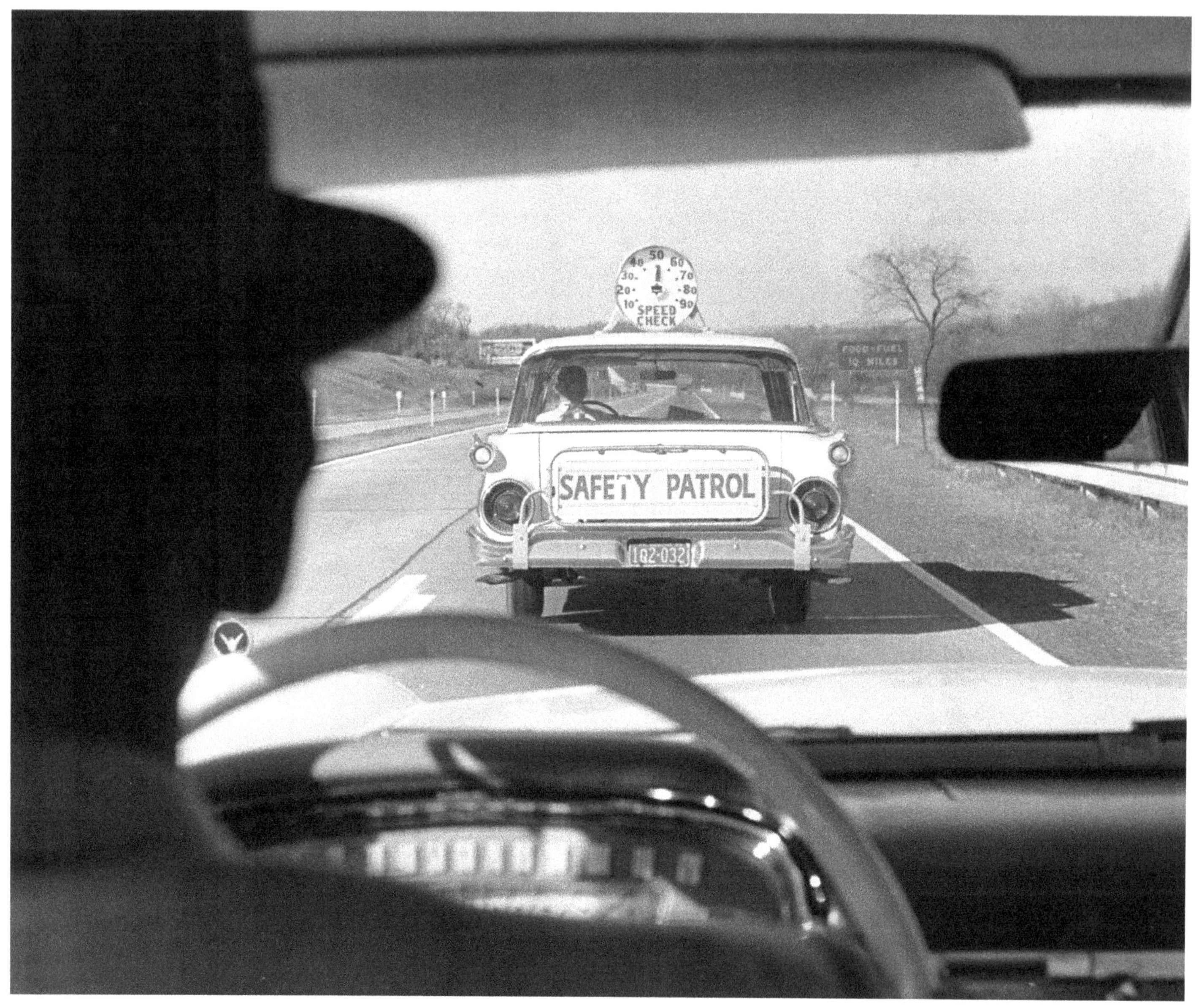

In a temporary effort to emphasize proper speed limits and increase safety along the Pennsylvania Turnpike, an oversized speedometer is placed on a safety patrol car in 1960.

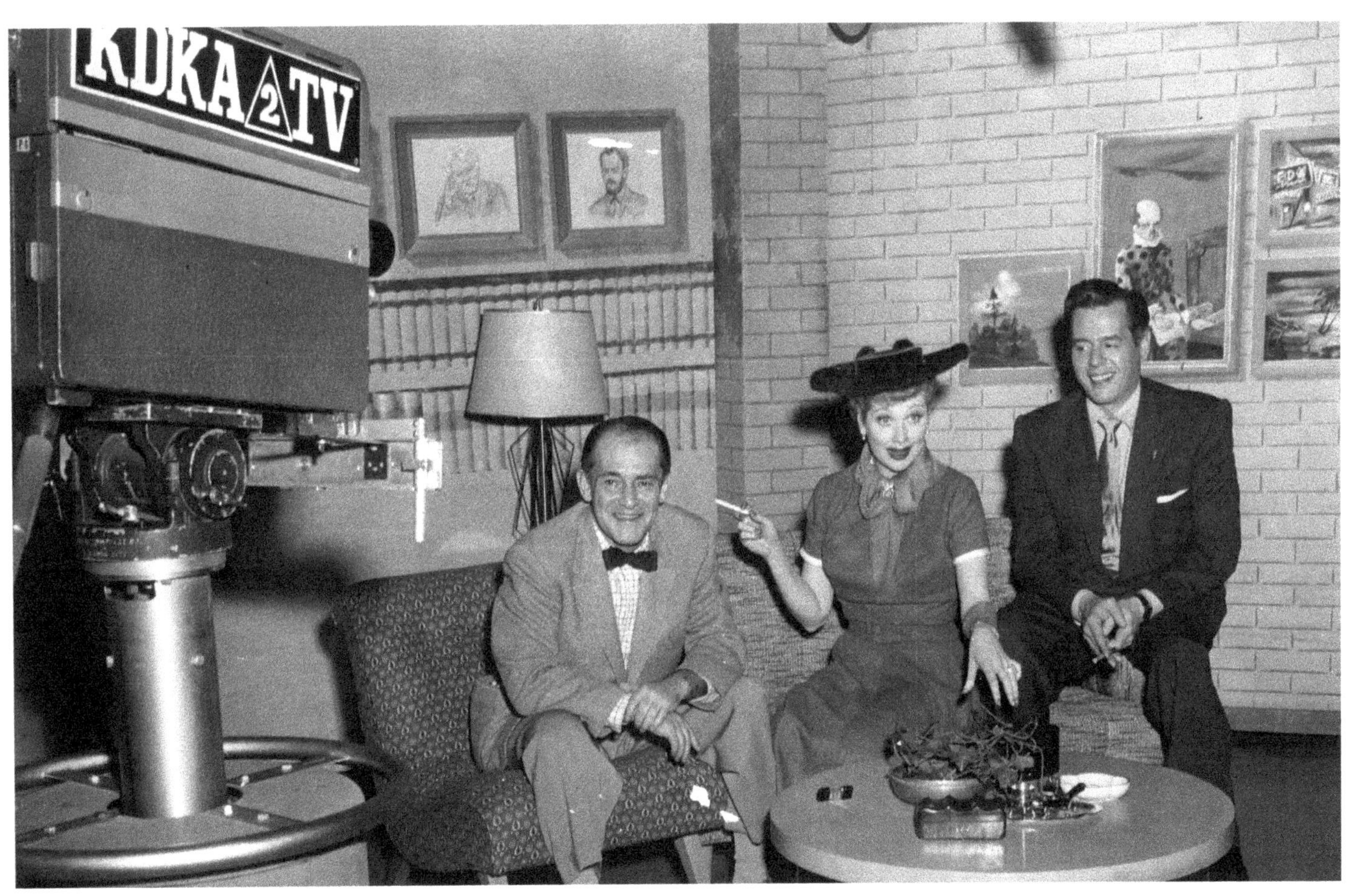

Harold Cohen (at left) chats with radio and television personalities Lucille Ball and Desi Arnaz, circa 1960.
Cohen was a popular television broadcaster with KDKA-TV in Pittsburgh.

Completed in 1886, the Allegheny County Courthouse features an interior courtyard and is a fine example of Richardson Romanesque design, named after the architect H. H. Richardson.

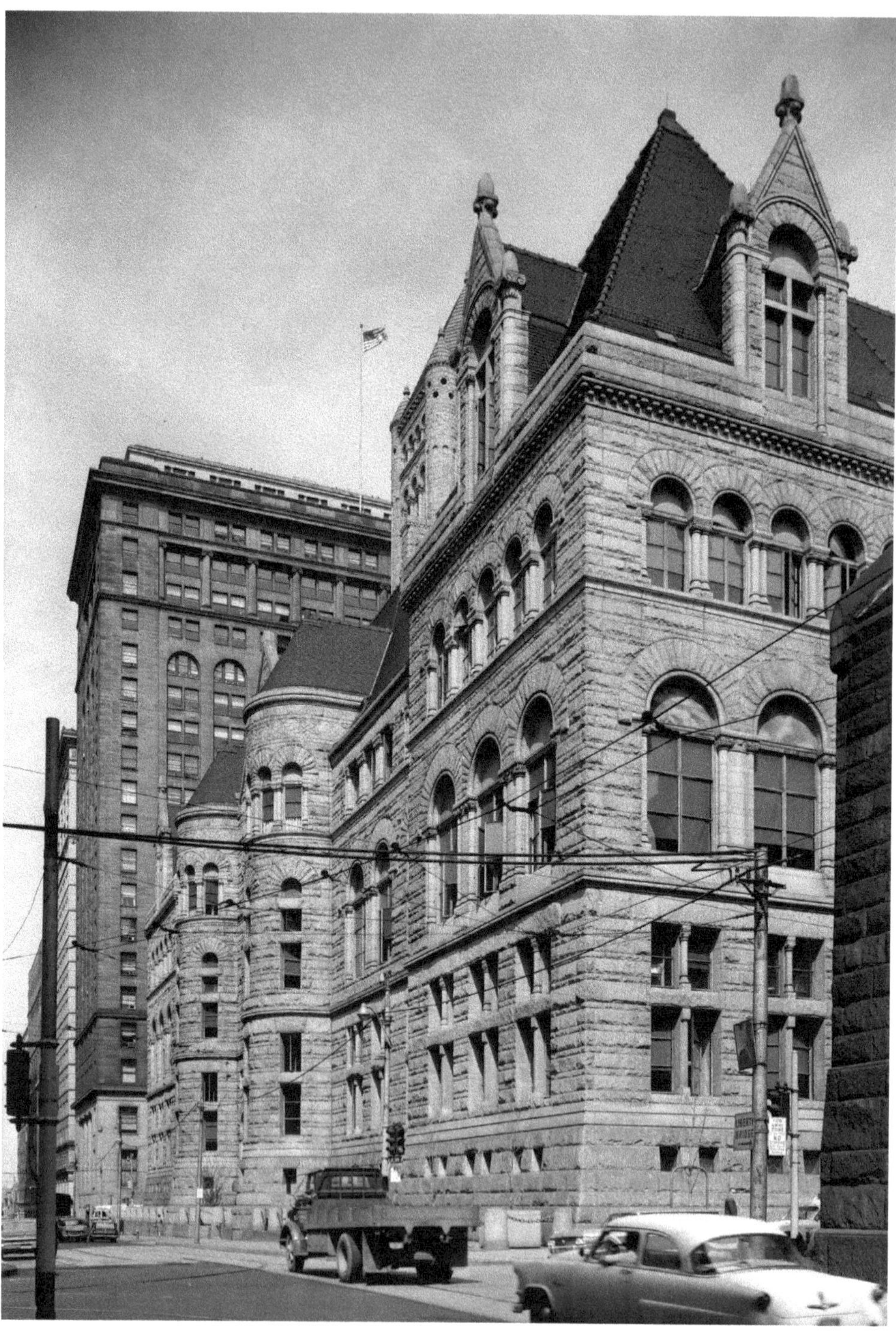

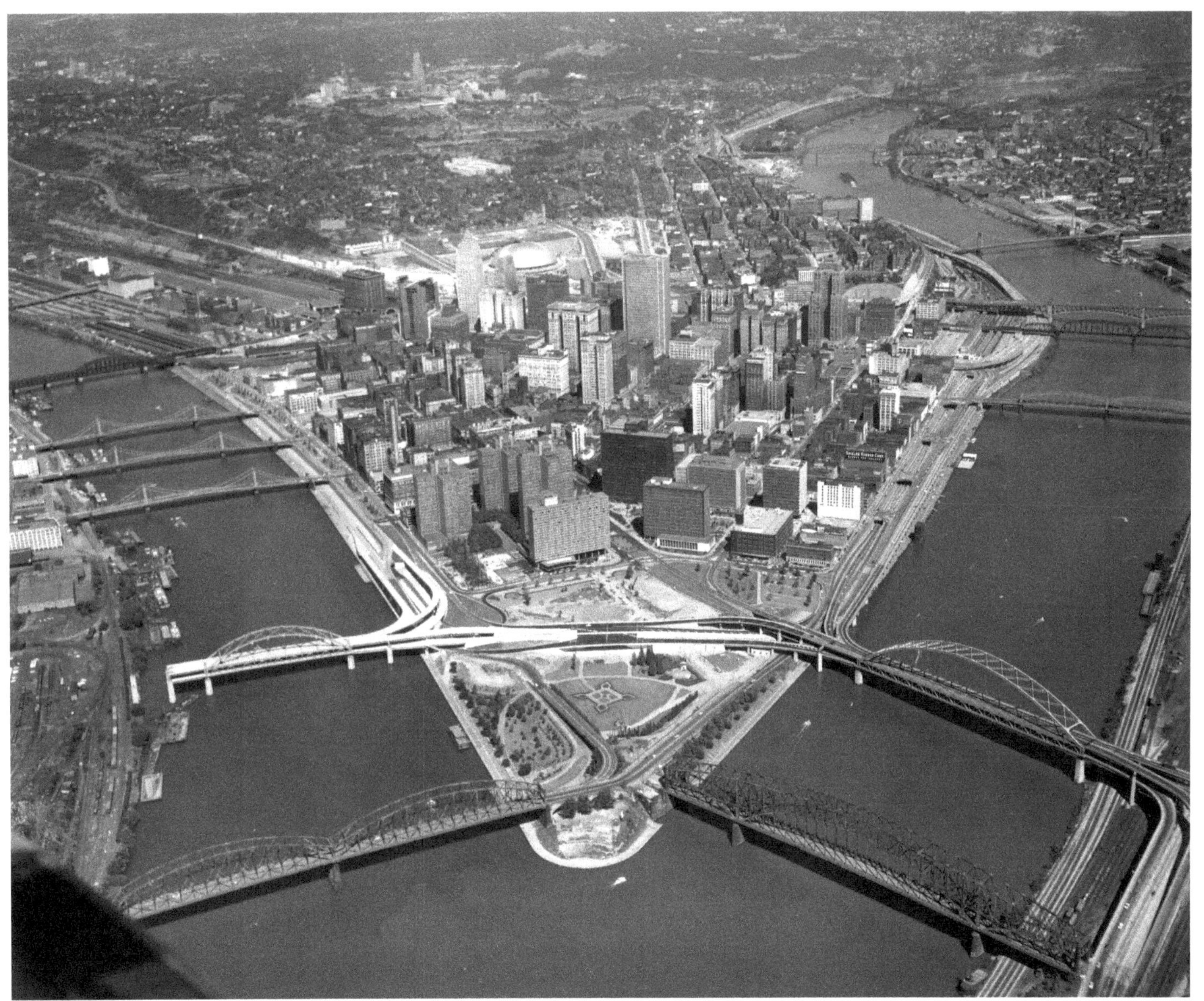

The "Golden Triangle" of downtown Pittsburgh, where the convergence of the Allegheny River (left) and the Monongahela River (right) forms the Ohio River, as it appeared in the mid-1960s. The two lower bridges were demolished in 1970 to make way for Point State Park.

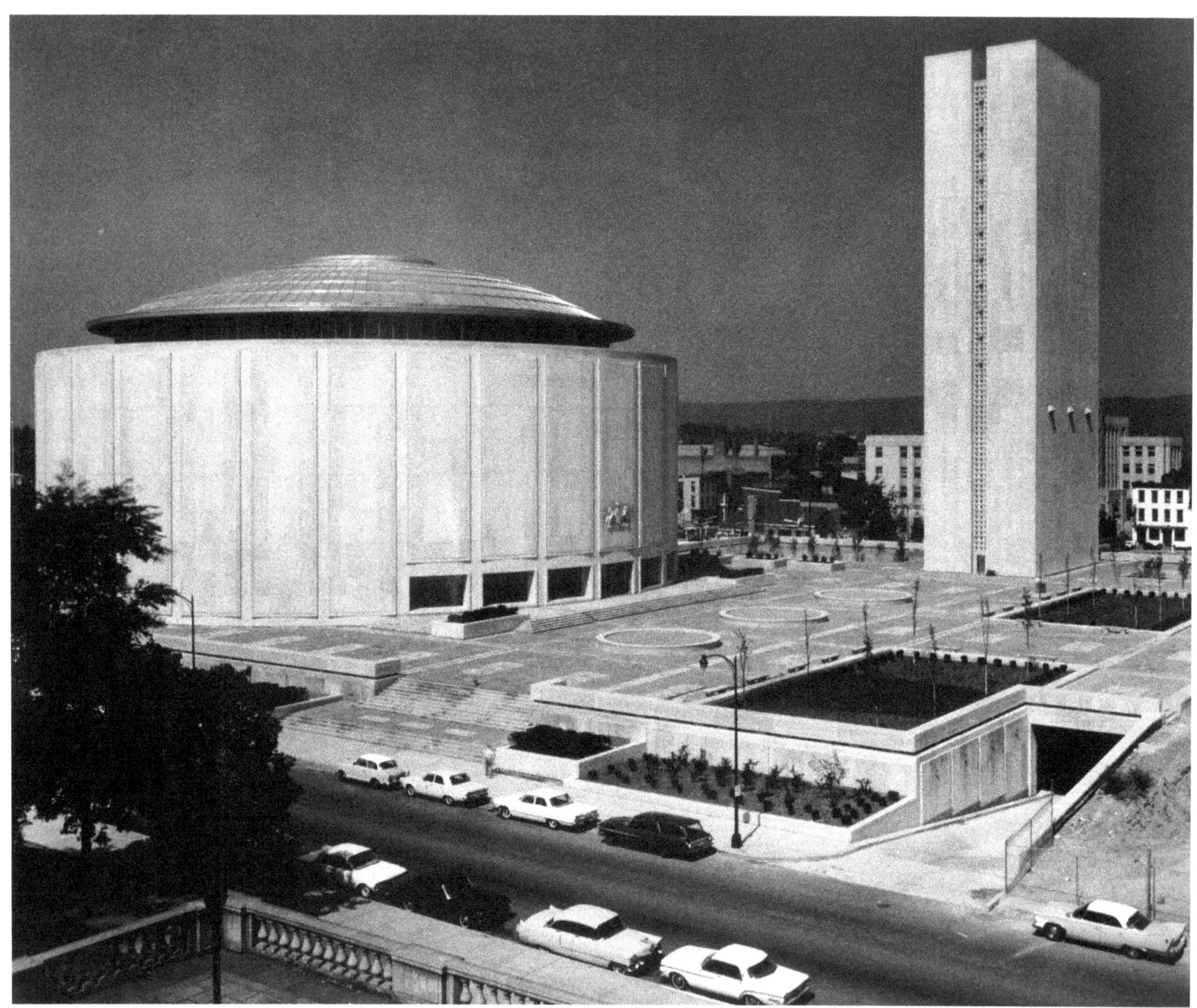

A view of the newly completed William Penn Memorial Museum (at left, now the Pennsylvania State Museum) and the Pennsylvania State Archives Building in Harrisburg, circa 1965. The design of the buildings is said to have been inspired by the iconic Trylon and Perisphere of the 1939 New York World's Fair.

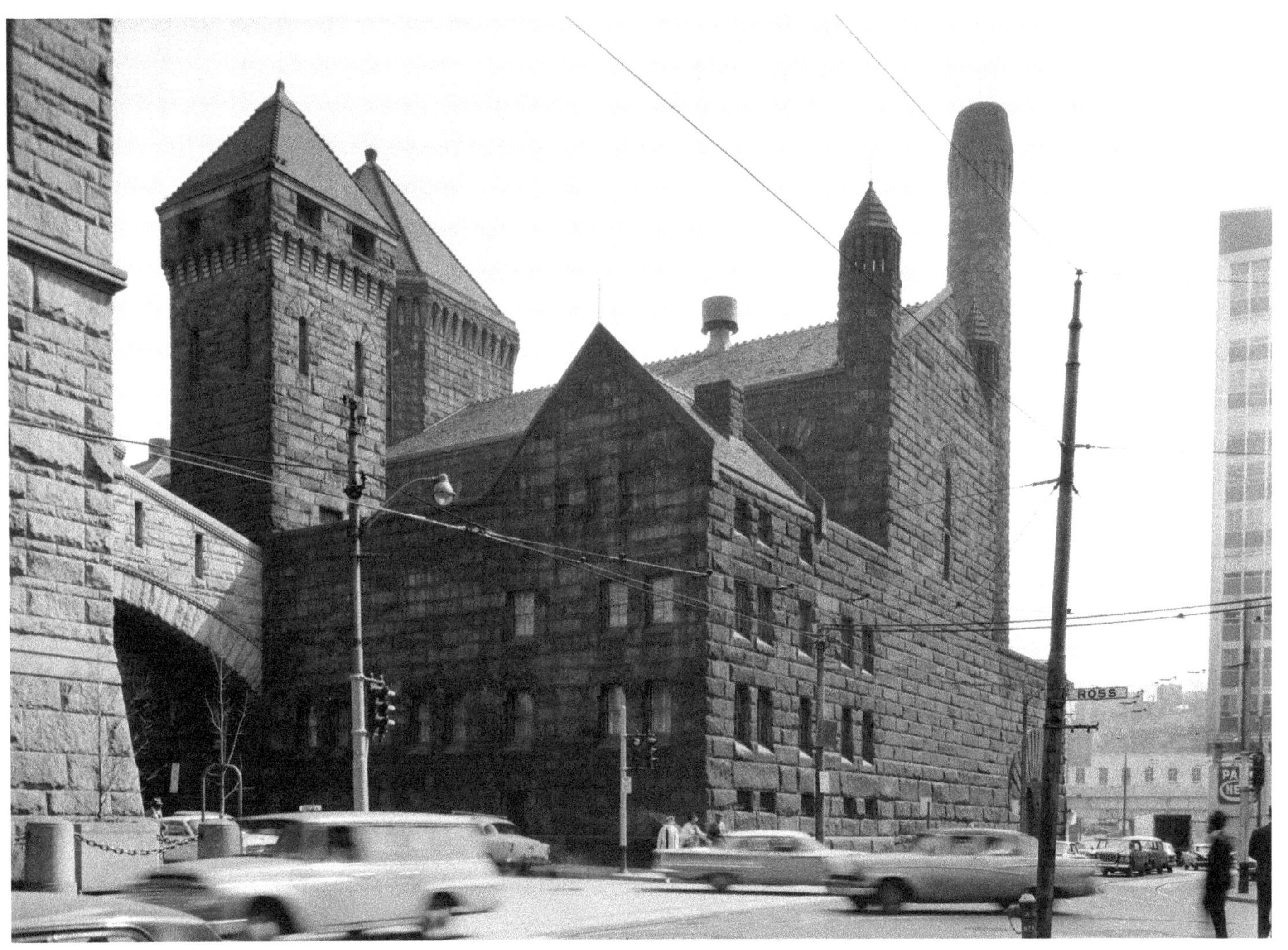

Attached to the Allegheny County Courthouse by a second-story bridge called the "Bridge of Sighs," the old Allegheny County Jail is now used as an extension of the courthouse.

Ice cream appeals to everyone, as expressed in this magical moment when the final product was revealed at the Pennsylvania County Fair in 1965. "Homemade" ice cream was created in hand-cranked contrivances like the one shown here.

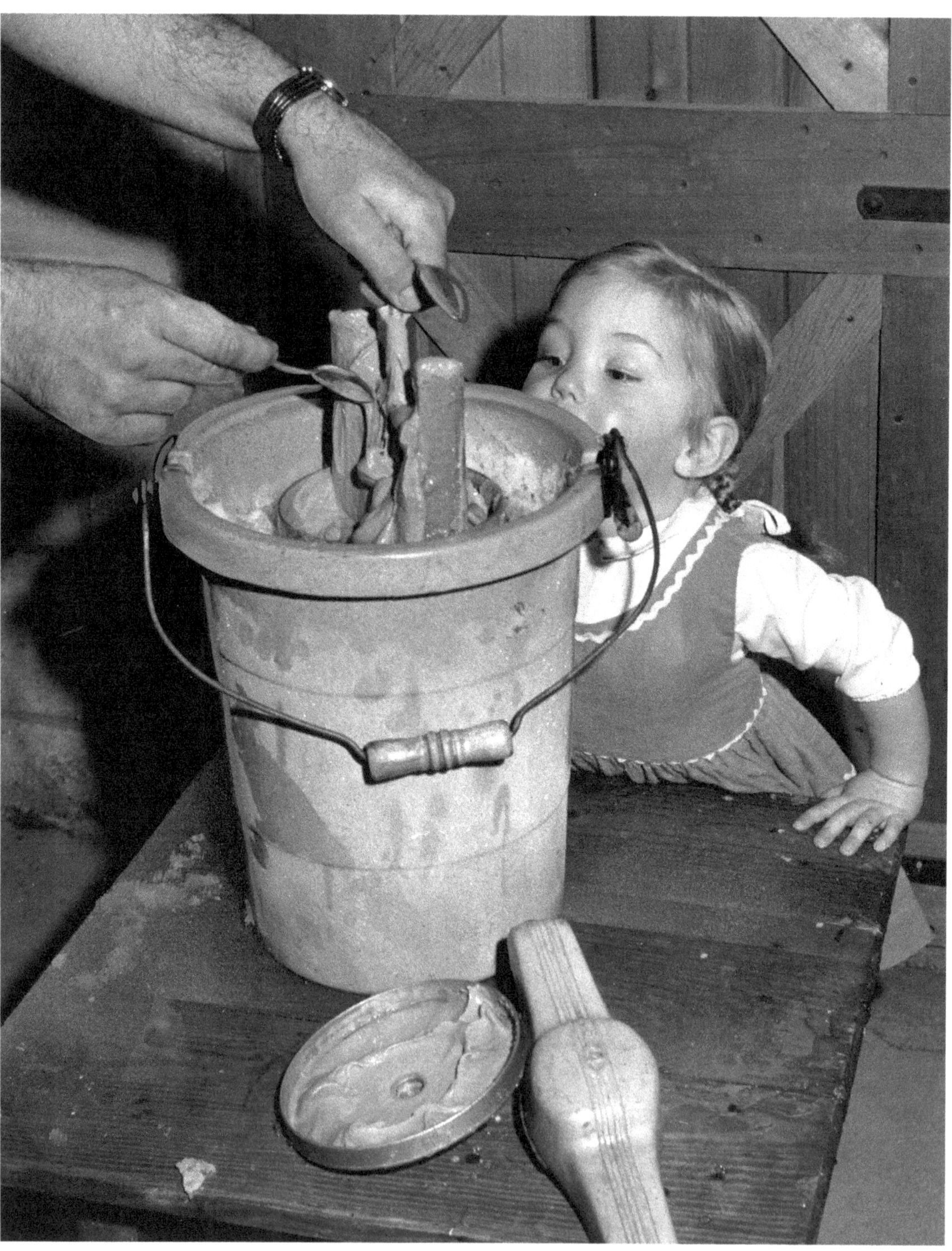

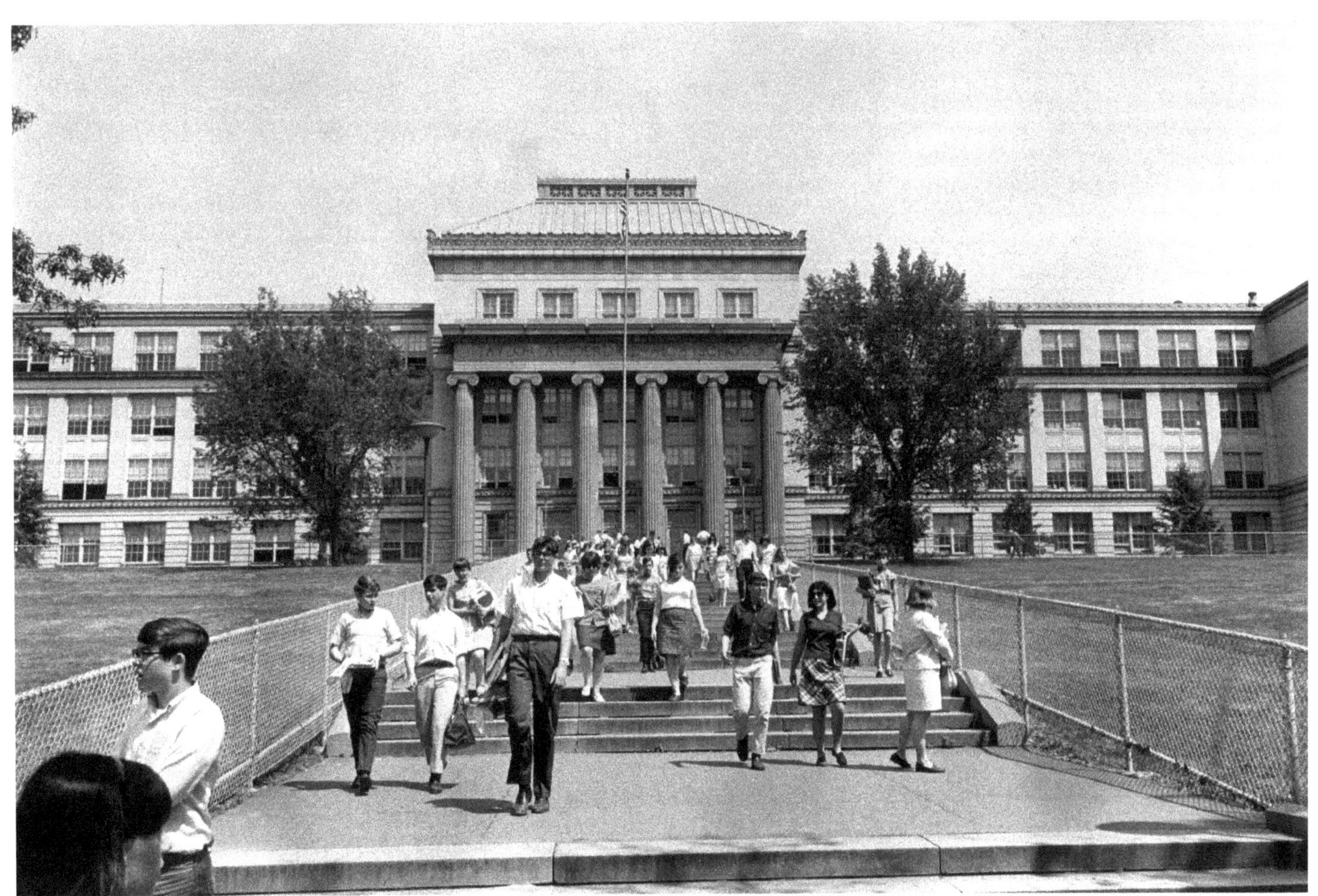

Students leave Allderdice High School at the end of the school day, 1967. Allderdice is still the largest high school in the Pittsburgh School District.

Two children enjoy a moment beside the lake at Camp James Weldon Johnson in 1965. The camp was founded in 1939 by the Urban League of Pittsburgh as one of the first camps in the country to serve African American children.

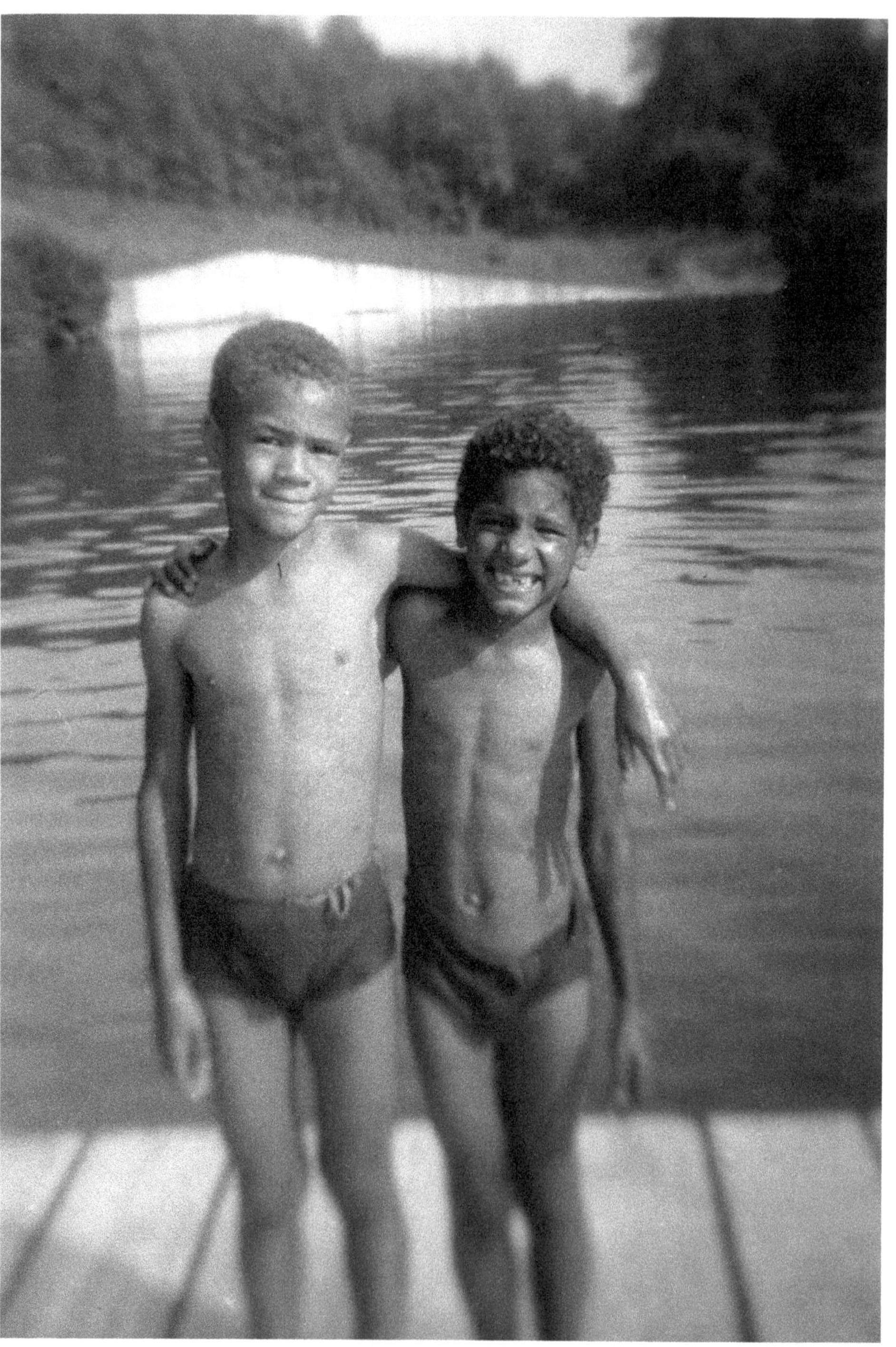

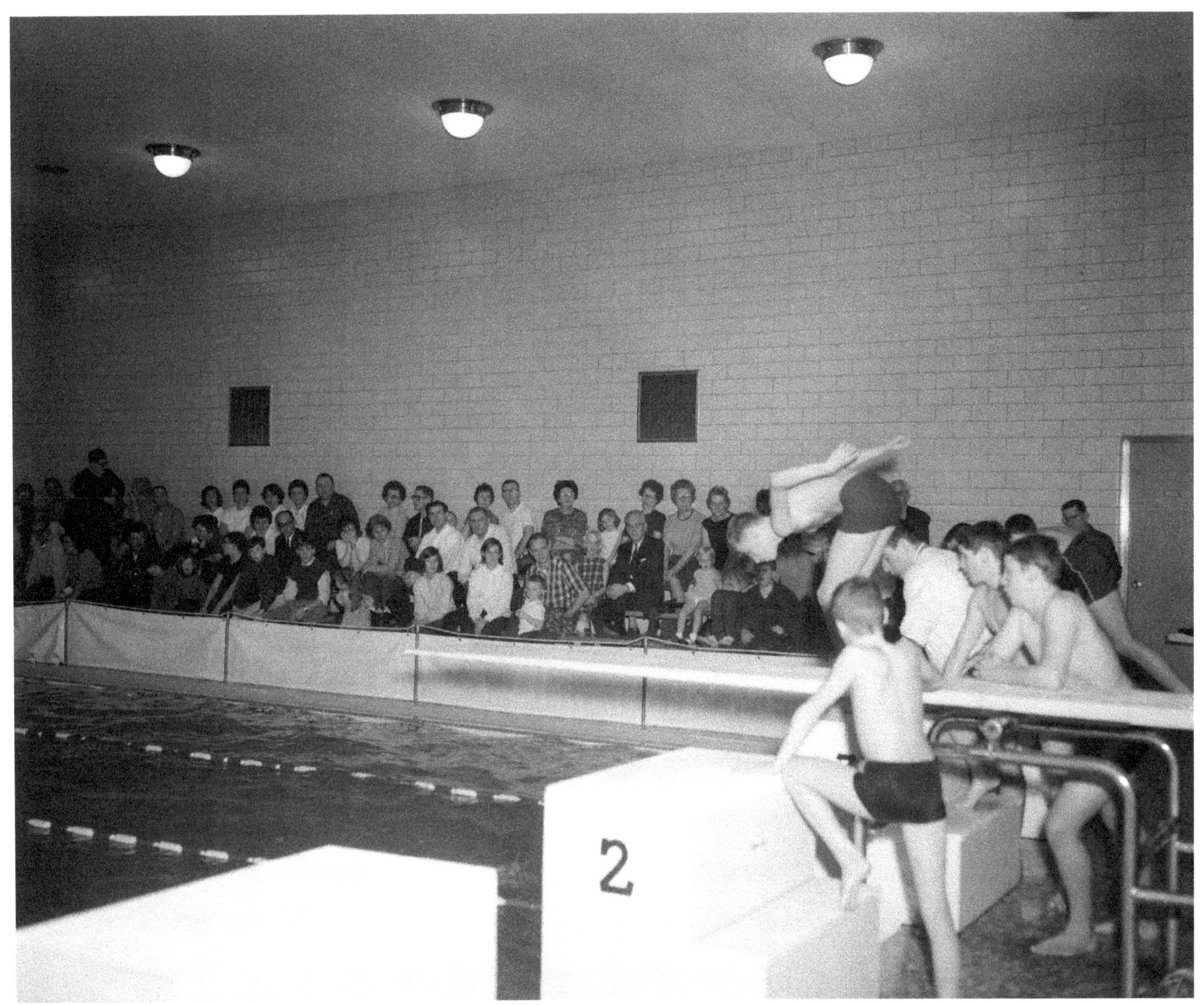

Boys participate in a swimming competition at the local Young Men's Christian Association in Warren County, 1967.

Completed in 1897, Dental Hall at the University of Pennsylvania in Philadelphia was the first "purpose-built" school of dentistry in the United States. Later, it housed the university's School of Architecture.

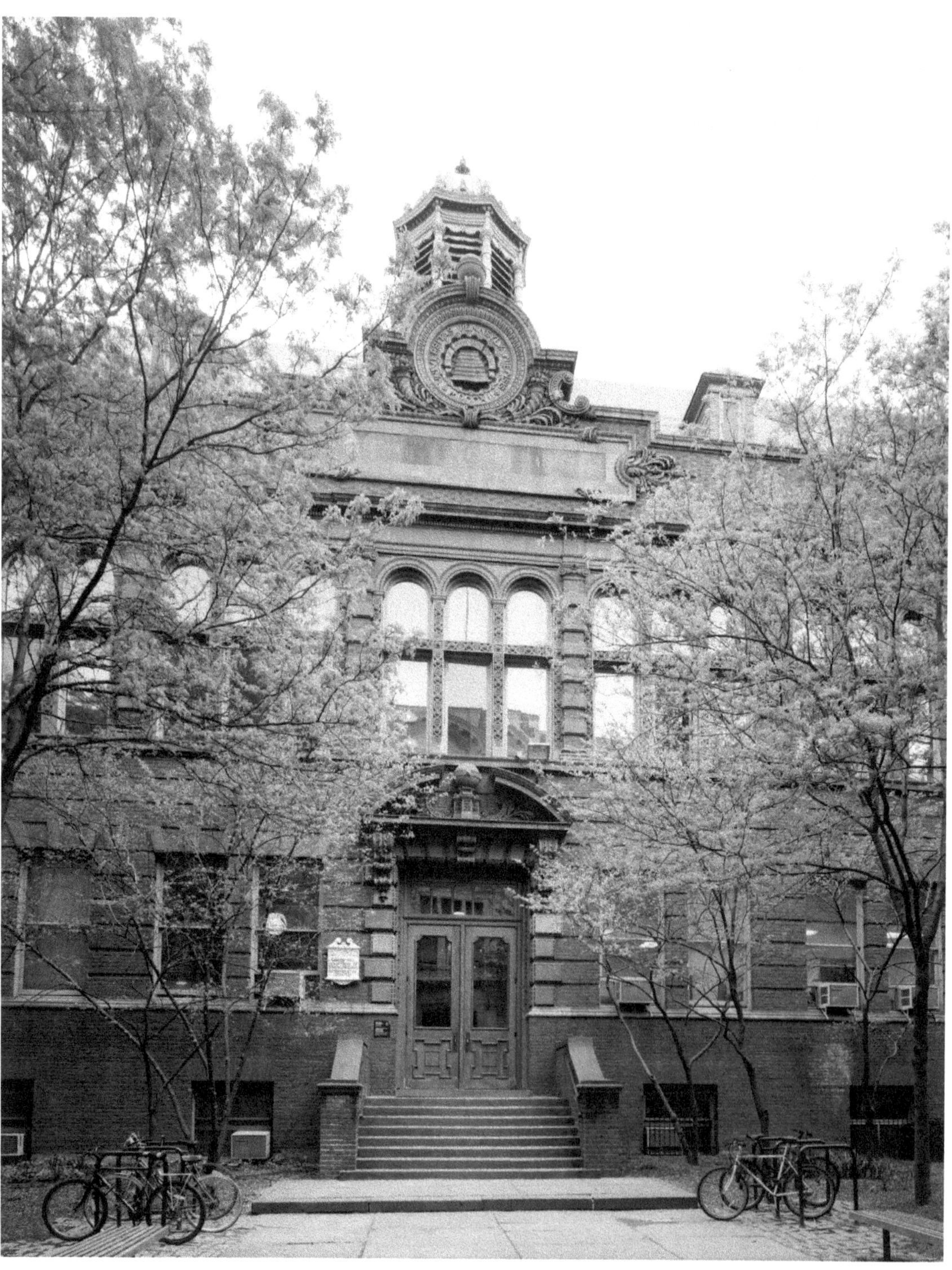

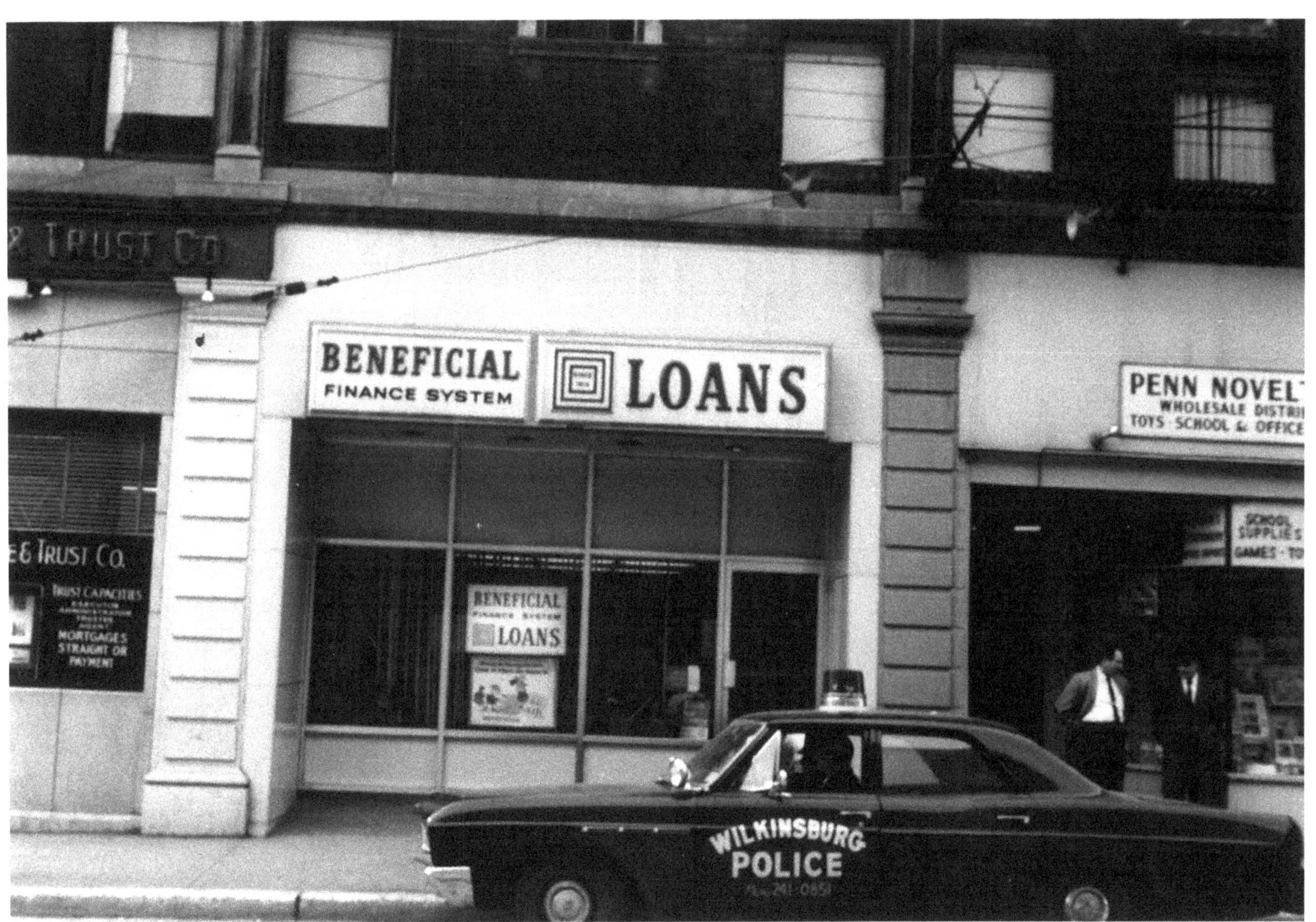

A police cruiser in Wilkinsburg, once annexed to Pittsburgh but now an independent borough.

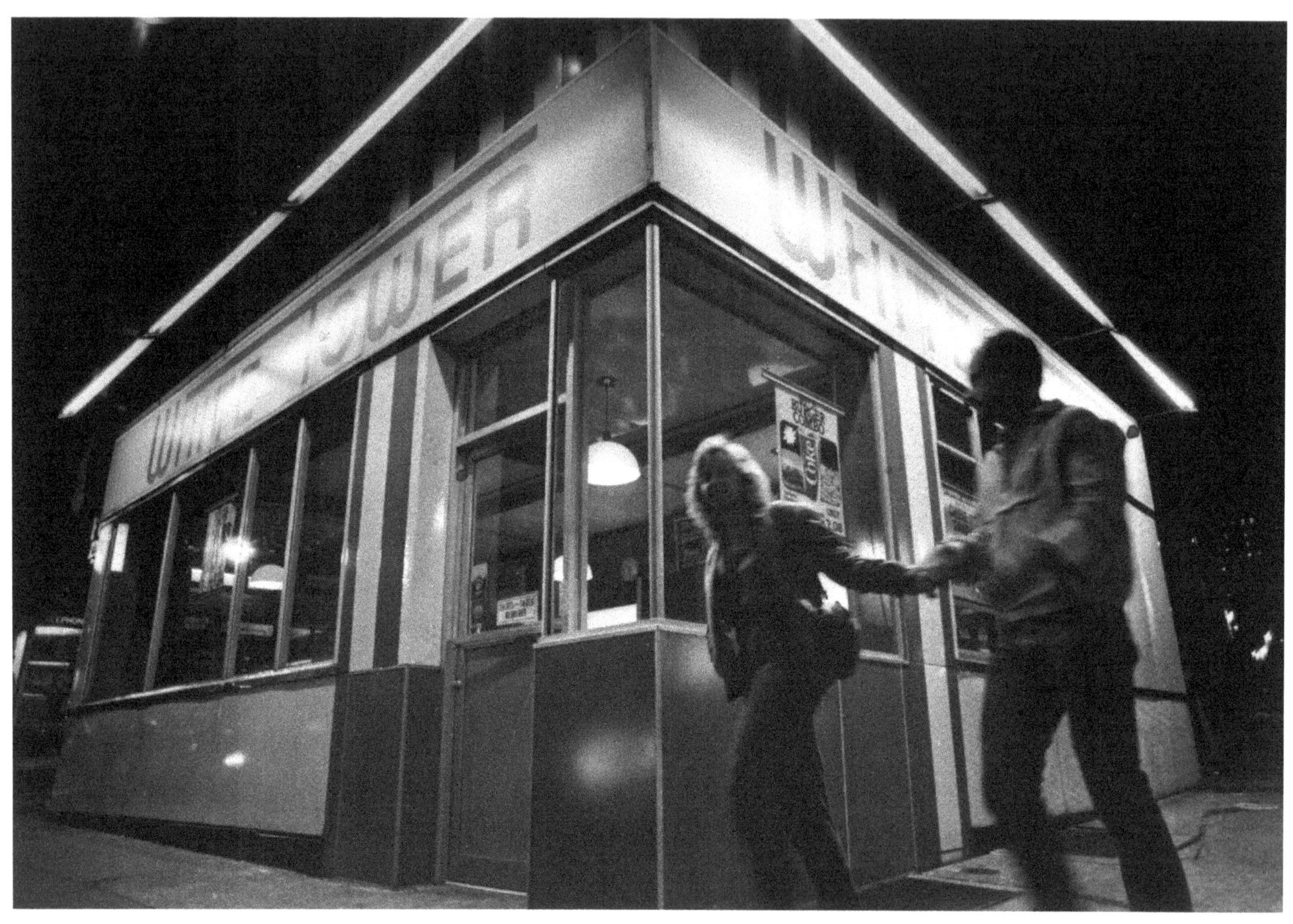

A local couple makes a late-night visit to a White Tower fast food restaurant in downtown Pittsburgh, circa 1970.

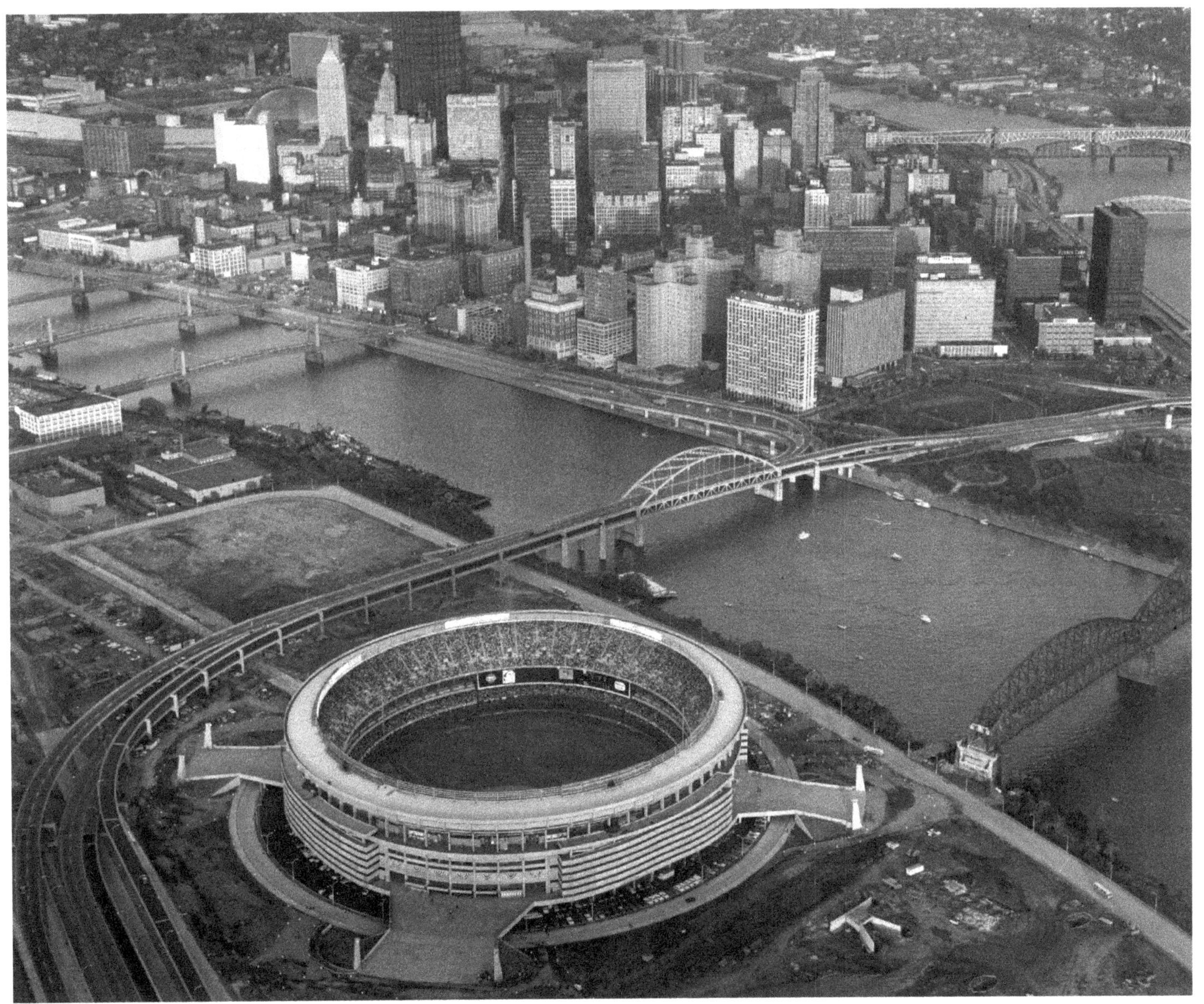

Three Rivers Stadium in Pittsburgh, shortly before completion in 1970. Home to the Pittsburgh Pirates and the Pittsburgh Steelers, the stadium was demolished in February of 2001.

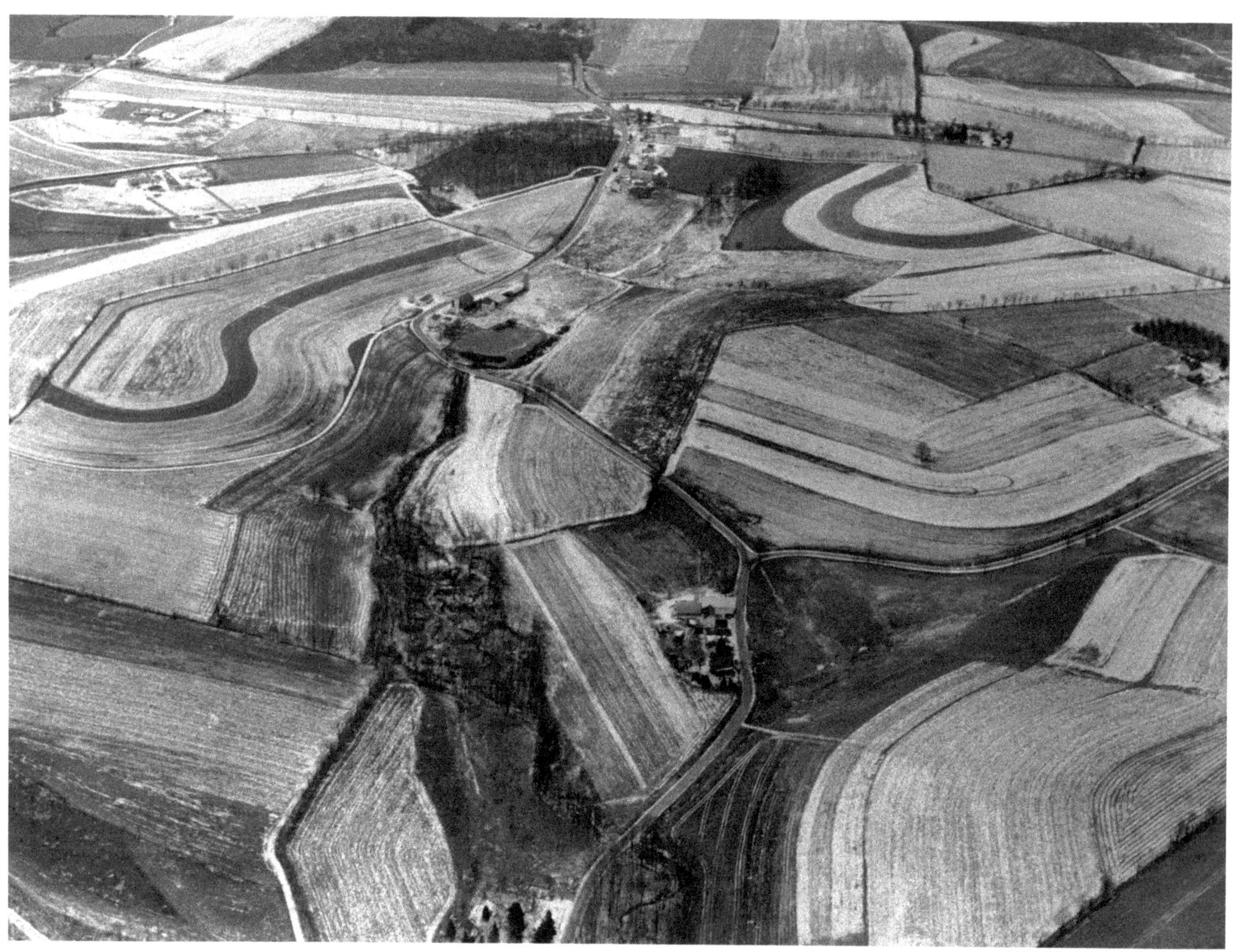

This dramatic aerial view of the farmlands of central Bucks County after a light snowfall in 1974 highlights the significance of agriculture to the county. In the last three decades, the rural landscape in Bucks County has been threatened by increased residential developments, and efforts are ongoing to preserve some of the area's agricultural traditions.

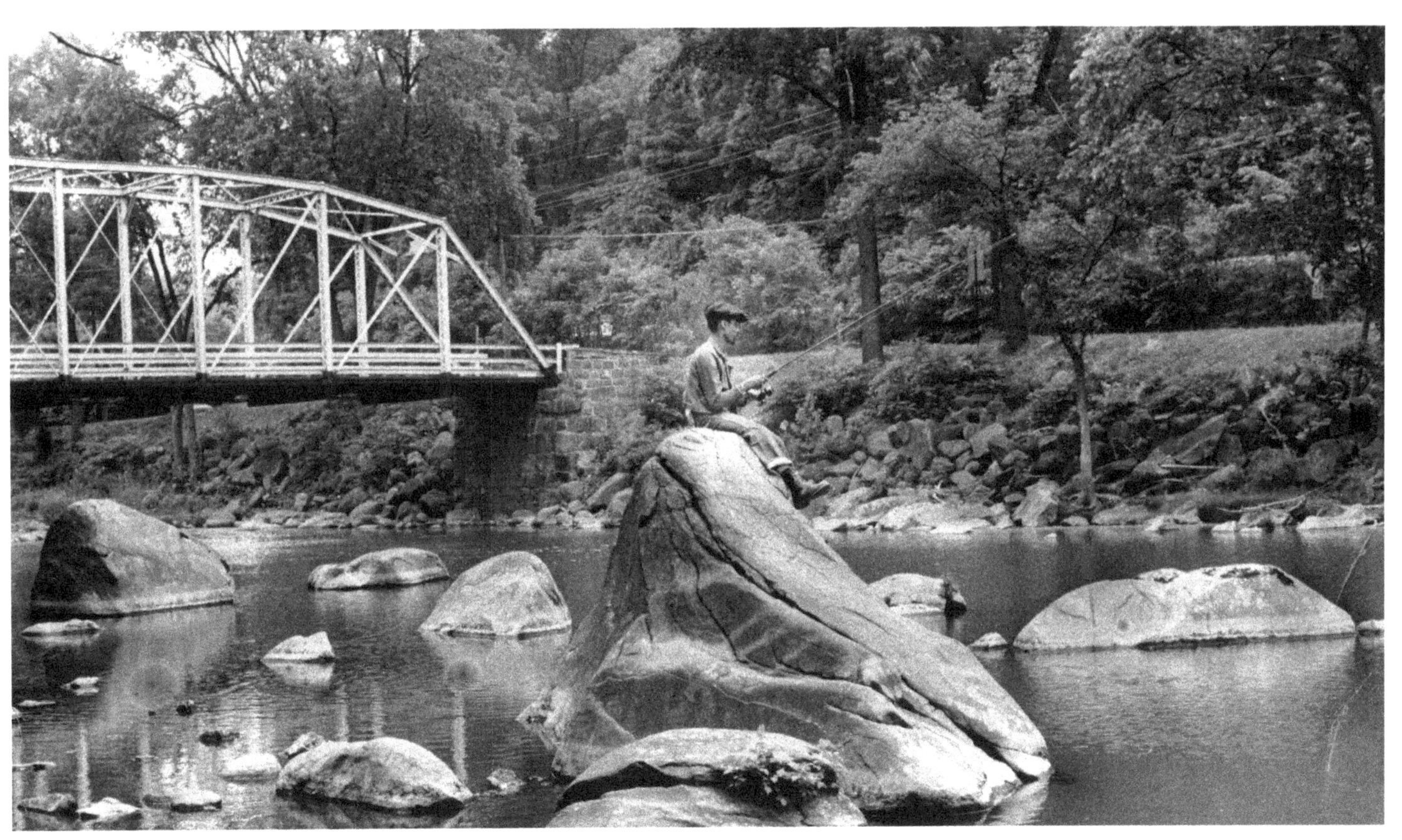

A young man enjoys a quiet moment of fishing along the Perkiomen Creek in Montgomery County, June 1974.

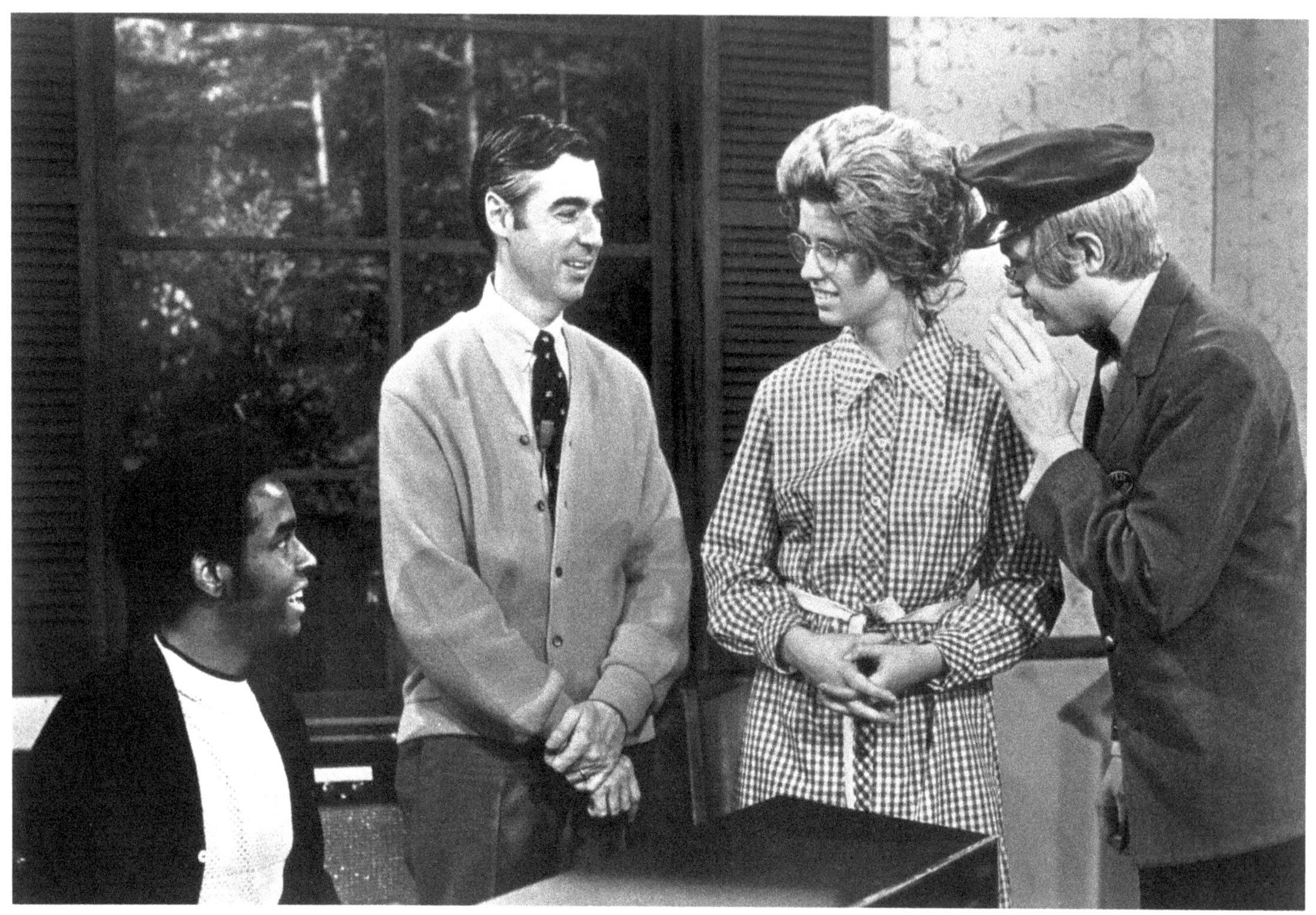

Recognizable to children and adults all over the world, Fred Rogers of *Mister Rogers' Neighborhood* developed the children's program in Toronto, but made it famous on Pittsburgh's WQED-TV, one of the first public television stations in the nation. Mr. Rogers, who was born in Latrobe and died in Pittsburgh in 2003, is often remembered as one of the city's most beloved residents.

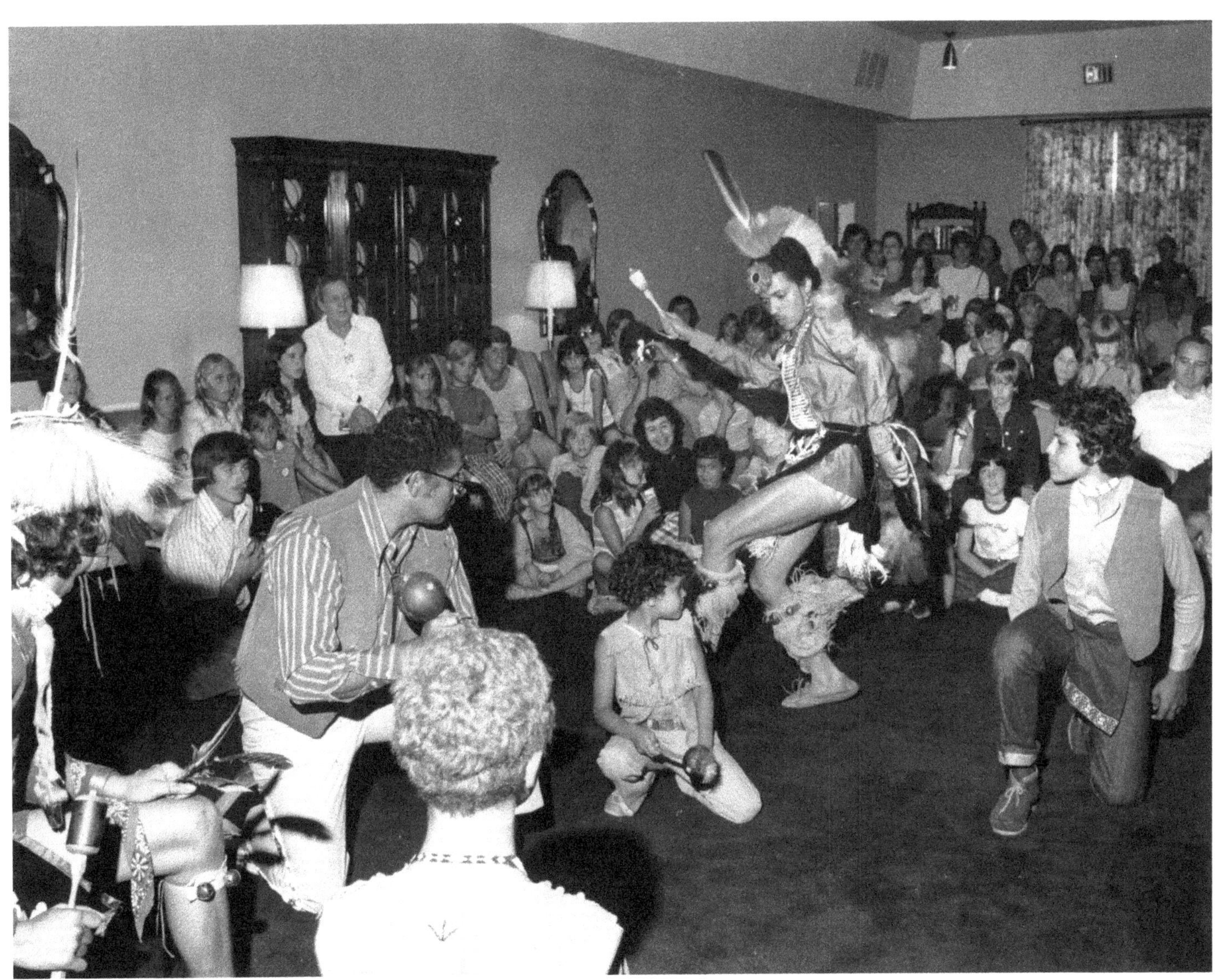

A dancer with the United American Indians of the Delaware Valley performs for schoolchildren in Bensalem, July 22, 1975.

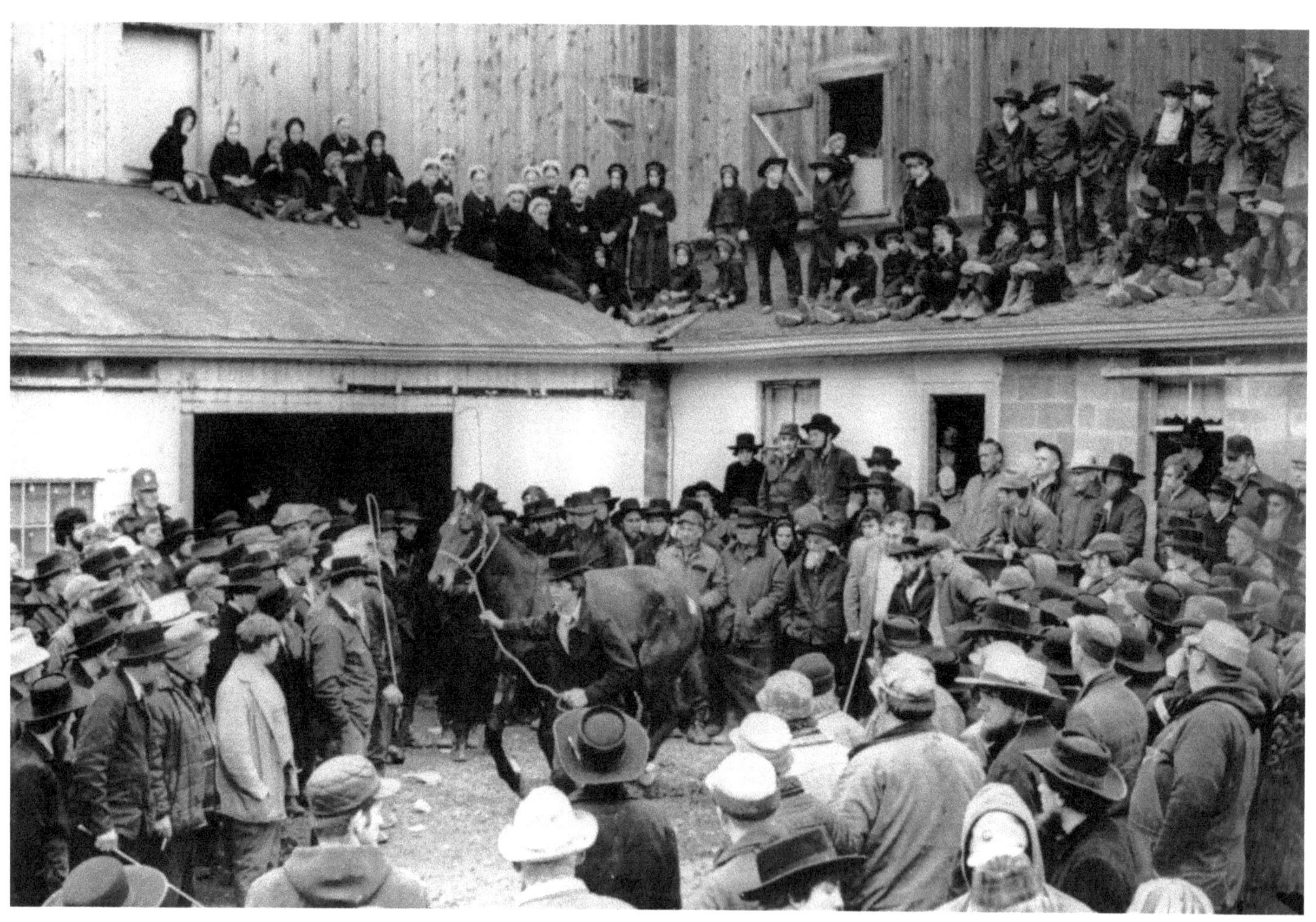

Members of an Amish community attend a horse sale in Madisonburg.

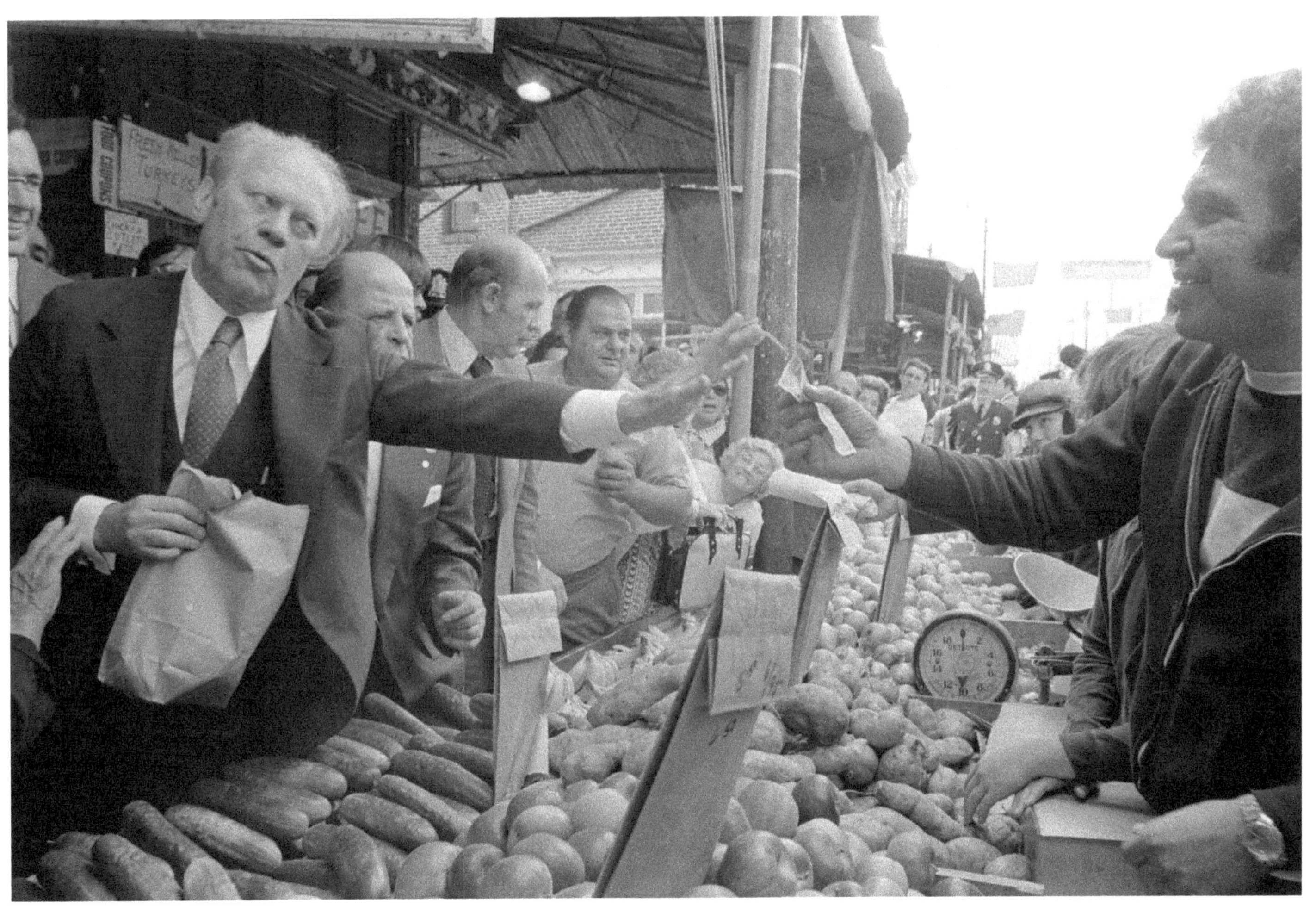

In Philadelphia to participate in the first presidential debate of 1976 against Democratic candidate Jimmy Carter, President Gerald Ford visits the Ninth Street market popularly known as the Italian Market.

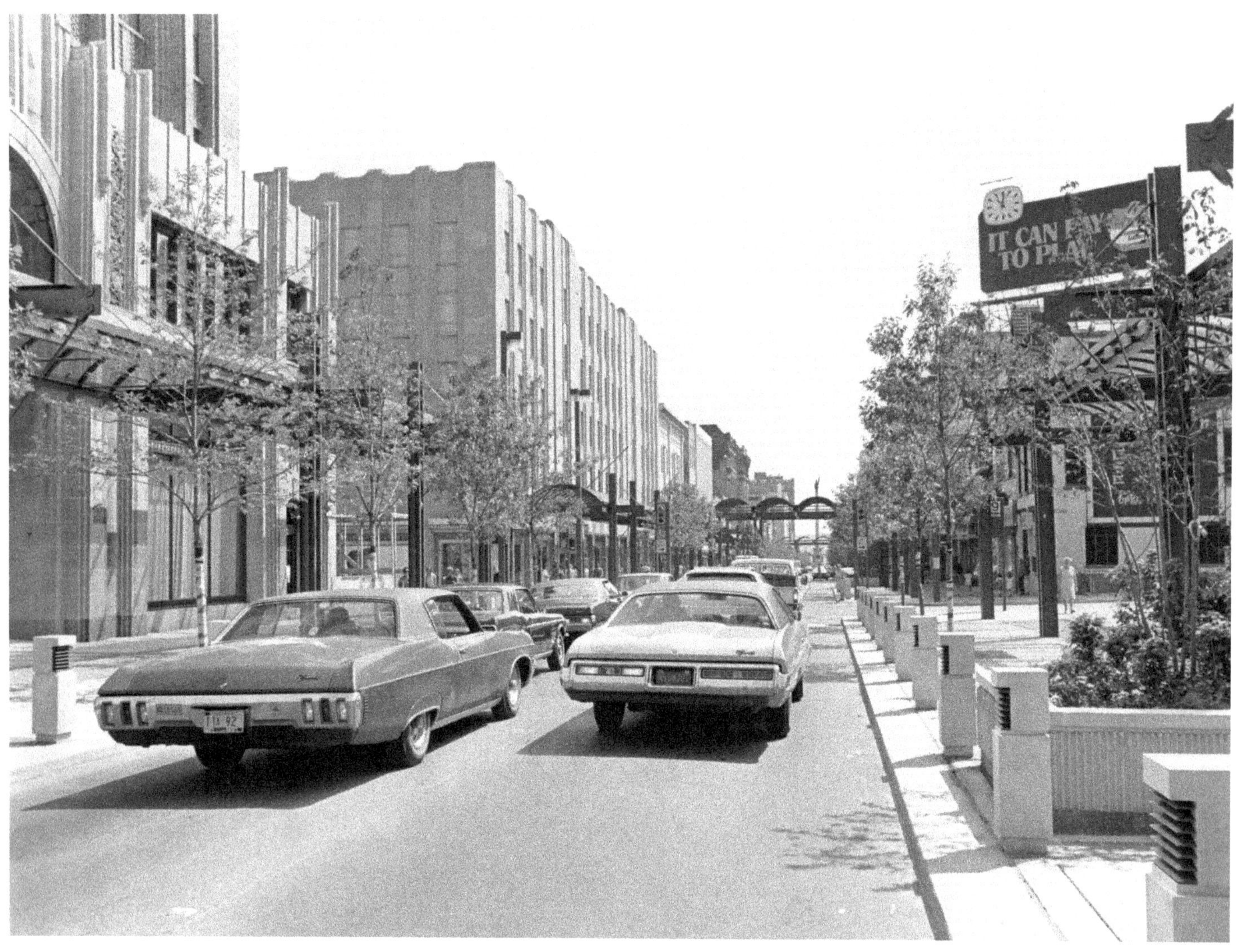

Hamilton Mall in Allentown was created in the mid-1970s in an effort to draw retail business and shoppers to the downtown area. The design featured an innovative canopy (now removed) that ran the length of all four blocks of the mall.

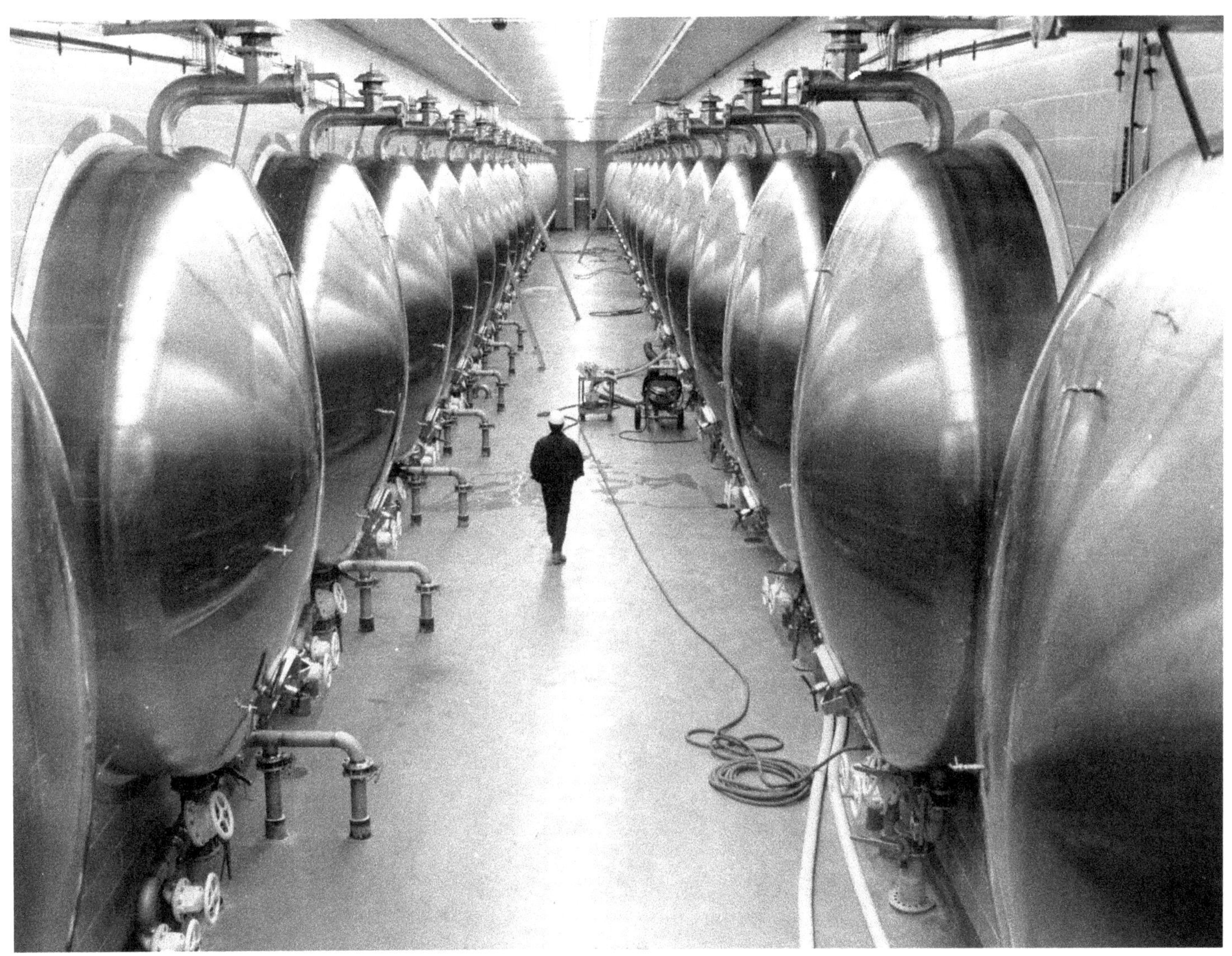

A worker walks along the ultra-modern processing tanks in the new brewery plant of the F&M Schaefer Company in Fogelsville, 1980. Originally based in New York City, Schaefer built the Pennsylvania plant in an effort to compete nationally. It was later bought by the Pabst Brewing Company.

Three months after the worst nuclear-related accident in American history, visitors to the area near the Three Mile Island power plant enjoy a summer excursion in July 1979. While no deaths occurred as a result of the core's overheating, the accident nevertheless resulted in dramatic changes in regulation, planning, and training within the nuclear industry. TMI-2, the tower involved in the accident, remains closed today.

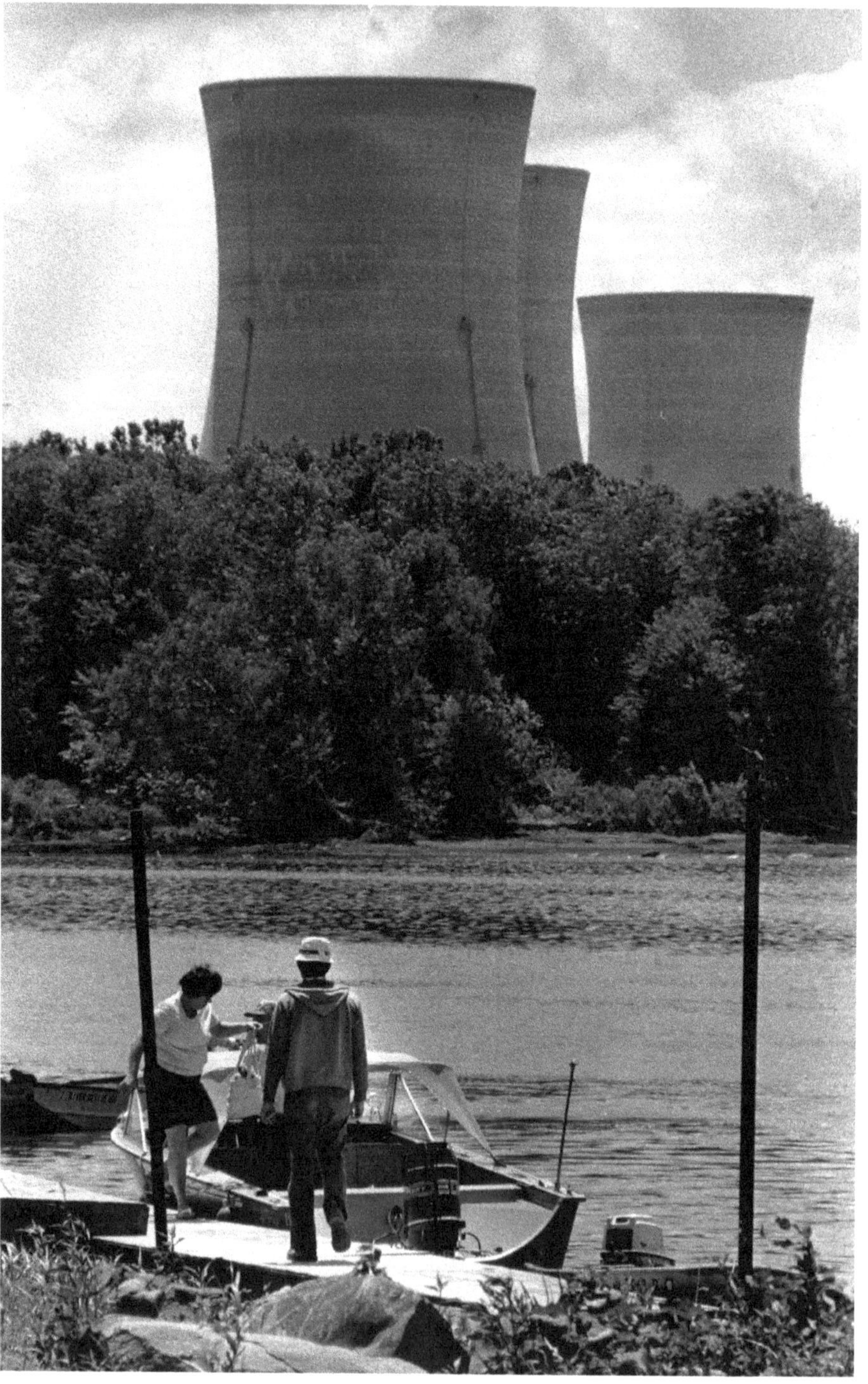

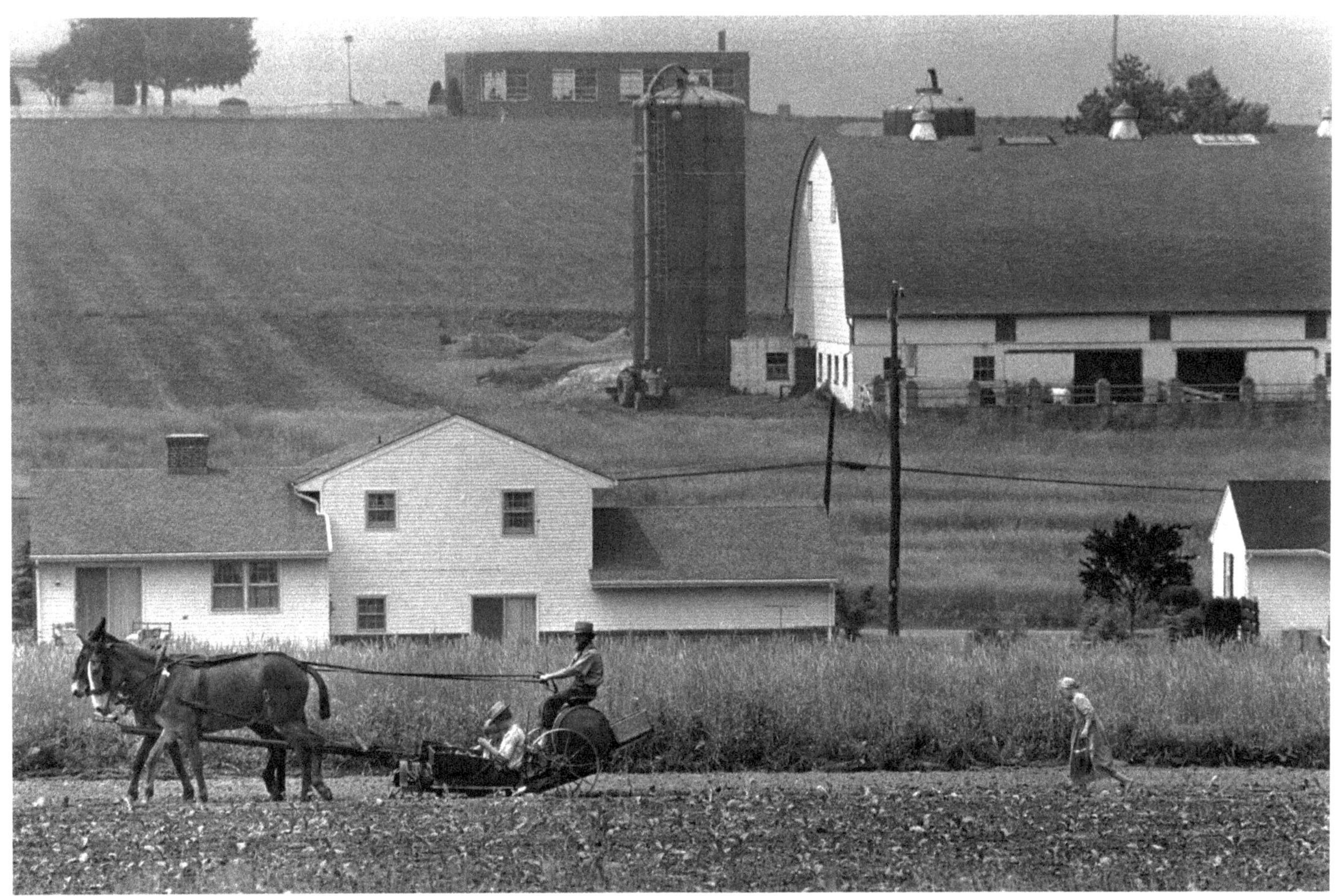

In a 1979 photograph that illustrates the diversity and interesting contrasts of Pennsylvania, an Amish farmer uses a traditional horse-drawn plow to work his fields near New Holland in full view of modern tract housing.

Notes on the Photographs

These notes, listed by page number, attempt to include all aspects known of the photographs. Each of the photographs is identified by the page number, a title or description, photographer and collection, archive, and call or box number when applicable. Although every attempt was made to collect all data, in some cases complete data may have been unavailable due to the age and condition of some of the photographs and records.

II **Williamsport**
The Historical Society of Pennsylvania

VI **York Springs**
The Historical Society of Pennsylvania

X **View from Downtown Pittsburgh**
Library of Congress
LC-USZ62-114463

2 **Philadelphia's Central High School**
Library and Archives Division, Sen. John Heinz History Center
Db781

3 **Town of Norwood**
The Historical Society of Pennsylvania

4 **Pennsylvania Hospital for the Insane**
Library of Congress
LC-DIG-ppmsca-09418

5 **Reverend Jehu Curtis Clay**
Library of Congress
LC-DIG-ppmsca-09246

6 **Oil Derrick**
Library of Congress
LC-DIG-stereo-2s01748

7 **Miners**
The Historical Society of Pennsylvania

8 **Hanover Junction**
Library of Congress
LC-USZ62-124420

9 **Chambersburg**
The Historical Society of Pennsylvania

10 **Carpenters**
The Historical Society of Pennsylvania

11 **Moravian Chapel**
The Historical Society of Pennsylvania

12 **Family on Welsh Mountain**
The Historical Society of Pennsylvania

13 **Kennedy Covered Bridge**
The Historical Society of Pennsylvania

14 **Mounded Charcoal Burner**
The Historical Society of Pennsylvania

15 **East King Street Near Center Square**
The Historical Society of Pennsylvania

16 **Timber Trestle**
The Historical Society of Pennsylvania

18 **Aztec Club**
The Historical Society of Pennsylvania

19 **West King Street**
The Historical Society of Pennsylvania

20 **Stone Bridge Over Cocalico Creek**
The Historical Society of Pennsylvania

21 **Waterfall in Delaware Water Gap**
The Historical Society of Pennsylvania

22 **Moravian Church**
The Historical Society of Pennsylvania

23 **Oil Companies' Headquarters in Rouseville**
Library of Congress
LC-DIG-stereo-1s01738

24 **Remains of Lewistown Bridge**
Library of Congress
LC-USZ62-91474

25 **Harvesting Straw**
The Historical Society of Pennsylvania

26 **Frozen Falling Spring Near Campbell's Ledge**
The Historical Society of Pennsylvania

27 **Overhanging Rock at Gulph Mills**
The Historical Society of Pennsylvania

28 **Devastation of Johnstown**
The Historical Society of Pennsylvania

29 Johnstown
The Historical Society of Pennsylvania

30 Williamsport Flood
The Historical Society of Pennsylvania

31 Williamsport's Third Street
The Historical Society of Pennsylvania

32 Cornerstone of the New State Library
The Historical Society of Pennsylvania

33 Nazareth Inn
The Historical Society of Pennsylvania

34 Religious Parade in Scranton
The Historical Society of Pennsylvania

35 Chinese General and Statesman Li Hung Chang
Library of Congress
LC-DIG-ppmsca-08924

36 Company C of the 118th Regiment Pennsylvania Volunteers
The Historical Society of Pennsylvania

37 Dingmans Ferry
Library of Congress
LC-USZ62-108175

38 Voters Gathering on Election Day
The Historical Society of Pennsylvania

39 Center Square and Queen Street in Lancaster
The Historical Society of Pennsylvania

40 Old Capitol Building in Harrisburg
Library of Congress
HABS PA,22-HARBU,1-1

42 Delaware Water Gap
The Historical Society of Pennsylvania

43 Fifth and Chestnut in Mifflinburg
The Historical Society of Pennsylvania

44 Electric Tower Looking Over Monarch Park
The Historical Society of Pennsylvania

45 Library of the University of Pennsylvania
Library of Congress
LC-DIG-ppmsca-15371

46 The Carlisle Indian Industrial School
Library of Congress
LC-USZ62-119133

47 The Carlisle Indian Industrial School #2
Library of Congress
LC-USZ62-47083

48 Strike Arbitration Commission
Library of Congress
LC-USZ62-95897

49 Bald Eagle Mountain and the Muncy Valley
The Historical Society of Pennsylvania

50 The Wabash Railroad Bridge
Library of Congress
LC-USZ62-110668

52 Lake Erie
The Historical Society of Pennsylvania

53 Hershey Chocolate Factory
Courtesy of Hershey Community Archives, Hershey, Pa.
4B13012.1

54 Coal Breaker in Westmoreland
Library of Congress
LC-USZ62-94996

55 Baldwin Locomotive Works
Library of Congress
LC-USZ62-103609

56 President Theodore Roosevelt
Library of Congress
LC-USZ62-100445

57 State Capitol in Harrisburg
Library of Congress
LC-USZ62-91537

58 Governor's Reception Room
Library of Congress
LC-USZ62-91540

59 Steel Plant in Homestead
Library of Congress
LC-USZ62-107971

60 Freight Trains West of Altoona
Library of Congress
LC-USZ62-93787

61 Bridge Spanning Susquehanna River in Berwick
Library of Congress
LC-USZ62-110689

62 Willow Grove Park
Library of Congress
LC-USZ62-104916

63 Willow Grove Park Lake
Library of Congress
LC-USZ62-95805

64 Homestead Steel Mill
Library of Congress
LC-USZ62-110748

65 Bijou Theatre on Penn Street
Library of Congress
LC-USZ62-101840

66 Pin Boys
Library of Congress
LC-DIG-nclc-04676

67 Coal Barge on the Ohio River
Library of Congress
LC-DIG-ppmsca-17700

68 **Braddock's Road and White Oak Level Road**
Library of Congress
LC-USZ62-99503

69 **The William Henry Family Factory and Homestead**
Library of Congress
HABS PA,48-BOLT,1-2

70 **Forbes Field**
Library of Congress
LC-DIG-ppmsca-18454

71 **Pittsburgh Pirate John Peter "Honus" Wagner**
Library of Congress
LC-USZ62-71743

72 **Girard Trust Building**
Library of Congress
LC-USZ62-98735

73 **Newsboys**
Library of Congress
LC-DIG-nclc-03631

74 **Wire Mills in Donora**
Library of Congress
LC-USZ62-131258

75 **Young Pennsylvania Coal Company Workers**
Library of Congress
LC-DIG-nclc-01103

76 **Miner Wearing Draeger Oxygen Helmet**
Library of Congress
LC-DIG-nclc-01122

77 **Shaft No. 6 in South Pittston**
Library of Congress
LC-DIG-nclc-01113

78 **Delaware River at Dingmans Ferry**
Library of Congress
LC-USZ62-108176

80 **Dumont's Opera House**
Library of Congress
LC-USZ62-113365

81 **York Firehouse and Union Engine No. 3**
Library of Congress
LC-USZ62-101290

82 **Campus of Pennsylvania College**
Library of Congress
pan 6a09318

83 **Chocolate Avenue in Hershey**
Courtesy of Hershey Community Archives, Hershey, Pa.
2A008.1

84 **Wormser's Glass Works**
Library of Congress
LC-DIG-nclc-01305

85 **Philadelphia's City Hall**
Library of Congress
LC-USZ62-98734

86 **Members of the Grand Army of the Republic**
Library of Congress
LC-DIG-npcc-32840

87 **Home of Horatio Gates Lloyd**
Library of Congress
LC-USZ62-94871

88 **Waterfall in Bushkill Falls**
Library of Congress
LC-USZ62-108179

90 **Monongahela River**
Library of Congress
LC-USZ62-133437

91 **Snake Hollow Section of McKeesport**
Library of Congress
pan 6a14440

92 **Wilkes-Barre**
Library of Congress
pan 6a09226

94 **St. Peter's Episcopal Church**
Library of Congress
HABS PA,51-PHILA,108-12

95 **Marion Morgan Dancers**
Library of Congress
LC-USZ62-102959

96 **Millersville State Normal School**
Library of Congress
pan 6a14450

97 **Whitemarsh Hall**
Library of Congress
LC-USZ62-94961

98 **Pershing Family Reunion**
Library of Congress
pan 6a35734

100 **Stanley Harris and Connie Mack**
Library of Congress
LC-USZ62-103758

101 **Bing Miller and Herold "Muddy" Ruel**
Library of Congress
LC-USZ62-135437

102 **Forbes Field**
Library of Congress
LC-USZ62-98704

103 **Oscar Hammerstein's Philadelphia Opera House**
Library of Congress
HABS PA,51-PHILA,540-1

104 **St. David's Episcopal Church**
Library of Congress
HABS PA,23-RAD,1-5

105 **Atwater Kent Company Factory**
Library of Congress
LC-DIG-npcc-27303

106 **A. Atwater Kent**
Library of Congress
LC-DIG-npcc-27300

107 **Philadelphia Museum Construction**
Library of Congress
HABS PA,51-PHILA,335-4

108 **Philadelphia Museum of Art**
Library of Congress
HABS PA,51-PHILA,287-2

109 **President and Mrs. Herbert Hoover**
Library of Congress
LC-DIG-npcc-27629

110 American Ornithologists' Union
Library of Congress
LC-USZ62-116081

111 Lock and Dam No. 8
The Historical Society of Pennsylvania

112 Chantler's General Store
Library and Archives Division, Sen. John Heinz History Center
2001.0193-I01

113 Fourth of July Parade in Clymer
Library and Archives Division, Sen. John Heinz History Center
MSP344-B1-F14

114 George Westinghouse Bridge
Library and Archives Division, Sen. John Heinz History Center
GPC-B011-F40-I01

115 Couple Enjoying Stroll
Library of Congress
LC-USF34-001603-ZB

116 The Horseshoe Curve at Altoona
Library of Congress
pan 6a09300

118 Old United States Customs House
Library of Congress
HABS PA,25-ERI,2-1

119 St. Peter's United Lutheran Church
Library of Congress
HABS PA,22-MIDTO,1-2

120 Mining Town in Westmoreland County
Library of Congress
LC-USF342-T01-000859-A

121 Bethlehem, Pennsylvania
Library of Congress
LC-USF342-T01-001174-A

122 Bethlehem Steel Plant
Library of Congress
LC-USF342-T01-001167-A

123 Johnstown
Library of Congress
LC-USF342-T01-001159-A

124 Miller Family Homestead
Library and Archives Division, Sen. John Heinz History Center
M1-A

125 Woodframe Homes
Library and Archives Division, Sen. John Heinz History Center
GPC-B002-F08-I01

126 Town of Sunbury and the Susquehanna River
The Historical Society of Pennsylvania

127 Double-deck Privy
Library of Congress
LC-USF344-007504-ZB

128 Susquehanna Trail
The Historical Society of Pennsylvania

129 Antietam Reservoir
The Historical Society of Pennsylvania

130 Boys from Nanty Glo
Library of Congress
LC-DIG-fsa-8a17113

131 Port Royal
Library of Congress
HABS PA,51-PHILA,5-3

132 Town of Ambridge
Library of Congress
LC-DIG-fsa-8b17091

133 Homemade Pool
Library of Congress
LC-DIG-fsa-8a10004

134 Buttercup Cottage
Library of Congress
LC-USZ62-136628

135 The Liberty Bell
Library of Congress
LC-USW33-029971-C

136 Bridge Spanning the Allegheny River
Library of Congress
LC-USZ62-134598

137 Working Family in Mauch Chunk
Library of Congress
LC-DIG-fsa-8c28740

138 Tri-County Farmers Co-op Market in DuBois
Library of Congress
LC-USF34-041230-D

139 Boat Racer Mary Altman
Library and Archives Division, Sen. John Heinz History Center
1997.0375-I01

140 Celebration of Lebanon's Bicentennial
Temple University Libraries, Urban Archives, Philadelphia, Pa.

142 Family in Aliquippa
Library of Congress
8c18799u

143 Pine Grove Mills Swimming Hole
Library of Congress
LC-DIG-fsa-8b30846

144 Allegheny Ludlum Steel Corporation Factory
Library of Congress
LC-DIG-fsa-1a35063

145 Women Unloading Lumber
Library of Congress
LC-USW33-025823-C

146 Brookline Elementary School
Library and Archives Division, Sen. John Heinz History Center
GPC-B009-F14-I01

147 Dean Fullerton's Farm in Allegheny County
Library and Archives Division, Sen. John Heinz History Center
M13-A

148 Eliza Furnace
Library and Archives Division, Sen. John Heinz History Center
1999.0061.I03

149 Miner Near Hendersonville
Library and Archives Division, Sen. John Heinz History Center
A.1993.0242

150 Coffee Pot Restaurant
Library of Congress
LC-USW3-036894-E

151 The Old Forks Inn
Library and Archives Division, Sen. John Heinz History Center
GPC-B23-F15

152 National Record Mart
Library and Archives Division, Sen. John Heinz History Center
MSP342-B01-F04-I01

153 Young Men's Christian Association
Library of Congress
HABS PA,62-WAR,2-9

154 Streets of Pittsburgh
Library and Archives Division, Sen. John Heinz History Center
MSP285-B21-F17

155 Women Wearing Surgical Masks in Smog
Library and Archives Division, Sen. John Heinz History Center
MSP285-B21-F20

156 A Gulf Service Station
Library and Archives Division, Sen. John Heinz History Center
MSP238-B2-F4

158 Marasco's Grocery
Library and Archives Division, Sen. John Heinz History Center
1995.0348

159 McConnell's Mill State Park
Library and Archives Division, Sen. John Heinz History Center
MSP285-B18-F31

160 Kennywood Amusement Park
Library and Archives Division, Sen. John Heinz History Center
MSP285-B18-F25-I01

161 Kennywood Rowboats
Library and Archives Division, Sen. John Heinz History Center
MSP057-B006-F12-I03

162 Diamond Market
Library and Archives Division, Sen. John Heinz History Center
GPC-B002-F18-I01

163 Commercial Warehouses
Library and Archives Division, Sen. John Heinz History Center
MSP080-B001-F16-I01

164 Pennsylvania Power and Light Headquarters
Temple University Libraries, Urban Archives, Philadelphia, Pa.

165 Lee Tire Company
Temple University Libraries, Urban Archives, Philadelphia, Pa.

166 The Alcoa Building
Library and Archives Division, Sen. John Heinz History Center
MSP285-B1-F5

167 Covered Bridge Over Whiteley Creek
Library and Archives Division, Sen. John Heinz History Center
MSP197-B009-F008-I5737

168 Hayden's Restaurant
Library and Archives Division, Sen. John Heinz History Center
MSP285-B22-F22

169 Miss Pennsylvania Beauty Pageant Contestants
Temple University Libraries, Urban Archives, Philadelphia, Pa.

170 West Chester's Bank of Chester County
Library of Congress
HABS PA,15-WCHES,13-1

171 Saving Fund Society
Library of Congress
HABS PA,51-PHILA,589-2

172 Heidelberg Raceway
Library and Archives Division, Sen. John Heinz History Center
MSP285-B18-F19

173 State Little League Champions
Temple University Libraries, Urban Archives, Philadelphia, Pa.

174 Lincoln University Students
Temple University Libraries, Urban Archives, Philadelphia, Pa.

175 Virus Research Laboratory
Library and Archives Division, Sen. John Heinz History Center
MSP285-B21-F9

176 Safety Patrol Car
Temple University Libraries, Urban Archives, Philadelphia, Pa.

177 **Harold Cohen, Lucille Ball, and Desi Arnaz**
Library and Archives Division, Sen. John Heinz History Center
MSP334-B001-F01-I02

178 **Allegheny County Courthouse**
Library of Congress
HABS,PA,2-PITU,29-3

179 **The Golden Triangle**
Library and Archives Division, Sen. John Heinz History Center
MSP285-B06-F05-01

180 **William Penn Memorial Museum**
The Historical Society of Pennsylvania

181 **Bridge of Sighs**
Library of Congress
132859pu

182 **Homemade Ice Cream**
Temple University Libraries, Urban Archives, Philadelphia, Pa.

183 **Allderdice High School**
Library and Archives Division, Sen. John Heinz History Center
MSP117-B005-F4-I01

184 **Lake at Camp James Weldon Johnson**
Library and Archives Division, Sen. John Heinz History Center
MSP229-F01-I01

185 **Young Men's Christian Association**
Library of Congress
HABS PA-62-WAR,2-10

186 **Dental Hall**
Library of Congress
HABS PA,51-PHILA,566E-1

187 **Wilkinsburg Police Cruiser**
Library and Archives Division, Sen. John Heinz History Center
ACC.1997.0097.B6.I02

188 **White Tower Fast Food Restaurant**
Library and Archives Division, Sen. John Heinz History Center
GPC-B002-F17-I01

189 **Three Rivers Stadium**
Library and Archives Division, Sen. John Heinz History Center
GPC-B011-F11-I01

190 **Farmland in Central Bucks County**
Temple University Libraries, Urban Archives, Philadelphia, Pa.

191 **Perkiomen Creek**
Temple University Libraries, Urban Archives, Philadelphia Pa.

192 **Fred Rogers**
Library and Archives Division, Sen. John Heinz History Center
MSP285-B04-F01-I01

193 **United American Indians of Delaware Valley**
Temple University Libraries, Urban Archives, Philadelphia, Pa.

194 **Horse Sale**
Temple University Libraries, Urban Archives, Philadelphia, Pa.

195 **President Gerald Ford**
Library of Congress
08510u

196 **Hamilton Mall**
Temple University Libraries, Urban Archives, Philadelphia Pa.

197 **F&M Schaefer Company**
Temple University Libraries, Urban Archives, Philadelphia, Pa.

198 **Three Mile Island Power Plant**
Temple University Libraries, Urban Archives, Philadelphia, Pa.

199 **Amish Farmer**
Temple University Libraries, Urban Archives, Philadelphia, Pa.

HISTORIC PHOTOS OF PENNSYLVANIA

The birthplace of both the Declaration of Independence and the United States Constitution, Pennsylvania is steeped in history as deep as that of the United States as a whole. Founded by William Penn in 1682, Pennsylvania would see America's first public protest against slavery, its first colonial constitution to ensure freedom of conscience, and a daguerreotype image of Philadelphia's Central High School that remains the oldest known photograph taken anywhere in the United States. That landmark image is among the many highlights of *Historic Photos of Pennsylvania*.

Reproduced in vivid black and white, the nearly 200 photos in this volume showcase Pennsylvania's natural beauty, industrial might, and advances in education and the arts. Farmlands and waterfalls, coal mines and steel mills, museums and universities—all contribute to the tapestry that is Pennsylvania's landscape and history. Most of all, the images in this collection pay tribute to the people who have made up Pennsylvania's storied past, even as the state looks ahead to a hopeful future.

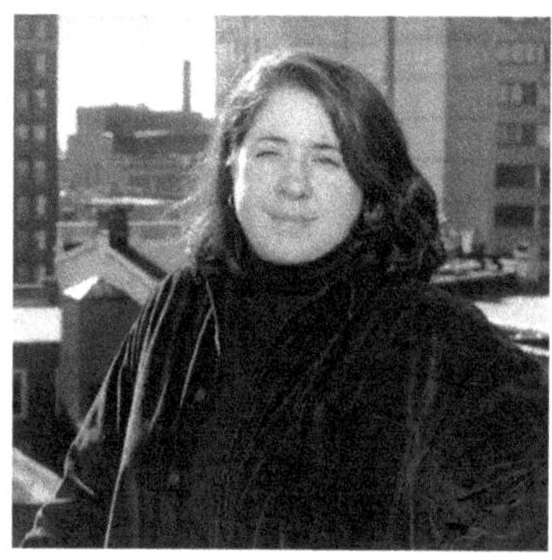

Laura E. Beardsley earned a master of arts degree in public history from Rutgers University– Camden. She is the former Director of Graphics and Research Services for the Historical Society of Pennsylvania in Philadelphia. Previously she worked as a park ranger and interpretative specialist at Independence National Historical Park. In recent years she has pursued a career as a freelance researcher and consultant. She has written *Historic Photos of Philadelphia* and *Historic Photos of the Main Line*, both available from Turner Publishing Company. Beardsley lived in Philadelphia for 20 years. She now resides in the quiet suburb of Drexel Hill.

WWW.TURNERPUBLISHING.COM

www.ingramcontent.com/pod-product-compliance
Lightning Source LLC
LaVergne TN
LVHW060606110826
845154LV00003B/45
9781684420636